D0488172

Politics in Israel

Politics in Israel

Governing a Complex Society

BRENT E. SASLEY
and
HAROLD M. WALLER

New York   Oxford

OXFORD UNIVERSITY PRESS

Oxford University Press is a department of the University of Oxford.
It furthers the University's objective of excellence in research,
scholarship, and education by publishing worldwide.

Oxford New York
Auckland   Cape Town   Dar es Salaam   Hong Kong   Karachi
Kuala Lumpur   Madrid   Melbourne   Mexico City   Nairobi
New Delhi   Shanghai   Taipei   Toronto

With offices in
Argentina   Austria   Brazil   Chile   Czech Republic   France   Greece
Guatemala   Hungary   Italy   Japan   Poland   Portugal   Singapore
South Korea   Switzerland   Thailand   Turkey   Ukraine   Vietnam

Copyright © 2017 by Oxford University Press

For titles covered by Section 112 of the US Higher Education
Opportunity Act, please visit www.oup.com/us/he for the
latest information about pricing and alternate formats.

Published by Oxford University Press
198 Madison Avenue, New York, New York 10016
http://www.oup.com

Oxford is a registered trademark of Oxford University Press

All rights reserved. No part of this publication may be reproduced,
stored in a retrieval system, or transmitted, in any form or by any means,
electronic, mechanical, photocopying, recording, or otherwise,
without the prior permission of Oxford University Press.

The CIP Data is On-File at the Library of Congress.

ISBN: 978-0-19-933506-0

Printing number: 9 8 7 6 5 4 3 2 1

Printed in Canada
on acid-free paper

TABLE OF CONTENTS

v

LIST OF FIGURES

LIST OF TABLES

ABBREVIATIONS

CEC	Central Elections Committee
DMC	Democratic Movement for Change
FSU	Former Soviet Union
GDP	Gross Domestic Product
HCJ	High Court of Justice
IDF	Israel Defense Forces
IDI	Israel Democracy Institute
INES	Israel National Election Studies
MK	Member of Knesset
NRP	National Religious Party
OECD	Organisation for Economic Co-operation and Development
PA	Palestinian Authority
PLO	Palestine Liberation Organization
PM	Prime Minister
UN	United Nations
UTJ	United Torah Judaism
WBG	West Bank and Gaza
WZO	World Zionist Organization

PREFACE

✦

I sraeli politics is one of the most interesting topics to study in the world. It is also, because of the relevance of the Arab–Israeli conflict to millions of Jews, Christians, and Muslims around the world, the subject of enormous media attention. Commentary in the public sphere, particularly in the United States, is filled with analyses of it. General pundits, analysts of the Middle East and of international affairs, journalists, politicians, students of higher education—most have an opinion on Israel.

Yet there remain profound misunderstandings of the country itself and the nature of its politics. Casual observers, for instance, often refer to the "religious parties" without differentiating between the Religious Zionist and the non-Zionist parties. Yet while these groups share concerns about the role of Jewish law in the public sphere, they disagree on the role of the state and feel differently about policy toward the Palestinians. Similarly, the concepts of "right" and "left" in Israeli politics is often conflated with Western conceptualizations of right (conservative) and left (liberal). Likud, as the leading right-wing party, does share the conservative preference for less government involvement in the economy, while Labor, the main left-wing party, shares the liberal preference for more government support for social welfare programs. But at the same time there has been a convergence between the two on economic policy over the years, toward a general acceptance of a free market economy. More often "right" and "left" in Israel refer to the parties' position on the peace process with the Palestinians and an independent Palestinian state in the West Bank and Gaza.

When we first looked into the possibility of writing this textbook, we were both surprised and encouraged by what we found. There has been a veritable explosion of courses directly about Israel or that incorporate Israel into their curricula in colleges and universities across the United States and Canada, as well as around the world. This is particularly evident in the United States. According to one study, there was a 69 percent growth in courses about Israel in the United States from 2006 to 2009.[1] The evidence indicates that six years later, the numbers continue to increase, though by smaller amounts.

The growing number of courses in North American universities and in countries besides Israel requires textbooks on Israeli politics in English. The field of Israel *studies* does have a number of relevant books on the topic, but they tend to be grouped according to specific themes: the history of Israel (stretching back to the nineteenth century or even earlier), Zionism, state building during the period of the *Yishuv* (the Jewish community in Palestine before 1948), societal divisions, politics and public opinion, and foreign policy. None of these is useful as a text on Israeli *politics*, because they are all too narrow in scope or are primarily historical.

To this end, our goal was to create a text that was readable, touched on major contemporary issues and debates in Israeli politics, and did so by grounding our explanation in a historical-sociological approach that emphasized the processes that led to the creation of the Israeli political system and continue to influence the conduct of Israeli politics. Without this grounding, we contend, students of Israeli politics will not obtain the depth of understanding that they need to make informed analyses and arguments about various issues or propose viable policy ideas. Indeed, in one innovation of our textbook, we demonstrate the importance of understanding the underlying structures, histories, and identities within the Israeli polity in order to achieve a deeper knowledge of Israeli policymaking in the economic arena and foreign affairs. We also decided to cite English-language resources only, so that readers will be able to follow the sources more easily and to utilize them for their own research.

The book has six underlying themes, or six dimensions that structure the conduct of Israeli politics: the weight of historical processes, the struggle between different groups over how to define the country's identity, changing understandings of Zionism, a changing political culture, the influence of the external threat environment, and the inclusive nature of the democratic process.

By emphasizing these six variables we hope that the text answers some of the questions students will have about Israel. But, as with any effort in the academy, our primary goal is to provide readers with the background knowledge and understanding of the relevant processes, structures, and actors so that they may reach their own conclusions regarding questions that interest them but that may or may not be addressed here.

It bears mentioning that we have contributed equally to this book. Indeed, such a large project, covering so many facets, makes such collaboration necessary.

Brent Sasley, Arlington, Texas
Harold Waller, Montreal, Quebec

NOTE

1. Annette Koren and Emily Einhorn, "Searching for the Study of Israel: A Report on the Teaching of Israel on U.S. College Campuses 2008–09," Cohen Center for Modern Jewish Studies, Brandeis University, January 2010. http://www.schusterman.org/wp-content/uploads/Searching-for-the-Study-of-Israel_January-2010.pdf

ACKNOWLEDGMENTS

One cannot write a book about a topic as complex as Israeli politics without help; nor, even, can two people. We have had plenty of support from many colleagues and friends, on both the professional and the personal levels.

The following individuals helped introduce us to Israeli politicians, activists, civil servants, and scholars: Dan Arbell, Amihai Bannett, Joel Braunold, Jesse Ferris, Assaf Halperin, David Halperin, James Morris, Michael Pitkowsky, Mitchell Plitnick, and Dahlia Scheindlin.

To those who gave freely of their time discussing specific issues in Israeli politics we are most grateful: Dan Ben-David, Eyal Chowers, Stuart Cohen, Avraham Diskin, Amir Fuchs, Itzhak Galnoor, Elli Gershenkroin, Reuven Hazan, Tamar Hermann, Paul Hirschson, Menachem Hofnung, Efraim Inbar, Ofer Kenig, Mikhael Manekin, Peter Medding, Mordechai Nisan, Nimrod Novik, Alon Pinkas, Gideon Rahat, Andrew Sacks, Jeremy Saltan, Dahlia Scheindlin, Tal Schneider, Danny Seidemann, Noam Sheizaf, Yair Sheleg, Shaul Shenhav, David Starr, Gerald Steinberg, Chaim Waxman, David Weinberg, and Uri Zaki. Many others have requested anonymity, but we are no less thankful for their insights.

We are very grateful for those who read specific draft chapters and provided valuable feedback and suggestions: Sarah Acker, Michael Brecher, Udi Eiran, Itzhak Galnoor, As'ad Ghanem, Zvi Gitelman, Tamar Hermann, Csaba Nikolenyi, Jeremy Pressman, Shmuel Rosner, Norrin Ripsman, Aviad Rubin, Jonathan Rynhold, Shmuel Sandler, Dahlia Scheindlin, Sammy Smooha, and Mira Sucharov.

Our editor at Oxford, Jennifer Carpenter, is greatly appreciated for supporting this project from the beginning, answering all our questions, and shepherding the process to the end. Matthew Rohal at Oxford and Production Manager Kelli Jauron were also instrumental in the publishing process, and we thank them as well. Anonymous reviewers provided thoughtful, and therefore helpful, comments and suggestions.

Brent would like to thank the following people. For debates about and parsing of Israel over the years: Zev Cohen, Dan Levine, Oded Löwenheim, Jeremy Pressman, Mira Sucharov, Dov Waxman, and Guy Ziv. All of them pushed back when I made arguments about Israeli politics, and therefore sharpened my thinking about the topic and the country itself. My regular conversations (more like passionate disagreements verging on a war of attrition) with Mira, especially, have helped shape my personal views and scholarly approach to Israel.

I want to emphasize my thanks and appreciation to Hal. Before he was my coauthor, he was my teacher and advisor. We approached some of the issues under discussion from different perspectives, but that never impeded the scholarly process. In fact, Hal encouraged me and gave me space to pursue my ideas—the mark of a true colleague and friend.

The Department of Political Science, the McDowell Center for Critical Languages and Area Studies, and the College of Liberal Arts, all at the University of Texas at Arlington, provided research support for trips to Israel. At different times Ilan Troen and Michael Koplow facilitated my presence in Israel and interaction with scholars of Israel through the Summer Institute for Israel Studies and the Israel Institute Leadership Summit, respectively.

My mother, Shelley, and my father, Ken, encouraged me throughout my academic career, as did my in-laws Issy and Bonny. I am not sure whether they would agree with all of my own conclusions about Israel, but that has not stopped them from supporting me. This is my first major project since my father passed away; I wish he could have seen the finished product.

I'm more grateful than I can put into words to Yael, Arielle, Samara, and Shai. Their laughter kept me grounded, while their curiosity, patience, and kindness sustained me. Without their presence, my work would be much, much poorer.

Hal first of all expresses his thanks to Brent. Nothing can be more satisfying to an educator than to watch a student mature as a scholar and then to be able to collaborate with him. It has been a distinct pleasure to work with him on this project. On the subject of former students, Sarah Acker, Bernard Avishai, Eyal Chowers, Mordechai Nisan, and Aviad Rubin have brought me only satisfaction and pride as I have watched them embark on their own careers, each engaging with Israel in a different way.

I owe an incalculable debt of gratitude to Daniel J. Elazar z"l, a dear colleague, friend, mentor, and collaborator. Dan first introduced me to the serious examination of Israeli politics and always impressed me with his profound insights. His memory has been a constant inspiration. Moreover, the Workshop on Jewish Political Studies, which he founded and led for so many years, afforded me an opportunity to get to know Israel as a scholar. It was an invaluable experience. The Jerusalem Institute for Public Affairs, which he also founded, has always provided me with a stimulating intellectual environment, whether I was in Israel or staying in touch from a distance.

My colleagues in the Canadian Institute for Jewish Research, notably Fred Krantz, David Bensoussan, Julien Bauer, Baruch Cohen, Feige Kaplan, Csaba Nikolenyi, Norrin Ripsman, and Ira Robinson, have been a constant source of stimulation regarding Israeli politics.

The students in my Israeli politics course at McGill have always challenged me to explain the most difficult aspects of the subject while approaching the study of Israel with energy, enthusiasm, and intense interest. I am most grateful to them.

Ilan Troen and his colleagues at Brandeis University's Schusterman Center for Israel Studies offer an outstanding Summer Institute for Israel Studies. My participation in it proved invaluable in so many ways. I also learned a great deal from my diverse group of fellow participants in the 2014 program.

I owe so much to my late parents, Allan and Lillian Waller, but in particular I always recall how they made me aware of Israel and stimulated my interest in all the changes that took place there over the years. Eugene and Pearl Goodman, my late in-laws, did much to encourage me to think about so many different dimensions of Israeli society.

Finally, but most importantly, my beloved Diane has been incredibly supportive of this project and has shown great interest in every aspect. There is no way that I can thank her enough. Sharon, Dahvi, and Jeffrey for years have had to put up with a dad who could not seem to stop talking about Israel. I am grateful to them for their patience, of course, but also for their abiding interest, encouragement, and enthusiasm.

⤳

CHAPTER 1

Israel in Historical and Comparative Perspective

Few countries are subject to as much intensive debate, among country-specialists as well as nonspecialists, as Israel. In part this is because of the complexity of Israel. The Israeli political system is the product of a long historical and sociological process, in which past Jewish experiences in Europe and Mandatory Palestine have shaped the structures, rules, and norms of its politics. At the same time, Israel remains a country in transition. Questions about the reconcilability of the Jewish and democratic facets of its identity and politics, the contemporary meaning of Zionism, the geographic-cultural split between Jerusalem and Tel Aviv, the blurring of the line between the domestic (Israel within the Green Line) and the foreign (Israel's presence in the West Bank), and the growing number of distinct and politically mobilized social groups within the country all condition the conduct of Israeli politics and public debate. This makes a book on the politics of Israel urgent, and so we have sought here to begin providing some structure to think about these questions.

If a book on Israeli politics is necessary, it is also potentially a political minefield. Because Israel occupies a prominent role in the public discourse outside the country, efforts to understand the country are often seen as supporting "one side" of a heated dispute over the other. We reject this too-easy labeling even while we recognize that observers will have different perspectives and priorities when it comes to thinking about Israel. Our purpose in this textbook is to provide a study of the main institutions, actors, processes, and questions that animate Israel's politics in order to supply students of the country with a solid foundation to think about Israel and consider their own answers to all of the aforementioned pressing questions.

STUDYING ISRAEL

In a 1996 edited volume, Michael Barnett contended that Israel was an in-between country in geographic, theoretical, methodological, and normative terms.[1] It is the only Jewish state in the world, yet it is located in a region composed of Muslim-majority states. It shares the same political system and high levels of development as countries of the West, yet its high levels of militarization and engagement in protracted conflict make it more like a developing state. Its political system is highly evolved, yet the question of how to separate religion and state remains unresolved. Finally, its history is a mix of experiences: it emerged from a colonial framework but underwent considerable autonomous development and continues to exercise control over much of a territory—the West Bank—that most of the world today recognizes as part of another people's state. The national liberation movement that led to the establishment of the modern state, Zionism, was unique in that it led to a *return* to a land where the Jews had once enjoyed a sovereign existence. As a young society, Israel had to adjust to the absorption of hundreds of thousands of new immigrants in the middle of a war. And its foreign policy has continued to be driven by existential threats from all its neighbors. It is hard to find a country that has endured similar conditions. Meanwhile, Israeli scholars have reinforced this perception to some degree. Many who have focused on Israel's establishment, the development of its society, and its foreign policy have highlighted the uniqueness of its situation.

Thinking of Israel as too different, though, has undermined a comparative approach to the country, which in turn deprives scholars and researchers of the insights gleaned from examination of other countries' experiences, as well as from the application of insights from the Israeli experience.

In truth, Israel has never been completely isolated in academic study. But its integration into scholarly research has often occurred only in one direction: Israeli scholars have for decades studied Israel alongside other countries, comparing it to other experiences and drawing on general theoretical models and approaches. This has particularly been the case in fields examining the development of political systems and political parties, the nature of interest group activity, the impact of conflict on political development, and state formation. But non-Israeli scholars have tended to neglect Israel, even in these areas.[2]

This situation has changed over the years, and Israel is increasingly being integrated into broader academic study, including in political science. But the process is slow and uneven—for example, the country continues to be seen primarily as *sui generis* in international relations—and most researchers are generalists who do not have an in-depth knowledge of Israel's history, culture, and politics. While of course generalists play an important role in the production of knowledge, understanding, and policy formation, there is still a need for a better—and deeper— understanding of Israel and its politics.

Israel continues to sit uneasily at the juncture of Jewish studies and Middle East studies, but there is evidence of change at the pedagogical level. It remains the case that Israel does not always fit comfortably into courses on the Middle East in general, which tend to focus on broad patterns of identity, culture, and politics; this leads to an emphasis on the Arab world especially (Turkey and Iran are often neglected in this approach as well). Israel is brought up when regional history or regional conflicts are discussed, but its politics are rarely compared to those of its neighbors in these classes. Nevertheless, there have been several improvements. The emergence of a specific field of Israel studies, facilitated by a host of new chairs and Israel studies centers at American universities, is proof of this change;[3] so too is the growth of educational programs for faculty to learn more about Israel, including those that incorporate visits to the country. Other evidence is found in the increase in the number of courses on Israel being offered on North American campuses and in the growing number of visiting professorships for Israeli scholars since the 2000s. One report concluded from these changes that the study of Israel has become "normalized" at U.S. institutions.[4]

Yet at the same time, the study of Israel and activities related to Israel and the Israeli–Palestinian conflict have become increasingly politicized on North American college and university campuses. This is best represented by the emergence and expansion of campus branches of the Boycott, Divestment, and Sanctions (BDS) movement;[5] public debates about hiring and promotion decisions related to professors who are active in these issues in the public sphere; and efforts by academic associations to boycott Israeli academic institutions and blacklist their scholars. It would not be an exaggeration to say that Israel has become a battleground within higher education in North America. Organizations have sprouted up to promote one set of ideas over others and to "defend" against such ideas. These developments have undermined the true meaning of academic freedom. Yet evidence indicates that university and college students are still very much interested in learning more about Israel, and most are simply uninterested in making their study of the country an ideological or political issue.[6]

The attention paid to Israel in North American and world media, in the public discourse, in commentary on social media, and in policy discussions in world capitals is also relevant.[7] For example, few analysts at Washington, D.C., think tanks or research institutes specialize in Israel. This might not be unusual—few countries have a devoted set of researchers and programs—but Israel is more prominent in American political debates and foreign policy than many of these other countries, even on issues that do not seem directly connected to it. The tendency is to hire analysts who focus on either regions or issues; those who work on the Middle East or on conflict, for example, are presumed to be able to write on Israel as well. The result is public commentary by observers who are not adequately familiar with the key actors and major ideas that shape the country's politics and policies, leading to a tendency for most of these analysts' writings and pronouncements on Israel to be ahistorical, driven by contemporary events, and viewed through a prism of American foreign policy priorities.[8]

Finally, there have been efforts in world politics to isolate Israel in the name of the Palestinian cause and the Arab–Israeli conflict. At the United Nations, for example, Israel is the only country that is subject to an annual package of resolutions against it (approximately 20 every year), typically focusing on Palestinian refugees (and Israel's presumed role in keeping them in a state of limbo) and Israeli occupation of what is regarded as Palestinian territory. Countries in the United Nations are also grouped according to geography, yet Israel was long refused membership in blocs representing the developing regions of the world as a result of Arab and Muslim opposition. (Today it is a member of the West European and Other Group.)

For all these reasons, a text on the politics of Israel—one that covers its political system; its main actors and political processes; the big questions animating its politics; and its social, economic, and cultural trends as they are refracted into the political arena—is necessary to build a more informed citizenry. A secondary purpose is to build the foundation for a more useful and effective comparative analysis of Israel. In this book we take the position that Israel is certainly different from other countries—as each country is different from every other—but it is not so unique as to preclude comparison with other countries, to draw on general theories and models to understand its politics, or to use it as a case study in general theory development. By laying out the basic elements of Israeli politics through the use of common concepts we hope readers can use the information to more directly compare the Israeli experience to those of other countries. We now suggest some ways this can be done.

ISRAEL IN A COMPARATIVE FRAMEWORK

Israel shares the colonial experience with most of its regional neighbors. Before the establishment of the state in 1948, what is today Israel, Jordan, the West Bank, and the Gaza Strip was governed by the British under the Palestine Mandate. The Jewish community in the Mandate—known as the *Yishuv* (literally, settlement)—had control over its own internal affairs, such as religious practices and communal organization, but was ultimately subject to British rule and priorities. Like the Turks—and, thinking beyond the Middle East, like many African liberation movements—some of the Zionist Jews living in the Mandate took up arms against the British. Indeed, Zionism—Jewish nationalism—explicitly absorbed the ideas and priorities of Russian, Polish, and Italian nationalism and, insofar as it represents the longing of a particular ethno-national community for its own state, reflects the same experience that characterized the establishment of many European, African, Asian, and Middle Eastern states. The historical processes that led to the establishment of Israel, then, can be compared to state formation processes that have occurred in other countries, with implications for the development of the political system and its components.

Israel struggles with the tension between religion and state that characterized several Western countries in the past and reflects the problems some of its regional neighbors are contending with today. Iran, a theocracy, faces complaints from many citizens about the oppressive role of Islamic rules in its society, while Saudi Arabia struggles with demands for greater freedoms for women and Shia Muslims in a system in which the Wahhabi *ulama* (religious establishment) exerts considerable influence over the country's politics. Turkey has seen a resurgence of conservative Islamic preferences among much of the population, which helped bring the Islamist Justice and Development Party to power in the 2002 national elections. And those Arab states whose rulers have been overthrown in the wake of the 2011 uprisings (namely, Tunisia, Egypt, and Libya) have been dealing with domestic strife as Islamist parties (among others) have increasingly participated in elections and sought to shape the countries' governing systems and social rules. The identity of the Israeli state can, therefore, be a useful comparative point when examining the development of a specific religious identity and subsequent efforts to define political rights and belonging.

Israeli society is composed of multiple, and diverse, social groups. Some of these communities are distinguished according to ethnicity (e.g., Russians, Mizrachim [Jews from the Middle East and Spain], Ethiopians), some according to religious orientation (e.g., *haredim* [ultra-Orthodox], Religious Zionists), and some according to national community (e.g., Arabs, Jews). The state itself has long been dominated by one specific ethno-national-religious group: the secular Ashkenazim, made up of European Jews and their descendants. All of these communities are struggling to define their own identity and place within the larger polity. This search for communal identity within a larger state identity parallels politics in several Western democracies (e.g., Canada, Belgium, and Spain) as well as in some Middle Eastern states (e.g., Lebanon, Iraq, and Turkey). As a data point, Israel can be useful for conceptualizations of national identity and the development of national symbols and hegemonic discourse.

Much is made of the fact that Israel is a Jewish state and therefore has nothing in common with other countries. To the extent that norms, history, and laws specific to Jews as an ethno-national-religious community play the dominant role in shaping Israeli politics, this is true. But most states are dominated by a specific ethno-national group (a very brief list would include Turkey, Iran, Japan, Germany, all of the Central Asian countries, and several African states). It is useful to compare how each has reacted to minorities within its borders and how the different states have balanced ethnic identity and citizenship rights.

The lack of resolution of the Arab–Israeli and Israeli–Palestinian conflict has kept conflict and war on the Israeli policy agenda. Though there is debate over how militarized Israel is under these conditions, the security community (composed of the intelligence agencies and the Israel Defense Forces) has played a prominent role in the country's decision-making. Force continues to be viewed as an integral element of the policy toolkit. This is the same outlook adopted by other states engaged in protracted conflicts or living under a heightened state of threat, including Turkey, most of the Arab states, and Pakistan. What effect conflict, hostility, war, and regional instability have on social development and on policy is an important avenue for exploration, and certainly Israel can be included in such discussion.

Israeli politics is affected by the Jewish diaspora—particularly in the United States—in much the same way other diasporas play a role in their ancestral homeland's politics. In the case of Israel, the role of the diaspora is most prominent in terms of defining what it means to be Jewish, but the growing divisions within the American Jewish community on how to support Israel has also had some impact on the state's politics. This same process plays out for other states that remain connected to large diasporas living elsewhere, especially in Western countries. India, Armenia, and Croatia are but three prominent examples in which emigrant or foreign-born Indians, Armenians, and Croats have sought to use their attachments to their ancestral homelands to participate in those states' decision-making processes and/or to influence their behavior by advocating on issues related to them in their "host" countries.

MAJOR THEMES OF THE BOOK

To better think about these questions, the book follows six themes in Israeli politics. First, the weight of historical processes has conditioned the contemporary political system. The Jewish experience in Europe, the onset of politically motivated immigration into Palestine, and the need to set up communal organizations that would both protect the small group of Jews living in the area and lay the ground-work for eventual statehood led to the construction of a political system that was transferred from the Yishuv to the state once it was created. Living as a separate community within Europe encouraged Jewish villages and communities, especially in eastern Europe, to construct institutions that would look after the community and represent it to the authorities of the land. Heavily influenced by European nationalism in particular, but also by Enlightenment ideas about human progress and representative democracy, the early Zionists created a system built on collectivist, statist, and socialist ideas that were drawn from the eastern European experience but followed western European political structures.

Second, the struggle between different groups over how to define the country's identity continues and in some ways has intensified. Though a small community of Jews lived in the area for hundreds of years, they had no political aspirations. The idea of renewed Jewish sovereignty was only seriously pursued beginning in the 1880s. Israel was created by immigrant Jews who came from Europe. These Jews, however, came in different "waves" of immigration (*aliyot*, the plural of *aliya*, literally, "going up"), each one representing a different community of European Jews. After 1948, large-scale immigration of Jews from Arab states commenced and was followed later by immigration from Russia and the republics of the former Soviet Union as well as from Ethiopia. The Arab community was at first depoliticized but became increasingly mobilized and assertive in its communal demands by the 1990s. Other communities that have become relevant for Israeli political discussion and policymaking are foreign workers from Europe and Asia—who replaced Palestinian laborers from the West Bank and Gaza in the aftermath of the First Intifada, the popular uprisings against Israeli rule in the West Bank and Gaza—and refugees and migrants from several African states (particularly Sudan, South Sudan, and Eritrea). All these groups have, to greater or lesser degrees, engaged in politics to shape the country's laws, political system, and social rules to either better accommodate their needs and demands or mold it to their own particular expectations. Thus the political system is suffused by these groups' efforts to change the state's laws, norms, and identity according to their particular preferences. This makes it difficult to construct a singular national identity and sense of belonging.

Third, Zionism has heavily shaped the political culture of Israel. As the organized expression of Jewish nationalism, Zionism was a very big tent. Zionists were grouped into different factions representing positions on the economic, political, and ideological spectrums. The structure of Zionist politics in the World Zionist Organization and later in the Yishuv was effectively transferred over into Israel, and Israeli institutions and political practices followed the lines set down in these earlier periods. But Zionism engendered a collectivist ethos among the Jewish community. When this ethos began to shift in the 1980s to a more individual-oriented framework, questions about the Zionist project and whether it had been completed began to be discussed with more urgency. In the aftermath of this shift, different Jewish groups in Israel—the political right, the political left, the religious communities—have sought to redefine what it means to be a Zionist state.

Fourth, Israel has undergone a shift from the early commitment to collectivism to an increasingly widespread and assertive individualism. The transition from a socialist to a free market economy (spurred in part by the growing relevance of technology to the economy) played an important role in this process, and the party system has changed as a result. This is particularly evident in the emergence of the political center—a mass of Israeli voters less interested in attaching themselves to any particular end of the political spectrum or any particular party. This has upset the longstanding balance in Israeli politics between the left, represented by Labor, and the right, represented by Likud. These shifts have also affected attitudes toward the state, the military, and Zionism itself.

Fifth, the external threat environment has had a profound effect on Israeli politics. Established in a hostile neighborhood—David Ben-Gurion read out the state's declaration of independence in the middle of an intercommunal war between Jews and Arabs in Mandatory Palestine, and a number of Arab state armies invaded the next day—Israel was from the start viewed as an alien infection in the body of the Arab and Muslim Middle East. The regional environment, then, shaped the political culture, affected relations between Jews and Arabs in the state, enhanced the defense establishment's role in policymaking, and foregrounded a sense of eternal insecurity.

Sixth, despite social divisions and a crowded political system, Israeli politics has been remarkably inclusive. Not every group that participates in the political arena is able to translate its interests into policy—Arab political parties have had the most difficult time—and the competing interests of different groups have led too often to deadlock and instability. Nonetheless, the democratic procedures and pluralism at the heart of this process are important elements of Israeli politics.

These threads have conditioned the development of Israeli politics, shaping its institutions and practices. We have divided the book into separate chapters that explain each of these processes, tracing their evolution and how they have affected Israeli politics. In this way we hope to provide a deeper sense of what animates Israel.

A NOTE ON TERMINOLOGY

Given the prominence of Israel in public discourse, various terms to describe events and actors have come to be associated with one "side" or "cause" over the other. But as a book written for a broad audience, we must write using the norms and most effective language for that audience. On the other hand, this is a book on Israel, and we want to reflect the predominant terminology and nomenclature used by Israelis. So, for example, to refer to the territory captured by Israel in 1967, we use the politically neutral term "West Bank" alongside the name used in official Israeli government discourse and among much of the public, "Judea and Samaria." The various wars that we reference are mentioned according to their year (e.g., the 1948 or 1947–1949 War, the 1967 War, the 1973 War) as well as how they are commonly known in Israel (e.g., the War of Independence, the Six-Day War, the Yom Kippur War). Other terms are explained throughout the text as they are explored.

Finally, we must define what we mean by *Israel* here, because there is often confusion regarding the country's boundaries on the basis of its presence in the West Bank. For our purposes, we mean Israel as it is bounded by the Green Line— the armistice lines set at the end of the first Arab–Israeli war in 1949. Though neither Israel nor the Arab states regarded these borders as permanent, they delineate the country accepted into the United Nations that same year. However, the expansion of settlements in the West Bank, which requires the imposition of Israeli law there and the protection of the state military, certainly raises questions, and many Israelis do not consider the Green Line a specific border either. Many of the political disputes discussed throughout the book and especially in Chapter 18 demonstrate that this remains an important policy issue in Israel today. But it is also clear that Israeli politics is centered on the space within the Green Line—sometimes called *Israel proper*—and this book follows that assumption accordingly.

KEYWORDS

comparative framework, Israel as unique, colonial experience, religion and state, collectivism, nationalism

NOTES

1. Michael Barnett, ed., *Israel in Comparative Perspective: Challenging the Conventional Wisdom* (Albany: SUNY Press, 1996).
2. Joel S. Migdal, *Through the Lens of Israel: Explorations in State and Society* (Albany: SUNY Press, 2001).
3. A separate discussion is whether a single country should be its own field of study, with all the consequent programs associated with a field of study. One response is that Israel has been so neglected and isolated until now that this is a necessary corrective.
4. Janet Krasner Aronson, Annette Koren, and Leonard Saxe, "Teaching Israel at American Universities: Growth, Placement, and Future Prospects," *Israel Studies* 18 (2013): 158–178.
5. The BDS movement, begun by Palestinian civil society groups, aims to penalize Israel's economic development until the country satisfies BDS activists' demands for resolving the Israeli–Palestinian conflict.
6. Annette Koren, Nicole Samuel, Matthew Boxer, and Ellie Aitan, *Teaching and Learning about Israel: Assessing the Impact of Israeli Faculty on American Students* (Waltham, MA: Cohen Center for Modern Jewish Studies, February 2013).
7. See, for example, Shira Pindyck, Moran Yarchi, and Amnon Cavari, "The *New York Times'* Coverage of Israel: 1981–2013" (presentation at the Annual Convention of the Association for Israel Studies Meeting, Sde Boker, Israel, June 2014).
8. Brent E. Sasley, "Still Going Strong," *Foreign Affairs*, December 6, 2013, http://www.foreignaffairs.com/articles/140328/brent-e-sasley/still-going-strong.

Chronology of Key Events in Israel's History, 1882–2015

1882–1903	First Aliya
1897	Theodor Herzl organizes the First Zionist Congress in Basel
1904–1914	Second Aliya
1909	Tel Aviv established
November 1917	Balfour Declaration
1919–1923	Third Aliya
1922	Assignment of the Palestine Mandate to Britain
1924–1929	Fourth Aliya
1929–1939	Fifth Aliya
1936–1939	Arab Revolt in Palestine
1939	British Government issues White Paper on Palestine
1942	Biltmore Program announced by Zionists
November 1947	United Nations General Assembly adopts Partition Plan
May 14, 1948	Declaration of Independence issued
May 15, 1948	Israel becomes independent; War of Independence begins
1949	Election of Constituent Assembly/First Knesset won by Mapai; David Ben-Gurion becomes Prime Minister
1950s	Terrorist attacks by Egyptian-supported Fedayeen
1954–1965	Lavon Affair roils Israeli politics
October 1956	Suez War—Israel, Great Britain, and France invade Egypt
June 1967	Six-Day War—Israel defeats Jordan, Egypt, and Syria, and gains control of east Jerusalem and the West Bank, the Sinai Peninsula and Gaza Strip, and the Golan Heights
1968–1970	War of Attrition between Israel and Egypt

October 1973	Yom Kippur War—Egypt and Syria launch surprise attack on Israel
1977	Labor loses a national election for the first time; Likud wins and Menachem Begin becomes Prime Minister
1978	Camp David Accords between Israel and Egypt
1979	Israel and Egypt sign peace treaty
1982	Israel attacks Palestine Liberation Organization in Lebanon; massacres at Sabra and Shatilla refugee camps by Christian Phalangists leads to forced resignation of Defense Minister Ariel Sharon
1987–1993	First Intifada — *Palestinian uprising against Israeli occupation*
1993	Declaration of Principles (Oslo Accords) signed between Israel and the Palestine Liberation Organization, leading to the establishment of the Palestinian Authority
1994	Israel and Jordan sign peace treaty
November 1995	Prime Minister Yitzhak Rabin assassinated by a religious zealot opposed to his policies toward the Palestinians
1995–1996	Palestinian terror campaign across Israeli cities
May 2000	Israel withdraws all forces from Lebanese territory
July 2000	Camp David Summit between Ehud Barak, Yasser Arafat, and Bill Clinton
2000–2005	Second Intifada; high levels of violence; Israeli forces enter Palestinian cities and towns in the West Bank to regain control
October 2000	Arab citizens protest, then riot; 13 killed by police
January 2001	Israeli–Palestinian negotiations continue at Taba
2005	Prime Minister Ariel Sharon implements unilateral disengagement from the Gaza Strip
March 2006	Kadima wins the election and forms the government, the first time a party other than Labor or Likud has assumed power
July–August 2006	Lebanon War between Israel and Hezbollah
2007	Hamas takes over Gaza Strip
December 2008–January 2009	Israel–Hamas war
July 2011	Social justice protests begin but peter out by middle of 2012
November 2012	Israel–Hamas war
July–August 2014	Israel–Hamas war

Hamas – Palestinian Sunni-Islamist fundamentalist organization

CHAPTER 2

✣

Zionism and the Origins of Israel

Despite being founded only in 1948, the State of Israel views itself within a long historical context dating back three millennia. After a brief examination of the country's historical background, this chapter focuses on the Zionist movement, which emerged in the late nineteenth century, and especially the contributions of Theodor Herzl, the founder of Zionism. It then examines the various Zionist ideologies that emerged during the twentieth century and how they affected the development of Israeli political parties. Finally, it considers the achievement of the initial Zionist goal through the recognition conferred by the Balfour Declaration and the initiation of the British Mandate for Palestine.

[handwritten margin notes: 1917; became by Britain; part of international law with the Palestine Mandate]

JEWISH HISTORY BEFORE ZIONISM

Modern Israel was created by the Zionist movement. *Zionism* is the Jewish national liberation movement, taken from the liturgical name for Jerusalem and for *Eretz Yisrael*, the Land of Israel. Its roots lie in the history of the Jewish people, dating back to biblical times. Israelites, later Jews, settled in Eretz Yisrael and lived there during the last millennium BCE. They established a sovereign political existence and a religious presence centered on the Temple in their capital, Jerusalem. In those biblical times the source of authority, both political and religious, was divine revelation. Temporal rulers operated within a framework established through the religious tradition and were meant to be subject to that tradition.

According to the Bible, the sovereign existence of the Jews was first interrupted by the destruction of the First Temple by the Babylonians in 586 BCE and the subsequent exile of the Jews. After several decades they were able to return and eventually built a Second Temple. Several centuries later the land fell under the control of Rome. During a revolt by the Jews against the Romans, the latter destroyed the Second Temple in 70 CE. That, and the bloody suppression of a rebellion some 65 years later, extinguished Jewish sovereignty. The bulk of the remaining Jews were sent into exile, while a small number remained in what the Romans called Palestine. Yet the desire to return was nurtured throughout the centuries,

11

[handwritten: Jews kicked out by 1st Babylonians, 2nd Romans]

anchored in Jewish liturgy, prayer, and collective memory. Specific references to the yearning to return to Zion or for the rebuilding of Jerusalem were part of daily prayers, and on both Yom Kippur and Passover, two of the major Jewish holidays, Jews concluded solemn rituals with the ringing call, "Next year in Jerusalem." By building on that desire to return, the Zionist movement was able to capture existing interest in and excitement for a renewal of Jewish independence.

THE JEWISH PREDICAMENT
IN THE NINETEENTH CENTURY

By the beginning of the nineteenth century, Jews lived primarily in Europe and throughout the Middle East and North Africa. Only a small number, perhaps 10,000, lived in Ottoman-controlled Palestine, motivated primarily by the religious consideration of being close to the four holy cities of Jerusalem, Hebron, Safed, and Tiberias. Some Jews did immigrate to Palestine in this period, but they too did so for religious reasons—to study or to spend the end of their days in the Holy Land. During the early part of the century, western European Jews gradually achieved emancipation, though not necessarily total equality. Jews in eastern Europe, especially the Russian Empire, lagged behind their brethren in terms of social advancement and the achievement of political rights. Despite some improvements, by the end of the century anti-Jewish discrimination remained a major problem for the various Jewish communities throughout Europe, and especially in Russia.

During the last half of the century, especially toward the end, the Jewish community was in intellectual ferment. As early as the 1860s some Jews were beginning to imagine a radical change in the Jewish condition. Early writers on the subject included Rabbi Zvi Hirsch Kalischer (1795–1874) and Moses Hess (1812–1875). In 1862 Kalischer published *Seeking Zion*, which focused on the idea of redemption of the Jewish people through a return to the Holy Land. Hess was another precursor of Zionism. His book, *Rome and Jerusalem*, also appeared in 1862 and anticipated a socialist approach to what became Zionism. He even referred to the "restoration" of the Jewish state.

Later in the century many Jews became involved in different political and social movements as a reaction to their oppressed conditions. These included socialism and communism, Bundism, assimilation, *haskalah* (Jewish enlightenment), and state nationalism. As a result of the failure to gain equality, and from a growing desire to have their own political independence, some Jews, especially in Russia, began to consider reconstituting Jewish life in another location, away from the threats of anti-Semitism. Over 2 million eastern European Jews who sought to leave their homes immigrated to America, with the heaviest flow occurring between 1881, the beginning of a wave of Jewish repression in the aftermath of the assassination of Czar Alexander II, and 1914, when war engulfed Europe. But in the wake of the terrible pogroms (organized attacks on Jews by non-Jews, often motivated by anti-Semitism) of the 1880s, a minority of the Jews in Russia began to think about emigration to the traditional Jewish homeland and the reestablishment of Jewish life there.[1] Among the early Russian-Jewish writers who developed what we might term pre-Zionist themes were Peretz Smolenskin (1842–1885), Moshe Leib Lilienblum (1843–1910), and Leon Pinsker (1821–1891).[2] The main themes of their writings were the idea of Jews as a national group, the grim prospects for the Jews if they remained in Russia, the rootlessness and abnormal condition of the Jewish people without their own sovereignty, and the necessity of some kind of collective action to resolve the conundrum. Pinsker's pamphlet *Auto-Emancipation* (1882) in particular encouraged Jews to think of controlling their own destiny and rebuilding their national life, preferably, but not necessarily, in the Land of Israel. In addition to the efforts of these writers, Jews in several Russian cities began to form proto-Zionist clubs known as *Hovevei Zion* (Lovers of Zion), in which members studied the Hebrew language, learned about Eretz Yisrael, and even began to plan to relocate to Palestine.

Jewish immigration into Palestine after 1882 is divided into a series of politically motivated waves called *aliyot*.[3] By 1882 there were about 25,000 Jews living in Palestine. The early pioneers who began to immigrate to Palestine, which was then divided into different administrative districts within the Ottoman Empire, after 1882 were not numerous; perhaps 35,000 arrived over the next 20 years (see Table 2.1). Their efforts were facilitated by their acceptance by the Ottoman rulers, who allowed them to purchase land for their settlements. But these Jews were different from those who were already residing in the four holy cities. They were motivated by a desire to escape pervasive anti-Semitism and by a sense of national identity, were not necessarily religiously observant, and saw their role in their new home as one of developing new communities. Many of them engaged in agricultural pursuits, which was usually a sharp break from their occupations in their countries of origin. Politically unorganized and generally focused on their local communities, they might be known as *proto-Zionists*. Nevertheless Zionists came to view this group as the first wave of immigration to the Land of Israel in modern times, the First Aliya. But unlike those who headed west to America, these Jews were among the early dreamers of a revived Jewish national life in the ancient homeland.

Table 2.1 Immigration of Jews to Palestine, 1882–1948

PERIOD	APPROXIMATE NUMBER OF IMMIGRANTS
First Aliya, 1882–1903	35,000
Second Aliya, 1904–1914	40,000
Third Aliya, 1919–1923	40,000
Fourth Aliya, 1924–1929	82,000
Fifth Aliya, 1929–1939	250,000
Aliya Bet, 1933–1948	110,000
Total Before Statehood	**557,000**

Notes: Aliya means immigration. A numbered aliya is a wave of immigration. Aliyah Bet was an illegal immigration operation run by groups connected to the Yishuv institutions.

THE FOUNDING OF THE ZIONIST MOVEMENT

During the 1890s a major turning point in the history of European Jewry occurred with the beginning of the Zionist movement. By the end of the decade its political goals were clear: to foster national identity among Jews, to bring Jews back to Zion in substantial numbers, to establish a Jewish communal presence in Palestine, and to lay the groundwork for eventual political autonomy, if not statehood. Indeed, Theodor Herzl (1860–1904), the founder of Zionism, wrote presciently in 1897 that he foresaw the creation of a Jewish state in Palestine within 50 years.

Herzl was a nonreligious Jewish Viennese journalist and playwright of Hungarian background who was highly assimilated and immersed in the German-language culture, especially its written works and theater, and not particularly active in Jewish life when he first began to think in Jewish national terms. Some observers ascribe his transformation to his experiences in Paris while covering the Dreyfus trial and its aftermath in 1894;[4] others attribute it to internal grappling with personal identity issues.[5] Whatever the reason, by 1896 he had committed himself totally to what became the Zionist cause. During the remaining frenetic eight years of his short life he devoted himself indefatigably and single-mindedly to the Zionist project. Some would say that he became obsessed with the Zionist idea.

Herzl's efforts to build the Zionist movement had three main foci: to establish an international Zionist organization to represent Zionist communities around the world and serve as the main political institution of the movement, to develop and publish the main ideas of the movement, and to conduct personal diplomacy on the highest levels with heads of government and heads of state in order to garner support for the establishment of a Jewish homeland. There is no doubt that the later success of Zionism owes a great deal to Herzl's efforts. In particular, his unique brand of personal diplomacy, which he pursued tirelessly, eventually gave the movement considerable credibility with various rulers and leading political figures. Herzl made the movement into an international political actor that promoted the concept of Jewish peoplehood to the Ottomans and to the most important European leaders. Although Herzl's period of personal leadership was cut short by his death in 1904, he succeeded in building a respected and effective international organization with diplomatic credibility that enabled his successors to carry out the program that had been laid out through his leadership.

Implications of Zionism

The goals of the early Zionists under Herzl were audacious in comparison to historical Jewish religious precedents. The Zionists took advantage of the fact that by the end of the nineteenth century the identity of Jewish individuals was no longer confined to their religion. Prior to the Emancipation—the period in Europe from the late eighteenth to the late nineteenth century during which Jews gradually gained more citizenship rights—Jews generally had no opportunity to identify as Jews in anything other than a religious sense. But as the social, economic, and political restrictions on Jews diminished, many options became available. The most significant for Zionists was that it became possible for Jews to think of themselves in national terms—as a nation—and not only as members of a religion.

A national identity, expressed through the idea of Jewish peoplehood, had always been available since the exile from Palestine forced by the Romans. But it had little practical significance while the Jews were concentrated in other nations' empires and states, a situation that led to the development of religious identity as the primary means of Jewish identification. Meanwhile, various forms of nationalism emerged throughout Europe during the last half of the nineteenth century. Zionists were aware of these movements and especially followed developments in Italy. By emphasizing national identity, Zionist Jews made it possible to claim international legitimacy as a separate people deserving its own national homeland.

The significance of this development in terms of Jewish tradition cannot be overestimated. Although an integral part of the tradition since the exile by Rome in the form of a yearning for a return to Zion, the general belief was that only God could bring about that return. God would send a Messiah to lead the Jews back to their ancestral homeland. Thus any national aspirations were understood passively. It was long accepted that pursuing such aspirations through human agency was an audacious challenge to God's will. Consequently, the traditional religious view was inherently skeptical of Zionist activity and plans; that view persists among many *haredi* (ultra-Orthodox) Jews living in Israel and elsewhere today.[6] However, by the time that Herzl began to articulate a Zionist position, large numbers of European Jews no longer held the traditional view and thus were open to the Zionist argument that it was not only appropriate but indeed necessary for Jews to take it upon themselves to actively inaugurate a new chapter in their history.

The Zionist stress on national identity, advantageous in an age when many Jews had abandoned traditional religious commitments, created difficulties in terms of the relationship of Zionists with other Jews. Indeed, most of the Orthodox religious leadership rejected Zionism as contrary to religious law; they believed that Jews were obligated to wait for the Messiah to bring them back to the Land of Israel. Zionism was, in their view, a "sin"; some referred to the establishment of Israel as a "satanic act."[7]

Another opposing position on the basis of religion emerged among Reform Jews in Germany and the United States, who also rejected Zionism. For decades it was a cardinal tenet of the Reform movement that Judaism was only a religion and that Jews were not a people or nation. In Germany that view was expressed in terms of the concept of German citizens of the Mosaic persuasion. This conviction, that German Jews owed national allegiance only to Germany, proved to be tragically ironic during the Holocaust. American Reform Jews, concerned about their status in America and fearing accusations of dual loyalty if they supported Jewish nationalism, took a similar position. In their Pittsburgh Platform of 1885, they stated, "We consider ourselves no longer a nation, but a religious community, and therefore expect neither a return to Palestine . . . nor the restoration of any of the laws concerning the Jewish state."[8]

In addition to theologically based opposition, some Jews (especially in Germany) did not share Herzl's assessment of the dangers of anti-Semitism. Therefore, they were not convinced that Zionism was needed. Nevertheless, on balance it is fair to conclude that the emergence of Zionism as a popular ideology among the Jewish masses of Europe represented a veritable revolution in Jewish life, rejecting the passivity of the traditional wait for the Messiah for an activist approach in which Jews took historical change into their own hands.[9] But precisely because it represented such a revolutionary step, most Jews did not yet identify with the movement.

Herzl's Path to Zionism

Herzl had shown little interest in Jewish matters before his experience covering the Dreyfus case. Indeed, as late as 1893 Herzl had even argued in favor of mass conversion, observing that Jews (like himself) had tried in vain to assimilate to their adopted societies but had been rejected, remaining what he termed "aliens" in their native lands. He thus concluded that assimilation could not solve what was known as the *Judenfrage*—the Jewish Question.[10] The Jewish Question (also called the Jewish Problem) was widely discussed in central and western Europe in Herzl's time. It arose because Christian Europe had to deal with the relatively new question of the place of Jews in its societies. Prior to the Emancipation, Jews had been severely restricted in most of Europe and denied the benefits of full citizenship in the countries in which they lived. Once they began to emerge from the ghettos (urban neighborhoods where Jews were confined by the local or national authorities), the question of rights became relevant. Essentially the question was whether Jews could ever be equal citizens, enjoying equal rights and opportunities, in Christian societies.

Perhaps it was not coincidental that anti-Semitic political doctrines began to emerge during the last third of the century, in Germany and elsewhere. Anti-Semitism was particularly rampant in Herzl's Vienna. It was an anti-Semitism that was racially based, which differed from the traditional religion-based model. By the 1890s the combination of violent anti-Semitism in Russia and the more genteel but no less potent variant in central and western Europe had created a crisis in Jewish life, a crisis that in the view of many Jews necessitated a reexamination of the basic assumptions about Jewish life in Christian societies. This was the context in which Herzl began to act.

Once Herzl made the transition to a Zionist identity, he focused mainly on the Land of Israel as the objective. He had the audacity to propose a solution to the Jewish Problem that no one before him—except perhaps Pinsker—had: a Jewish state. As he saw things, first he had to convince his fellow Jews that his vision was not naïve dreaming, but rather a realistic goal. And then he had to persuade the rest of the world that his plan was justified and feasible. He argued that a Jewish state was needed in order to alleviate the suffering of the Jews, mainly those in the Russian Empire, but also eventually Jews more broadly. If anti-Semitism would not go away even in the high civilization of Vienna, it would certainly not diminish in the less civilized areas of eastern Europe. Given this, he became convinced that the only way to resolve the Jewish Question was to remove the Jews from Europe, to take them away from the anti-Semitism that threatened their physical well-being and civic status. Since such a solution was necessary, he was convinced that it would certainly happen. This view was encapsulated in his famous aphorism, "If you will it, it is no dream."[11] His words were more than a catchy slogan; he deeply believed in them, emphasizing the mobilization of the will of the Jewish people as the way to move forward.

Despite his grandiose dreaming, Herzl acknowledged that not all Jews would join his struggle. In addition to those who were opposed on religious grounds, there were many who sought Jewish autonomy within Russia or other countries, many who sought refuge in the New World, and still others who tried to make the best of things where they lived without expecting a fundamental change in their status. So the Zionists of Herzl's time were a minority of the world's Jews and a minority of European Jews as well. That was probably still the case in 1948, when his dream was realized with the creation of the State of Israel.

Herzl's dream envisioned the building of a modern state, comparable to the states with which he was familiar. He recognized that this would be a gradual process and not an easy one. He and his followers knew that their task was twofold: they would have to build up the Jewish community in the traditional homeland by gradually bringing in Jewish immigrants, and they would have to gain international legitimacy for their project. Herzl began to articulate his vision in books and articles, notably *Der Judenstaat* (*The Jewish State*) and his novel *Altneuland* (*Old New Land*).

At the outset of his quest European Jews gave Herzl a lukewarm reception. Nevertheless, he devoted himself completely to the cause, even at the expense of his marriage, his financial well-being, his health, and eventually his life. He became a man of action, constantly on the move on behalf of his cause. During his eight years at the head of the Zionist movement Herzl proved to have outstanding leadership ability. He remained the dominant personality in the organization until his death. But he was hardly an autocrat: he was committed to democracy and stressed the democratic process in the various Zionist congresses that were held.

Organizing the Zionist Movement

Herzl organized the first Zionist Congress, which convened in Basel, Switzerland, in 1897, despite considerable opposition within various Jewish communities. The Congress set up the World Zionist Organization (WZO), which ran the affairs of the movement and set the path for the Zionist cause. Before the establishment of the British Mandate of Palestine and a Jewish community in Palestine with official status (the *Yishuv*), which occurred after World War I, the WZO was the main focus of Zionist organizational activity. Only after the Yishuv began to mature politically during the 1930s did the WZO begin to lose its dominant position.

The congresses were held on a regular basis, and Zionist communities from around the world sent delegates to participate in the debates over the movement that took place there. Representatives were democratically elected from their home communities, and the business of the congresses was conducted according to democratic rules. Elections to the Zionist Congress were conducted using a proportional system: voters cast their ballots for slates of candidates that were allocated representation in proportion to the votes received. Such a system was necessary because of the difficulty of defining meaningful constituency boundaries in the face of geographic dispersion. Furthermore, in order to provide coherence to the discussions, it was desirable to have slates that transcended local concerns and instead represented ideological positions, since voting was taking place in many countries. Thus the pattern was set for subsequent elections in the Yishuv and later Israel, in which ideologically oriented lists or parties gained seats in proportion to the votes received. Herzl also recruited key aides, such as David Wolffsohn (1856–1914) and Max Nordau (1849–1923), who were instrumental in helping him to attract the eastern European Jews who became the backbone of the movement.

The program that the first Zionist Congress adopted consisted of four main elements:

1. Creating the organization and structure to provide continuity
2. Developing Zionist identity through education
3. Planning settlement activities in Palestine to create a Zionist Jewish community there
4. Carrying out diplomatic initiatives to try to persuade international leaders to support the cause

During the early years of Zionism the congresses met annually. One of the most important was the sixth Zionist Congress, held in 1903. The Kishinev Pogrom[12] against the Jews in Bessarabia (then part of the Russian Empire) gave added impetus to the deliberations, which focused on the British government's proposal to establish the Jewish homeland in what was then Uganda (actually part of the Kenyan highlands). Precisely because of the desperation felt by eastern European Jews at the time, some Zionists, including Herzl, toyed with the idea of settling another land. These Jews came to be known as Territorialists. Herzl himself for a short time had considered locating the new homeland in an undeveloped part of Argentina. The discussion at the Congress did not resolve the issue, but intense debate continued until the Uganda proposal was voted down at the next Congress in 1905. From that point on, although a few Zionists, such as Israel Zangwill, continued to seek alternative options, there was never any doubt that a homeland in Eretz Yisrael was the objective. The memory of Zion and the national and religious attachment to the Land of Israel was deep, so ultimately advocates of settling the Holy Land prevailed in the debate about where Jewish sovereignty should be exercised.

Until his death in 1904 Herzl put much of his energy into high-level diplomacy. He met with many heads of state and government leaders throughout Europe, including the Pope, the Italian king, the Ottoman sultan, and even the German Kaiser, whom he personally welcomed on the latter's visit to Palestine. While he was engaged in diplomatic efforts the Zionist Organization engaged in "Practical Zionism," laying the groundwork for the actual immigration of Jews to Palestine, which became a significant factor with the advent of the Second Aliya in 1904. This wave of immigration consisted mainly of working-class eastern European Jews, among them the future Israeli leaders David Ben-Gurion (1886–1973) and Yitzhak Ben-Zvi (1884–1963), who arrived in 1906 and 1907, respectively.

ZIONIST IDEOLOGIES

Within a few years of the creation of Zionism, several theoretical or ideological approaches to Zionism had emerged. These were the antecedents of the political parties that came to characterize Zionist, and later Israeli, politics for decades.

Herzl termed his own ideas "Political Zionism," which was not really an ideological position but rather a concept that reflected his pragmatic diplomatic approach. However, most of the people who involved themselves in Zionist politics in the early years generally identified with a socialist, liberal/free market, religious, or cultural approach. Later on a right-wing approach emerged.

Labor/Socialist Zionism

One of the most significant ideological orientations in Zionism by the end of World War I was based on the socialist ideas that had been so successful in European politics in the late nineteenth and early twentieth centuries. Socialist attitudes were quite common among working-class Jews in Russia (the bulk of the community), which linked them to mainstream Russian socialism. Two main groups emerged among socialists who tried to integrate their Jewish concerns with their social and economic goals: the Bundists and the Labor Zionists. The supporters of the Bund sought an autonomous but nonterritorial Jewish national existence in Russia based on socialist principles. They strongly opposed Zionism and became irrelevant in the development of the Zionist movement and later Israel. The Labor Zionists, in contrast, attempted to integrate their Zionist aspirations with their socialist beliefs and became the dominant faction on the left side of the Zionist movement. A third alternative, followed by many left-leaning Jews, was to totally subordinate their Jewish backgrounds to their socialist political affiliations and give their support to Russian parties or revolutionary movements like the Bolsheviks and Mensheviks.

One Zionist ideologue, Nachman Syrkin (1867–1924), perceived that Jews could not really expect to flourish in Russian society because of discrimination. His analysis led to calls for an independent Jewish labor movement. Syrkin believed that the socialist revolution would not solve the Jewish Question, though he did advocate a classless society. Ironically, he believed in internationalism, a common idea among socialists at the turn of the century, but felt that the Jews would first have to become an independent nation. To Syrkin a state was a necessary historical step, but he contended that it could only be formed as the result of a genuine mass movement. Though decidedly socialist, Syrkin was not a committed Marxist like Ber Borochov (1881–1917), and he did believe that it was feasible to fuse socialism and Zionism, ultimately promoting a brand of socialism that had much in common with the democratic socialism that emerged in western Europe early in the twentieth century.

Borochov was an activist and organizer as well as a thinker. In his writings he attempted to synthesize Marxism and Zionism and articulated a critique of Jewish class structure in Russia. He believed that Zionism would provide the means to transform that structure because he expected that the immigration of middle-class Jews to Palestine would create opportunities for workers, which would in turn attract proletarian immigrants. Toward that end he helped to create *Poalei Zion* (Workers of Zion), the first Socialist Zionist mass political organization. Though he died in 1917, before any of his theories were translated into action, his ideas inspired the more left-wing elements of Labor Zionism for years to come.

Labor Zionism received a big boost because of the Second Aliya, following the failure of the 1905 revolution in Russia. Those immigrants, about 40,000 in number, were mainly adherents of Poalei Zion or *HaPoel HaTzair* (the Young Worker Party). The former followed much of Borochov's thinking, especially with respect to class and nationality-based struggles. It stressed the need to create a Jewish working class in order to take steps toward the revolution, which was to be both Zionist and socialist. But under the leadership of two key figures in the Second Aliya, David Ben-Gurion and Yitzhak Ben-Zvi, the Palestinian Poalei Zion modified and adapted Borochov's positions, becoming more pragmatic and less reliant on immutable historical laws. By the second decade of the twentieth century they had succeeded in transforming their organization into a social democratic party with a sense of the real and the possible, as well as a strong ideological basis.

In contrast, HaPoel HaTzair was very pragmatic and avoided grand ideological theory. Its supporters, such as the writer Aaron David Gordon (1856–1922), believed that the new Jewish society had to differ from European Jewish communities in fundamental ways. Hence they emphasized the importance of Jewish manual labor and the need for Jews to form a working class that would build the new society. The development of such a class would be an essential precursor to national liberation. Many of the party's adherents were also pacifists who objected to the formation of Jewish self-defense groups by other Palestinian Jews. What tied the various Socialist Zionist groups together, then, was their emphasis on work as necessary for constituting the Jewish nation. In historian Howard Sachar's words,

> The emphasis of the Second Aliyah was upon physical labor on the soil of Palestine. The youthful visionaries who fled the misery of the Pale evinced a genuine sense of guilt for having been alienated from the land. It was a Russian, no less than a Jewish, reaction. Slav writers, from the populist Narodniki to the universally venerated Tolstoy, had been accustomed to extol the peasant as the repository of all virtue; and … the Jewish intelligentsia subscribed to this romanticized image. Their obsession with the soil also expressed unconscious resentment at the creeping industrial revolution in eastern Europe, a social transformation that dislodged the Jews economically and confronted them with the new and more vicious anti-Semitism of the urban lower-middle class. Agriculture alone, then, would make the Jew independent. As members also of Poalei Zion, the newcomers appreciated that Socialist thinkers from Marx to Lenin had cited the absence of a Jewish peasant class as evidence that the Jews were not a nation, but rather a peculiar social or functional entity.[13]

Liberal/General Zionism

Whereas the various Labor Zionist groups reflected the collectivist orientation of socialism, other Zionists based their political goals on the bourgeoisie, and so were oriented toward a more free market economy. Herzl himself leaned toward a liberal approach to Zionism, a perspective that was carried forward by Nordau and then Chaim Weizmann (1874–1952). The Liberal Zionists tended to be rather centrist politically. They were less concerned with promoting a specific ideological agenda, arguing that the focus should be on building up Zionist institutions in preparation for independence. The highest-profile faction among such groups was the General Zionists. Their most prominent spokesman was Weizmann, who later became Israel's first President. A British scientist who had come from Russia and emerged as the leader of Zionists outside Palestine, he became the head of the World Zionist Organization and the spokesman for Zionism internationally. Although he certainly did not share Ben-Gurion's socialist stance, the two of them were instrumental in leading the Zionists toward the goal of Jewish statehood, with Weizmann acting on the outside and Ben-Gurion emerging as leader of the Yishuv.

Religious Zionism

Even though the initial position of the Orthodox community was to reject Zionism as a repudiation of key religious beliefs, some Orthodox Jews did see merit in the movement and formed a Religious Zionist organization (*Mizrachi*) in 1902. This group, which claimed that the hand of God was acting in history through Zionism, became an integral part of the Zionist movement. Though its adherents, such as its founder, Rabbi Isaac Jacob Reines of Lithuania, may have had some doubts about the relationship of Zionism to traditional Jewish theology, they eventually embraced it enthusiastically, seeing the return to the traditional homeland as part of the long-promised process of national redemption. This was a radical departure from the traditional view and led to a split within Orthodoxy and the formation of the anti-Zionist and ultra-Orthodox *Agudat Yisrael* in 1912. The split has persisted and has direct implications for contemporary Israeli politics. Both Religious Zionism and the Aguda, as Agudat Yisrael is often identified, are represented in Israeli political parties today; their differences sometimes become policy issues, such as the question of conscription of the ultra-Orthodox (see Chapter 6).

The Religious Zionists tried to combine religion and nationalism, stressing the sanctity of the land and the combination of land, peoplehood, and religion as the core of modern Judaism and Jewish identity. Although they preferred establishing the Jewish national home according to the principles of *halacha* (religious law), they understood that as a relatively small minority within Zionism they would have to compromise their principles. Thus they were pragmatic associates of the nonreligious elements in the Zionist movement, though they remained wary of the socialists, secularists, and liberals and were often unhappy with Weizmann's leadership.

Rabbi Abraham Isaac Kook (1865–1935, also known as Rav Kook) was the major thinker of the Religious Zionists. The British appointed him as one of the two Chief Rabbis of Palestine in 1925. But he was also a prolific writer who integrated the centrality of Eretz Yisrael in the Jewish religious tradition into Zionist thought and even expressed the view that the Jews were facing the dawn of the messianic era. One of his main contributions was to reinterpret the significance of the Land of Israel, contending that from a religious perspective it was not only preferable, but indeed obligatory, to live in Eretz Yisrael. Another key element of his thinking was his view that secular Zionists served as an instrument of God's will, which imbued their endeavor with religious meaning. His ideological position ensured that Orthodox Jews could feel themselves to be an integral part of the Zionist enterprise and could work together with nonreligious Zionists, despite the intense criticisms of the haredim.

Cultural Zionism

Zionism without the political dimension was also a possibility to the followers of a Russian-born writer and essayist named Asher Zvi Ginsberg (1856–1927), better known by his pen name Ahad Ha'am (Hebrew for "one of the people"). His thought focused on what he called Cultural Zionism, the idea that the purpose of Zionism was to foster the revival of Jewish spiritual life and the flowering of Jewish culture, including language, literature, education, and Jewish knowledge. Ahad Ha'am was skeptical of Political Zionism because he doubted that enough Jews would immigrate to Eretz Yisrael, thereby precluding that solution to the Jewish Question in Europe. Essentially, he wanted the Land of Israel to be a national spiritual center of Judaism, a center of study, literary creativity, and learning. He feared that Herzl's vision would produce a "state of the Jews" but not necessarily a Jewish state, foreshadowing debates in decades to come. Ahad Ha'am also considered the existence of the Arab population in Palestine and wondered about its effects on the Zionist effort.

Revisionist Zionism

The main ideological challenge to Socialist Zionism that developed during the Mandate period was articulated by the journalist Vladimir Jabotinsky (1880–1940), who immigrated from Russia to Palestine. More than most Zionist thinkers, Jabotinsky believed that the use of force would have to be an integral part of efforts to establish Jewish sovereignty in Palestine because of the existence of another community already living there. He anticipated clashes with the Arabs and advocated Jewish military preparation and the eventual formation of an army.[14] That conviction led him to form a Jewish Legion that fought on the British side against the Ottomans in 1917 and to stress the value of military training and discipline. As a result he is often viewed as a militarist, though his followers contended that his commitment to military preparedness was motivated by defensive considerations. Jabotinsky was also inspired by the liberal nationalism that appeared in many European countries, especially Italy, during the nineteenth century. He believed deeply in individual rights for all inhabitants of the coming Jewish state.

Jabotinsky had major policy differences with the mainstream Zionist leadership and was especially critical of what he saw as Weizmann's policy of gradualism, compromise, weakness, and lack of initiative. In contrast, he believed in bold strokes, without which he did not think the Zionist movement could succeed. This discontent led him to resign from the Zionist Executive (the top leadership group of the World Zionist Organization) in 1923 and establish the Revisionist movement. He claimed to be the true heir of Herzl and Nordau's Political Zionism. During the 1920s the Revisionists were the only Zionist group actively advocating a Jewish state. The rest more cautiously called for a Jewish "national home," echoing the language of the Balfour Declaration (see Appendix C). The Revisionists also advocated a more maximalist state. Jabotinsky spoke of a state with a Jewish majority on both sides of the Jordan River. Like the Cultural Zionists, Jabotinsky also openly discussed the dilemma posed by Arabs who would oppose the Zionist movement on the basis of their own nationalism, but where Ahad Ha'am was less clear about how to resolve this issue, Jabotinsky firmly believed the Jewish case to be morally stronger.

Ideological Politics

The ideological developments of the early part of the twentieth century had a lasting impact on the Israeli political system. All of the major Zionist ideologies, especially Labor Zionism, General Zionism, Religious Zionism, and Revisionist Zionism, became the bases of Israeli political parties later on, to the extent that by 1948, when statehood was achieved, the country already had a well-developed party system. Currently, Labor Zionism is carried on by the Labor and Meretz parties, General Zionism and Revisionist Zionism by the Likud party, and Religious Zionism by *Bayit Yehudi* (the Jewish Home party). As we shall see in the next chapter, the Palestinian Jews during the Mandate period also developed their own political institutions and electoral system.

Other countries have also developed ideology-based party systems, including states as varied as the United States, China, the Soviet Union (before 1991), and various European countries. Although there are some parallels between these countries, there are significant differences as well. In the United States, for example, there has been an overarching ideology of liberalism: variants inform competing political positions, but there is an implicit consensus about the basic meaning of liberalism. Both China and the Soviet Union have based their politics on the hegemony of the Communist Party and its ideology, which does not allow any party competition. And European countries, to the extent that their parties are ideological, have generally divided along conventional left–right lines. Israel, in contrast, subscribes to a defining ideology, Zionism, but each party defines that ideology differently, and not necessarily in terms of the same variables. Thus one can classify contemporary Israeli ideologies along three distinctly different axes: a conventional left–right economic distinction; a religious or secular distinction; and in terms of security and attitudes toward the Arabs (see Chapter 9).

It should be noted that early Zionist thinkers did not confront the question of how the Arab residents of Palestine, a very large majority that numbered about 300,000 in 1900, would respond to Jewish immigration in pursuit of Zionist goals. This, of course, proved to be a serious oversight, especially since the Arabs believed that Britain and France had promised Palestine to them during World War I.[15] Zionists tended to view Palestine as "a land without a people for a people without a land."[16]

There were three main views of the Palestinian Arabs among the Zionists. The Socialist Zionists mostly saw them as competitors for labor, and as roadblocks to the creation of a Jewish economy necessary for the reconstitution of peoplehood. The bulk of the secular Zionist community, which was guided by universal humanism, believed that the building up of a modern state in a backward region of the Ottoman Empire would bring technological advancements to the Arab population. Thus they viewed the Arabs in more paternalistic terms. Only the Revisionists saw the Palestinian Arabs as a people with their own communal identity that would not welcome—indeed, would challenge—the Zionist effort to establish a Jewish political entity in the area. For this reason the Palestinian Arabs were seen as enemies and antagonists. It was not until years after the state was established that its political leaders began to confront the dilemma of a substantial resident Arab population.

THE PALESTINE MANDATE

Zionism began to move from theory to practice with the significant immigration associated with the Second Aliya. Externally, the cause began to progress toward the end of World War I. Most importantly, the British government issued the Balfour Declaration in 1917, which committed the government to back the establishment of a Jewish national home, though pointedly not an independent Jewish state:

> His Majesty's Government views with favor the establishment in Palestine of a national home for the Jewish people, and will use their best endeavors to facilitate the achievement of this object, it being clearly understood that nothing shall be done which may prejudice the civil and religious rights of existing non-Jewish communities in Palestine or the rights and political status enjoyed by Jews in any other country.

The significance of the statement was underscored by the victories of the British army under General Allenby, which drove the Ottomans out of Palestine and brought the territory under British control.

There are two important points to make with regard to the Declaration. First, despite its cautious wording about a national home, many Zionists understood that implementation of the Declaration would eventually provide them with an opportunity to transform that national home into a full-fledged independent state, even if that was not the official goal at first. Second, the Declaration addresses the "national" rights of the Jewish people but only refers to the "civil and religious" rights of the Arabs of Palestine. This wording reinforced the view of the Zionists that Jewish nationalism would take precedence over Arab nationalism in Palestine, even though the Arabs greatly outnumbered the Jews in 1917 and indeed throughout the Mandate period.

What motivated the British government to issue the Balfour Declaration? There are various explanations, including the desire to solidify Jewish support, including American Jewish support, for the Allied war effort; British colonial ambitions in the Middle East; a response to pressure from Weizmann and the Zionists; and firm beliefs (what we today call Christian Zionism) held by key members of the Cabinet. The October Revolution in Russia, which ultimately led to the Bolsheviks taking that country out of World War I, also had an impact. Britain wanted to keep Russia in the war and might have believed that Jews would be able to influence the new government toward that goal.[17]

After the war the various nationalities in the former empires of the defeated Central Powers (Germany, Austria-Hungary, and the Ottoman Empire) as well as the Russian Empire turned to the international community for recognition of their national rights. The Jews were among them. The Paris Peace Conference in 1919 recognized the Jewish people as one of the peoples seeking national self-determination. The resolution of the question of what would happen to the former Ottoman territories in the Middle East, as agreed upon by the victorious Allies at the San Remo Conference and in the Treaty of Sèvres (1920), and reaffirmed in the 1923 Treaty of Lausanne, provided for three mandates, or trusteeships, as approved by the League of Nations: Syria and Lebanon, under the oversight of France, and Mesopotamia (modern-day Iraq) as well as Palestine, under the oversight of Britain. The Palestine

Mandate at first included both sides of the Jordan River, including what is today the Kingdom of Jordan. The text of the Palestine Mandate incorporated verbatim the Balfour Declaration, thereby making the establishment of a Jewish national home a primary purpose of the Mandate and enshrining it in international law. The Palestine Mandate, like those in Syria and Mesopotamia, also emphasized the duty of the Mandatory power to prepare the entire population for self-government. Arguably, the contrast between the Zionist objective of building a Jewish national home and the Palestinian Arab objective of achieving self-government based on their majority status made the British task impossible.

Shortly before the beginning of the Mandate in 1922, the British government decided that the provisions regarding the Jewish national home would not apply east of the Jordan River. What is today Jordan was severed from the original Palestine Mandate and eventually made into its own state. Nevertheless, as the Mandate went into effect, the Zionists were optimistic and hopeful that their project would flourish under British rule. The Arabs of Palestine, backed by the Arab states, were generally opposed to Zionism and in particular put strong pressure on the British to limit Jewish immigration to the territory.

SUMMARY

In just 25 years, Zionism had come into being as a movement, produced several ideological approaches to the overall general goal, established Jewish communities and settlements in various parts of Palestine, achieved international recognition and support for its goals, and was ready to embark on the next stage of building a state. The movement had a permanent organization, the WZO, and fostered an intellectual ferment that generated numerous ideological writings and disputes. It produced several organizations that implemented those ideologies and became the basis for party politics later on.

As the Mandate began, the Jews of Palestine were ready to begin the long struggle that culminated in statehood. Until that point they had focused their attention on the European powers, and especially Britain. Few Zionists anticipated the way in which conflict, at times violent, would be a central part of Jewish–Arab relations during the Mandate period. The 25 years of the Mandate ultimately provided the opportunity for statehood, though progress toward that goal was hardly smooth, as will become clear in the next chapter.

KEYWORDS

Labor Zionism, Religious Zionism, Revisionist Zionism, Theodor Herzl, Ahad Ha'am, British Mandate for Palestine, Yishuv

NOTES

1. Barry Rubin, *Israel: An Introduction* (New Haven, CT: Yale University Press, 2012), 19.
2. Arthur Hertzberg, ed., *The Zionist Idea: A Historical Analysis and Reader* (Philadelphia: Jewish Publication Society, 1997), 143, 167, 179.

3. *Aliya* means going up in two senses. The first is literal—in order to travel from the sea coast to Jerusalem, the traditional capital, one must ascend in altitude. The second is spiritual—Jerusalem (Zion) was traditionally centered on the religious experience. Hence Jews considered immigration to the Land of Israel to be an experience of ascent in both senses of *aliya*.

4. French army captain Alfred Dreyfus, a Jew, was falsely accused of passing sensitive information to Germany. He was convicted in a court-martial in 1894 and sentenced to a long prison term. His supporters continued to fight to clear his name, a goal that was ultimately achieved. For Herzl and other Jews, the main significance of the Dreyfus Affair was the anti-Semitism that it brought to the surface in many parts of French society. As a result, some became convinced that there was no future for the Jews in Europe.

5. Jacques Kornberg, *Theodor Herzl: From Assimilation to Zionism* (Bloomington: Indiana University Press, 1993), 190. Herzl grappled with his identity as a Jew and the problem of how to resolve the dilemma of Jews not being fully a part of the general European culture. At various points in his life before Zionism he considered assimilation and conversion as solutions to this dilemma.

6. The term *haredi* translates into "one who trembles before God," but is more loosely understood as "God-fearing." It is commonly used as a synonym for ultra-Orthodox.

7. Aviezer Ravitzky, *Messianism, Zionism, and Jewish Religious Radicalism*, trans. Michael Swirsky and Jonathan Chipman (Chicago: University of Chicago Press, 1993).

8. Central Conference of American Rabbis, "The Pittsburgh Platform—1885," https://ccarnet.org/rabbis-speak/platforms/declaration-principles/.

9. Shlomo Avineri, *The Making of Modern Zionism: Intellectual Origins of the Jewish State* (New York: Basic Books, 1981), 13.

10. Theodor Herzl, *The Jewish State* (New York: Dover Publications, 1988), 85–97.

11. The phrase was adapted from his novel, *Altneuland*.

12. The Kishinev Pogrom occurred when a mob was whipped up using the old accusation of blood libel—that Jews were using the blood of Christian children for ritual purposes. It shocked Jews throughout the world and attracted the attention of many governments. What was particularly distressing to the Jews was the vicious character of the attacks, which resulted in 49 deaths and over 500 injuries, combined with the instrumental role of the authorities in the violence. In the aftermath of the pogrom Zionists approached their work with intensified commitment and a sense of urgency.

13. Howard M. Sachar, *A History of Israel: From the Rise of Zionism to Our Time*, 3rd ed. (New York: Alfred A. Knopf, 2007), 74. The Pale of Settlement was the western part of Czarist Russia where Jews were allowed to live.

14. Alain Dieckhoff, *The Invention of a Nation: Zionist Thought and the Making of Modern Israel,* trans. Jonathan Derrick (New York: Columbia University Press, 2003), 212–213.

15. The Arab claims were based on the McMahon-Hussein correspondence (1915) and the Sykes-Picot agreement (1916). The Zionists later contended that the Balfour Declaration and the Palestine Mandate superseded any commitments to the Arabs.

16. Anita Shapira, trans. by William Templar, *Land and Power: The Zionist Resort to Force, 1881–1948* (Stanford: Stanford University Press, 1992), 42.

17. It was certainly true that many Russian Jews found the Bolshevik cause attractive. But during the early years of the Soviet Union it became clear that neither the Communist Party nor the Jews who were active in it had any interest in the Zionist cause, which was ideologically contrary to the international emphasis of Marxist-Leninist thought. In light of this history there is a certain irony in the fact that the Soviet Union backed the 1947 Partition Plan that led to the creation of Israel.

CHAPTER 3

꒰ㅂ꒱

Yishuv Politics During
the Mandate Period

B ritain's Palestine Mandate, established by the League of Nations, lasted from 1922 until Britain relinquished its role on May 15, 1948, when the Mandate was to have been divided into an Arab state and a Jewish state, according to the United Nations Partition Plan. Knowledge of the quarter-century during which Britain governed Palestine is critical for an understanding of Israel's political development as well as the still-unresolved Arab–Israeli conflict for a number of reasons. Primary among the events of the Mandate period are the challenges and opportunities afforded the Yishuv to mature politically and prepare for statehood, the escalating conflict between the Jewish and Arab communities within the area, and the manner in which the Mandate ended. On the day that the Mandate ended and the British departed, the State of Israel declared its independence.[1] The Palestinian Arabs, however, failed to establish their own state and instead joined forces with neighboring Arab countries to abort the nascent Jewish state by military means and extend Arab rule over all of what had been the Mandate territory.

From the perspective of Israeli politics after 1948, developments during the Mandate period helped to determine a number of features of the political system. Indeed, by 1948, the Jews had a functioning political system anchored by widely accepted democratic procedures, a defense force (the *Haganah*), a diplomatic corps in training, an active party system, experienced voters, a highly motivated and loyal citizenry, and a functioning legal system, including a body of laws and courts to apply them. It is noteworthy that participation in Yishuv politics was voluntary, as it was not a state and had no coercive power over its population. Nevertheless, almost all Zionist and Jewish groups participated in political life. All of the aforementioned institutions were transformed into Israeli state institutions with relative ease after 1948. It was the accomplishments of the Mandate period that enabled the Jews to make the most of the opportunity to transition into statehood.

This chapter traces developments during the Yishuv period, beginning with a description of the efforts to construct a viable Jewish society under the Mandate, particularly those focusing on the development of the party system and a national identity. It then outlines the intercommunal conflict that characterized the later Mandate era, the Zionist–British conflict, and events during the end of the Mandate.

CONSTRUCTING A JEWISH SOCIETY

One of the key characteristics of the Mandate period was the dual nature of social and political life in Palestine. There were two distinct communities, one Jewish and the other Arab. The communities generally lived separately, with the exception of a few mixed towns like Jerusalem, Jaffa, and Haifa. Both groups had relationships with the Mandatory government, but cooperation was minimal, in part because the government was run from London, leaving little scope for participation by the two local communities. Since neither community wanted to remain under British control, this situation suited each one's common goal of preparing for independence by governing itself. In these preparations, each had outside help. The Arabs enjoyed support from the Arab states and nationalist movements elsewhere in the Middle East, while the WZO and Jewish communities in the diaspora backed the Yishuv.

In reality, Palestine was a binational polity throughout the British Mandate with little to hold it together except formal British authority. This meant that there was scant support for the idea of a binational state when some Jews did propose it during the 1920s and again during the early 1940s.[2] The two societies differed in manifold ways, including religion, language, ethnicity, culture, social structure, and economic organization. Each community tried to exercise authority over its own members. Thus, while the Mandatory government operated the official state structure, the two communities had their separate voluntary polities. There was no sense of shared political or economic institutions or geographic space (they had largely separate economies, and the Hebrew- and Arabic-language school systems were also kept separate). Although the political leadership on each side exercised considerable communal authority, even in the absence of sovereign status, the Jews were more successful in creating institutions and processes that could be transformed into a functioning state in 1948.

During the first half of the Mandate period, approximately from 1922 to 1936, there was an emphasis in both communities on consolidation and building political infrastructure. All of the major Israeli institutions—the party system, the political system, the military, the educational framework, organized labor, and so on—were created in this period. This era also saw the creation of representative institutions, eventually leading to what amounted to a government of the Yishuv. There were two main institutions. The more powerful and significant was the Jewish Agency (successor to the Jerusalem office of the Executive of the World Zionist Organization), which enjoyed formally recognized legal status by the League of Nations and the Mandatory Government. Its executive included both Zionists and, after 1929, non-Zionists, but was dominated by the leadership of the WZO. The other institution, which was much weaker, was the *Knesset Yisrael* (Jewish Assembly), which also held recognized status. This was a voluntary political structure to which any Palestinian Jew could belong. Those who joined formed a broad Jewish electorate that selected members of an assembly, known as *Asefat HaNivharim* (Elected Assembly), through a proportional representation electoral system based on the practices used in the WZO. Elections were held among the Jews in 1920, 1925, 1931, and 1944, with turnouts as high as 70 percent, thereby conferring democratic legitimacy on the new institutions. The Assembly selected a smaller *Va'ad Leumi* (National Council), which in turn selected its own executive.

All of these bodies were temporal and secular; they had no religious authority. A separate Chief Rabbinate, created by the British in 1925, dealt with religious matters, which included personal status issues such as marriage and divorce. This was the continuation of Ottoman policy, which had divided the Empire's population into *millets* (religious communities) and granted each millet authority over its own religious affairs. Recognizing the different cultural and doctrinal positions of the two communities, the British established a separate Chief Rabbi for the Ashkenazi population (Jews of European descent), and one for the Sephardi population (technically, Jews of Spanish descent but at the time used to refer also to Jews of Middle Eastern descent). The Jews grasped the opportunity to build a political community based on a nationalist ideology and to establish the necessary institutions to maintain an autonomous existence.[3]

The Palestinian Arabs, too, created a political body to represent their interests in negotiations with the Mandatory power, but the Arab Higher Committee was self-appointed by prominent landholding Palestinian Arab families. Because it was not an elected or representative body, it could not serve as the focal point for a broadly based Palestinian nationalism.

It was quickly apparent that one of the main issues, and perhaps the most contentious, that separated the two communities was immigration. The Zionists sought maximum immigration of Jews, primarily from Europe; indeed, for many early Zionist thinkers, the "ingathering of the exiles" was a primary function of Jewish statehood. Once the Nazis took power in Germany in 1933, the need for immigration to Palestine became more urgent. The Arabs generally opposed Jewish immigration, fearing that the resulting population growth would overwhelm their community. Each side pressed the Mandatory government to give preference to its view. By the end of the 1920s friction between the two communities was very high, with Arab protests turning into violent riots and even massacres in places like Jerusalem and Hebron.

Fostering a Jewish-Zionist National Identity

In addition to specific political and economic institutions, the Zionist leadership sought to revitalize Jewish identity. This was necessary, according to early Zionist thinkers, to make of the Jews a "normal" nation, but it was also a way of fostering a sense of belonging among members of what was an increasingly besieged community. Most of the community was drawn, or drawn in, to this Jewish identity, with the exceptions of the far-left Communists and the haredim, both of whom largely remained either anti- or non-Zionist.

One important way this unified identity was achieved was by reconstituting Hebrew as the language of the Yishuv. Long used only in Judaism's liturgy, prayer, and study, Hebrew had been dormant as a living, usable language. Cultural Zionists saw in it a powerful proof of Jewish peoplehood and a way to revive Jewish spirituality and culture. They led the way in modernizing the language, and no one contributed more in this regard than Eliezer Ben-Yehuda (1858–1922), who made it his personal mission to reconstruct this ancient language for modern usage.[4] Most immigrants to the Yishuv either did not speak Hebrew or understood it primarily from religious texts. When the British declared Hebrew one of three official languages of the Mandate (alongside English and Arabic), its use became more formalized and necessary. The Cultural Zionists, Labor Zionists, and Revisionist Zionists especially encouraged the use of Hebrew in everyday activity, creating new words to describe modern objects, concepts, and actions.

Another way that the Zionists sought to bind the community together was through the reimagining of Jewish history and the creation of the "new Jew." Yael Zerubavel demonstrates how the early Zionist leaders identified three periods in Jewish history: antiquity (Jewish origins up to the destruction of the Second Temple), exile (from the end of Jewish sovereignty in Eretz Yisrael to the late nineteenth century), and rebirth (the onset of Zionism to the present).[5] For Zionists trying to reestablish Jewish statehood in their biblical and historical homeland, the period to which they looked for inspiration was antiquity. In this era Jews were warriors, leaders, masters of their own fate. The Zionists thus looked past exile, averting their eyes in disgust and humiliation at what the Jews had become. Jews of the exile were viewed as physically weak and too religious (and therefore emotionally weak). The Jews of the Zionist era would be strong again. Posters of deeply tanned men and women, now called *halutzim* (pioneers), carrying rifles and farming implements were used for recruitment purposes in Europe and America.

In order to create new collective memories to inspire the new Jew and create a new Hebrew identity, early Zionists reinterpreted Jewish history and religious texts. They emphasized the martial elements of ancient and biblical stories. Jews who were killed as martyrs for remaining true to their beliefs were transformed into heroes fighting for Jewish rights and independence. For example, the story of the Bar Kochba rebellion was viewed very differently by rabbinic leaders and by the secular Zionists. From 132 to 135 CE, Bar Kochba led an unsuccessful rebellion against the Romans. Whereas religious Jews saw him as a ruthless, mean-spirited, violent man who bullied his followers into war—or as something like a heretic for pretending to be a Messiah-like figure—secular Zionists saw in him a warrior willing to take up arms to reclaim Jewish sovereignty, taking action rather than waiting passively for God, despite the failure of his rebellion and Rome's subsequent violent reaction against the Jews. The Revisionist Zionist youth movement took its name, Betar, from one of his strongholds.

The Zionists did not look just to the Bible or to antiquity; they drew on more recent events as well. The battle at Tel Hai in 1920 became a near-mythic tale of the ultimate sacrifice for the greater good. When the small settlement became engaged in a fight with an Arab band, the one-armed Joseph Trumpeldor—already a hero in the Yishuv—led the defense. He was mortally wounded in battle and on his deathbed allegedly uttered what became a rallying cry: "Never mind, it is good to die for one's country."[6]

DEVELOPMENT OF A PARTY SYSTEM

During the Mandate a political party system based on the ideological divisions in the Zionist movement developed within the Yishuv. Some of the parties had their origins in the days of the Zionist congresses, well before the establishment of the Mandate. In this way they served as the building blocks of the national institutions by providing a linkage between their supporters and the collective political expression of the Yishuv. By the 1930s a professionalized political leadership that was selected on the basis of merit and achievement had emerged from the political parties that competed in Yishuv elections. Since this party system carried over into Israeli politics after 1948, it is important to examine the origins and activities of the parties that composed it.

At first those parties concentrated on establishing themselves and looking after the needs of their members. Indeed, parties became more than political organizations. They constructed a wide variety of agencies to serve their members' needs, including youth and women's groups, reading clubs, health clinics, and paramilitary organizations. Divided by ideology and different interpretations of Zionism, parties were essentially "sub-centers" within the Yishuv.[7] But subsequently they entered into electoral competition and participated in the self-government of the Yishuv.

Since workers were in the vanguard of the Second and Third Aliyot, they formed the first parties in Palestine, which gave them the advantage in the construction of both Yishuv and Israeli institutions. As mentioned in Chapter 2, the two main parties were Poalei Zion (later *Achdut Ha'avodah*, Unity of Labor) and HaPoel HaTzair. These parties joined to form the *Histadrut* (General Federation of Laborers in the Land of Israel) in 1920 and then *Mapai* (a Hebrew acronym for *Mifleget Poalei Eretz Yisrael*, or Party of the Workers of the Land of Israel) in 1930, which became the most successful of the political parties, with the strongest and most talented leadership. David Ben-Gurion became its leader in 1935 and led it throughout the rest of the Mandate period, becoming Israel's first Prime Minister in 1948. Mapai is the antecedent of today's Labor Party.

These parties helped to provide work and social services to their members. As national institutions developed, the parties continued to play that role. They also allocated resources and provided linkages between individuals and the central institutions. An important principle that emerged during the early 1920s, originally in the context of British-issued immigration certificates, was the party key, a method of proportional allocation of resources through the parties. This encouraged the development of party machines, especially in Mapai, which provided for the needs of its members in exchange for unquestioned support. As a result Mapai pioneered the distribution of patronage in the broadest sense, patronage that often went well beyond the allocation of official government jobs. Other labor or socialist parties that emerged during the 1920s were to the left of Mapai and included *HaShomer HaTzair* (The Young Guardsman), which was oriented toward a segment of the *kibbutzim*, or collective agricultural communities; and *Poalei Zion Smol* (The Left Workers of Zion), which was committed to class struggle. There was also an anti-Zionist Palestine Communist Party, which advocated for binationalism and was illegal (though it did compete in Histadrut elections). But by the end of World War II, by which time many of the Zionist parties had consolidated into a few large organizations, Mapai emerged as one of the largest groups and was able to dominate both Yishuv and Zionist politics. It still faced some opposition from other leftist parties, particularly *Mapam* (*Mifleget HaPoalim HaMeuhedet*, the United Workers Party).

Three other broad political groupings were each influential in Yishuv politics. One, known simply as *Ezrachim* (Citizens), brought together a number of elements that did not share the working-class identity of the labor parties. These were mainly the Farmers Association, the Artisans Association, and the General Zionists (a secular, liberal, and free market–oriented group). The General Zionists later split into two factions. The A faction, led by Chaim Weizmann from abroad, cooperated politically with Mapai, while the B faction was very antagonistic toward labor politics.

The second grouping was composed of Sephardim. This community was distinct from the Ashkenazi community, particularly culturally. The Sephardim during the Mandate period constituted a small portion of the Yishuv but generally traced their lineage in Eretz Yisrael back for many generations. They were not numerous enough to have their own party, so they divided their votes between the labor parties and the Ezrachim.

The third grouping was religious and consisted of Mizrachi (the name given to the organization of the Religious Zionists) and the haredim. However, the latter were generally hostile toward Zionism. They withdrew from Yishuv politics in the early 1920s, which led the Mizrachi to join forces with the Ezrachim in specific elections and on specific issues. The Mizrachi later split into two factions, one retaining the name and the other labeling itself as *HaPoel HaMizrachi* (The Mizrachi Worker). The latter was more willing to work with Mapai and became an important ally of that party after 1935.

Finally, there were groups on the right end of the political spectrum. Here the dominant party was the Revisionist organization, led by Vladimir Ze'ev Jabotinsky until his death in 1940, after which Menachem Begin inherited the leadership mantle. The Revisionists withdrew from participation in Yishuv politics for parts of the 1920s and 1930s. They had their own social, labor, and health organizations, paralleling those established by Mapai, though with much smaller numbers.

Zionist elections were held in the Yishuv and in the WZO through the 1930s and again in 1946. Within Palestine, labor parties generally won between 60 and 70 percent of the vote. The General Zionists began with less than 10 percent of the vote, but that figure increased to between 12 and 17 percent after middle-class immigrants began to arrive during the 1930s. Support for Religious Zionists was also in the single digits before 1935, but thereafter this faction won between 10 and 15 percent of the vote. The Revisionists polled between 12 and 16 percent during the early 1930s, boycotted the elections between 1935 and 1939, and then won nearly 14 percent in 1946. The haredim did not compete in elections, as they viewed human-created institutions as a violation of God's will.

WZO election results that combined both Palestinian and diaspora Jewish voters produced much different outcomes. Generally, labor parties led in total votes, but the General Zionists were also competitive. The Religious Zionists and Revisionists did not come out much differently than they did in elections in Palestine. The implication is clear: Yishuv politics was decidedly oriented toward the labor Zionists because of the composition of the population in Palestine, which was dominated by workers, whereas international Zionist politics was much more balanced between Labor Zionists and General Zionists, reflecting the different population structure in the diaspora. Bearing that history in mind, it is not surprising that labor parties dominated Israeli politics during the early years of statehood.

CONFLICT BETWEEN ARABS AND JEWS IN MANDATORY PALESTINE

Arab–Jewish intercommunal relations deteriorated badly during the 1920s and 1930s, mainly because of intense policy differences. For the Jews, immigration of their brethren was their top priority, especially once the Nazi threat loomed larger in Europe, while the Arabs remained implacably opposed to Jewish immigration. The British were caught in the middle and learned that they could not please either side. Killings and reprisals became common, punctured by outbreaks of major violence in 1920 and 1929 and culminating in the Arab Revolt of 1936–1939. Paradoxically, the violence contributed directly to the formation of a series of Jewish defense organizations and paramilitary groups, which later became the core of the Israel Defense Forces, the state's official military.

The Nazi threat to European Jews, a major part of world Jewry, conferred urgency on the Yishuv's efforts to increase immigration to Palestine. From the perspective of Palestine's Arabs, the country belonged to them, and the Jews were gradually taking it away. Since the British governed the country and were allowing this to happen, the British, too, became a target for Arab protests. The Jews also had major complaints against the British. Based on international treaty obligations and Britain's commitment in the 1917 Balfour Declaration, they believed that the purpose of the Mandate was to build up the Jewish national home. When the British limited immigration (discussed below), they were, the Zionists argued, undermining the Zionists' attempts to achieve that goal.

Eventually violence against the British emerged in the form of the Arab Revolt (1936–1939). It was the responsibility of the British forces to control the revolt, a task that required three years. The violence of the period led the British to establish a Royal Commission in 1937. Known as the Peel Commission, it investigated the causes of the violence and the overall situation in the country, and recommended that Palestine be partitioned into an Arab state and a Jewish state. The Arabs rejected the plan totally, consistent with their conviction that all of Palestine should be an Arab state, not least because the Arabs were the larger part of the population. The Jewish response was less definitive. Although the proportion of the land that the Commission assigned to the Jews was quite small, the official Zionist leadership ultimately leaned toward accepting the plan, albeit reluctantly, in order to have a

Jewish state that could accept desperate immigrants who wanted to flee Europe. The Revisionists, who were not part of the official leadership, opposed the proposal. However, as war in Europe approached, the British turned their attention away from the partition idea, reflecting a cooling of relations between the British and the Yishuv that had been developing since 1937.[8]

DETERIORATING ZIONIST–BRITISH RELATIONS

From the perspective of the Jews, relations with the British deteriorated in 1939 as the British tried to shore up their relations with the Arab world before the outbreak of war in Europe. This led the Mandatory government to view the Haganah as an obstacle to its goals. But the main policy development of 1939 was the issuance of a White Paper by the British government that represented a sharp turning away from the idea of partition and foresaw an Arab state eventually emerging in Palestine. Moreover, at precisely the moment of maximum need, it sharply limited Jewish immigration into Palestine to 75,000 over five years, with an Arab veto over further Jewish immigration after that. The policy shift turned the Yishuv against Britain even as the Jews understood that they had to support Britain in its fight against Germany. Ben-Gurion stated the dilemma succinctly: "We must fight the White Paper as if there were no war and we must fight the war as if there were no White Paper."[9] In reality this meant that the struggle against the policies enunciated in the White Paper was put off until the end of the war. Haganah members did fight alongside the British in operations against pro-German forces in the Middle East. A supplementary aspect of this collaboration was the opportunity to gain valuable combat experience.

As a result of the Nazi assault on European Jewry, the Zionist leadership came to view the cause of Jewish statehood as increasingly urgent. To this end the Zionists convened what came to be known as the Biltmore Conference in New York City in 1942. It was there that they formally decided that statehood was now the goal, a decision that put Britain squarely in their way and prompted many Zionists to see Britain as the enemy.

During the early 1930s the Yishuv had consolidated most of the disparate self-defense forces into the Haganah, which became the community's primary paramilitary force. In response to the Arab Revolt, control over the Haganah was centralized in the hands of the executive of the Va'ad Leumi, the government of the Yishuv, which was dominated by Mapai. The Haganah maintained generally good relations with the British and made some contributions to the war effort in the region. It helped that the organization was advised unofficially by the British officer Orde Wingate.

The Revisionist Zionist leadership, which opposed Mapai, kept its own forces out of the Haganah, organizing them instead into the *Irgun Zvai Leumi* (National Military Organization, often known by its Hebrew acronym Etzel). Another paramilitary group was *Lohamei Herut Yisrael* (Fighters for the Freedom of Israel, or Lehi).[10] During the early 1940s the left-wing *Palmach*, associated with Mapam, also remained separate from the Haganah.

The fact that the various defense and paramilitary organizations were controlled by bodies or groups that were opposed to each other led to rivalries and suspicion. This made it impossible for the de facto government of the Yishuv, led by Ben-Gurion, to control the activities of Etzel and Lehi, both of which were pursuing their own agendas as active anti-British underground movements by 1944. This competition sometimes led to developments that greatly complicated Ben-Gurion's effort to govern the Yishuv and instill community discipline. For example, in 1944 Lehi assassinated British Minister Lord Moyne, while in 1946 Etzel blew up British military headquarters at the King David Hotel in Jerusalem. Lehi and Etzel's military attacks against the British were regarded by many as terrorism and underscored the difficulties of exercising centralized authority in what was not yet a state.

Animosity between Mapai and its allies on one side and the Revisionist-oriented paramilitary organizations on the other led to the so-called Season during 1945–1946, when elements of the former groups leaked information to the British that led to the arrest of many of the fighters in the latter groups. The 1948 *Altalena* incident, described in the next chapter, was the culmination of this competition. The resultant animosity between the Mapai and Revisionist leadership persisted for years after statehood was achieved—Ben-Gurion even refused to grant permission for Jabotinsky's remains to be brought to Israel for burial—and had a profound effect on Israeli politics more generally. The Mapai–Revisionist rivalry became the Labor–Likud competition that has characterized the Israeli political system since 1977.

With the advent of statehood, veterans of Etzel formed the *Herut* (Freedom) party under Begin's leadership. Herut at the outset maintained a commitment to the idea of an Israel that not only stretched from the Jordan River to the Mediterranean Sea but extended to the other side of the river as well. Within a few years of 1948 it became the major ideological opponent of Mapai but for the next several decades was not able to muster enough support to challenge Mapai seriously. Begin maintained his leadership throughout and finally found a route to power through mergers with center and farther-right parties. The result was Likud, which finally gained power for the first time in 1977.

THE END OF THE MANDATE

While the Haganah generally steered clear of anti-British activity until the end of the war, the election of an anti-Zionist Labor government in Britain in 1945 encouraged all Zionist groups in Palestine to confront the Mandatory power with armed force, though in the case of the Haganah, military actions was closely oriented toward specific political objectives; Etzel and Lehi were less strategic about their attacks. The Arab community in Palestine, supported by the surrounding Arab states, continued to staunchly oppose any Jewish entity in the area, particularly as the pan-Arab movement became more organized.

At the end of World War II the fate of refugees from Europe, the survivors of the Holocaust, became a top policy concern. The British continued to limit legal immigration, which spawned operations, mainly conducted by the Haganah, to land immigrants in Palestine against their wishes. These missions were known as *Aliya Bet*, the euphemism for illegal immigration. Essentially, the British were caught between the two competing nationalisms and were not up to the task of keeping the Jews and the Arabs under control. Consequently Britain decided to terminate the Mandate and placed the problem into the hands of the newly founded United Nations (UN). It is not clear if the British truly meant to give up Palestine, or if they hoped that the UN would itself be unable to resolve the problem and would return a strengthened Mandate to Britain.

In 1947 the UN sent a Special Committee on Palestine (UNSCOP) to the region to investigate and recommend a way out. UNSCOP was divided on the best way to resolve the competing nationalisms, and so produced a majority report and a minority report.[11] The majority report recommended a new partition, one that was somewhat more favorable to the Jews in terms of territory than the Peel plan.[12] The timing may have been propitious for the Zionist cause because of widespread sympathy for the Jews in the wake of the Holocaust. The well-known plight of refugees—mainly survivors—only intensified support, though considerable lobbying was also required. On November 29, 1947, the UN General Assembly voted to accept the majority recommendation, officially termed the UN Partition Plan for Palestine, by a vote of 33 to 13, with 10 abstentions. The Zionists welcomed the vote—indeed, many were overwhelmed with emotion at what they considered the first real step toward Jewish sovereignty in nearly 2,000 years[13]—while the Palestinian Arabs and the Arab states were opposed and rejected the decision. Though prior to the vote intercommunal violence had been increasing, the vote immediately intensified Jewish–Arab fighting in Palestine as each side tried to gain territory, while the British, unable to assert control, generally held back. The Yishuv, basing its policy on the UN decision, leaned heavily toward declaring statehood at the expiration of the British Mandate on May 15, 1948. However, it should be noted that while there was some uncertainty in the Zionist leadership as May 15 approached, this plan prevailed thanks to the assertive leadership of Ben-Gurion. The Palestinian Arabs, in contrast, decided to attempt to force the abrogation of the Plan and abort Jewish statehood.

During the five and a half months between the UN vote and the end of the Mandate there was open warfare between Jews and Arabs in a number of places in Palestine. At first the Palestinian Arab irregulars appeared to have the upper hand, though an offensive during the spring of 1948 enabled the Haganah to gain the advantage. Certainly, however, the outcome of the fighting had not been determined definitively by the time the Mandate expired on May 15, 1948. On the day before, Ben-Gurion convened the Va'ad Leumi and the leadership of the Yishuv in Tel Aviv in front of a large picture of Herzl, read Israel's Declaration of Independence (see Appendix D), and announced that the Va'ad Leumi would now function as a provisional government for the State of Israel pending the election in 1949 of a parliament (called the *Knesset*), which would also act as a constituent assembly. It was clear that the Jewish national institutions had acquired legitimacy, recognition, and the backing of the Jewish population. These factors provided them with the authority to act on behalf of the entire Yishuv. Moreover, as the Declaration of

Independence made clear, the founders of the state saw themselves as acting not just for the Jews of Palestine, but for the Jewish people as a whole.

Despite often-intense internal political divisions, the experiences of the Yishuv during the Mandate period and the horror of the Holocaust combined to give the people of the Yishuv a strong sense of national unity at that critical moment. When the time came for the expiration of the Mandate, there was across-the-board unanimity in support of independence, despite the reservations that some political actors may have had in the days and weeks leading up to the decision.

THE MANDATE PERIOD IN PERSPECTIVE

By 1948 the differential level of political development between the Jews and the Arabs in Palestine was apparent. The Zionists were sufficiently organized to establish a government that could control and govern the Jewish population. The Arabs were not and yielded to external Arab leadership instead of declaring the state authorized by the UN resolution. As a result, the plan for creation of an Arab state itself was aborted, which delayed the development of a separate and distinctive Palestinian Arab identity. By the end of the war in 1949, Israel had conquered more territory than had been allotted to it under the Partition Plan, while what became known as the Gaza Strip was seized and held by Egypt and the West Bank was annexed by Jordan. As a result Jordan came to occupy the bulk of the land that had been allocated to a Palestinian Arab state. Jerusalem was divided into a western Israeli part, which became the capital, and an eastern Jordanian-held section, which contained the Old City and the holy sites. The loss of the local Arab political leadership, most of whom had fled, adversely affected the structure of Arab society in Palestine. The ensuing war, regarded by Israel as its War of Independence, was largely fought between the Israel Defense Forces (a renamed Haganah that incorporated most of the leftist and rightist paramilitary groups) and the armies of several Arab states, upon which the Palestinian Arabs primarily relied for the defense of their homeland.

Later the Palestinian Arabs called these events *al-Nakba*, the Catastrophe. Most of Palestinian Arab society collapsed and some 700,000 Palestinian Arabs became refugees as the result of the upheaval of 1948. Unlike refugees from other countries during the same period, the Palestinian refugees have generally not been absorbed elsewhere. They and their descendants have been encouraged to believe that they will ultimately be able to return to the areas where they lived before 1948 in Israel. Israel, on the other hand, wanting to preserve its Jewish majority, has resisted pressure to allow any return. The Palestinians, insisting on what they regard as a right of return, have made that issue one of the key points of contention in Israeli–Palestinian peace negotiations.

Demographic Changes in Palestine During the Mandate

From 1922 to 1948 Palestine underwent major demographic changes. According to regular British censuses, which are considered reliable, the Jewish population grew slowly at first and then more rapidly as conditions in Europe deteriorated. In 1922 there were nearly 84,000 Jews out of a total population of about 744,000, but by

1945 that number had grown to 554,000 out of a total of 1,795,000. The Muslim and Christian populations also grew, but not as rapidly. In 1922 there were some 589,000 Muslims and 71,000 Christians in Palestine, whereas in 1945 the totals were 1,102,000 and 139,000, respectively. Some of the growth among the non-Jews reflected natural increase, but at least part is due to immigration across land borders. During the 23 years from 1922 to 1945, the Jewish proportion of the settled population increased from 12.9 percent to 31.8 percent. At the time of partition, Jews were still a minority in Palestine, which bolstered the Arab preference for a solution based on one state in which individuals would vote equally.

SUMMARY

By the termination of the Mandate the Jews had established a substantial community of about 600,000 people with considerable cohesion, though they were still a minority in Palestine. The Yishuv had a participatory political culture with a multiparty system and a clearly understood voting method, national institutions with widespread legitimacy, the beginning of a national language and culture, a military force that was able to transform itself quickly into an army, and a governmental apparatus that was ready to manage the institutions of the new state. Hence the transition to statehood in 1948, though implemented during a major war, went reasonably smoothly and enabled the nascent state to focus on repelling the existential threat that it faced from the moment of its birth. During a relatively short period of 25 years the Yishuv had successfully engaged in a nation-building process that equipped it very well for the existential struggle that it faced in 1948.

KEYWORDS

Yishuv, British Mandate for Palestine, Mapai, party system, voluntary institutions, democracy, Histadrut, Jewish–Arab violence, collective myths

NOTES

1. Technically, Israel declared its independence the day before, on Friday, May 14, to come into effect on the 15th. This was done in order to avoid desecrating the Sabbath, which began at sundown on Friday.
2. The main backer of binationalism among the Jews was an organization called *Brit Shalom* (the Covenant of Peace), which dated back to the late 1920s. Its followers believed that the Zionists should be prepared to make some concessions in order to reach agreement with the Palestinian Arabs regarding a binational state. Among the leading Jewish advocates of binationalism in the early 1940s were Martin Buber and Judah L. Magnes, a professor and President, respectively, at the Hebrew University of Jerusalem.
3. Anita Shapira, *Israel: A History* (Waltham, MA: Brandeis University Press, 2012).
4. For decades, the most popular Hebrew-English dictionary used in Hebrew instruction abroad was based on Ben-Yehuda's work.
5. Yael Zerubavel, *Recovered Roots: Collective Memory and the Making of Israeli National Tradition* (Chicago: University of Chicago Press, 1995).

6. Cited in Mira Sucharov, *The International Self: Psychoanalysis and the Search for Israeli-Palestinian Peace* (Albany, New York: State University of New York Press, 2005), 61. Ironically, a 1987 Israeli film, *Late Summer Blues*, depicted high school youth about to enter the army ridiculing Trumpeldor's exclamation and its use in Israeli culture.

7. Dan Horowitz and Moshe Lissak, *Origins of the Israeli Polity: Palestine Under the Mandate*, trans. Charles Hoffman (Chicago: University of Chicago Press, 1978).

8. Shapira, *Israel: A History*, 87.

9. Cited in Jewish Virtual Library, "David Ben-Gurion: Select Quotations." http://www.jewishvirtuallibrary.org/jsource/Quote/bg.html

10. An offshoot of Etzel, Lehi was considered to be further to the right, even extremist. Led at first by Avraham Stern, following his death in 1942 the group was helmed by Yitzhak Shamir (later Prime Minister), Israel Eldad, and Nathan Yellin-Mor together. The British pejoratively labeled it the Stern Gang.

11. While the majority report recommended partition of Palestine into two separate states, the minority recommended the establishment of a federal union, with Jerusalem as its capital.

12. The plan gave the Jews 56 percent of the Mandate territory and the Arabs 43 percent. The Jewish section was to include a roughly equal number of Arabs and Jews (407,000 to 498,000, respectively), while the Arab part would have contained 725,000 Arabs and 10,000 Jews. Jerusalem was to be placed in an international zone.

13. In his autobiography, prominent Israeli author Amos Oz—in 1947 a little boy—captures well the unbridled, tearful joy the Jews in Palestine felt, celebrating late into the night. See Amos Oz, *A Tale of Love and Darkness*, trans. Nicholas de Lange (Orlando: Harcourt, 2004), 353–359.

CHAPTER 4

State Building After 1948

The establishment of the state forced Israeli leaders to confront a number of challenges, including how to absorb hundreds of thousands of new immigrants coming mostly from Muslim countries in the region, regulate an internal market, and sustain a functioning political system at the core of which would be an authoritative government—all while the country was at war with its neighbors. But because the Zionists had already constructed a political system and an economy that was inclusive of most parties and groups within the Yishuv, their task was made much easier. Indeed, the process of state building after 1948 continued along the same lines as it had in the pre-state period.

Israeli leaders also had to engage in a process of *nation* building among the Jewish public (the Arab minority was largely left out of this process). In addition to making sure that the state had a functioning government and systems of management, they had to ensure that the system retained legitimacy among the population, and that it would be viewed as having credible authority to make decisions and laws and have them be obeyed. There was also a need to balance central authority with communal autonomy for the Jewish, Arab Muslim, Arab Christian, Druze, Bedouin, and other populations within Israel.

Finally, all of these processes took place while the state remained under constant threat as the Arab–Israeli conflict intensified. A series of wars and skirmishes that took place after the first Arab–Israeli war ended in 1949 forced the government to consider security measures as part of the expansion of its authority, which in turn affected other programs. The Arab community, for example, was put under military administration until the end of 1966, which impeded the democratic process.

The state sought to extend its authority in five key areas: the political arena, defense, education, the economy, and personal status issues. This does not mean, however, that it sought to serve as the controlling authority in all of these areas; in some, it preferred to set the parameters of the system while providing different communities considerable independence to govern their own affairs. This approach was both a continuation of existing practice and an effort to carefully balance the different elements of a varied society. By the 2000s, though, the effort to balance national and communal authority proved too difficult as different communities and groups tried to assert their autonomy from the state or "capture" the state for their own purposes.

This chapter begins with a discussion of the process of state building (*mamlachtiut*). It then moves on to the five main areas in which the state, led by the Labor Zionists, sought either to exert central authority over the processes that governed each activity or, if they could not be directly controlled by the state, to structure them. The last section highlights a handful of other areas that the state worked to bring under its authority.

MAMLACHTIUT

The shift from a set of autonomous "sub-centers" built on voluntary communal institutions, described in Chapter 3, to a series of hierarchic, compulsory systems dominated by a single authority (the state) required not only considerable effort on the part of state leaders and bureaucrats, but also agreement among those who were being incorporated into the new structure. David Ben-Gurion, who became the country's first Prime Minister, led these efforts, and in many ways it was his resolve that kept the process of consolidation going. Indeed, he saw it as his personal mission to break centuries of Jewish tradition and impose unity on a historically fractious people, arguing that in the past it was this fragmentation that prevented the Jews from maintaining their biblical kingdoms.[1] He was determined to avoid this outcome in modern Israel.

The process by which Ben-Gurion and others accomplished this consolidation is called *mamlachtiut*, a term that refers to "state building," that is, the creation of state institutions. More broadly, though, mamlachtiut means statism: the centralization of power in the hands of the state, mostly at the expense of existing political parties and movements. The state becomes the locus of citizens' loyalty, and it sets the boundaries of acceptable action within the polity. The obligatory nature of state authority meant that groups that had had the option of staying out of the Yishuv's labor-dominated institutions could not do so anymore. The Revisionists, the non-Zionist haredi parties, and the Communists now had to participate if they wanted a chance to be represented in the political arena and to share in the distribution of power. Later, too, the Arab community organized its own political parties and joined the system.

Ben-Gurion and his colleagues succeeded in asserting the jurisdiction of the state over the sub-centers in several arenas. But because this process was itself decidedly political, led by Mapai,[2] they did not succeed in establishing control over all of them. In some areas they "failed" on purpose by deciding that some autonomy from the state was needed in service to the larger cause of maintaining Jewish unity and ensuring the overall success of the state-building project. Though this might have seemed to be an appropriate strategy at the time, many of these decisions caused considerable problems in later decades. In some cases, segments of the population tried to expand the political space allotted to them, moving further away from state control. In education the haredi community, for example, sought to downplay the importance of a secular curriculum—such as mathematics, science, and secular history—and focus more on the study of religious texts.

THE POLITICAL ARENA

The state was very successful in transforming the voluntary political system of the Yishuv into a compulsory one. As the previous chapter noted, strong political parties and a functioning political process already existed in the Yishuv while Palestine was governed by the British Mandate. At independence it was relatively easy to maintain most of these systems, which avoided the need for a drawn-out and distracting contest between competing ideas at a time when the new state was in the middle of a war. The transition included adopting the Yishuv's system of proportional representation and organizing the country as a single voting district. This effort was facilitated by the dominant position of Mapai, the main Socialist Zionist party and the strongest party in the Yishuv. Mapai was eager to maintain the existing institutions because the party had been dominant under their rules; retaining the same rules and processes would thus maintain Mapai's hegemony.

Myron Aronoff has argued that those who built the institutions of the Yishuv relied on majoritarian rule and consensus democracy.[3] By that he means that the Zionists agreed that the party with the largest share of communal support should naturally form the senior partner in the government. At the same time, given the multiplicity of parties and streams of Zionism operating in the Yishuv, the political system would have to ensure that all groups were represented and would have significant say in community decisions. He notes that after 1948, given Mapai's entwinement with the state, the system came to reflect majoritarianism at the expense of consensus. In fact, Ben-Gurion did not want Israel to adopt the proportional representation system, preferring the British parliamentary system both out of familiarity and because he thought it would help cut down on the sectoral loyalties that had divided the Yishuv. Ultimately, he could not convince his colleagues to agree, and the two systems were combined into the new Israeli arrangement.

The shift from voluntary to compulsory politics overseen by an authoritative state was guided by Mapai in three ways. First, Mapai had played the lead role in forming the institutions of the Yishuv. The party argued that a Yishuv-wide political system was needed to present a united front against the British and the Arabs, as well as to facilitate a strong Jewish community that would be able to mobilize its resources, defend itself when the time came, and assert the Zionist claim to Palestine. In fact, maintaining the Yishuv systems contributed to the success of mamlachtiut, because all of the parties and movements that existed in the Yishuv continued to operate after 1948 and were familiar with these institutions and rules. They agreed to give up much of their independence and power in return for serving as vehicles for political representation in the new parliament and party system.

Second, as the largest party, Mapai always won a plurality—but never a majority—of the vote during elections; in fact, no Israeli party has ever won a majority of seats in the Knesset (Israel's parliament). All governments of Israel have been coalition governments, composed of multiple parties (typically three to five, but sometimes more) that have to agree on a government platform and a distribution of ministries. Mapai was able to claim the right to negotiate the formation of a government because of its size and share of the vote, and therefore to act as senior partner in the coalition. At the same time, because it occupied a center-left position, Mapai was able to attract partners from either side of the political spectrum. Parties further to the left and to the right were unable to tame their ideological opposition and cooperate with each other, allowing the party to strengthen its claim to the central position in the coalition. Mapai's hegemonic position in this process is reflected in the quip that Israeli elections were held to determine not who would be asked to form the government, but who would be Mapai's coalition partners. Being at the center of the bargaining process also allowed Mapai to claim the top decision-making positions in government in addition to the prime ministry, such as the powerful defense ministry.

Third, in addition to dominating the political process, Mapai had long supplied the Yishuv with the equivalent of civil servants. By the time the state was established, only Mapainiks had the requisite experience and knowledge to run the bureaucracy. It was a simple matter for the party to shift these officials to the state's institutions, thereby ensuring the continuation of its priorities in the state period.

Ben-Gurion and the other leaders of Mapai never intended to relinquish their dominant position in the Israeli polity—indeed, they never conceived that their hegemony might be challenged or come to an end. Ben-Gurion purposely excluded from his coalition governments those groups that would not submit to his and his party's domination (particularly Menachem Begin's Herut party). It was easy, then, for Mapai to control the state's political and governmental institutions, shape them according to their socialist-collectivist-Zionist vision, and guide the country through its major crises during the early years of its existence.

DEFENSE

The biggest threat to the state's nascent authority came from paramilitary organizations that belonged to Mapai's Zionist rivals in the pre-state period. But the threat was short-lived: a concerted effort led, within a matter of months, to the establishment of a single national military and the subordination of competitors to its authority.

A monopoly on the use of force has long been considered a hallmark of a stable and functioning state; alternate centers of military power are otherwise able to challenge the state and resist its writ. When these potential power centers are affiliated with organizations or ideologies at odds with the state or with the groups that control the state, the potential for broader conflict is enhanced. To this end, the provisional government issued simultaneous with the declaration of the state an order at the end of May 1948 for the creation of the Israel Defense Forces (IDF), later codified in the 1976 Basic Law: The Military. Ben-Gurion was especially insistent that in this area the new state could not afford to dilute its authority. As in the political arena, the state was successful, though at a cost: the outbreak of intra-Zionist violence and a number of deaths.

Several Zionist parties had militias associated with them during the Yishuv period. The Revisionists' fighting force was the Irgun, also known as Etzel (introduced in Chapter 3), led by Menachem Begin. Begin was a fierce champion of Revisionist ideas and policies, and this put him squarely at odds with Ben-Gurion, who was equally committed to Labor Zionist ideas and policies. Though Begin shared Ben-Gurion's commitment to state authority, he was more reluctant to give up complete independence in the military arena. This disagreement was exacerbated by longstanding arguments between the Revisionists and Mapai over the conduct of the 1947–1949 War and different priorities over where to set the borders of the Jewish state. It took a direct clash of arms between the IDF and the Irgun for the dispute to fully resolve itself.

Begin understood the importance of a single authority within the state, and as the war between Israel and the Arab states proceeded after May 1948 he agreed that the Irgun be folded into Israel's official new military. But the city of Jerusalem was left out of the Revisionist–Mapai agreement as a special issue. Besieged by Arab forces during the war, the Jewish neighborhoods of the city were considered to warrant special attention, and Begin wanted the freedom to rescue them if he could.

The contradiction of and threat to state authority inherent in this arrangement came to a head during the *Altalena* affair in June 1948. The ship was hired by the Irgun to bring weapons and men from France to Israel before the agreement to incorporate the Irgun into the IDF had been made. Begin and Ben-Gurion were able to come to an agreement on how to distribute the transport's equipment and weapons. They initially decided that 20 percent of the weapons would go to the Irgun's forces in Jerusalem. But Begin wanted some of the rest of the arms to go to specific Irgun units within the IDF, and this contributed to a breach of the Revisionist–Mapai agreement.

By the time the ship landed on June 20, 1948, at Kfar Vitkin, many former Irgun members who had joined the IDF had returned to their partisan loyalties; they went to protect the ship from the IDF and to show their support for their independence. When Begin refused to comply with the IDF's order to surrender the ship, fighting broke out. Perhaps caught up in the moment, Begin boarded the ship and sailed it to the port at Tel Aviv, which Ben-Gurion had determined should not be allowed to happen.

Fearing the precedent of an independently supplied militia, Ben-Gurion ordered the IDF to fire on the ship to prevent it from landing at Tel Aviv and its arms from going to the Irgun. Though there were some claims that the ship was only hit accidentally, a shell did strike it, and a fire broke out. A firefight also began as soldiers jumped from the burning ship and swam to the beach.

By the end of the affair, three IDF soldiers and 16 Irgun members were killed, while scores of Revisionists were arrested. Many were upset at the intra-Jewish bloodshed, particularly while the war was continuing, and the event contributed to the deep tensions between the Revisionists and Mapai and their political heirs Likud and Labor. Though it was not a direct cause of the decision, the lingering resentment over the *Altalena* affair made it easier for Ben-Gurion to exclude the right-wing parties from government coalitions for most of the first 30 years of the state's existence.

While the right-wing organizations posed the greatest threat to both the IDF's authority and the hegemony of Mapai within it, even among the left there were serious divisions that manifested in a reluctance to submit to a single military authority. The *Palmach*, the Yishuv's "strike force" associated with the far-left Mapam party, was unwilling to give up its independence as the select unit of the Jewish forces. Palmach officers saw themselves as elite members of the Yishuv's, and then the state's, fighting force. The disbanding of the Palmach was not marred by violence as was the subordination of the Irgun, but it was a struggle to absorb it, too, into the IDF. Tensions between former Palmachniks, many of whom became officers, and the rest of the IDF persisted for many years.

EDUCATION

During the Yishuv period, different Zionist parties, as well as the ultra-Orthodox, ran their own educational institutions. Unlike in the political and military arenas, though, the government decided after 1948 that a single authority in the sphere of education might be more harmful than not. On the assumption that it was necessary to allow religious groups and the Arab minority some autonomy in their own education systems, the government allowed for different educational streams servicing different communities, though the state would provide funding for them and, ostensibly, thereby be able to control some of the content of the schools' curricula.

The purpose of this program was to account for communal loyalties within a framework of a larger national identity. Four educational streams[4] were designed and implemented under the State Education Law (1953): *mamlachti* (state) schools; *mamlachti dati* (state religious) schools; *HaHinuh HaAtzmai* (independent education) haredi schools, which are subsidized by the state but receive minimal state supervision; and schools oriented toward the Arab community. While decentralization was thus a conscious decision, the state failed to establish adequate authority over schools catering to the haredi, which contributed to a breakdown in its jurisdiction and ability to enforce national curricula and standards. At the same time, the state came to exert more authority over the Arab schools, placing emphasis in the curriculum on the Jewish experience in Israel over the Arab experience and diluting that community's control over its own education. In both cases, education policy became highly politicized.

The state school system concentrates on secular subjects and is the stream that most Israeli students have entered. In these schools students receive a combination of "civics" or general instruction (e.g., math, science, social studies) and what can be called Jewish studies (e.g., biblical studies, Jewish history, Hebrew literature). This stream is under close state supervision. State religious schools are attended primarily by Religious Zionist (*dati leumi*) and modern Orthodox pupils. These schools have instituted a full curriculum of general instruction with an emphasis on Judaism, Jewish identity and history, and Jewish texts. Considerable weight is given to study of the concept of Eretz Yisrael as well. In this network, too, the state exercises authority, although as some groups within the national religious community, such as Kiryat Moshe in Jerusalem and certain settlements in the West

Bank, have become disillusioned with the state's settlement policy, some of their rabbi-teachers have made efforts to distance themselves from the state's writ. Much of the opposition to the withdrawal of Israeli civilians and soldiers from Gaza in 2005 came from these schools. Reports suggest that in some state religious schools there has also been a growing commitment to haredi norms, such as the imposition of more modest dress codes similar to those enforced at haredi schools.[5]

The state is also responsible for underwriting haredi schools that agree to adopt the state's curriculum. But while it provides the bulk of the funds for their operation, it has little control over curriculum or even educational policy. For all intents and purposes, this stream operates independently from the state. It neglects the sciences and other general studies topics in favor of study of the Torah and the Talmud, Judaism, and other Jewish-oriented (as opposed to Israel-oriented) topics. A 2013 study found that students in these schools receive only about four hours per week of general studies.[6] In addition, because most haredim are non-Zionist, a sense of identity with and loyalty to the State of Israel is often absent from discussion. State holidays, for example, are not observed. This rejection of secular subjects has been mitigated somewhat in recent years as the community's consistently high levels of poverty have led to the recognition that employment outside the haredi world is necessary—which in turn requires knowledge of secular subjects. This recognition has been manifested most clearly in the earlier age at which some haredi students are now leaving their educational institutions compared to previous years—that age is increasingly closer to 22 than the previous norm of 30 or older.

Though the motivation behind the creation of different streams was to facilitate national unity and identity among the Jewish population, in reality the absence of a single educational system, governed by the same standards and curriculum, has enabled the entrenchment of separate communal loyalties. The state's authority has been diluted, and as the proportion of students in nonstate schools has increased relative to that in the state system, questions about how students perceive Israel have increasingly come to the fore.

The last stream was designed to serve the Arab community. In these schools Arabic is the language of instruction, and students learn more Arab history and culture, although the national curriculum in math, science, and other general subjects is required to be incorporated into this teaching. Unlike the state's attitude toward the state religious and haredi systems, however, where it has declined to enforce its authority when schools ignore state-sanctioned general curricula, the state has been keen to emphasize its control over the educational process in Arab schools. Arab culture and history have been downplayed as the government has sought to entrench identification with the state. Jewish instructors have been hired at the expense of Arab teachers, while the infrastructure for this stream has been underdeveloped compared to the state school system.[7]

The most prominent example of this process occurred in 2011. As leaders of the Arab community have, since the 1990s, emphasized a more nationalist orientation in their politics, institutions within the community have sought to recognize and commemorate the *Nakba* (Catastrophe), which is how Arab citizens view the period of Israel's independence and the 1947–1949 War. In response, the Knesset, at the direction of the Binyamin Netanyahu government, in 2011 passed Amendment Number 40 to the Budgets Foundations Law. This amendment allows the Finance Ministry to withhold from or reduce state monies to publicly funded institutions that hold any activity that calls into question Israel's existence as a "Jewish and democratic state" or commemorates Israel's Independence Day as a "day of mourning." The amendment has been commonly referred to as the "Nakba Law" because it prevents Arab schools and other bodies from organizing public activities around this experience, which is a distinctly different experience from that of the Jewish majority.

For Arab citizens of the state, Israeli history is not one of redemption, return from exile, and Jewish sovereignty, but rather one of war, dispossession, loss of national identity, and a severing of ties with Palestinians in the West Bank and Gaza. This has raised questions about the effectiveness and even correctness of multiple education streams. How, for example, can the state balance out its emphasis on Jewish liberation and independence with the Arabs' collective memory of the Nakba? Which history, memories, and narratives should be taught to whom? Coupled with an understandable inability of the Arab population to identify with the state's Jewish symbols (the flag's Star of David, the menorah on the coat of arms, the national anthem evoking the redemption of Zion), these questions have implications for the status of the Arab community and intracommunal relations within Israel.

According to recent government projections, the proportion of Jewish-Israeli students at the elementary level in state schools will drop to 49 percent, less than a majority, by 2019, with the proportion of students in state religious and state-funded haredi schools rising (albeit slowly) to 19 percent and 32 percent, respectively.[8] The bulk of an expected increase in the Israeli student population will come from the haredi and Arab sectors, and combined the two groups will comprise about 50 percent of the total enrollment in Israeli schools.[9] Growing percentages of students in nonreligious state schools, combined with moves by some in the non-secular or non-Zionist communities to challenge the state curriculum, in turn raise questions about new generations of students' identification with the State of Israel in its current form and portend struggles over how to define it.

ECONOMY

A state cannot function without a united internal market. The different Zionist movements, while continuing to maintain separate health clinics and run smaller economic cooperatives, kibbutzim, and other party-run economic institutions, participated fully in the general economy of the Yishuv.[10] When Israel was established, then, there was already a community-wide set of economic structures that the state could take over, although it faced some resistance on the part of the sub-centers.

One of the Zionists' priorities during the Mandate was to construct an economy based on Jewish labor and Jewish economic transactions that was separate from the rest of the economy in Palestine, which was dominated by the majority Arab population. This division was sought not only to allow the Jewish community to survive and thrive, but also because the dominant parties—Labor and Socialist Zionists—believed that the Jewish people, and therefore the Jewish state, could only be revived by work, and particularly by agricultural labor. A third reason for such a move was the desire of the Labor Zionists to control the Jewish community's economy.[11]

Toward these ends the Histadrut (the General Federation of Laborers in the Land of Israel) was formed in 1920 by Achdut Ha'Avodah and HaPoel HaTzair, two of the Yishuv's main Labor Zionist groups. From its founding until the 1980s, the Histadrut was at the center of a socialist political economy in which the main government-affiliated organizations regulated Jewish businesses and served as a patronage resource for whichever Zionist group controlled it. After the establishment of the state, the socialist-collectivist ethos of the Labor Zionists continued to predominate. It made sense, then, for the Histadrut to continue to act as the core of the Israeli economy, and it remained closely tied to the state. For many years, the head of the Histadrut was an official from Mapai. The Histadrut also facilitated and channeled licenses, workers' fees, and contracts, and it owned firms in different industries, such as health care, banking, and construction. All of this meant that its officials often acted on behalf of the government.

Because the state's economic power was tied so closely to the Histadrut, it did not try to disrupt its services. This decision was, of course, made easier by the fact that Mapai was the dominant party in both the government and the Histadrut. The labor federation was subsequently supplemented with a new Ministry of Labor designed to provide direct state oversight of the economy. The arrangement worked well at first. It provided the government with control in key industries, allowing it to channel the economy toward necessary national ends at a time of great threat and in the face of the pressures of constructing a functioning polity. The collectivist nature of the system enabled a greater sense of belonging among much—though certainly not all—of the population. And because the Histadrut was already well established, with branches throughout the Jewish community, the Israeli economy was able to continue functioning relatively well, particularly as the country had to intensify the war effort.

But few countries with a state-run economy have lasted more than a few decades without becoming entrenched in waste and corruption. Eventually the weight of mismanagement collapses the entire system, as occurred in the Soviet Union. Alternately, some states that have consciously decided to shift from a state-run economy to a market-oriented one, such as South Korea, have done well. Both outcomes—either failure or flourishing—are made more likely when the country is plugged into the global economy, for example, through the export of specific goods and services, or through exchange of rents for raw materials. For its part Israel became increasingly involved in the international market as Israeli government firms and private businesses engaged in international transactions (see Chapter 15). In addition, as the country prospered and the population grew wealthier, demand for consumer goods from outside of Israel grew. These developments, in turn, weakened the Histadrut.

Despite its connection to the government through Mapai, the Histadrut tried to remain independent. Disagreements soon arose over budgetary issues:

the government sought to reduce expenditures while the Histadrut tried to maintain or increase levels of pay to its unionized workers. Other issues related to working conditions—such as time off, compensation, and working conditions—cropped up alongside disputes over salaries and wages. Because it was a labor federation with branches throughout the country and in different service and industry sectors, the Histadrut was able to launch workers' strikes whenever it felt it necessary, mobilizing groups such as teachers unions, dock-workers, telephone and electricity providers, and transportation federations. The result was often paralysis of specific sectors of the economy and sometimes, if the strikes occurred in key areas like transportation, across the state as a whole. The ability to strike in key sectors and industries made it difficult for the government to ignore the Histadrut's demands and often forced it to the bargaining table when it would otherwise have resisted.

The weakening of the Histadrut began in the 1980s when the Labor–Likud unity government sought to control rampant inflation, which required cutting back on salaries and budget expenditures affecting many workers around the country. The second Yitzhak Rabin government (1992–1995) passed a new health care law that removed one of the more important institutions of the Histadrut, its health care organization *Kupat Cholim Clalit* (General Sick Fund). In the 1990s and 2000s the Israeli government sought to privatize the economy, breaking apart state- and Histadrut-run enterprises and breaking down the power of the unions. Under the concerted efforts of Binyamin Netanyahu in his roles as Prime Minister (1996–1999, 2009–present) and Finance Minister (2003–2005), the state sold off many of its assets in different sectors of the economy, including banking, telecommunications, heavy chemicals and natural resources, construction, and transportation.

In the economic arena, then, the state has been largely successful at curtailing the power of the Histadrut in major industries and sectors. Its ability to completely disrupt the Histadrut has been constrained by the lingering effects of a socialist economy and a collectivist culture, and the federation continues to clash with the government over budgetary and fiscal issues. The 2011 social justice protests—which focused on the high cost of living—seemed to provide the Histadrut with an opportunity to reinvigorate itself and its role in the political economy, but whether its power will be revived will depend on whether the government moves ahead with recommendations to address the demands raised by the protests.

PERSONAL STATUS ISSUES

During the Mandate, the British allowed the Jewish and Arab communities considerable autonomy, particularly in religious affairs and areas of personal status such as birth, marriage, divorce, conversion, and burial. In the Jewish community, halacha (the corpus of Jewish religious law) provided the rules according to which individuals passed through their life cycles. In the Arab community, Muslims and Christians governed their own personal relationships. As noted in Chapter 3, the British approach to these issues had its roots in the millet system of the Ottoman Empire, in which protection of religious minorities translated into autonomy in personal affairs for the major religious communities.

After the state was established, Ben-Gurion and Mapai saw no reason to change the system. First, it had worked well enough under the Ottomans and the British, and its success had allowed the Jewish community to maintain its separation from the Arab community. Second, Israeli leaders were keenly aware that in addition to the national divide between Jews and Arabs, the new state had a number of religious groups coexisting under its authority, and the Jewish state could not force non-Jews to follow Jewish laws and rituals. Third, the system established during the Yishuv had allowed a delicate balance between secular and ultra-Orthodox Jews to be maintained. The latter dynamic was enhanced in the "status quo agreement," a letter exchanged between David Ben-Gurion, as leader of the Jewish Agency, and the premier haredi body, Agudat Yisrael (see Chapter 6). In the letter, Ben-Gurion indicated that Orthodox Jewish religious practices would be facilitated in certain areas such as education and public dietary laws. Thus, in this arena, the state purposely avoided imposing a single religious authority over all its citizens, deeming it better to grant priority in the public sphere to Judaism while maintaining religious autonomy for other religious communities. There was no single standard for everyone, either based on civil law or on a single set of religious precepts. The major innovation was that the state agreed to recognize life cycle events that occurred abroad (e.g., marriage) but would not require its religious authorities to do the same.

As in the economic arena, as the existential threats to the state receded and the country prospered, dissatisfaction with the secular–religious balance and the status quo grew. Among Jewish Israelis, growing individualism led to discontent with the more conservative and traditional interpretations of scripture that governed the community. The issue of civil marriage became especially problematic. Precise numbers are difficult to come by, but the Central Bureau of Statistics recorded recognition of over 12,000 marriages that took place abroad in 2010. This number includes marriages of Israelis living abroad, but it also includes the civil marriages of several thousand Jewish Israelis who traveled abroad for marriages they could not get in Israel. (Cyprus is a particularly popular marriage destination because it is not far away.)

The state's authority in the arena of personal status issues is increasingly being questioned. More Israelis are identifying as not having a religion, and more are demanding civil marriages to correspond to their secular inclinations. The influx of hundreds of thousands of immigrants from the former Soviet Union in the early 1990s brought these issues into starker relief. Many of these new immigrants were not considered Jewish by the state's rabbinical authorities, either because they were Christians married or related to Jews or because their Jewish life cycle events (such as conversions or marriages) had been conducted by non-Orthodox rabbis. Yet these individuals were admissible into the country under the Law of Return, which does not rely on a halachic definition of Jewishness. The question of their belonging in the national community was thus thorny. Though they could immigrate into the country and obtain automatic citizenship, they were legally restricted from other benefits and were viewed by the haredi religious authorities as not Jewish according to halacha. For example, some Russian immigrants who entered the Israeli military and were killed during their service could not be buried in Jewish cemeteries. A conversion to Judaism required that they follow Orthodox conversion rituals—something most were opposed to because of that denomination's strict requirements and rules. In addition, non-Orthodox religious groups have been pushing the state to recognize the diversity of Jewish legal opinion and denominations, and to facilitate the application of non-Orthodox Jewish rules in cases in which citizens have asked for it. This remains one of the more troubled arenas in which the Israeli state has had to balance out the various elements of Jewish identity and Jewish religious laws among its citizens.

OTHER STATE-BUILDING EFFORTS

The state, led by Mapai, tried to consolidate its authority in other arenas as well, and this broader record has been similarly mixed. The state was successful in integrating several hundred thousand new immigrants in the late 1940s and early 1950s, most of whom came from the Arab world, where the establishment of Israel contributed to an increase in persecution of and ill-will against the Jewish populations. The Israel Defense Forces played a critical role here, absorbing the newcomers into one of the premier state institutions, helping them to settle in areas around the country, and teaching them the language of the state, Hebrew.

At the same time, though, the state carried out this integration with little sensitivity to the specific needs or cultural patterns of these incoming communities.[12] The urgent need to find homes for the many immigrants, to continue fighting the war, and to consolidate the state's presence around the country, further complicated by a thinly veiled sense of superiority among the secular Ashkenazi Jews who had founded the country, led to some humiliating experiences for the Mizrachim. Many were forced to undergo decontamination treatments (often in the form of hurried showers during which clumps of powdered disinfectants were thrown at them). Much of this population was moved to "development towns," which were for the most part small, hastily constructed villages with little in the way of modern housing or technology. Others recall being passed over for certain types of jobs, treated as second-class citizens in the procurement of government services, and a general lack of interest among the existing Israeli population in their cultural traditions, such as music.

An effort was also made to write a constitution for the state. This process was hindered by intense disputes among the political parties. Though the Declaration of Independence stated that a constitution would be created by October 1, 1948, some argued that it was too difficult to write such a document in the middle of a war and while there was so much uncertainty about the future of the state, including whether the Jewish people as a whole—on whose behalf Israel had been created—would ever reach the country. Others believed a constitution was simply unnecessary: the haredi parties, for example, contended that the Jewish state already had a constitution in the Torah.

In the interim, Israel adopted the "Harari proposal." In June 1950, Yizhar Harari of the Progressive Party suggested that the Knesset give the task of preparing a constitution to the Constitution, Law, and Justice Committee. The committee would write up a "basic law" covering a specific issue, and it would then be issued as a separate chapter. Once all necessary chapters were written, they would be brought to the Knesset as a whole constitutional document. This proposal made it easier for the different parties to put off the need for what would clearly be a divisive debate over the shape of a constitution. Over the course of the next several decades, the Knesset passed 15 Basic Laws, to which the Supreme Court in 1995 gave constitutional status. To date, the process established by the Harari proposal continues to govern Israeli constitutional lawmaking.

Finally, the capture of the West Bank and Gaza Strip in the 1967 War posed numerous problems for the Israeli state. The beginning of the settlement enterprise, in which the government facilitated the moving of Israeli citizens into the West Bank, blurred the borders of the country[13] and distorted the application of Israeli sovereignty and Israeli law across different regions.[14] Such settlement has led to intense legal and political battles in Israel over its presence in the occupied territories, but particularly in the West Bank after Israel disengaged from Gaza in 2005.

SUMMARY

The establishment of the state in a period of great uncertainty and flux, including a war for survival, posed many problems for Israel. Its ability to manage them successfully, however, was enhanced by the existence of a series of rules, systems, and institutions built during the Yishuv. It was relatively simple to transform these elements into Israeli institutions. The difficulty came in making them compulsory, as opposed to the voluntary nature they had maintained in the pre-state period. This was accomplished by an approach that combined the imposition of state authority (in politics and defense) with the granting of autonomy to different groups and institutions (in education, the economy, and personal affairs). The process was facilitated by the dominance of Mapai, but its role in constructing the new arrangements meant its own interests and priorities were embedded within the transformed institutions. This contributed to a struggle between various factions over the state and the bureaucracy for some time to come.

It was a delicate balance, and while it seemed successful in the first decades of the state's existence, there were too many problems inherent in the approach. The politicization of most segments of society and the arrival of new immigrant communities have challenged the state's ability to serve as the ultimate, binding authority in some arenas. The conduct of Israeli politics in later years has been shaped to a large degree by efforts to either maintain or change these systems.

KEYWORDS

Mamlachtiut, David Ben-Gurion, Mapai, Altalena affair, compulsory authority, Histadrut, separate school systems

NOTES

1. Nathan Yanai, "Ben-Gurion's Concept of *Mamlahtiut* and the Forming Reality of the State of Israel," *Jewish Political Studies Review* 1 (1989): 153–156.

2. Mapai—a Hebrew acronym for the Worker's Party of the Land of Israel—was the biggest and most important party of the left, and the largest in the Israeli political constellation. It merged with other socialist groups to form the Labor Party in 1968.

3. Myron J. Aronoff, "The Origins of Israeli Political Culture," in *Israeli Democracy Under Stress*, ed. Ehud Sprinzak and Larry Diamond (Boulder, CO: Lynne Rienner, 1993), 47–48.

4. There are other sectoral-operated schools as well, servicing specific religious communities. For example, different Christian denominations in Israel run their own educational institutions, while the Shas party maintains a network of independent schools for ultra-Orthodox education.

5. See Ilan Ben Zion, "Religious Zionist Schools Adopt Stricter Modesty Rules," *Times of Israel*, August 20, 2012, http://www.timesofisrael.com/religious-zionist-schools-adopt-stricter-modesty-rules/.

6. *Israel Hayom* staff, "Study: Haredi Schools Teach Less Than an Hour a Day of Core Studies," *Israel Hayom*, July 2, 2013.

7. See Majid al-Haj, *Education, Empowerment, and Control: The Case of the Arabs in Israel* (Albany: SUNY Press, 1995); Riad Nasser and Irene Nasser, "Textbooks as a Vehicle for Segregation and Domination: State Efforts to Shape Palestinian Israelis' Identities as Citizens," *Journal of Curriculum Studies* 40 (2008): 627–650.

8. Yarden Skop, "Forecast: Only 40% of Israeli Students Will Attend Nonreligious Schools by 2019," *Haaretz*, August 7, 2013.

9. At the same time, both sectors' share of the student growth rate has been declining over time. See Nachum Blass, *Trends in the Development of the Education System: Pupils and Teachers*, Policy Paper No. 2013.11 (Jerusalem: Taub Center for Social Policy Studies in Israel, 2013), 5, http://taubcenter.org.il/wp-content/files_mf/trendsinthedevelopment2013.pdf.

10. Ilan S. Troen, *Imagining Zion: Dreams, Designs, and Realities in a Century of Jewish Settlement* (New Haven, CT: Yale University Press, 2003).

11. On Labor Zionism's efforts and successes in the Yishuv and early Israel, see Michael Shalev, *Labour and the Political Economy of Israel* (Oxford: Oxford University Press, 1992); and Yonathan Shapiro, *The Formative Years of the Israeli Labour Party: The Organization of Power, 1919–1930* (London: Sage Publications, 1976).

12. Baruch Kimmerling, *The Invention and Decline of Israeliness: State, Society, and the Military* (Berkeley: University of California Press, 2001).

13. Israel's de facto border in the east between 1949 and 1967 was the Green Line, so named for the green ink pen used to draw the armistice line between Jordan and Israel in 1949. It was never established or recognized as a formal border, though Mapai governments had generally accepted it as such.

14. Shlomo Gazit, *The Carrot and the Stick: Israel's Policy in Judaea and Samaria, 1967–68* (Washington, D.C.: B'nai B'rith Books, 1995); Gershom Gorenberg, *The Accidental Empire: Israel and the Birth of the Settlements, 1967–1977* (New York: Times Books, 2006); and Idith Zertal and Akiva Eldar, *Lords of the Land: The War Over Israel's Settlements in the Occupied Territories, 1967–2007*, trans. Vivian Eden (New York: Nation Books, 2007).

CHAPTER 5

✍

Political Culture and Demography

Describing Israel's political culture is challenging, because Israel is a relatively new society, most of whose members are descended from immigrants who were not indigenous to the territory when the foundation for the Israeli state was laid. At the same time, changing patterns of immigration bring new communities into the polity on what seems to be a regular, if intermittent, basis. As a result, the Zionist movement, the institutions and people of the Yishuv, and eventually the Israeli state all contributed to the construction of a new political culture as well as a state. In addition, the Arabs of Israel have a history that developed largely independent of the Jews and never became fully integrated into Israeli political culture.

The term political culture, as used in comparative politics, describes the attitudes, orientations, and beliefs that are held by the citizens of a country with regard to their political system and shape the environment in which a country's politics operates. Israeli political culture has been subject to two trends, similar to those experienced by other multicultural and immigrant societies led by a dominant ethno-national group. On the one hand, the need to construct the boundaries of the community for security purposes and to create the momentum needed for statehood led to the imposition of the identity of the "new Jew"—a member of a Hebrew society in which all individuals shared the same language, values, and identity. On the other hand, the country was dominated by a secular Ashkenazi elite that mostly reinforced its hegemony while leaving other communities out. Some of these communities felt alienated and marginalized, but certainly all tried to maintain their separate identities at the same time that they adapted to Israeli identity. This led to periods of tension and political conflict that continue into the contemporary era.

This chapter begins with a discussion of political culture in the Yishuv in Mandatory Palestine before the state was established. It then notes the importance of immigration for the development of a national political culture, which leads to a discussion of the main political values held by citizens. The next section examines the effects of the watershed events of 1967—the conquest of the West Bank and east Jerusalem—on Israel's political culture. The difficulty in maintaining a national consensus follows directly from the implications of these events. One main thread running through Israeli political culture has been the shift from a collectivist ethos to a more individual-oriented one, and this is discussed in the next section. Political culture in the Arab community—which has largely remained separate from the majority Jewish culture—is also explored. The chapter ends with some notes on demography in the state, because of the importance demographic trends have had, and continue to have, on Israeli political culture.

THE PRE-STATE PERIOD

One of the problems that confronted the early Zionists and later the Israeli leadership was that Jews had not been able to exercise sovereign power for the nearly 2,000 years since the last revolt against the Roman Empire. The lack of the political experience that an independent existence would have provided left the Jews without any model for what a Jewish national polity should look like. Models based on biblical experience were not especially helpful to those who sought to create a democratic state in line with emerging twentieth-century values and methods of governance. Jews around the world did have considerable experience in running their own local communities, or *kehilot*, but that was not easily transferable to a national arena. The Jewish population that settled in Palestine early in the century lacked experience with modern democratic values and practices because the vast majority came from countries without democratic traditions at the national level; whatever political experience these groups had came from participation in community organizations, which were not necessarily run democratically. A subsequent related challenge concerned how to integrate newcomers into this new society and foster their internalization of democratic norms. *in a secular sense*

An integral part of Zionist ideology was its goal of creating a new society, both in theory and in practice. This society would be a Jewish society, but one that was populated by "new Jews" who would differ from the European Jews in significant ways. This desire did not reflect only a theoretical ideal; it was to be implemented in practice, a goal that has been substantially achieved by the transformation of Jewish society. One of the key elements of the new Jewish society was the determination of its people not to be powerless anymore, a view that was reinforced by the fate of European Jewry at the hands of the Nazis. Since the creation of the state Israeli Jews have felt compelled to go to great lengths to demonstrate the ways in which they have achieved the goal of creating a new society and ensured that they will not meet the fate of Europe's Jews. The trauma of the Holocaust became embedded in the common Israeli experience early in the years of statehood. The character of the military response to various kinds of security provocations, which was usually quite tough and energetic, reflected a determination to reinforce the reality that the Jews would no longer be victims but instead would fight back against those who would do them harm.

In order to accomplish their goals, the Zionists had to impose a Western democratic regime on a society that had limited experience with democracy. Interestingly, the goal of a democratic polity was accepted from the beginning, even though most of the Jewish immigrants to Palestine had little personal experience with that form of national government. That attitude maintained the commitments envisioned by Theodor Herzl and his colleagues from the beginnings of the Zionist movement. Even during the Mandate period, the Zionists set up noncoercive institutions that were legitimated by regular elections, as discussed in Chapter 3. The experience with the British governmental system in this period also exposed the community to the liberal values of British institutions, despite considerable dissatisfaction with the content of British policy. By the time that the state came into being, these institutions and political processes were well established and not questioned, even if some of the practical techniques employed by the politicians were derived from their political experience in eastern European countries before coming to Palestine.

The Israeli experience, in which hundreds of thousands of immigrants, overwhelmingly from nondemocratic countries, have been socialized into a democratic system, is a vivid example of successful political learning. It is even more remarkable when we consider the fact that the commitment to a democratic system has been maintained under consistent conditions of war and threat, and in a region where there are almost no other democracies. Yet there is no indication that the commitment to democracy is conditional. For example, the Israel Democracy Institute's 2013 Israel Democracy Index showed that about 66 percent of Israel's Jews say that "democratic" or "Jewish and democratic" are key identifying characteristics of Israel.[1] Why has the commitment to democracy been so strong in the face of such challenges? For one thing, the Jewish political tradition, as it had developed over two millennia of dispersion, was never receptive to authoritarian rule. Furthermore, the founders of the modern Israeli political system were staunch democrats who developed the society's institutions accordingly.

FOUNDATIONAL VALUES OF THE STATE

Numerous elements that had become part of the political culture of the Yishuv by 1948 were simply accepted by Israelis at the establishment of the state. Since that time the emphasis on the various elements may have changed, but the broad themes remain largely intact. These themes can be grouped into three broad categories.

A Jewish State. The overriding purpose of Israel was to create a Jewish state, one that not only provided refuge for Jews who needed it but would further the development of Jewish peoplehood in all its dimensions. Thus Israel was created not just as a state *of* the Jews but most decidedly as a *Jewish state*, one that would embody and promote Jewish values and provide an environment in which Jewish culture, learning, and creativity would flourish. Toward those ends a modernized Hebrew would become the national language and the predominant means of communication. Although the state would be officially secular and religious observance would not be required, support for the Jewish religion and religious institutions would be a concern of the government, and public policy would facilitate personal religious observance. Furthermore, as the reconstituted Jewish state, Israel would welcome Jewish immigrants from anywhere and would maintain an attitude of skepticism about the long-term viability of the Jewish diaspora communities.

A Democratic State. From the outset a key goal of the founders of Israel was to create a state that would embody democratic values and be committed to an open political process. Voting and participation were encouraged, a highly representative voting system was taken for granted, and political parties became an integral part of the life of the society from an early stage. However, because of the emphasis on collective goals during the pre-state period, less emphasis was placed on individual liberty than in other Western democratic systems. This relative neglect of individual rights also reflects the emphasis in the Jewish political tradition on obligations rather than rights, as well as the socialist stress on the needs of the collectivity before the needs of the individual.

A Civic Society. The new society not only stressed the achievement of collective goals but also strove to identify and promote goals that would help engender a commitment to the nation and the state. Among those were the promotion of agriculture and a return to the land (distinguishing Israelis from their European forebears, who did not have access to agricultural pursuits), the subordination of individual achievement to the needs of the society as a whole, the creation of strong governmental and quasi-governmental institutions, a statist preference in public policy and economic policy in particular, the cultivation of patriotic virtues, self-defense through the deployment of military force, and the maximization of a spirit of national self-reliance. The idea that individuals would realize their personal aims through collective action was an underlying theme of most of the goals explicitly recognized at the time of independence. Consistent with that orientation was the weakness of civil society and the underdevelopment of a sphere of action outside the influence of a strong state.

After the state was created, the government, led for 13 of its first 15 years by Prime Minister David Ben-Gurion of Mapai, took a number of steps to shape the emerging political culture. In addition, several developments had important impacts. By the time of the Six-Day War in 1967 it was possible to clearly identify the elements of the political culture, including those that dated back to the pre-state period and those that developed after 1948.

The Effect of Immigration

One of the most striking factors in the development of Israeli society during its early years was the massive immigration of Mizrachim, Jews from Middle Eastern countries. Although there had been Mizrachi and Sephardi Jews living in what became Israel for many centuries, they were quite small in number. The Zionist movement, which sparked the bulk of immigration before 1948, was almost exclusively led by Ashkenazi Jews of Europe. As a result, the Yishuv that began to take shape during the first third of the twentieth century was dominated by Ashkenazim, as were the institutions that they created, which therefore reflected their experiences and goals.

During the early years of statehood, however, the Mizrachi immigrants, or Middle Easterners (often referred to in Israel's early years as Sephardim) became a significant faction in the society, the effect of which was to define Israel as a partnership (if an unequal one at the start) between these two groups of Jews. Although both groups were Jewish, they came from significantly different cultural backgrounds and had different historical experiences. Even their experiences of anti-Semitism, which culminated in the Holocaust for European Jews, were different. Anti-Semitism in Europe was manifested most often in persecution, expulsion, and mass murder; in the Arab world it was often found in the second-class citizenship and restrictions of civil rights imposed on the Jews, though there were also examples of violence directed against Jews. The Jews from Arab countries came from very conservative and traditional societies, while the European Jews came from societies that were changing more rapidly as they began to modernize. Each group had its own variation of the religious tradition, including some liturgical differences, its own scholars and role models, and its own objectives. Even musical and culinary traditions were quite different. The Zionist pioneers who came from Europe tended to be idealistically motivated, certainly through the early years of the Mandate, and saw themselves as part of a collective mission, though later Ashkenazi immigrants were simply trying to escape the Nazi threat. Mizrachi immigrants, on the other hand, largely came to seek refuge from persecution in their home countries. Once the latter group arrived, however, the dual Ashkenazi/Mizrachi character of Israeli society became a feature of the political culture that had important implications for such phenomena as voting behavior.

Some sixty years later it appears that the divide between Ashkenazim and Mizrachim is breaking down. In part this is due to marriages that involve partners from both groups becoming increasingly common, and in part it is due to the increasing Mizrachi integration into the state. Yet there is ample evidence that Mizrachi Jews still lag behind the Ashkenazim in socioeconomic terms. It can be anticipated that as a source of division, ethnicity will gradually decline in importance in the future.

Democracy and Political Values

As the new state formalized its main political institutions and processes, the preference for democratic governance, based primarily on European parliamentary models, was evident. These values were eventually codified in a series of Basic Laws (an alternative to a constitution) that were enacted piecemeal over the years and concretely expressed the societal consensus about how the country would be governed. Furthermore, the development of political parties during the Mandate and the Yishuv's experience with elections made political participation highly valued from the start of statehood. Political involvement was crucial during the Mandate period because it helped to make the emerging state a credible idea. As a result, most citizens of the new state felt that they had a real and continuing personal stake in the success of Israel, thereby producing high rates of participation. Finally, the development of the state's institutions and practices over a period of decades allowed them time to evolve organically rather than being imposed within a short period of time. This evolution of political institutional practices was identified by Daniel Elazar and Stuart Cohen as a key element of the Jewish political tradition.[2]

In terms of policy, the government under Ben-Gurion emphasized the process of mamlachtiut, or statism (see Chapter 4). Essentially this meant that the government would pursue policies to increase the centralizing role of the state in everyday life and diminish the role of subnational organizations, which were often party oriented. As a unitary state, Israel tended to focus power in the hands of the national government, with little significant policy authority left to municipal governments. The pursuit of mamlachtiut by Ben-Gurion and his Mapai party had a dual effect: it provided a way for a diverse citizenry (at least the Jewish part) to relate to the state and it strengthened the state's ability to pursue public policy goals. Because the political culture was new to everyone, any Israeli could become a part of it without having to defer to some other part of the society. Both individual identity and the potential for state action were advanced by the policy of mamlachtiut and were important goals for political and economic development. Given the persistent external threats and the challenge of coping with large-scale immigration, mamlachtiut was both necessary and successful.

The emphasis on the state was reinforced by other traditions that had been established well before 1948. For example, the kibbutz, the communal and collective agricultural settlement, became an important symbol of the character of the Jewish renaissance during the Mandate and into the 1950s, even if only a small minority of Israelis actually lived on kibbutzim. Not only were the accomplishments of the kibbutz movement celebrated by the dominant Mapai party, which itself had ties to a segment of the kibbutzim, but kibbutzniks came to exemplify the best of the Israeli community. They symbolized the Jewish return to the land, pioneered in farming it, helped to make the desert bloom, and contributed disproportionately to the ranks of IDF soldiers, especially in the elite combat units. Underlying their activities was the belief that the best way to achieve their desired ends was through collective action.

Related to mamlachtiut was the development of the army. The urgency of the security situation necessitated a rapid development of the IDF during the early years. But Ben-Gurion and his colleagues saw in the army not just a defensive instrument but also an opportunity to forge greater national unity through an intense socialization experience. Just after independence Ben-Gurion and his government had ensured that independent fighting groups associated with different Zionist streams would be integrated into the army. Once that happened and the War of Independence was successfully concluded, the IDF became a major force for integration as a result of a conscription policy that brought virtually all men and women (excluding haredim, Orthodox women, and Arabs) into the army at age 18. During the first 20 years of statehood the prestige of the military was quite high, buoyed by the impressive victories in the 1956 Suez War and the 1967 Six-Day War.

Nearly all young Jewish Israelis shared the same experience of army service that helped facilitate their identification with the nation, its history, and its aspirations. The army experience gave most young people a sense of national unity because of the way that it broke down background differences, particularly ethnic ones. That helped to foster a sense of national identity, both as a modern Israeli and as part of the Jewish nation. Arguably, Israel was consciously developing a melting pot society consisting of immigrants from dozens of different environments.

Israel's political culture is also marked by a high degree of informality, particularly among the Jewish population. This stems from several experiences. First, in the Yishuv, Zionist activists sometimes had to operate in a way that would avoid notice by the British authorities, particularly when it came to military and illegal immigration operations. Thus they had to rely on personal relationships and interactions to transmit information and equipment from one leader or group to another. Second, the small size of the population increased the chances that people in and out of government and the civil service would be familiar with each other. Third, the nature of the (near) universal draft meant that many Israelis who worked together during their active and reserve service maintained those contacts in their civilian lives. It is common, for example, for parliamentarians and government ministers to know each other from military experience as one another's superiors or subordinates in uniform. The ongoing security situation also required that Jewish Israelis constantly make decisions about war and peace under very stressful conditions, which in turn generated a sense of camaraderie they carried with them once they left their defense posts. All of these experiences together have highlighted Israeli culture's reliance on self-sufficiency, tendency toward improvisation, and disregard for hierarchy. These characteristics have become accepted parts of Israelis' daily lives.

The most interesting example of the way these traits play out in the political arena is the common use of Jewish politicians' nicknames by journalists, the public, and other politicians—even in direct conversations. Use of nicknames implies a level of familiarity across Jewish Israeli society; Arab politicians, too, sometimes use them. Labor leader Isaac Herzog is regularly referred to as "Buji," a term of endearment his mother used when he was a child. The late Rehavam Ze'evi, of the far-right *Moledet* party, was called "Ghandi" for the resemblance he bore to the Indian pacifist. Prime Minister Binyamin Netanyahu is widely known as "Bibi," and Defense Minister Moshe Ya'alon is "Bogie." It is noteworthy, though, that nicknames have been applied only to male politicians, and primarily only to Ashkenazi and Mizrachi Jews. A different manifestation of informality applied to female politicians is the use of first names, as in the case of Golda (Meir).

Civil Religion

Finally, through the army and other institutions the government began to shape a number of national observances that were independent of any religious practice. Some were related to key points in army service, while others were related to national holidays. They include *Yom Hashoah* (Holocaust and Heroism Remembrance Day, often shortened to Holocaust Memorial Day), *Yom HaZikaron* (a memorial day for fallen soldiers and victims of terrorism), and Independence Day, all three falling within a short period of time in the spring. These dates are distinctly different from the other national holidays that come from the religious calendar and generally involve little formal religious observance. Both Holocaust Memorial Day and the memorial day for fallen soldiers are sad occasions, an opportunity for the entire community, not just family members, to mourn the victims of the Holocaust, members of the IDF and security services who gave their lives in defense of the country, and, in recent years, civilians killed by terrorism. Thus the atmosphere throughout the country is solemn on those days. At the beginning of the memorial days, at sunset, sirens sound across the country. Most Jewish citizens stop what they are doing, stand at attention, and contemplate what the siren signifies. Traffic on the highways comes to a near-complete halt, and most citizens will stand outside their cars. The siren ritual is repeated at 11 a.m. the following morning. On the memorial day for fallen soldiers there are many ceremonies at military cemeteries, as well as visits by family members to the graves of departed husbands, fathers, and children. Independence Day, which immediately follows the memorial day, is a day of frivolity and celebration. Families get together for recreational activities. The almost-instant transition from mourning to celebration is a remarkable phenomenon that is considered to represent the Israeli way of life.

The way in which these occasions are structured means that both secular and religious Israelis can participate equally in such events. However, Arab citizens feel that they have no reason to mourn or to celebrate on any of these occasions and generally do not participate. In addition, most haredim do not recognize the government's designation of these days for special purposes. They mark the Holocaust on a different date and, as non-Zionists, do not mark either the memorial day for fallen soldiers or Independence Day. Such action only accentuates the divide between haredim and Zionist Israelis. Nevertheless, these observances and other civic rituals, coupled with the appropriation of traditional symbols with religious roots, gradually became recognizable as components of a civil religion that served to unite the disparate parts of the Jewish population.[3] Zionism as a core value also became an integral part of the civil religion.[4]

Because citizens felt connected to the state, participation in elections was highly valued in the years following independence, especially because of the prominent role played by the political parties, which dated back to the Mandate period. Voter turnout was high for the first several decades of Israel's existence, even in the Arab sector. For about two decades, turnout in the Jewish sector ranged from the high 70s to the mid 80s, while voting rates in the Arab sector were equally high, even reaching 90 percent in 1955.

By 1967, then, a year that proved to be a key turning point in Israeli history because of the Six-Day War, the political culture was well established. Israel was a Jewish state based on traditional Jewish values and a Zionist ideology that was committed to vibrant party politics and a lively democratic political system. An Israeli civic identity had been defined, in part because of the almost universally shared army experience among the Jewish population. A strong state had emerged with only modest opposition from those who believed in a more active private economy, and the state had been instrumental in establishing the elements of a civil religion. In a sense, the 19 years between 1948 and 1967 provided the political, military, and civil leadership the opportunity to put the new state on firm footing, to forge a common identity that would unite a largely immigrant population, and to clearly align the country with that part of the world community that was dedicated to democratic principles. But as a new state that was still developing, Israel had a political culture that was still in flux and indeed underwent major changes in the decades that followed.

CHANGES SINCE 1967

Since 1967 there have been numerous developments that have affected the shape of Israel's political culture. Many reflect departures from the patterns that were established in the pre-state period and after independence. In their totality the changes that have taken place have substantially reshaped the prevailing attitudes, although many continuities do remain.

Perhaps the most important development was the Six-Day War in 1967, which entailed a stunningly rapid victory over three Arab countries and the acquisition of territory that had been ruled by Jordan, Egypt, and Syria. For at least six years after this conflict, until the Yom Kippur War in 1973, Israelis felt a security that they had not felt during the previous 19, based on the conviction that no combination of Arab foes represented a threat to the basic security of the state. That complacency was shattered by the surprise attack carried out by Egypt and Syria in 1973. But even though the ultimate outcome of that conflict was battlefield supremacy by Israel, the state's initial setback and its high number of casualties were traumatic and reverberated throughout the political system during the ensuing years, contributing to the first Likud electoral victory in 1977. In the longer-term perspective, 1973 marked the end of the conventional military threat that had been posed by the country's close neighbors and prompted Israelis to broaden their concerns from their prior narrow focus on conventional military threats.

The 1967 victory brought several territories under Israeli control, notably eastern Jerusalem, the West Bank (historic Judea and Samaria), the Gaza Strip, the Sinai Peninsula, and the Golan Heights. The first three of these brought substantial numbers of Palestinians under Israeli rule. Although Sinai was later returned to Egypt in the 1979 peace treaty, Israeli citizens and soldiers did not pull out of Gaza until 2005, and the issue of Israeli control in the West Bank has proved to be controversial and divisive. Moreover, even though eastern Jerusalem and the Golan Heights were later formally annexed, their status has not been resolved definitively.

In a larger sense, the questions of what to do with the territories that Israel captured in 1967 and, more specifically, whether to agree to a Palestinian state and under what conditions have created a fault line in the Israeli population and the political system. This division represents a sharp departure from the pre-1967 situation, in which there was a broad consensus about security and how to deal with military and terrorist threats from neighboring countries, as well as about identity and values. While most Israelis want their government to be prepared to use force to protect the state against terrorist attacks, there is no consensus about how to resolve the territorial issue. This split contributed to the public's erratic voting patterns in the 1990s and 2000s, as Labor and Likud (and then Kadima) were alternately carried into power over these very questions.

This cleavage over fundamental questions has altered a political culture in which support for government security policies was long understood to be critical. Until the 1980s Israel never had an organized opposition to its basic security and territorial policies. But by the middle of that decade considerable ferment had emerged on the left, including within the Labor Party, that revolved around the notion that in the long run Israeli security would be enhanced if the state could make peace with the Palestinians and withdraw from much, if not most, of the territory acquired in 1967. Groups like Peace Now were instrumental in bringing about a substantial change in attitudes. The articulation of such views by a significant part of the population, including the elite sectors, demonstrated that Israel no longer enjoyed a consensus on many key security questions, a view that was reinforced by Labor's 1993 embrace of the idea that peace with the Palestinians was attainable, captured by the Oslo Accords signed that year. Likud and the right were highly skeptical of this contention. Ever since, attitudes toward the peace process with the Palestinians have been a major line of cleavage among Israeli Jews.

The Normalization of Dissent

The general consensus on defense and security matters in the early years of statehood spilled over into the economic and social arenas as well. With a weak opposition led by Menachem Begin's Herut party, Prime Minister David Ben-Gurion's Mapai–Labor party led the government continuously between 1948 and 1977. Most Israelis did not perceive their views about economic and social organization as partisan. Rather, the strong role of the state in such matters was generally accepted and was not subjected to a great deal of scrutiny. In fact, the idea of dissenting from the broad consensus was seldom put forth among the public with any success. For nearly 30 years Herut, the General Zionists, and the Progressives (and later the Liberals) were unable to gain enough support to challenge Labor electorally. However, that changed in the years after 1967. The capture of the biblical and historical Jewish kingdoms made the ideas once promoted only by a small number of Israelis at the political level (particularly Herut) now possible and legitimate. While Israel did annex and expand the environs of Jerusalem, it did not annex the rest of the West Bank—but neither did it commit to withdrawing from all of it. The beginning of settlement in the region, for ideological and religious reasons, also anchored the claim that at least part of this territory belonged to Israel. Once dissent on military and security issues became legitimate, it was possible to question economic and social policies as well. Begin, through the efforts of Ariel Sharon, was able to bring the Herut view on the territories and the Liberal view on the economy together in the formation of Likud in 1973, which finally made a right-of-center party a plausible alternative to Labor.

These expressions of dissent from the prevailing political orthodoxy took different forms at different times. They were sometimes a reflection of elite concerns and at other times issues that energized the mass public. Often new parties sprang up to promote one of these causes or an existing party embraced the cause. Examples include the Democratic Movement for Change (DMC), which promoted electoral reform in the 1977 election; *Shinui* (Change), which advocated for secular Jews against the Orthodox establishment in the 2003 election; Labor and Meretz, which mobilized concerns about the tent cities and street protests against high consumer prices, especially for housing, in 2011; and Yesh Atid, which campaigned against preferential treatment of haredim in the 2013 election. The appearance of protests, such as those against high consumer prices, which often resulted in the formation of new political parties, reflected a much greater willingness on the part of average Israelis to express dissenting views.

A more profound expression of dissent from prevailing values is the expression of support for what is called post-Zionism on the part of some leftist academics, intellectuals, and activists (see Chapter 18). Some post-Zionists advocate separating Israel from its connection to Jewish peoplehood and treating the country as a "state for all its citizens." In other words, they support the idea that Israel should stop viewing itself as the state of the Jewish people and instead adopt a neutral stance that treats Jewish and Arab citizens equally. Obviously this represents a radical departure from core Israeli values that antedate statehood by 50 years, and it is not an idea that has attracted a large following. But because the post-Zionists are concentrated in occupations that allow their views to be publicized, the movement has attracted some attention, particularly abroad. Dissenting from the Zionist consensus is a highly consequential act that has been tolerated by society despite the controversy that it engenders.[5]

A development on the other end of the political spectrum has been the increasing radicalization of elements of the Religious Zionist community. This shift began with the euphoria of the victory in the Six-Day War of 1967 and was followed by the embrace of the settlement enterprise based on a religious interpretation of those events. But as the prospect of relinquishing substantial parts of the West Bank became real after 1993, some within that sector began to raise the question of which authority took primacy, religious imperatives as presented by some rabbis or decisions of the government. It was not coincident that Yigal Amir, the assassin of Prime Minister Yitzhak Rabin in 1995, came from a Religious Zionist background. The decision to withdraw from Gaza in 2005 exacerbated tensions, in part because many of the settlers there were Religious Zionists and in part because their confreres in West Bank settlements became concerned that a similar decision might apply to them in the future. As a result of the Rabin assassination, the Israel Security Agency (*Shin Bet*) had to turn more of its attention to possible terrorist threats from Israeli Jews. The question also arose of whether religious soldiers could be depended upon to follow orders in the event that Israel decided to withdraw from parts of the territory of Judea and Samaria, as the West Bank is referred to by Israel. That, plus the appearance of settler factions acting outside the law, suggests that what Ehud Sprinzak described as *illegalism*, a willingness to operate beyond the bounds of the law, had become part of the value system of a segment of the population.[6]

In general the national religious sector has become decidedly more prominent since 1977. Once the dominance of Labor ended, groups that had played secondary roles in politics, such as Mizrahim, Arabs, and various types of religious Jews, began to become more assertive politically. This did not happen all at once, but looking back the trend is clear. Today, the national religious group is now much more strongly represented in politics and in the army than it ever was, which means that religious values have become more of an issue politically.[7]

FROM COLLECTIVISM TO INDIVIDUALISM

One of the most significant developments during the last several decades has been the move away from the traditional Israeli focus on collective goals and achievements toward a more individualistic value system.[8] During the early years of statehood the economic and security needs of the state were so great that citizens were implicitly, and sometimes explicitly, urged to subordinate their individual needs to the needs of the collectivity, a prerogative the public accepted. This was true even before 1948, as the Yishuv endeavored to build the foundations of the state. Through the years citizens were encouraged to find fulfillment through collective accomplishments, both civilian and military. In a sense the kibbutz movement of collective agricultural communities, which played a key role in the development of the land during the Mandate period and afterwards, served as a template for the society at large, even though the number of Israelis who lived on kibbutzim was never a high proportion of the overall population. But the kibbutz lifestyle came to symbolize what was expected of Israelis: to do their work to the best of their ability but to find rewards only in the accomplishments of the community as a whole.

Despite the salience of such views for decades, it can be argued that in recent years the evident divisions in, and perhaps even fragmentation of, society have led to a diminution of social solidarity in the population. This phenomenon has been accompanied by an increase in antipolitical feelings in the general public. Perhaps the most distinct arena in which this shift has taken place is in the military/security sphere. When the military must mobilize to fight, Israeli Jews generally do report to their units. But in quieter times there have been increases in avoidance of military service in some sectors of the population, notably secular Ashkenazim. To date this has not caused serious manpower problems for the IDF, but it is an issue that sparks concern in official quarters.

Under the Labor governments from 1948 through 1977 the economic emphasis was on state or quasi-state enterprises in which private interests played a very minor role. The net effect of this environment was to stifle individual initiative and promote the value of delayed gratification. Ironically, although the army was obviously a collective enterprise too, it was a place where soldiers were allowed—and often encouraged—to exercise leadership individually. Indeed, many of Israel's heroic military leaders of the post-1948 generation made their reputations through such actions.

After 1977 more changes began to occur, especially in terms of economic activity. Government policies shifted toward encouraging private enterprise and individual initiative, thereby creating the possibility of economic gains for entrepreneurs and businesspeople. By the 1990s much of that individualism had been manifested in the high-tech sector, which was taking off and which enabled many individuals to reap personal fortunes. In the 2000s, as Finance Minister and Prime Minster, Binyamin Netanyahu made privatization a top priority. Not incidentally, the country as a whole experienced solid economic growth through the first decade of the twenty-first century, eventually achieving status as an advanced economy that warranted membership in the Organisation for Economic Co-operation and Development (OECD). During the 1990s and 2000s there was growth of private radio and television stations and a transformation of the newspaper and online media industries. Some traditional newspapers that had been oriented toward political parties, such as *Davar*, a Labor Zionist outlet, were unable to survive and were eventually replaced by privately owned papers.

The radio and television industry is a particularly interesting example of government involvement in cultural issues. In the early years of the state, and for many years thereafter, radio broadcasting was dominated by the government-run Voice of Israel. The advent of television in the country was delayed considerably because Ben-Gurion was opposed to making it available; television broadcasting did not begin until the late 1960s. As with radio, television was publicly owned. It was only much later, in the 1980s and 1990s, as government influence in the economy was declining and private enterprise was coming to be seen in a more favorable light than it had been in the days of Labor hegemony, that private radio and television stations began to broadcast; in addition, many pirate radio stations came to operate outside of any government supervision. Today citizens have access to three primary television stations, two of them private. In addition, the appearance of cable and then satellite TV during the past two decades has greatly increased the choices available to the Israeli consumer and reduced the ability of the government to use the media as a way to shape the national culture.

The evolution of the film industry also underscored the trend toward greater individualism. Instead of the 1950s style of patriotic films, often with military subject matter, the newer films began to depict the lives of ordinary Israelis to a much greater extent, and to explore once-taboo topics and contemporary controversies. The net effect of all these changes was a flowering of individual creativity in innumerable fields. On balance that was surely a positive development, but it also made it much more difficult for the government to demand personal sacrifices from its citizens.

Concomitant with this trend toward greater individualism was the increasing awareness of issues of individual liberties. The pressing needs of state building during the early years of statehood led to little emphasis on rights and liberties. Indeed, as the government enacted the elements of a constitution on a piecemeal basis during the 1950s and 1960s there was a notable absence of any statement of rights in the liberal sense. If anything, citizens' obligations were stressed, a value that also reflected the Jewish tradition's priorities. But as society progressed, there was increasing public recognition that Israel's aspirations to join the ranks of the Western liberal democracies required attention to the issue of individual rights and liberties. Two developments reflected the shifting emphasis. First, the Knesset enacted two Basic Laws in 1992 that dealt, at least in part, with individual liberties (the Basic Law: Human Dignity and Liberty and the Basic Law: Freedom of Occupation). Second, the Supreme Court took a more activist stance by upholding individual rights in the face of government assertions of compelling state interests. This was especially true during the period when Aharon Barak served as President of the Supreme Court (see Chapter 14).

The new emphasis on individualism in various spheres led to a decline in ideology, which had traditionally defined and demarcated Israeli society. Individuals were encouraged to develop an ideological orientation and identification at a relatively early age, often through partisan youth groups, and to seek adult opportunities that reinforced the adopted ideological position. The political parties, of which there were many, were often divided by fine ideological distinctions. However, after 1977 the party system began to change, eventually leading to a broader center than had existed previously. The traditional left and right parties (Labor and Likud) modified their positions on central issues, and various centrist and specialized parties emerged (although the centrist groups were often short-lived). In contrast, the division between secular and religious Israelis hardened, especially as haredi parties became more assertive beginning in the 1980s. The reaction to haredi assertiveness was a growing support for avowedly secular parties that committed themselves to curbing the power of the religious sector. Yet the 2013 election demonstrated that secular politicians, and presumably their supporters in the general public, could not only distinguish between haredim and national religious Jews, but could form alliances with the latter. This is precisely what occurred within the new Yesh Atid party, and between that party and *Bayit Yehudi* (Jewish Home).

Finally, the massive immigration from the former Soviet Union (primarily from Russia) of the 1990s noticeably affected the political culture. The new immigrants, of whom there were over a million, were overwhelmingly secular, and a substantial proportion was not even Jewish from the perspective of Jewish religious law. Although the Russians' indifference to religion did not in itself have a major effect on the political culture, it did increase sensitivity within the country to the presence of such a large population that did not share some knowledge of Jewish tradition with the majority. In a more direct way, it increased support for greater distance between the state and religious interests and created pressure for modification of conversion procedures in order to enable more of the immigrants to regularize their status as Jews. At the same time, it prompted Orthodox organizations and authorities, especially haredim, to press for stricter rules for processes such as conversion and burial and definitions of who is a Jew. Over time, the immigrants—and, to a greater degree, their children—began to come together into a unique Israeli identity. But since the definition of membership in the Jewish people is a religious question that is in the hands of the rabbinate (which is increasingly controlled by haredi interests), the conversion question barred full resolution of the identity problem for those who were not halachically Jewish. At the same time, the Russian community in Israel has tended to be highly skilled and has contributed to its own well-developed culture, manifested, for example, in the large number of Russian-language media.

POLITICAL CULTURE IN THE ARAB COMMUNITY

Although the creation of a political culture to which Jewish Israelis could relate proved successful, the Arab sector of the population was largely left out of this undertaking. Despite the fact that Arab citizens were granted full political rights and elected representatives to the Knesset, politics and government were essentially the preserve of the Jews, who had set up the state as a vehicle for the realization of Jewish and Zionist values, and who constituted a large majority of the population. Hence the content of the political culture had a number of Jewish elements, while those that were not explicitly Jewish did not prove meaningful to Arab citizens. For example, army service was mandatory for most Jews but not required for Arabs. The symbols of the state, such as the flag, the national anthem, and the state emblem, all had explicit Jewish content. The flag features the Shield of David, harking back to biblical times, on a field that resembles a prayer shawl, while the anthem, *HaTikvah* (The Hope), speaks of the Jewish soul yearning for a return to Zion and Jerusalem. The national emblem features a candelabrum from the Temple. Arab society in Israel has also long been conservative, which has put it further at odds with a Jewish society increasingly adopting Western norms of individualism, such as those related to dress, the status of women, and family expectations.

Given the prominence of Jewish themes and concepts in the dominant political culture, it has been difficult for Arab Israelis to become part of that culture; indeed, the increasing acceptance of their identity as *Palestinian* Israelis is in part a reaction to the Jewish character of the state. In addition, during the first 18 years of statehood the Arabs were under military government, which further distanced them from the Jewish population and did nothing to lessen their sense of alienation. In sum, the political culture that developed in Israel was very much one in which Jews participated to a great extent but which offered little with which Arab citizens could identify.

Clearly the Arabs have a divided identity based on ethnicity, peoplehood, culture, language, and religion. The last category, religion, has become more salient during the past two decades with the rise of Islamism elsewhere—reflected in Israel by the growing strength of the Islamic Movement—but differences in all of these categories have set Arab Israelis apart from their Jewish fellow citizens. Legally they are Israeli, though many might also identify as part of the Palestinian people. There is no sign that the Israeli government or Israeli society at large is interested in conferring official minority status on the Arabs in the sense of making the state binational. As a result, individual Arabs are left to choose the elements of the Israeli political culture that they find meaningful. Political and legal rights can be exercised readily: voting rights and an Arab presence in the Knesset are obvious examples. But Arab Israelis perceive that they lack political efficacy, that they are unable to achieve concrete results for their community. Nor can they truly share in the close connection that Jewish Israelis feel to their state. On balance they can participate on the margins of the political culture while developing their own Arab Israeli political culture. In addition, their relationship to the emerging Palestinian polity creates challenges for them: as Israelis, they are not truly part of the political process of their Palestinian brethren in the West Bank and Gaza. Rather, they are a community in limbo, one that is ambivalent about political participation and is constantly trying to conceptualize its relationship to the state and to the dominant group within that state. Consequently they face a double dilemma, not truly fitting in either in Israel or in the Palestinian polity. Indeed, they are often at great pains to stress both parts of their political identity (see Chapter 7).

DEMOGRAPHY

Finally, it is important to note Israel's demographic trends. Demographically Israel has undergone considerable change since its founding, largely as a result of immigration, and this has had a considerable effect on the state's political culture. At the

Table 5.1 Population of Israel, 1948–2014

YEAR	JEWS	NON-JEWS	TOTAL	PERCENT JEWISH
1948	716,700	156,000	872,700	82.1
1950	1,203,000	167,100	1,370,100	87.8
1960	1,911,300	239,100	2,150,400	88.9
1970	2,582,000	440,100	3,022,100	85.5
1980	3,282,700	639,000	3,921,700	83.7
1990	3,946,700	875,000	4,821,700	81.9
2000	4,955,400	1,413,900	6,369,300	77.8
2010	5,802,900	1,892,200	7,695,100	75.4
2014	6,102,000	2,488,000	8,132,000	75.2

Sources: Jewish Virtual Library and Israel Central Bureau of Statistics.

beginning of statehood in 1948 there were about 600,000 Jews living in Israel. By the end of the War of Independence some 156,000 Palestinian Arabs also remained on the Israeli side of the 1949 armistice line. Massive waves of immigration over the decades since have sharply increased the Jewish population, reported by the Central Bureau of Statistics (CBS) in 2015 as over 6 million (see Table 5.1). The non-Jewish population has grown substantially as well, largely by natural increase, to about 2 million. In April 2015, the CBS estimated the total population to be 8,345,000, of whom 74.9 percent were Jews, 20.7 percent Arabs, and 4.3 percent "Other." The last category includes non-Arab Christians, Bahai, and non-Jewish family members of Jewish immigrants from Russia.[9] An estimate by the Ministry of Immigrant Absorption suggested in 2011 that about 750,000 Israeli citizens lived abroad, while the government estimated between 800,000 and 1,000,000.[10]

For decades, the Arabs experienced a much higher birthrate than the Jews, though in recent years there has been a convergence. This is due in part to a sharp decline in the Arab birthrate because of modernization and women's entry into the workforce and in part to an increasing birthrate among Jews, both religious and secular.

Among the Jews, Ashkenazim dominated the Yishuv before statehood. However, most of the immigrants during the two decades after 1948 came from the Middle East or North Africa, called Mizrachim. By the 1980s the Mizrachim had become a majority of the Jewish population but lagged behind their Ashkenazi brethren economically and socially. Those differences have declined slowly. In the meantime, the influx of immigrants from the former Soviet Union during the 1990s brought the Ashkenazim to nearly half of the Jewish population. The immigration of Jews from Ethiopia, who now constitute over 2 percent of the population, further added diversity to the state. See Table 5.2 for immigration figures.

The overall birthrate among Israelis is higher than those of other OECD countries. One result of the high birthrate is that Israel has a younger population than the OECD average. For example, 28 percent of the population is under 15, compared to 18.5 percent in the OECD at large. And in the over-65 category Israel falls

Table 5.2 Immigration of Jews to Israel,
Selected Years, 1948–2014

YEAR	NUMBER OF IMMIGRANTS
1948	101,828
1950	170,563
1955	37,528
1960	24,692
1965	31,115
1970	36,750
1975	20,028
1980	20,428
1985	10,642
1990	199,516
1995	76,361
2000	60,201
2005	21,183
2010	16,633
2014	26,500
Total	**3,152,146**

at 10.3 percent, compared to 15 percent for the OECD. Life expectancy is also higher than the OECD average.

SUMMARY

Given the many lines of cleavage within Israeli society, some might argue that there is no overarching or homogeneous Israeli political culture. The divisions between Jews and Arabs, Ashkenazim and Mizrachim, religious and secular, and haredim and non-haredim all make it difficult to make generalizations. Nevertheless, the way in which the political system has developed does allow some generalizations, such as those discussed previously, about those who are the most active political participants. Moreover, such generalizations do help to establish the context within which Israeli politics operates.

Political culture is important because it helps to set the boundaries of political activity. In Israel, given the history of the Jews and their lack of experience of national self-governance, the political culture developed organically during the Mandate period but more consciously after 1948. The leadership of the Yishuv and then the state were very conscious about the need for Israelis to have shared values, goals, and purposes, and the means to achieve their objectives. By the early years of statehood it was clear that the values of a Jewish and democratic state that featured a civic society had been widely accepted.

At first the values of the political culture were largely oriented toward collective success. Ben-Gurion and Mapai's emphasis on mamlachtiut and the emergence of the army as both a fighting and a socializing organization both contributed to the development of a political culture that was largely collectivist in orientation. However, over time Israel evolved in a more individualistic direction, driven in part by changing government policy as well as the aspirations of the citizenry. The Arabs of Israel, while generally approving of some of the features of the political system, such as the emerging emphasis on civil liberties, do not share the national aspirations of the Jews. Consequently they are only marginally part of the Israeli political culture.

KEYWORDS

political culture, Zionism, collectivism, capture of the West Bank, socialism, Jewish state, democratic state, demography

NOTES

1. Tamar Hermann, Ella Heller, Nir Atmor, and Yival Lebel, *The Israeli Democracy Index, 2013* (Jerusalem: Israel Democracy Index, 2013), 62. http://en.idi.org.il/media/2720081/Democracy%20Index%20English%202013.pdf.
2. Daniel J. Elazar and Stuart A. Cohen, *The Jewish Polity: Jewish Political Organization from Biblical Times to the Present* (Bloomington: Indiana University Press, 1985), 1–44.
3. For a broader discussion of this process, see Charles S. Liebman and Eliezer Don-Yehiya, *Civil Religion in Israel: Traditional Judaism and Political Culture in the Jewish State* (Berkeley: University of California Press, 1983).
4. Thanks to Shaul Shenhav for emphasizing this point.
5. For some discussion of post-Zionism, see Lawrence Silberstein, *The Postzionism Debates: Knowledge and Power in Israeli Culture* (New York: Routledge, 1999).
6. Ehud Sprinzak, *Brother against Brother: Violence and Extremism in Israeli Politics from Altalena to the Rabin Assassination* (New York: Free Press, 1999). For a broader discussion, see Ami Pedahzur, *The Triumph of Israel's Radical Right* (Oxford: Oxford University Press, 2012).
7. Tamar Hermann, Gilad Be'ery, Ella Heller, Chanan Cohen, Yuval Lebel, Hanan Mozes, and Kalman Neuman, *The National-Religious Sector in Israel 2014: Main Findings* (Jerusalem: Israel Democracy Institute, 2014), http://en.idi.org.il/media/3863902/Madad-Z-English_WEB.pdf.
8. Yaron Ezrahi, *Rubber Bullets: Power and Conscience in Modern Israel* (Berkeley: University of California Press, 1997).
9. "On the Eve of Independence Day, Israeli Population Stands at 8,345,000," *Jerusalem Post,* April 21, 2015.
10. Joseph Chamie and Barry Mirkin, "The Million Missing Israelis," *Foreign Policy* July 5, 2011.

CHAPTER 6

⤳

Religion and Politics

Technically and officially, religion and state are separated in Israel in the sense that the state does not operate according to halacha. Laws made by the Knesset are the basis of governance, with the exception of personal status law, which is applied by the various religious authorities to their communicants. In practice, however, religion is deeply intertwined with politics and government. Israel is hardly unique in that regard, but since it is the only Jewish state in the world, with a population that is about 75 percent Jewish, there are characteristics of the Israeli system that vary from practices elsewhere. But even though the religious dimension is essential to an understanding of Israeli politics, it is not the main explanatory factor.

In this chapter we examine the connection between the Jewish religion and Zionism from the beginning of the Zionist movement through the present. Over the years of statehood—and even before—there was an effort in the political arena to define the parameters of the religion–state relationship, an issue to which we give great emphasis here. The chapter then looks in some detail at the politics involving the haredim, or ultra-Orthodox Jews, who frequently play a key role in politics. Other topics that will be discussed include changes in the religion–state relationship over time, issues within that relationship in both the past and the present, and the role of religious parties in coalition politics.

RELIGION AND THE IDEA OF A JEWISH STATE

Israel was founded to be a Jewish state, the political expression of Jewish peoplehood. Historically, Jews understood that there was an inherent connection between the Jewish people (a national group), its homeland (the biblical Land of Israel), and the practice of Judaism (the religion of the Jewish people). Thus religious identification and national identification coincided, which has not necessarily been the case with other peoples. This convergence was emphasized in the Zionist view of Jewish history, propounded, among others, by the early Zionist leaders, who were staunch secularists. As a result, in principle people who were Jews in the national sense practiced the religion of Judaism. Actual individual practice ranged from the meticulously observant to the totally nonobservant, with most Jews in the last two centuries being located somewhere in between. Those who decided to convert to another religion were generally considered to have severed their ties with the Jewish people (though that was not the position of religious law), while those who became totally nonobservant retained the option of remaining Jews in a national, cultural, or communal sense, or even of dropping out of the community altogether. The option to choose the extent of one's religiosity may not always have been available,[1] but it certainly was available by the time the Zionist movement began.

The early Zionists had an expansive view of who the Jewish people comprised. Most of them held the view that both Jews who professed the Jewish religion in some way and those who had become nonreligious were Jewish in the national sense, unless they had converted to another faith. Moreover, as Zionism developed it responded to the dual challenges of cultural assimilation in western Europe and anti-Semitism in eastern Europe.[2] These are the foundations of the very complex relationship between religion and nation in Zionism.

Understanding this complex connection, and therefore the role of Judaism in Israeli political life, requires an understanding of how most Jews conceptualized Jewish history. Until the advent of Reform Judaism in the first half of the nineteenth century, few Jews conceived of their religion as denominational. Practicing Jews were, for all intents and purposes, what we now call Orthodox. As an oversimplified version of their worldview, they conceived of Jewish history since the termination of Jewish sovereignty by the Romans as divided into the period of *galut* (exile) and redemption. Exile referred to the destruction of Jewish life in Eretz Yisrael, which meant in political terms the end of Jewish sovereignty, while redemption meant the return of the Jews to their homeland—that is, the reestablishment of Jewish sovereignty.

But for Orthodox Jews, that redemption was part of God's plan for the Jewish people, as explained in the Bible. The emergence of Zionism forced religious Jews to confront the possibility of a renewal of Jewish sovereignty in their homeland, but through human rather than divine action. Some embraced the human initiative and saw Zionism in religious as well as national terms, while others emphatically rejected Zionism based on their interpretation of Judaism. For both groups, though, the existence of Israel posed several problems regarding their interaction with the state—issues like their degree of participation in the state's politics and the role of religion in the state's laws and norms. Many of these issues remain unresolved to this day.

SETTING THE PARAMETERS OF THE RELIGION-STATE RELATIONSHIP

Because of both the close relationship between Judaism and Jewish peoplehood and the active participation of religious Jews in the Zionist movement, the idea that religion and politics in the State of Israel might be practically separated was never entertained seriously, even though the haredim shunned involvement in the Zionist movement. During the Yishuv period, David Ben-Gurion, as political leader of the community, felt that it was important to spell out some of the terms of the connection between religion and the new state and did so in 1947 in a pact with the ultra-Orthodox Agudat Yisrael leadership of the time that came to be known as the Status Quo Agreement. This agreement created a framework for the religion–state relationship that remains relevant today and consisted of four key provisions:

1. The Sabbath, which stretches from sundown Friday to sundown Saturday, will be the official day of rest.
2. All state-run facilities will observe *kashrut*, the halachic dietary regulations.
3. Laws on personal status matters (e.g., marriage and divorce) will be applied to satisfy the "deep need of the religiously observant."
4. The government will supervise a state religious educational system in addition to the state secular system. Every educational network will have autonomy but must offer a minimum curriculum in basic secular subjects.

Several laws and policies, mostly established during the early years of statehood, fleshed out the meaning of the four provisions. Thus, dietary laws were observed in public institutions, a state religious school system was established and funded, Jewish religious holidays became official days of rest, and the religious court system assumed jurisdiction over personal status matters. There were other manifestations of ties between religion and the state that were incorporated over the years. The national flag drew on religious symbolism, as the Star of David has long been associated with the Jewish community, and the Jewish lunar calendar was given official status in public life. In the formal, legal arena the latter development meant that both the Jewish and civil dates would be used for official purposes. In everyday practice, however, only the civil date is used. Furthermore the normalization of the participation of religious parties in politics right from the start signified that the connection between religion and the state was important for a segment of the population.

One of the advantages of Ben-Gurion's approach was that it neutralized potential religiously based opposition to a declaration of statehood. The agreement was also consistent with Jewish tradition, which did recognize different realms of authority for religious and political leaders, albeit within a single unified system stemming from the Torah. Ideas about a system that featured separate domains for religious and political authority were also in keeping with widespread practices throughout the Middle East, into which the Zionists were moving, and in other parts of the world, including Europe, from which the Zionists were coming.

The state that was created in 1948 was defined as a secular state in the sense that the source of laws was definitely the legislature and not religious documents or authorities. The Declaration of Independence, for instance, refers to a "Jewish state" but makes no mention of halacha. Moreover the state would not coerce citizens into religious observance. From the start the state protected freedom of religion, which was clearly understood to include the freedom not to be religiously observant or to be observant to an extent determined by each individual. The founders of Israel did not, then, create a religious state or a state based or operating upon religious principles. Instead Israel was to be a state where private religious practice would be allowed, even supported, and where the main questions regarding Judaism in the public sphere would be about whether the state would reflect religious values and traditions, and if so, what kind. Indeed, most of the political leadership at the state's founding—and, for that matter, ever since—was not religiously observant; rather, they were predominantly secular Jews. In the Israeli context this meant that they were totally nonobservant or observant only to a limited extent. Nevertheless, the secular Mapai regularly included the National Religious Party (a Religious Zionist party) in its coalitions, an arrangement that was beneficial to both parties.

The one sharply defined exception to this generalization about the separation of religion and the state is that the state reserved to the religious authorities control over personal status issues. This was in keeping with both the Status Quo Agreement and the millet system in place under the Ottoman Empire and the British Mandate. The various religious communities, including Jews, Muslims, and Christians, were given autonomy over their own affairs as well as control of personal status matters such as marriage, divorce, and conversion. In practice, this meant that more orthodox or conservative interpretations became the official rule for Jews (see Chapter 4). In effect the state delegated such powers to the religious authorities.

At the outset there was broad acceptance of this framework. The religiously observant Jews knew that they were a minority who could not expect to impose a religious state on the secular majority, whereas the secular Jews like Ben-Gurion understood that, given Zionism's emphasis on the connection between religion and nationhood, there would be manifestations of religion in public life. It was also understood, of course, that individuals could do as they pleased in their private lives.

As the state evolved, certain terminology came into use. In Israel the term *religious Jews* generally means Orthodox Jews—those who follow Judaism's laws and norms closely. Other denominations or movements such as Conservative and Reform Judaism, which are prominent in North America, were only slightly represented in Israel at its founding, a situation that enabled the Orthodox Jews to appropriate the term *religious*. Other Jews were generally referred to as *secular*, although many Israeli Jews who were not Orthodox practiced some elements of the religious tradition. Often those who practiced some but not all of the religious requirements were classified as *traditional*. At the present time, the best estimates of the religious preferences of the Israeli Jewish population place the national religious Jews (Orthodox) at 9 percent of the population, haredi at 9.4 percent, "traditional religious" at 13 percent, "traditional nonreligious" at 15.1 percent, and secular at 49.1 percent (see Figure 10.3 in Chapter 10).[3]

The Haredim and Religious Zionists

The haredim, or ultra-Orthodox, are a rapidly growing segment of the population, primarily because their practices encourage early marriage and large families. When Zionism first became a movement around the beginning of the twentieth century, the ultra-Orthodox groups in Europe were generally opposed to the project, sometimes rather vehemently, on the grounds that only a Messiah sent by God could lead the Jews back to the Land of Israel, and thus a secular government for the Jewish state was a contradiction in terms. Hence they perceived Zionism as a *crowy*

perversion of Judaism and a challenge to the Orthodox view. This led other religious Jews to differentiate themselves through an explicitly Zionist self-definition and to establish the *Mizrachi* Religious Zionist movement in 1902. Ever since, Religious Zionism has signified a fusion of Orthodoxy with Zionist values. That form of Zionism has stressed the integration of modernity into its ideology, and as a result, its followers wear ordinary clothing (as opposed to the distinctive garb of the ultra-Orthodox); attend state religious schools that include the same general studies curriculum as other state schools; participate fully in the activities of the society, including politics, economic activity, and military service; attend universities; and occupy a range of occupations in the labor force. Its values have found political manifestation in the National Religious Party (NRP, sometimes known by its Hebrew acronym *Mafdal*).

In contrast, the haredim emphatically rejected Zionism from the start; formed an anti-Zionist organization in Europe to represent them—Agudat Yisrael, led in part by individuals who had split from Mizrachi over doctrinal issues; and generally rejected modernity in a variety of ways. Over time most of the ultra-Orthodox, especially those who lived in Palestine before statehood, gradually moderated their views and became non-Zionists, a designation that signifies that they see no religious significance in the Jewish state but in the wake of its creation have accepted citizenship and participate in political life to some extent.

The distinction between non-Zionists and anti-Zionists remains important in haredi circles today. Anti-Zionists, such as the *Neturei Karta* or the *Satmar Hasidim*,[4] adamantly reject Zionism, publicly oppose the State of Israel, and often consort with Israel's declared enemies. A few have even attended conferences in Iran that feature Holocaust denial or have protested against Israel alongside non-Jews opposed to Israel's existence as a Jewish state. These groups would prefer to live under the rule of non-Jews until God's plan comes to fruition. As a result, they have little impact on Israeli politics. The bulk of the haredim, in contrast, while not identifying philosophically with Zionism and the Jewish state, had come to terms with the idea of a Jewish government by 1948. As a result, they have participated in the political system, formed political parties, and supported those parties at the polls. Haredi parties are represented in the Knesset and have been members of some governing coalitions. Members of Knesset (MKs) from the haredi *Shas* party (a Hebrew acronym for Sephardi Torah Guardians) have held ministerial positions since the party's first electoral success in 1984. Agudat Yisrael members held ministerial positions in the early years of statehood but have restricted themselves to Deputy Minister positions until 2015, when one became Minister of Health.

Haredim, in contrast to Religious Zionists, wear traditional, modest garb (black pants, jackets, and hats for men, and skirts and long sleeves for women); have their own educational system that emphasizes religious learning at the expense of general education (despite obligations to teach the core curriculum); normally do not attend universities or join the army (though technical colleges oriented toward a haredi clientele are becoming increasingly popular); and are usually underprepared to participate in the labor force. Indeed, the haredi community ranks alongside the Arab sector as among the poorest and least prepared for a modern economy in Israeli society.

Among the Ashkenazi haredim there are two main sectors: hasidim and followers of the Lithuanian *yeshivot* (academies of higher religious, especially Talmudic, learning). The former generally emphasize a more lively approach to study and prayer and follow the authority of various hasidic rebbes (rabbis), heads of dynasties named for specific towns of origin, that date back to eighteenth-century Russia. The latter are oriented to the rabbis of various yeshivot, the origins of which were in Lithuania. Today the two sectors cooperate politically through a party called United Torah Judaism (UTJ), which represents a merger between Agudat Yisrael (the Israeli successor to the European Agudat Israel) and *Degel HaTorah* (Banner of the Torah). Mizrachi haredim follow their own spiritual leaders, notably the late Rabbi Ovadia Yosef, and have their own political parties, especially Shas.

Finally, one other group of haredim should be mentioned here: the *hardal*, or nationalist haredim. Their religious practices are generally the same as those of other haredim, but they identify with Jewish nationalism and the idea of a Zionist state. They are not yet organized politically and are small in comparison to the other communities, but they have become increasingly visible in recent years.

GROWING INVOLVEMENT IN POLITICS

When we examine the interaction between state and religion in the political arena, we can identify an important turning point in 1984. Up to that year the main representative of the religious sector in politics was the National Religious Party, which partnered with Ben-Gurion's Mapai (now the Labor Party) to form the core of most of the governments of that period. For the NRP the most important ministries to control were the Ministry of Religious Affairs and the Ministry of the Interior. Influence in the Ministry of Education was also quite important. The main haredi party was Agudat Yisrael (now a component of UTJ), which was ambivalent about participation in government coalitions. When Aguda did join a government, which it did on several occasions in the early decades of statehood and then again after 1977, its members did not accept ministerial posts but would agree to become deputy ministers (as they did in the first three governments). But in 1984, the new Shas party won seats for the first time and was eager to join the government coalition and to hold ministerial positions as well.

State and Religion 1948–1984
Several points regarding the relationship between religion and state at the time of independence and in the next few years require elaboration. First of all, the Chief Rabbinate, created under the British Mandate, was continued into statehood and became a state institution, with the Ashkenazi and Sephardi Chief Rabbis at first elected by the Knesset but later chosen by an extended rabbinate council made up of local rabbis who serve congregations, regional chief rabbis for various cities, judges of the rabbinical courts, inspectors who ensure adherence to dietary laws in institutions and establishments that follow those laws, and bureaucrats who administer the policies of the rabbinate. Once elected, the Chief Rabbis are essentially autonomous in their spheres of action. Marriages between Jews are conducted under their auspices, divorces are granted under their authority, and conversions

follow their regulations and procedures. Non-Jewish religious authorities have similar powers relative to their communicants.

The religious school system (mamlachti dati) was in this period administered by a section of the Ministry of Education that was staffed by people from the national religious camp, which in those days meant the NRP. Its general curriculum paralleled that of the other state schools (mamlachti) but added the religiously oriented coursework that followers of the NRP believed to be essential elements of a Jewish education. It was funded by the government, just as the state system was. The haredi educational sector, known collectively as Independent Education (HaHinuh HaAtzmai), was not funded by the government during this period but was under the control of the various haredi groups that ran schools for their followers.

Sabbath observance was a general framework set forth by the government, but the specifics of how the society would operate on the Sabbath, a day of strict rest and withdrawal from ordinary weekday activities in the Jewish tradition, were vague. Most of the rules regarding work and whether various places of business might remain open were addressed by the law, but enforcement was left up to local authorities. This led to many inconsistencies, such as the availability of public transportation on the Sabbath in Haifa but not elsewhere (as had been the practice during the Mandate), the use of private jitneys operating along bus lines in places where buses were not running, nearly complete closures of restaurants and places of entertainment in Jerusalem but a much more relaxed atmosphere in Tel Aviv, and the operation of the main international airport while El Al, the national airline, was grounded. Other important rules, and debates, related to the provision of emergency services.

Religion–state relations existed in the context of a political system that included the formal expression of religious interests through political parties. The leading religious parties of the period were the NRP and Agudat Yisrael. The former embraced the political process and took a high-profile role in the Knesset and around the Cabinet table, while the latter took a low-profile role, did not accept ministerial positions from the early 1950s until 2015, and was not very active on the legislative front. The NRP was a party run largely by laypeople who shared a religious outlook but operated in much the same way as the secular parties. In contrast, Aguda's ambivalence about the state and its institutions was evident in its approach to politics. It took direction from a rabbinical council of senior Torah scholars and Hasidic leaders (called *Moetzet Gedolai HaTorah*—Council of Torah Sages). Indeed, many members of its all-male Knesset delegations were rabbis.

Religion and the State After 1984

A new period of relations between religion and the state was inaugurated in 1984. Subsequent events solidified the changes and made possible a different type of relationship. The catalyst for change was Shas, the newly formed party run by ultra-Orthodox Mizrachim (guided by a Sephardi Council of Torah Scholars) that was designed to appeal to voters who had long harbored resentment against the Ashkenazi political, economic, and social establishment. Shas had broken through the political system with a respectable four Knesset seats in the 1984 election and then increased its share of the vote (and therefore its number of MKs) in several subsequent elections, reaching a high of 17 seats in the 1999 election. Unlike Aguda, the other ultra-Orthodox party, Shas was eager to hold ministerial posts and to participate in debates around the Cabinet table and on the floor of the Knesset in order to advance its constituents' interests. Its first ministers were appointed in 1984. It grew during the 1980–2000 period, while the NRP was in decline, which made it the most important religious party by far; indeed, it replaced the NRP as the primary religious partner for both left-wing and right-wing coalitions. Its main foci were to obtain government funding for its schools while continuing to refrain from following the official curriculum and to tap government funds for social services for its constituents (i.e., economically disadvantaged Mizrachim).

Shas also took a strong line against any steps to remove marriage and divorce from the purview of the rabbinate, pressed for tougher standards for converts, used its control of the Ministry of the Interior to make it more difficult for non-Orthodox converts to immigrate, and pressed for the expansion of religious influence in various aspects of Israeli life. Its efforts in the area of conversion led to the intensification of the notorious "Who is a Jew?" debate, which began during the 1950s and 1960s but became much more salient during the late 1980s, when the haredi parties demanded that the Law of Return, a cornerstone of Israeli legislation designed to facilitate the "ingathering of the exiles," be amended to allow automatic immigration only for people who were born to a Jewish mother (the traditional criterion) or who had been converted according to halachic standards. The law was vague about the nature of acceptable conversions and, in direct reaction to the Nuremberg Laws during the Nazi period, offered admission to anyone who had at least one Jewish grandparent. The haredi proposal would have led to a tightening of the relatively permissive original version of the law, as interpreted by the courts. This proposed tightening led to a crisis during the coalition negotiations that followed the 1988 election. It also alienated the large non-Orthodox sectors of the American Jewish community.

In the end, the politicians found a way to avoid giving Shas what it wanted, but Shas had certainly made a point about its power and willingness to use it. Shas has been part of most governing coalitions since 1984, though not the 2013–2015 government, and it has achieved some of its goals, but not all. For over 25 years it dominated the religious part of the political spectrum, pushed Aguda to be more activist, and demonstrated that the haredi sector could be a consequential actor in the political system. The irony about Shas is that its leadership and Knesset members are decidedly haredi, but its electorate is a mixture of haredim (who compose perhaps 40 percent of constituents), traditional (somewhat religious but not strictly observant) voters, and even some secular Israelis, generally all of whom are Mizrachi. Moreover, many of its rank-and-file supporters identify with the Zionist character of the state.

ISSUES IN RELIGION–STATE RELATIONS AFTER 2000

An underlying trend that has affected religion–state issues is the growing control of haredim over the Chief Rabbinate, perhaps as a result of the shift in focus of the NRP away from strictly religious issues and toward the significance of the territories known in Israel as Judea and Samaria (the historical Hebrew terms for the West

Bank). The increasing stringency of rabbinate policy has affected several issues with religious implications. In addition to disputes over budgetary and political matters, three major ones have emerged since 2000. One involves hundreds of thousands of people from the former Soviet Union who immigrated to Israel during the late 1980s and early 1990s. These individuals qualified for immigration under the Law of Return because they had at least one Jewish grandparent or were married to a Jew, but under Jewish law they were not considered Jewish because Jewish identity can only be acquired by one who is born to a Jewish mother or undergoes conversion. Since immigration can lead to status as an Israeli citizen but not necessarily membership in the Jewish people, policymakers recognized the necessity of finding a route to Jewish status in addition to the existing path to Israeli status. Historically there has been no way for a non-Jew to become Jewish other than through religious conversion. There is no concept of converting to Jewish nationality. Since these (largely) Russian immigrants generally are not observant Jews and do not intend to become religiously observant by Orthodox criteria, the question of converting them has become a major political issue, especially because the rabbinate will not preside over a marriage unless both parties are Jewish according to halacha.

In 2014 a politically controversial bill that would have made it somewhat easier for people to convert to Judaism became a major challenge to the continuity of the governing coalition because of the opposition of Bayit Yehudi (see Chapter 5). Generally the haredi parties have resisted attempts to liberalize conversion standards, which, strictly speaking, require a convert to agree to be religiously observant. This is only a small part of the problem posed by the second-class status of non-Orthodox expressions of Judaism. Non-Orthodox groups can and do have their own synagogues, but their rabbis have no state-recognized status and therefore cannot perform weddings, preside over divorce proceedings, or convert people who wish to be recognized as Jews by the state. Thus a number of still-unresolved issues concern the Orthodox (and increasingly ultra-Orthodox) monopoly over a number of matters that are of great concern to Israelis who are not Orthodox or perhaps not even Jewish in a halachic sense but identify with and are effectively part of the Jewish population of Israel. This has led to the popularity of different political parties that have expressed firm opposition to haredi control over such decisions. These parties include very secular groups, such as Shinui, and very nationalist ones, such as *Yisrael Beiteinu*. Though the latter has drawn most of its support from Russian immigrants, it began to broaden its appeal in the 2013 election in part by focusing on an expansion of civil authority over personal status issues.

The second major issue with religious and political implications concerns the question of who is a Jew, which has been contentious for decades because of its highly symbolic significance. The ability to determine the answer to such a question is one of the reasons that religious parties seek to control certain key government departments, such as the ministries of Religious Affairs (today, Religious Services) or the Interior, and thereby exercise control over the religious establishment. In addition, matters of personal status have public religious consequences, which makes them key areas in which the Orthodox forces can demonstrate their power with respect to the non-Orthodox movements, especially those in the United States and Canada.

The third main issue that has come to the fore in recent years, and especially in the 2013 election, involves draft exemptions for haredi men. In 1950 Ben-Gurion acceded to demands from the haredi leadership to grant indefinite draft deferments to young men who were engaged in religious studies on the grounds that what they were doing was just as important to the Jewish people as what other young men did in the army. The need to maintain Orthodox traditions in the aftermath of the destruction of much of European Jewry gave added impetus to the decision. At the time some 400 haredi men were entitled to such deferments. Subsequently the numbers of haredim have grown tremendously, and now over 60,000 reportedly avoid army service by enrolling in an advanced yeshiva known as a *kollel* as late as into their thirties. This has led to a substantial backlash from the secular part of the population and efforts by governments to change the policy. There have been a number of proposals over the years to deal with the problem, but no lasting solution.

The issue of draft deferments remains a major point of contention between secular and haredi politicians and ordinary citizens. At times secular parties have been formed with the particular goal of doing something about this perceived injustice. For example, the late Tommy Lapid's Shinui party won 15 seats in the 2003 election and joined the government coalition, although it failed to achieve any permanent change in the policy. In the 2013 election his son Yair Lapid led a new party, *Yesh Atid* (There Is a Future), into the Knesset, with 19 seats. His pledge to do something about the haredi draft exemption was a key feature of the party's platform.

In 2002 the Knesset passed the Tal Law, which attempted to create incentives for yeshiva students to enter military service or perform alternative national service. The High Court of Justice struck down the law, causing it to expire in 2012, an action that led to a political crisis and the need for early elections. In 2014 the Knesset finally passed a new law that sharply reduced the number of deferments, effectively compelling many young haredi men to submit to the draft. The law, which does not come into effect fully until 2017, has been bitterly opposed by the haredi parties and their communities, raising the specter of civil disobedience. Not surprisingly the policy was reversed after the 2015 election, as a result of the coalition agreement between Likud and United Torah Judaism: penalties for avoiding conscription were removed, while efforts are underway to amend or repeal the law. Even had the policy remained in force it is likely that only about 3,000 young men per year would have been affected by the draft, with about half pursuing alternative national service rather than entering the armed forces.

Besides its aim of ensuring equality, a major objective of this law was also to help the young haredim to acquire the skills necessary to integrate into the workforce, and so it was considered important for broader social and economic trends as well. It is ironic that just as the draft law was about to come into effect, haredim were increasingly obtaining vocational training and going to work. It is estimated that over 40 percent are already working.[5] The beginning of entry into the workforce, a trend that would be reinforced if haredim were no longer exempted from the draft, is expected to enable these individuals to gradually become integrated into the larger society politically and socially. That might begin to attenuate the divisions between haredim and the rest of the society. But the process will also create ideological tensions for the haredim themselves, because many resist being integrated into a Zionist society.

The dispute over drafting haredim, as well as the policy of paying financial subsidies to members of those communities, often to support the males who are engaged in full-time religious study, has led to antipathy between them and the Religious Zionists. The latter group does serve in the army, and many of its members resent the haredim's use of religious obligations as an excuse for mass exemptions. This hostility was evident during the coalition negotiations in 2013, when Bayit Yehudi, which represents much of the Religious Zionist sector, joined with the secular Yesh Atid to exclude haredi parties from the coalition and to ensure that a law that would subject haredim to the draft became part of the coalition's program.

RELIGIOUS PARTIES AND COALITION POLITICS

The nature of coalition politics has been particularly helpful to the haredi parties. With the left and right parties fairly well defined, the haredi parties have often found themselves in a position in which they could join a coalition on either side, which gave them significant bargaining power. This was particularly true for Shas, which has usually had more seats than Aguda/UTJ. The haredi parties' leverage was highest during the 1980s, when the left and right were almost evenly split, allowing the religious parties to determine who would form the government. The demands of the haredi parties were so high after the 1984 election that archrivals Likud and Labor chose to form a unity government (a coalition of the two main opposing parties) rather than a coalition that involved Shas. Again, after the 1988 election, Shas demands on the "Who is a Jew?" issue prompted American and Canadian Jewry to warn Israeli political leaders against giving in to such demands. Again, the result was a unity government. Haredi leverage has diminished since 2000, but the haredim did succeed, at least through 2012, in staving off action to end draft deferments for their young men and in preserving public funding for their institutions without accountability. Moreover, they have held firm in opposition to the growing demand for civil marriage and in favor of rather stringent requirements for conversion. Both issues are quite sensitive politically.

The NRP, while diminished in terms of influence after 1984, did not disappear from the scene. It did transform itself into a party that primarily represented the interests of settlers in the West Bank (many of whom moved there because of religious motivations) but did not have enough seats to have more than a marginal influence during most of the post-1984 period. However, in the 2009, 2013, and 2015 elections it ran as part of a new party, Bayit Yehudi, which also incorporated secular settlers and is somewhat more moderate on religion and state issues than the haredi parties but more hardline on settlements, security issues, and negotiations with the Palestinians. After some internal maneuvering shortly before the 2013 election, a new, younger leadership team took over under the guidance of the charismatic Naftali Bennett and won 12 seats in the election, making it the fourth-largest party in the Knesset. By exceeding the 11 seats won by Shas, Bayit Yehudi established itself as a key religious party in the new parliament. Both parties declined in the 2015 election, to eight seats for Bayit Yehudi and seven for Shas (see Chapter 9). The advent of such a revived Religious Zionist party signals a shift in the political dynamics of the religious camp. For nearly 30 years the haredi Shas was the leading religious party and a key element in several coalition governments. Those governments understandably were receptive to Shas's requests, which generally were for money for their educational and social service activities. Bayit Yehudi, on the other hand, has a different emphasis—namely, Israeli control over the West Bank and the expansion of Jewish settlements there.

Issues that might appear to be primarily religious questions can become major political controversies in Israel. In 1976, for example, when new Air Force planes were flown from the United States, from which they were purchased, to Israel, the government, led by Labor Prime Minister Yitzhak Rabin, planned a major welcoming ceremony to mark the occasion. However, the flights were delayed and only arrived on Friday evening, after the beginning of the Sabbath. The NRP, which was part of the government at the time, left the governing coalition in protest of the official government event's Sabbath desecration, helping to bring about the 1977 election.

Many conflicts over religion are not as visible to the public because they are thrashed out around the Cabinet table. When questions of religious practice arise, the haredi parties in particular are reluctant to compromise because they see such questions as matters of principle. Moreover, there is often competition between parties to determine which one best protects religious interests by taking the most rigid position. The religious parties do see themselves as having a responsibility to preserve Jewish traditions in a secular Jewish state, whereas the other parties simply do not share the same concern. As a result struggles over such issues both within and outside the government can become quite intense and contentious. In recent years these conflicts have related to matters of draft deferments, gay rights, abortion, autopsies, archaeology, Sabbath observance, the Chief Rabbinate, local rabbinical councils, religious practices in the Israel Defense Forces, sale of bread during the Passover holiday, availability of pork products, nudity and suggestive advertising, and conversions. When a Prime Minister designate tries to form a government, he may try to put together a coalition without haredi parties, but arithmetical and political constraints usually compel their inclusion. This has led the haredi parties generally to oppose electoral reforms that might diminish their leverage. Indeed, it appears that they have maximum leverage under the current electoral system. However, it should be noted that the haredi parties strenuously opposed efforts to raise the voting percentage threshold for inclusion in the Knesset in 2014 but were unable to stop a determined coalition from doing so. The law raising that threshold to 3.25 percent did pass over their objections, deepening the divide between the haredi parties and the parties in the government. Internal disputes led to a breakaway party from Shas, which in the 2015 election did not pass the new threshold, although it would have passed the old one, contributing to a loss of seats for the party. Nevertheless, neither Shas nor UTJ hesitated to join the new coalition led by Likud in 2015, even though a Likud-led government had initiated measures that they had vehemently opposed during the previous two years. Bayit Yehudi, too, joined the coalition, potentially setting the stage for a clash over the issues mentioned previously.

While our focus has been on the formal and legal aspects of the religion–state relationship, it should be noted that in recent years many issues involving religion have been manifested outside the formal governmental arena. Some of these include the increasing assertiveness of haredim at the local level regarding such issues as separate seating for men and women on certain buses; pressure to conform to haredi norms in mixed neighborhoods; the religious dimension of the settlement movement in the West Bank, which has made threats of defiance of any possible withdrawal order; the encouragement by some Religious Zionist rabbis to their followers to put adherence to their religious beliefs above their obligations to the state; and religious–secular clashes in the military.

SUMMARY

In Israeli politics religious interests compete like any other interest in the political arena. However, the depth of religious commitments among parts of the society can make religion–state issues more salient. Sectors of the population, including the various religious communities, define specific interests, use their voting power to elect parties that will represent them, and then try to leverage their Knesset representation to gain a position in the governing coalition. It is around the Cabinet table that most of the key decisions are made, so entering the coalition is a crucial step. The religious parties have proven to be quite adept at achieving these aims ever since 1948. In addition, there are various techniques outside parliament that interest groups can use, such as demonstrations and protests, which haredim in particular have utilized.

The religious camp is varied, including national religious groups (Orthodox Zionists such as the NRP or Bayit Yehudi), dovish national religious groups (such as *Meimad*, a party that strove to represent that orientation without electoral success), Ashkenazi haredim (represented by UTJ), and Mizrachi haredim (represented by Shas). These different elements do not necessarily agree on much beyond a commitment to their interpretation of Orthodox Judaism and are usually in competition with each other to maximize their own leverage and their share of the benefits that government can bestow. Thus the parliamentary fragmentation of the religious camp reflects divisions in society. Looking ahead, a key question will be the extent to which the haredim will become more Israeli, as defined by loyalty to and identification with the state. These individuals are clearly a part of Israeli society, although they are far from fully integrated. Furthermore, there are some signs among them of growing openness toward Zionism.

Given the historical development of the Jewish people it is unlikely that complete separation of religion and politics is possible. There are some in Israeli politics who advocate such separation, while there are others who regard that as undesirable. While most observers would agree that improvements in the religion–state relationship might still be possible, obtaining a broad consensus on what to do remains an elusive objective.

KEYWORDS

Zionism, Judaism, Jewish identity, ultra-Orthodox, Religious Zionism, Hasidism, anti-Zionist, *galut*, redemption, *haredi* draft, religious parties, traditional, secular

NOTES

1. Before the Emancipation Jews did not have a lot of options regarding religious practice, and what we now call Orthodoxy was prevalent. But beginning in the early nineteenth century, individuals gained the freedom in many places to practice their religion as they saw fit. This development gave Jews the opportunity to determine their own level of religious practice. On the institutional level the Reform movement established itself in Germany and then in the United States, followed decades later by the Conservative movement. Both attracted adherents, thereby breaking the Orthodox institutional monopoly.

2. Shlomo Avineri, *The Making of Modern Zionism: Intellectual Origins of the Jewish State* (New York: Basic Books, 1981).

3. Israel Democracy Institute, *Israeli Democracy Index 2013*, 179, http://en.idi.org.il/media/2720081/Democracy%20Index%20English%202013.pdf.

4. Neturei Karta is a small sect of ultra-Orthodox Jews based in Jerusalem that is virulently anti-Zionist. Its members refuse to recognize the legitimacy of the Israeli state and often do so in a very public manner. The Satmar Hasidim are based in New York but also have a presence in Israel. They are anti-Zionist and do not hesitate to publicly manifest their attitudes.

5. Dan Ben-David, *A Picture of the Nation 2014: Israel's Society and Economy in Figures* (Jerusalem: Taub Center, 2014), 78.

CHAPTER 7

✃

The Politics of the Arab Minority

Israeli politics is primarily Jewish politics, and within that arena it is primarily Zionist politics. The political system is the result of decades of Jewish and Zionist experience, itself a response to the dispersion and political exclusion of Jewish communities around the world. It is bounded by Jewish symbols and calendrical events, and Jewish parties play the dominant role in the Knesset and in government policymaking. Yet Arabs make up Israel's largest non-Jewish community, constituting about 20 percent of the total population (1.683 million people by December 2013).[1] Among them, approximately 80 percent are Muslim, 10 percent Christian, and 10 percent Druze. As in countries like Canada, Spain, and Turkey, the existence of a large ethno-national community that is different from the dominant group has led to discrimination against the minority, alienation from the state, and tension between the minority and the majority. At the same time, the Jewish majority has typically viewed the Arab community through the prism of the Arab–Israeli and Israeli–Palestinian conflicts, which cast them as a hostile population. Finally, most Arab citizens do not identify with the State of Israel as a Jewish state; they are overwhelmingly anti- or non-Zionist, trying to find their place as citizens in a country at war with their ethnic kin. This nonidentification adds to the Jewish sense of threat and mistrust.

This friction has broader effects beyond the community, raising questions about what it means to be a Jewish state. For example, should Arab citizens be expected to sing the national anthem, *HaTikvah* (The Hope), which expresses the Jewish yearning for self-determination in the Land of Israel? If not, should they be allowed to sing a different song or simply stand silently in respect? Would doing either undermine the sense of national identity necessary for states to function and prosper?

Despite these myriad problems, Israel has not experienced widespread ethnic riots or regular violence between Arabs and Jews, though clashes between Arab citizens on one side and Jewish citizens and Israeli police on the other have broken out occasionally. At first martial law, imposed on the Arab community until the end of 1966, helped dampen the emergence of violent challenges to the state. But it is also because most Arabs in Israel explicitly identify as citizens of the Israeli state, rejecting political loyalty to the Palestinian cause even while embracing their ethno-national kinship ties. The political system has also served as an arena for Arab citizens to express opposition to Israeli policies, particularly through voting, political mobilization at the local level, and the establishment of parties devoted to issues of concern to the Arab community.

A critical event for understanding contemporary Arab politics in Israel occurred in October 2000.[2] Sparked by the intense violence of the Second Intifada (which began in September 2000), but building on years of simmering tension and resentment, several large demonstrations of Arab citizens broke out primarily in northern Israel. The protests quickly turned into riots, as stones and sometimes firebombs were thrown at Jewish police and civilians alike, leading to the death of one Jewish civilian. The riots spread throughout the country, and soon Jewish mobs began attacking Arab demonstrators and property. With numerous injuries and damage to property, Israeli police responded with rubber bullets and live fire. Over the course of about nine days, 13 Arab citizens were killed. In Dov Waxman's words, "never before in Israel's history had there been inter-communal violence on such a scale."[3] Comparing attitudes of the Arab community toward the state before and after this captures this shift: in April 2000, 55 percent of Arab Israelis stated that they were proud to be citizens of Israel; in February 2001, that figure fell to 21 percent.[4] Today, As'ad Ghanem argues, Arab politics is conditioned by four main areas of disagreement with the Jewish majority and the Jewish state: the identity of the minority and its subsequent relationship to the Jewish state; state policies on internal issues such as the distribution of resources and openness of the political system to Arab parties; policy toward the Israeli–Palestinian conflict; and the hegemonic Jewish character of the state.

This chapter therefore begins with a seemingly semantic issue, but one that matters for both social identity and political action: the term the Arab community uses to identify itself. It continues with an analysis of the major changes that have taken place within the community as they play out in the political arena, particularly the four main processes of Israelization, Palestinization, politicization, and Islamization. This discussion is followed by an analysis of Jewish Israeli attitudes toward the Arab minority, which provides some necessary context. The chapter then discusses the nature of Arab political representation and voter turnout. It ends with a reference to the prominent Arab Israeli writer Sayed Kashua, examining whether he can be seen as a barometer of the community's presence in and integration into Israel.

WHAT'S IN A NAME?

The term used to refer to the Arab community in Israel is highly politicized and is often seen as describing the ideas and priorities of the individual or group using that specific term rather than the community itself. For example, some argue that "Arab" is value-neutral, while "Palestinian" implies a political agenda. Arguing against this point, Dov Waxman has noted that Palestinian, as a term for the Arab community, is both commonly used in the academic literature and the term used by the community to describe itself.[5] In this book we use Palestinian Israeli and Arab Israeli (or some version of them, such as Israeli Arab) interchangeably.

Members of Israel's Arab community are those who remained within Israel's borders at the end of the 1947–1949 War—approximately 156,000 out of 1.2 million Palestinian Arabs at the end of the British Mandate—and their descendants. The rest fled and were displaced or expelled in the course of the war, moving into the West Bank and Gaza Strip (WBG), neighboring countries, and countries outside the Middle East.[6] Over time, this community has undergone a shift in how it has perceived itself.

For the first two decades of Israel's existence the community was referred to as Israel's Arabs, Israeli Arabs, or Arab-Israelis (and sometimes "the Arabs of 1948"). These terms signified an attachment to the Israeli state, separating the community from those who were called Palestinians, which denoted members of the community who lived outside the borders of Israel. This division was purposeful, since it implied that the Arabs in Israel had no claims to sovereignty, secession, or national distinction. At the same time, the community itself was largely traumatized by the 1947–1949 War, the severing of ties with their ethnic kin in the WBG, and the imposition of Jewish rule over them. Because they were viewed as a hostile fifth column by the (Jewish) state, a military administration was created to govern them directly until the end of 1966. These political, administrative, and psychological barriers inhibited the development of a clear sense of identity and political will, and made it difficult for members to mobilize politically.

As the community's political identity began to develop in the 1970s, they were sometimes called Arab citizens of Israel. This denoted a legal connection to Israel, but not an identification with the state. Indeed, it was a step toward an even more distinct separation that emerged with the capture of the WBG in 1967. The extension of Israeli control over the territories heightened Israeli Arabs' identification with their Palestinian brethren in the WBG. Today many in the community prefer to call themselves, and be known as, Palestinians, Palestinian citizens of Israel, or Palestinians who reside in Israel.

As the community has pulled away from the identity imposed on it at the beginning of the state, it has underlined its Palestinian identity but without completely severing its connection to the Israeli state. Israeli sociologist Sammy Smooha has conducted a series of surveys of Arab Israelis since the mid-1970s, tracking, among other things, how they identify themselves. From 1976 to 2009, the percentage of Arab citizens of Israel who self-identified as "Arab," "Israeli Arab," or even "Israeli" declined from 54.7 percent to 39.6 percent.[7] Interestingly, that figure has gone up during critical moments in Israel's relationship with the WBG Palestinians and the Palestine Liberation Organization (PLO). In 1995, during the heyday of the Oslo process, and in 2003, during the violence of the Second Intifada, that number increased to about 53 percent. These attachments may be bolstered by material factors, such as the Israeli state's provision of the Arab community with freedom of movement, political and civil rights, considerable resources for health, education, and other benefits, and some separate communal rights—many of which are denied to Palestinians in the West Bank and in other regional states. The 2014 Israeli Democracy Index, for example, found that

26 percent and 39 percent of Arab citizens are "very much" and "quite a lot" proud to be Israeli, respectively, compared to only 13.7 and 19.9 percent who felt "not so much" or "not at all."[8]

At the same time, Arab citizens of Israel have increasingly associated themselves with the broader Palestinian community in the WBG, even while they prefer to retain a connection to Israel. The percentage of those who identified as "Israeli Palestinian" or "Palestinian in Israel" rose from 12.4 percent in 1976 to 45.6 percent in 2004; in 2006 that figure reached a peak of 54 percent, before declining to 42.1 percent by 2009.[9] A different question on the same topic found a similar trend: from 2003 to 2009 the percentage of Arab citizens who ranked "Israeli citizenship" as their most important affiliation declined from 29.6 percent in 2003 to 12.2 percent in 2012.[10] The change in all these percentages is affected by the emergence of a third form of identity that has severed Arab citizens' identification with Israel.

This third type of identity is simply "Palestinian" or Palestinian Arab," and its strength seems to vary depending on external circumstances. For instance, at moments of heightened tension between the community and the Jewish majority as a result of ethno-national clashes, during demonstrations when Arab citizens are killed by state police or the military, or during periods of increased violence between Israel and Palestinians in the WBG, levels of identification with Israel drop. From 1976 to 2002 the percentage of the community identifying as "Palestinian Arab" or "Arab"—without "Israel" as any kind of marker—declined from 32.9 percent to 11.5 percent, with a jump from 1999 to 2001 up to 20 percent.[11] From 2003 to 2009, that percentage began to rise again, from 5.5 percent to 17.5 percent.[12] This increase coincided with a period of right-wing (Likud) or right-leaning (Kadima) governments that, the community felt, mostly ignored issues of concern to Arab citizens.

These trends denote the Arab community's separation from the hegemonic Jewish identity of the state and a close identification with their ethno-national kin in the WBG—but also their lack of a clear political identification. There is, in other words, a preference among most Palestinian citizens of Israel to maintain a legal attachment to the state.

The historical exceptions to these overall trends have been the Druze and Bedouin communities in Israel. The Druze have long maintained a close identification with the state, while the Bedouin have been more indifferent. Changes in both communities began in the 2000s as frustration with existing conditions emerged and led to confrontations with the state. The Druze are subject to Israel's compulsory military draft. This has earned them the benefits that accrue to all military veterans and confers on them a status of greater belonging to the Israel state than that enjoyed by the broader Arab community. But it has not translated into greater social equality with Israeli Jews, and a sense of neglect by the government has fueled some discontent and resentment.

The Bedouin have increasingly clashed with the state over displacement from their traditional living grounds in the south. At the creation of the state, the government took over hundreds of thousands of dunams of land the Bedouin had long seen as their traditional territories.[13] Some members of the community moved to officially recognized villages built for them, which have received little government attention or resources for development. Other Bedouin have refused to move and have instead constructed "unrecognized villages." These are often small collections of ramshackle huts and encampments built on state lands without the necessary permits and licenses, and as such they do not receive government support for basic necessities, including plumbing and electricity. The government has often bulldozed them to force the Bedouin to move to specially built cities. Village members normally return to the destroyed site to rebuild, which in turn prompts the state to destroy it again; some villages have been razed 10 or more times. As a result of these developments the Bedouin have been pushed to the bottom of most indicators of quality of life in Israel.

The relationship between the state and the Bedouin continued to deteriorate in the 2010s as a result of a government plan to relocate up to 70,000 Bedouin from the Negev Desert in the south to a series of approved sites. This proposal, presented in September 2011, was called the Prawer Plan, named after its chief architect, Ehud Prawer.[14] In June 2013 the Knesset voted to implement the plan. But the blueprint had been formulated with little input from the Bedouin themselves. Fearing the negative impact on their cultural traditions, and worried that their communities would subsequently be forgotten by the government while the Jewish communities slated to move into the area would receive all the government's attention, the Bedouin refused to move off their ancestral lands.[15] Public protests against the plan forced the government to announce its postponement in December 2013 while it considered its options on how to proceed.

CHANGING POLITICS OF THE COMMUNITY

Originally, the Declaration of Independence was meant to govern the state's policy toward the Arab minority. This document proclaimed:

> THE STATE OF ISRAEL will . . . foster the development of the country for the benefit of all its inhabitants; it will be based on freedom, justice and peace as envisaged by the prophets of Israel; it will ensure complete equality of social and political rights to all its inhabitants irrespective of religion, race or sex; it will guarantee freedom of religion, conscience, language, education and culture; it will safeguard the Holy Places of all religions; and it will be faithful to the principles of the Charter of the United Nations. . . .

> WE APPEAL . . . to the Arab inhabitants . . . to participate in the upbuilding of the State on the basis of full and equal citizenship and due representation in all its provisional and permanent institutions.

It thus asserted that there would be no discrimination among Israel's citizens, but it purposely made no mention of collective minority rights or recognized the existence of any other ethno-national group within Israel except the Jewish majority.[16] Some group rights were created for the Arab community, including the elevation of Arabic to an official language of the state, the establishment of a separate education system, the bestowal of cultural and religious rights for Muslim Arabs and Christian Arabs, and a claim—though largely unimplemented—to maintain fair representation in the civil service. For the most part, though, the Israeli state divided its citizens between the Jewish majority and the Arab minority, with most of its attention focused on the former.

When Israel won its War of Independence, the new Arab citizens found themselves members of a state they had not expected. Once part of a majority in Mandatory Palestine, this community was suddenly made into a minority in a country dominated by a people that had only a year before been the minority. Moreover, the Jewish majority was at war with the Arab minority's kin outside the borders of the new state. The political, religious, social, and economic institutions of the Arab community that had operated independently before the war had collapsed during the conflict. Some Jews considered the Arab population in Israel to be temporary—that in the next war, the community would likely move out of the state. Under such conditions, Arab citizens could hardly be expected to identify with the Jewish state.

Israeli policy toward the Arab minority at first reflected this sense of threat, which is not surprising given that only armistice agreements, not peace treaties, were signed in 1949. Virtually the entire Arab community was put under direct military rule until December 1966, on account of the Jewish majority's suspicions that its members remained hostile to Israel and would continue the fight. Arab citizens were put under surveillance, with the government even using Arab informants, while efforts were made to force the identification of the community with the Jewish state. This included the cooptation of Arab leaders from various family networks (*hamulas*) into political parties that were ostensibly autonomous but in reality affiliated with and directed by Mapai, the Labor Zionist party. These intrusive forms of control made it difficult for Palestinian Israelis to construct an independent politics of protest.[17] Low levels of education and the social and economic underdevelopment of the community also made it harder for members to organize. Leadership of the community during this initial period fell to the different localities' mayors, elite families, and Mapai satellite parties, and generally sought to accommodate the people to the realities of Israel. Arab politics at this time has been described, unsurprisingly, as "quiescent."[18]

Though some Arab citizens have achieved considerable success in Israel (in 2015, for instance, Salim Joubran served as a justice on the Supreme Court and as chairperson of the Central Elections Committee), the overall result of these processes has been widespread and persistent inequality and an imbalance in the distribution of state resources across the two communities. For example, the state has since 1948 actively appropriated and confiscated considerable amounts of Arab-owned land, including territory owned by Arabs who had remained in Israel and become its citizens.[19] The Or Commission (see Appendix F), charged with investigating the riots of October 2000, found—among other things, including some aggression within the Arab community itself—that

the state and generations of its government failed in a lack of comprehensive and deep handling of the serious problems created by the existence of a large Arab minority inside the Jewish state. . . .

Government handling of the Arab sector has been primarily neglectful and discriminatory. The establishment did not show sufficient sensitivity to the needs of the Arab population, and did not take enough action in order to allocate state resources in an equal manner. The state did not do enough or try hard enough to create equality for its Arab citizens or to uproot discriminatory or unjust phenomenon. . . .

As a result of this and other processes, serious distress prevailed in the Arab sector in various areas. Evidence of the distress included poverty, unemployment, a shortage of land, serious problems in the education system and substantially defective infrastructure. These all contributed to ongoing ferment that increased leading up to October 2000 and constituted a fundamental contribution to the outbreak of the events.

It bears mentioning that social and political patterns within the Arab community have also contributed to these conditions. The authority of communal leaders and local governing bodies is sometimes ignored or dismissed, while these leaders' and bodies' economic mismanagement and poor governance both undermine development and contribute to a lack of legitimacy. Traditional attitudes regarding the status of women in Arab society have made it difficult for that population to achieve higher levels of education and obtain the skills needed to enter the workforce in a modern economy oriented toward high-tech development—an experience similar, in many ways, to that found in the haredi community (though Arab women are a growing population in Israeli higher education).

Further evidence of this inequality can be found in measurements of quality-of-life categories across the Jewish and Arab sectors in Israel. Government spending on housing, social welfare, and employment for the Arab community lags behind expenditures for the Jewish population, while Arab representation in state institutions is far below its share of the population (see Tables 7.1–7.5 for selected indicators).[20] The overall effect of these processes in the Arab community has been anger, frustration, and a willingness to downplay identification with Israel. As the community became more mobilized, these resentments were channeled into an active politics.

Elie Rekhess, a close observer of Arab–Israeli politics, has identified four processes that have developed within the Arab community over time: Israelization, Palestinization, politicization, and Islamization. These processes have underlined the community's political mobilization, led by an activist political and intellectual leadership, which in turn has allowed its members to press their demands more vigorously at the national level. They are not strictly delineated categories, but

Table 7.1 Percentage of Publicly Initiated Housing Unit Starts (Residential) in Communities of 10,000 or More, 2009

	PERCENTAGE
Jews	16.3
Arabs	1.2

Source: Sikkuy, *The Equality Index of Jewish and Arab Citizens in Israel, 2009* (Jerusalem and Haifa: Sikkuy, December 2010), 40, http://www.sikkuy.org.il/wp-content/uploads/2010/12/sikkuy_eng09.pdf

Table 7.2 Unemployment Rate by Gender and Nationality, 2008

	PERCENTAGE
Jews	
Men	7.34
Women	8.54
Arabs	
Men	9.44
Women	14.28

Source: Sikkuy, *The Equality Index of Jewish and Arab Citizens in Israel, 2009* (Jerusalem and Haifa: Sikkuy, December 2010), 66, http://www.sikkuy.org.il/wp-content/uploads/2010/12/sikkuy_eng09.pdf

Table 7.3 Representation in the Israeli Civil Service, 2009

	PERCENTAGE
Jews	93.03
Arabs	6.97

Source: Sikkuy, *The Equality Index of Jewish and Arab Citizens in Israel, 2009* (Jerusalem and Haifa: Sikkuy, December 2010), 69, http://www.sikkuy.org.il/wp-content/uploads/2010/12/sikkuy_eng09.pdf

Table 7.4 Total Average Per Capita Expenditures for Social Welfare (National and Local Governments), 2009

	NEW ISRAELI SHEKELS
Jews	551.3
Arabs	375.8

Source: Sikkuy, *The Equality Index of Jewish and Arab Citizens in Israel, 2009* (Jerusalem and Haifa: Sikkuy, December 2010), 75, http://www.sikkuy.org.il/wp-content/uploads/2010/12/sikkuy_eng09.pdf

rather are general descriptions with some overlap between them. To some extent these processes are the result of forces beyond the community's control, pressing against them and pushing them in specific directions. But at the heart of each development has been the agency of the Palestinian citizens themselves, seizing the opportunities available to them; indeed, there are debates within the community over which of these processes is the appropriate direction for the community to take. Each process is described in the following section.

Table 7.5 Percentage of Households Under the Poverty Line According to Market Income, 2011

	PERCENTAGE
Haredim	70
Arabs	57
Non-Haredi Jews	27

Source: Dan Ben-David, ed., *State of the Nation Report: Society, Economy and Policy in Israel, 2013* (Jerusalem: Taub Center for Social Policy Studies in Israel, November 2013), 27, http://taubcenter.org.il/tauborgilwp/wp-content/uploads/Taub-Center-State-of-the-Nation-Report-2013-ENG-8.pdf

Israelization

The process of Israelization began by 1966–1967. Twenty years after the establishment of the state, the Arab population had grown from 156,000 to about 400,000. Because this increase was primarily the result of a high natural growth rate, it produced a larger, younger population. As education expanded across the community, this younger generation became increasingly well informed, comfortable operating within the Israeli state (including adapting to broader cultural and technological changes), and acclimatized to the Israeli political system. The end of direct military rule created more freedoms for Arab citizens at the same time that a new middle class composed of educated professionals and intellectuals emerged. Ilan Peleg and Dov Waxman note that "this new elite started to set the Arab public agenda, articulating the community's goals and organizing the means to achieve them."[21] This agenda shifted from the accommodation of the previous 20 years to a more assertive stance. Israelization, then, refers to a process of integration into the Israeli state and political system. More broadly, it entails a willingness to identify with the Israeli state on the basis of citizenship and residence while working to advance the community's specific interests.[22]

But it was not until the peace process of the 1990s that Israelization really took off. In September 1993, Israel signed the Declaration of Principles (commonly known as the Oslo Accords) with the PLO. Because the Oslo Accords laid the foundation for the principle of two states (Israel and Palestine) and brought the PLO to a position of autonomous government in parts of Gaza and the West Bank as the Palestinian Authority (PA)—in short, enshrined the principle of Palestinian self-determination—Arab citizens of Israel were forced to choose one of two options. Either they could push for a broader geographical notion of Palestine (some form of a single state between the Mediterranean and the Jordan River) or they could accept that the struggle for self-determination had been won and the focus should be on politics within Israel only—on what Majid al-Hajj called "the civic issue." The decline of the Arab–Israeli and Israeli–Palestinian conflicts facilitated the acceptance of an Israel-centric activism among most of the community. This was made easier by the fact that the PLO/PA did not claim to speak for Palestinian citizens of Israel.

Israelization has been weakened since the 2000s. The lack of major progress on a more equitable balance of resources from the state, the onset of the Second Intifada, the events of October 2000, and three wars between Israel and Hamas in Gaza (in 2008–2009, 2012, and 2014) renewed Arab suspicions about the Jewish majority's interest in accepting their community. Examples of overt Jewish Israeli racism toward Israeli Arabs during these events convinced many of the latter that even weak identification with the state remains problematic, while Arab Israeli protests against the wars in Gaza, which were supported by most Jewish Israelis, convinced many Jews that Arab citizens identify more with WBG Palestinians than with Israel.

Palestinization

At the same time the Arab community was becoming integrated into the Israeli system, it was developing an ethno-national consciousness. This process built on the developments described previously, but it was given added momentum by the outcome of the 1967 War and, paradoxically, the peace process of the 1990s and 2000s.

Palestinization has been the result of the Arab community's renewed connection to Palestinians in the West Bank and Gaza. As mentioned, the severing of that connection with the establishment of Israel in 1948 and the end of the war in 1949 was sudden and traumatic. Cut off from their brethren, Arab Israelis felt alone, outside of the larger Palestinian-Arab people. The capture of east Jerusalem, the West Bank, and the Gaza Strip in the 1967 War reversed that separation, bringing the two communities back together. Though different laws applied to each group, the Israeli state was the ultimate controlling power for both. The Green Line established by the 1949 armistice was all but erased, particularly by the 1980s, as Israelis crossed over the boundary for shopping, to eat at West Bank restaurants, and to have their cars repaired while WBG Palestinians crossed into Israel for work. The expansion of settlements in the territories brought with them Israeli infrastructure, military administration, and Israeli laws.

After the 1967 War, as the PLO engaged in an international campaign of terrorism while making the Palestinian cause a prominent issue on the global agenda, Israeli Arabs were increasingly open to identifying as one component of the Palestinian people. In 1974 the Arab League recognized the PLO as the "sole legitimate representative of the Palestinian people," bringing that identification into starker relief. Though Arab Israelis did not seek to either give up their Israeli citizenship or promote the end of Israel, they were galvanized into embracing a new sense of their national identity. The First Intifada, from 1987 to 1993, made it impossible for this community to ignore their ethno-national connection, since demonstrations, riots, and terrorist attacks were taking place in the WBG and in Israel itself.

But the community was unwilling to adopt one identity at the expense of the other, at least at first. The appearance of two early nationalist movements, *al-Ard* (the Land) in 1958 and the Sons of the Village in the early 1970s, captures this effort to chart a middle course. Both movements were radical in that they called for an aggressive effort to equalize rights for Jews and Arabs in Israel, and considered Palestinian Israelis part of the larger Palestinian nation. Yet neither group had much support within the community, and both faded away after a few years (al-Ard was also heavily constrained by the military government). The emergence of an Arab-led Communist party (*Rakah*) in the 1970s and 1980s as the primary national political body of the community is further evidence of this reluctance. Rakah advocated for a more equitable distribution of wealth on socialist principles rather than on the basis of minority politics, but within the state rather than as a replacement of it.

If the peace process begun with the Oslo Accords in 1993 at first gave the Arab community in Israel hope that their needs would be met, they were soon disappointed. As the peace process dragged on, the government's attention focused almost completely on the WBG Palestinians at the expense of Arab Israelis. The electorate's drift to the right (see Chapter 10), indicated by the election of either right-wing or center-right governments from 2003 to 2015, heightened the sense that Jewish Israelis were less interested in the plight of their fellow citizens. Continuing discrimination and the decision to ignore the recommendations of the Or Commission prompted Palestinian Israeli leaders to move toward a more nationalist, radical politics, a shift highlighted most clearly by the *Future Vision* document (discussed later).

At the political level, a series of amendments and bills proposed by right-leaning governments beginning in 2006 prompted the Arab community to feel specifically targeted. These included efforts to write another Basic Law making Israel the "nation state of the Jewish people"; a bill requiring all citizens to take a "loyalty oath" to Israel as a "Jewish and democratic state"[23]; the Nakba Law (2011), which prevents groups receiving funding from the state from commemorating the events of 1947–1949 as the Palestinian Catastrophe; and the Acceptance to Communities Bill, which allows small communities in the Negev and Galilee to reject applicants seeking to live within their areas.[24] Finally, developments in the peace process heightened this sense of exclusion. Former Foreign Minister Avigdor Liberman, for example, has promoted a plan to exchange with an independent Palestinian state Israeli territory and Palestinian citizens living there (in what is known as "the Triangle") for settlements and Israeli citizens in the West Bank. This, Israeli Arabs have argued, would amount to an unlawful and illegitimate stripping of their citizenship and their similarly unlawful expulsion.

For the most part, then, Palestinization means a greater identification with the Palestinian people and a concomitant effort to enhance the status of Arabs in Israel. In practical terms this has included a greater willingness to question Israel's nature as a Jewish state and to consider alternate options (such as a binational state); a move to promote indigenous collective rights for the community; a demand for "reopening the 1948 file"—that is, for a revival of the issue of the state's expropriation of land previously held by Arab Israelis and the return of some 250,000 "internal refugees" (including their descendants) to their homes in Israel; an emphasis on securing a full say in setting government policy; and the assertion of the community's right to commemorate Israeli Independence Day as their Nakba.[25] This process has been marked by the effort of Arab leaders and intellectuals to present a unified Palestinian Israeli community, arguing that the dominant Israeli distinction between "minorities" (such as Muslims, Druze, Christians, and Bedouin) fractures the community and makes it harder to achieve collective rights.[26] Indeed, according to Oded Haklai, Palestinian demands that they be recognized as an indigenous ethno-national minority "have become the centerpiece of [Palestinian citizens'] political activism in the last two decades."[27]

Politicization

Both Israelization and Palestinization have converged to foment a process of politicization—that is, an increase in Arab political involvement that aims to directly confront the Jewish majority in the political arena. This is evidenced by the rise of Arab political parties independent of the Zionist parties. Efforts to establish a separate Arab political identity began in the 1970s, when autonomous Arab political parties began to operate. The first Israeli Communist party (*Maki*) was a joint Jewish–Arab effort, but it split into a Jewish and an Arab Communist party. The Arab party, Rakah, became the main political vehicle for a more radical Arab politics. Rakah's primacy diminished by the 1980s as a new set of nationalist Arab parties, led by a younger generation of Palestinian Israelis, emerged to challenge the Jewish state. In the 2000s, four "Arab parties" operated in the political system: Hadash (the successor to Rakah, ostensibly a joint Arab–Jewish party, but dominated by Arabs), *Balad*, *Ra'am*, and *Ta'al*. In 2015 these four parties formed an electoral alliance called the Joint List (sometimes referred to as the Joint Arab List) (see Chapter 9).

These trends have been facilitated by changes within the community itself. As the Arab population has become better educated and younger, it has become more comfortable in the Israeli state and acclimatized to the political system even while frustration and resentment at decades of discrimination has grown. A series of clashes between Arabs and the Israeli police and military (e.g., Land Day 1976; October 2000; and during the 2014 Gaza war), some of which resulted in the killing of Palestinian citizens, have heightened the sense that Arabs are considered second-class citizens in Israel. Member of Knesset Ahmad Tibi (Joint List) captured the general feeling among the community after the deaths of 13 Arab citizens in October 2000 when he argued, "We were regarded not as demonstrators but as enemies and treated as such. Before seeing us as citizens, they saw us as Arabs. Jewish citizens demonstrate, but none of them [are] killed."[28]

Increasing nationalism and radicalism are also captured in public opinion surveys regarding how Arabs in Israel view Israel's nature as a Jewish state. Sammy Smooha's surveys of the Arab population in Israel indicate that such attitudes have been stable, remaining within a 10–percentage point range across the years but nonetheless rising and falling at moments correlated with the specific government in power, domestic changes, and external events. The picture painted is one of an uncertain Arab public struggling to reconcile its ethno-national identity with its Israeli citizenship, with an overall negative trend in attitudes toward Israel.

In 1976, 51.1 percent of Arabs agreed that Israel had a right to exist; that figure remained above 50 percent through 2004, reaching over 60 percent in 2003 and 2004.[29] But there has been some variation on the question of Israel's right to exist as a "sovereign state," as a "Jewish-Zionist state," and as a "Jewish and democratic

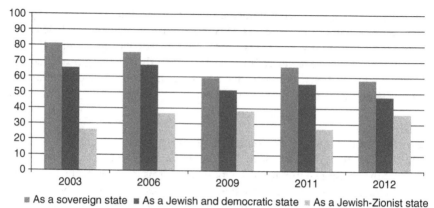

Figure 7.1 Arab attitudes toward Israel's right to exist, 2003–2012   SOURCE: Smooha, *Still Playing by the Rules*, 17.

state" (see Figure 7.1). Meanwhile, the proportion of Arabs denying Israel's right to exist "as a state" has been reported as 20.5 percent in 1976, 6.8 percent in 1995, 11.2 percent in 2003, and 24.5 percent in 2012.[30]

Also significant is that the percentage of Arab Israelis supporting violence to achieve Arab interests shrank from 17.9 percent in 1976 to 1.9 percent in 2004. Subsequently, however, under conditions of increased violence between Arabs and Jews across Israel, Gaza, and the West Bank—as a result of a lack of closure regarding the events in October 2000, as well as several "rounds" of violent conflict between Israelis and Palestinians during the Second Intifada (which began in September 2000) and three Israel–Hamas wars—it has steadily increased, to 10.6 percent in 2012 and 13.3 percent in 2008 (see Figure 7.2).

Smooha refers to the 2000s as a period of "toughening of Arab attitudes toward the Jewish character of the state and its Jewish majority" and a "lost decade" in terms of improving Arab–Jewish relations. It is difficult to disagree with him.

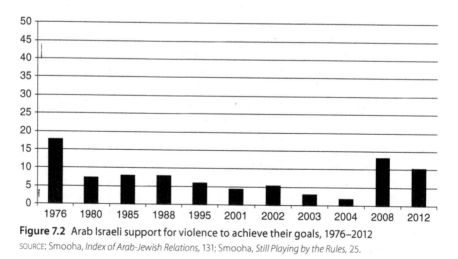

Figure 7.2 Arab Israeli support for violence to achieve their goals, 1976–2012
SOURCE: Smooha, *Index of Arab-Jewish Relations*, 131; Smooha, *Still Playing by the Rules*, 25.

Islamization

Islamization refers to the spread of loyalty to and identification with an explicit Islamic community that is separate from Israeli identity, and it is represented by the Islamic Movement in Israel. Of the four processes described here, it is the weakest, although because it is difficult to determine exact numbers of support for the Islamic Movement, we cannot know the precise motivations for voter support, attendance at Movement events, and participation in Movement institutions. Most analysts' working assumption is that the Movement's specific goals appeal directly only to a small segment of the Palestinian Israeli population.

Like all Islamist organizations, the Islamic Movement in Israel calls for the community's social norms, legal codes, and political rules to be structured by a stricter interpretation of Islam than has previously been in operation. Its slogan is *Al-Islam huwa al-hall* ("Islam is the solution"), which, as Rekhess notes, "embodies the Movement's entire philosophy: there is a crisis that cries out for solution, and the solution may be found in Islam; Islam has the power to alleviate the grievances of the individual, the ills of society, and the problems of mankind."[31] The focus on an Islamic identity is supplemented with a Palestinian nationalist agenda.

The Islamic Movement in Israel was founded in the early 1970s, when a few individuals who had been trained in Islamic institutions in the West Bank began to conduct *da'wa*, or outreach among the Israeli Arab community, to spread the value of the religion. At the time the community was just coming out of almost 20 years of military rule. As secular Palestinian radicalism failed to generate major improvements and Arab Israelis began to look for a new politics and a new identity, the Movement's appeal spread. Like other Islamist groups, the Islamic Movement expanded primarily by constructing a network of social and educational services, though it was restricted in its efforts across the Arab community by Israeli security constraints and limited resources.

The movement attracted few official followers until the 1980s, when it began to play a more prominent role in municipal politics across the community. In 1989, led by a few key individuals, it did very well in local elections, winning seats in municipal councils or mayorships in every election it participated in. But it was not until the 1990s that the Movement became strong enough to influence Arab Israeli politics, moving from the local to the national level.[32]

The electoral and political successes of the Movement contained within them the seeds of division. As it became more prominent, it had to confront critical questions about participation in national politics. These internal tensions came to a head in the 1996 national election, when the organization was torn over whether to participate or not, and were heightened by external developments, particularly the signing of the 1993 Oslo Accords, which required the Islamic Movement to take a position on the emergence of a recognized and accepted Palestinian nationalism, represented by the PLO.

The tensions could not be overcome, and the Movement split into a northern faction and a southern faction.[33] The northern branch, led by Sheikh Raed Saleh, is more radical and dogmatic on both religious and political issues, as well as uncompromising.[34] It opposes participation in either national elections or Israeli state institutions, on the grounds that doing so would legitimate the Jewish/Zionist-dominated secular system and undermine Arab rights and Islamic values. According to the International Crisis Group, it also opposes the existence of Israel as a Jewish state, viewing it as a temporary entity.[35] It wants to strengthen an independent Muslim-Palestinian identity and therefore limit, even sever, its connection to the Israeli state. The northern faction also rejects the *Future Vision* document, which most of the Arab leadership has accepted, in part because it does not give an important role to Islam. Many believe that the northern faction has grown stronger in recent years. This may be connected to the slowly growing radicalism in Arab Israeli opinion described previously.

The southern faction, led by Sheikh Abdullah Nimar Darwish, is considered to be more moderate and pragmatic. Though it, too, advocates a more autonomous Arab arena, it believes the community's needs can best be addressed by participating in the existing system. It argues that participation in elections and the consequent representation in the political arena is an important method for improving the position of Israeli Arabs. In the mid-1990s the southern faction joined with other groups to form Ra'am (the United Arab List). From 2006 to 2015 it formed an alliance with Ahmed Tibi's Ta'al that was called Ra'am–Ta'al. In the 2013 election, Ra'am–Ta'al won four seats in the Knesset, three of which were held by candidates from the Islamic Movement. This branch also accepted the *Future Vision* as a legitimate statement of the leadership of the Arab community, but one that requires revisions.

The Islamic Movement is not a major player in Palestinian Israeli politics, and especially not in Israeli politics, but it is an increasingly important one. The Movement has been able to mobilize growing segments of the Arab population, and its social-religious appeal transmits its radical positions across the community. In addition, the state's neglect of this sector has allowed it to fill a gap and become more relevant to the Arab population. Finally, its call for a more nationalist, separatist politics is close to the position of the secular parties and the intellectuals, creating a critical mass for these ideas.

But the internal division within the Movement does hamper its effectiveness. Each branch has established different organizations that serve the same purpose (e.g., protection of Muslim holy places, sports clubs, and so on). Their disagreements over participation in the Israeli system are principled and political. Yet should the state begin to address the Arab community's social, economic, educational, and infrastructure needs, it is possible that the Movement's ability to continue expanding might be checked.

JEWISH ATTITUDES TOWARD THE ARAB MINORITY

An analysis of Arab politics in Israel would be incomplete without some sense of the Jewish community's attitudes about these issues. If among Palestinian Israelis the trend has been toward greater confrontation and ambivalence, among Jewish Israelis it has been equally multifaceted. In some ways it is difficult to get a handle on Jewish attitudes: public opinion surveys suggest that attitudes toward Arab Israelis and attitudes toward the rights they should have within the Jewish state hover around the same percentages: between one-quarter and one-third of Israeli

Jews view Israeli Arabs negatively and suspiciously, while between one-third and three-quarters believe Arab citizens should have full rights, collective rights, and even some autonomy. Yet in the 2000s members of right-wing governments have put forward bills designed to anchor the identity of the state in its Jewish character at the expense of its Arab minority, and the bulk of the Jewish public has been silent. Furthermore, anecdotal evidence suggests that, while it might not be widespread, there has been an uptick in Jewish nationalism, chauvinism, and racism, particularly during moments of intense violence between Israelis and Palestinians of the WBG.

The most disturbing example of these attitudes occurred during the Israel–Hamas war in summer 2014. Triggered by the kidnapping and murder by a West Bank Hamas cell of three teenage Jewish students on June 12, the conflict progressed rapidly, with the escalation of rocket fire on southern Israel from jihadist groups in Gaza and an Israeli air and ground campaign that began on July 8. As the events unfolded, large crowds of Jewish Israelis protested against what they perceived to be the government's "soft" response to the murders. Multiple reports emerged of Israeli Jews attacking both Israeli Arabs and left-wing activists protesting the military campaign. The worst attack occurred on July 2, the day after the three teenagers were buried. Three men kidnapped 16-year-old east Jerusalem resident Mohammed Abu Khdeir and beat and burned him to death. In other instances, mobs actively searched out Arabs to attack, with some claiming that Jews went through the Jerusalem light-rail—which passes through east Jerusalem—asking passengers if they were Arabs. In both the West Bank and in Israel, violence escalated as crowds from both sectors attacked individuals from the other.

In the political arena, the most dramatic example of these attitudes came during the 2015 election. On Election Day, Likud leader and Prime Minister Binyamin Netanyahu warned in a Facebook post that "the rule of the right was in danger" because Arabs were coming out to vote "in droves." This remark raised concerns among many in the Arab community, as it seemed to imply that their participation in the democratic process was suspect and illegitimate, and led to accusations of incitement. Several days later Netanyahu apologized not for the content of the comment itself but for hurting Arab citizens. Though defenders of the post claimed that it was simply an expression of electoral politics, most Arab politicians rejected the apology as disingenuous.[36]

Indeed, according to Smooha's surveys, a significant portion of Israeli Jews would prefer to restrict Arabs' rights within the state. In 2012, 22.2 percent felt the state should deny "the right of existence of an Arab minority with full civil rights," while 28.3 percent wanted to deny Arabs the right to vote in Knesset elections.[37]

The Israel Democracy Institute's (IDI) Israeli Democracy Index is in line with these findings, particularly when it comes to questions of security and the Jewish character of the state. In 2014, 73.8 percent of Israeli Jews "strongly" or "somewhat" agreed with the statement, "Decisions crucial to the state on issues of peace and security should be made by a Jewish majority." Given the history of Israel and the continuing sense of threat among the Jewish community, this may not be surprising. But the IDI found that this number represents a decrease from 82.9 percent who agreed in 2010, although it is up from the 66.7 percent recorded in 2013.[38]

At the same time, though, the Jewish public does view the Arab community as part of Israeli society and thinks it should be accorded full rights. In 2012, 75 percent of Jews recognized the right of Arabs to live in Israel "as a minority with full civil rights," and 67 percent thought Arabs should be accepted as full members of Israeli society.[39] In 2013 the IDI asked Jewish respondents whether democratic principles or Jewish law should be given preference in cases in which they conflict, and 42.7 percent—a plurality—said, "It is preferable in all cases to uphold democratic principles." Similarly, in 2014, 42 percent of Jews disagreed "strongly" and 20.9 percent disagreed "somewhat" with the statement that "Jewish citizens of Israel should have greater rights than non-Jewish citizens."[40] Perhaps more important, according to a 2011 Sikkuy survey, 74 percent of Israeli Jews acknowledge that discrimination against Arab citizens exists, while 60 percent think that promoting equality is in the interests of Israel.[41]

We can surmise from these numbers that the increasing radicalism and nationalism found among the Israeli Arab public, and especially its leaders, is partly of a piece with Jewish Israeli attitudes regarding this community's place in the state. Exacerbating Jewish perceptions is a longstanding concern, reinvigorated during periods of violence and war, regarding the role of Arab Israelis in the Israeli–Palestinian conflict, namely, as a real or potential security threat. This unease stems from the historical circumstances of the establishment of Israel, when the Arab population of Mandatory Palestine was at war with the Jewish community and members participated in Arab Palestinian attacks on the new state.[42]

Still, while significant segments of Israeli Jews harbor uncertainty, suspicion, hostility, and some exclusionary preferences toward the Arab minority, even larger portions of the Jewish sector hold accommodationist attitudes. This may be a foundation that can be strengthened.

ARAB LEADERS AND THE ARAB PUBLIC

Though the Arab community as a whole has felt alienated from the state and has moved toward a more hostile and confrontational attitude toward it, there is some difference between how leaders and elites of the Palestinian community view themselves and their role vis-à-vis the Israeli state, and perceptions and expectations among the general Arab public.

There are three main areas of difference. First, the Arab public does not appear to believe the leadership's conceptualization of Palestinian Israeli identity to be of critical importance, although they are sympathetic toward it. Indeed, the general community, while ostensibly supportive of binationalism, seems more reconciled to Jewish hegemony than the leadership is. In 2012, for example, as Smooha reported, "55.9% of Arabs reconciled themselves to Israel as a state with a Jewish majority, 60.6% as a state whose language is Hebrew, 53.2% as a state with an Israeli-Hebrew culture, and 60.2% as a state where Saturday is the day of rest. Moreover, 54.7% of the Arabs would prefer to live in Israel than in any other country in the world."[43] Still, 69.6 percent of Arabs thought that it is not justified for Israel to maintain a Jewish hegemony. This belief appears to leave the door open to a more radical politics, if the leadership can successfully mobilize the Arab public. It is not clear that they can at this point.

Second, Arab politics seems to be more radical and nationalist than the general Arab population is interested in embracing. Arab political parties, academics, grassroots activists, and civil society, including the Islamic Movement (particularly the northern branch) and the High Follow-Up Committee for Arab Citizens of Israel (comprised of representatives of the main communal institutions), are all more radical than most of the community's members. Amal Jamal has noted that the bulk of the population is unaware of the political conceptualization of indigeneity, even though they might agree with the idea behind it.[44]

This difference is captured most strongly in the *Future Vision of the Palestinian Arabs in Israel*, a 2006 set of strategy documents written by Arab Israeli academics, political leaders, and intellectuals. The study begins with an explicit rejection of Israeli identity: "We are the Palestinian Arabs in Israel, the indigenous peoples, the residents of the State of Israel, and an integral part of the Palestinian People and the Arab and Muslim and human Nation." Though the document delves into discrimination in law, land and housing allocation, economic development, and education, it also discusses more abstract ideas of Arab identity and cultural development.

But even while it focuses on material concerns and sets out recommendations for addressing them, it does so by situating them in direct opposition to Israel's existence as a Jewish state. It argues, for example,

> Israel is the outcome of a settlement process initiated by the Zionist–Jewish elite in Europe and the west and realized by Colonial countries contributing to it and by promoting Jewish immigration to Palestine, in light of the results of the Second World War and the Holocaust. After the creation of the State in 1948, Israel continued to use policies derived from its vision as an extension of the west in the Middle East and continued conflicting with its neighbors. Israel also continued executing internal colonial policies against its Palestinian Arab citizens. Israel carried out the Judaization process in various forms, beginning with the expulsion of the Palestinian People back in 1948.

The confrontational tone of the document angered and appalled Israel's Jewish leaders and parties, and in many ways made them less open to hearing these demands and working with the Arab leadership to achieve them. The *Future Vision* represents a direct contradiction of the Israeli Declaration of Independence, which highlights the particular nature of the Jewish experience and enshrines Jewish identity alongside individual liberties, but not collective minority rights. As the former argues:

> The State should acknowledge responsibility of the Palestinian Nakba (tragedy of 1948) and its disastrous consequences on the Palestinians in general and the Palestinian Arab citizens of Israel in particular. Israel should start by rectifying the damage that it had caused and should consider paying compensation for its Palestinian citizens as individuals and groups for the damages resulted from the Nakba and the continuous discriminating policies derived from viewing them as enemies and not as citizens that have a right to appose the state and challenge its rules.

It is not clear, though, that the community as a whole believes such acknowledgment and restitution to be a priority. In addition to the polling data cited previously, other figures indicate that when local Arab governments have worked with the national government, improvements in economic, social, and educational conditions have been noticeable—even among Arab citizens.[45] Still, the *Future Vision* documents represent a critical development in Arab Israeli politics, and many argue they are a turning point in this community's relationship with the (Jewish) state.[46]

There has been particular frustration concerning Arab parties' focus on Israeli foreign policy, especially policy toward the West Bank and Gaza. The rhetoric of Arab political leaders, particularly those in Balad, has in recent years often been highly charged. Some, such as Azmi Bishara, a former MK and leader of Balad and a 1999 prime ministerial candidate, have publicly focused on foreign affairs, turning away from domestic issues. In the early and mid-2000s, for example, Bishara visited Lebanon and Syria and made a series of controversial statements criticizing Israel and praising Hezbollah. It was later revealed that Israeli security forces were so suspicious of him that they put him under surveillance, eventually determining that he was advising Hezbollah against Israel. He was questioned by police and in 2007 fled the country to the embassy in Cairo, where he resigned from the Knesset. In Israel he remains under indictment for supporting a terrorist organization.

This is not to say that none of the Arab politicians serve their constituents' expressed needs. Haneen Zoabi, also of Balad, is known for her strident rhetoric accusing Israel of racist discrimination; refuses to stand during the singing of the national anthem; and was aboard the *Mavi Marmara*, which belonged to the flotilla that in 2010 tried to break the Israeli blockade on Hamas-run Gaza. But she is also a staunch advocate for Arab women's rights in general and an outspoken opponent of violence against women in the community specifically.

Third, the Arab leadership, composed of politicians and intellectuals, is mistrusted by the Arab public to a great degree because of the former's focus on seemingly abstract issues of identity at the expense of material conditions. The community's frustration on this point is palpable and is captured most clearly in surveys of the Arab community. In 2012, Smooha found that 58.2 percent of Arabs did not trust Arab leaders in Israel, with 63.2 percent believing they did not advance solutions to the Arab population's problems, 61.1 percent believing they did not serve the Arab population in protesting against the state and its policies, and 76.0 percent believing they should focus more on settling Arab Israelis' daily problems and less on Israel's dispute with the Palestinians. As well, 62.4 percent supported, and only 25.5 percent opposed, prioritizing fighting for civil and socioeconomic equality over fighting for peace and a change of the state's character.[47] In February 2015 another survey of Arab citizens asked respondents to rank the areas they thought Arab MKs should focus on after the election the following month. Of the three most important areas identified by respondents, the largest group expressed the belief that MKs should focus on the community's internal problems (see Table 7.6).

Perhaps the general Arab attitude is best captured by the way one Arab citizen put it to the International Crisis Group: "Arab members of Knesset can do little

Table 7.6 Arab Public Beliefs About Most and Least Important Areas Arab MKs Should Focus On, by Percentage

	RANKING 1	RANKING 2	RANKING 3	TOTAL
Government and government institution policy on the Arab population	28.1	34.7	23.4	86.2
Internal problems of Arab society: Women's status, employment, education, violence, health care	44.3	22.1	17.6	84
Negotiations between Israel and the Palestinians	19.0	29.2	27.9	76.1

Source: Konrad Adenauer Program for Jewish-Arab Cooperation, "Main Findings of Public Opinion Survey on the Arab Vote to the 20th Knesset," Moshe Dayan Center, February 2015, http://www.kas.de/wf/doc/kas_15350-1442-2-30.pdf?150315131309

more than fill up a chair."[48] Yet the Arab public still seems to support the Arab leadership, particularly in elections—possibly because there is little other choice. That, in turn, might be affected by the recent electoral changes in Israel, discussed in the following section. The establishment of the Joint List, whose leader Ayman Odeh has worked to tone down such rhetoric, may indicate a realization that certain previous positions have been counterproductive.

VOTER TURNOUT

As with the Jewish public, Arab voter turnout has declined over time, though it increased in the 2013 and 2015 elections. From 1949 to 1973, turnout in the community hovered in the 80 percent range, standing at 79 percent in 1949 and reaching a peak of 90 percent in 1955. It is not clear how much of this high turnout was based on active participation versus explicit mobilization of local leaders and hamula heads by Mapai and other leftist parties. It is not likely, given the community's trauma (the end of the 1948 War, the separation of Israel from the West Bank, and the loss of majority status in the area) that Arab voters were eager participants in a new and unfamiliar political system. Indeed, the turnout rate steadily declined from 1955 until 2013. The 2013 election may have been the beginning of a renewed interest in voting: that year turnout was slightly higher, at 56.5 percent, and in 2015 it increased by a larger margin, to 63.5 percent.

The lowest turnout was in the 2001 direct election for Prime Minister, which pitted Labor's Ehud Barak against Likud's Ariel Sharon. Coming out of the Camp David and Taba negotiations with the Palestinian Authority, in which Barak had offered what were then unprecedented concessions, including withdrawal from most of the West Bank and a division of some sort in Jerusalem, Barak was fighting for his political life. Israeli citizens concerned with ending the conflict would have had considerable incentive to mobilize to keep Barak in power and make sure

Sharon—known as the grandfather of the settlements for his role in the 1980s in plugging them into the Israeli road system and electrical grid—was kept out.

This election also took place at the beginning of the Second Intifada, a vicious explosion of violence that killed many Israelis and WBG Palestinians. Israeli Arab turnout at the polls plummeted to 18 percent (with one-third of those voters casting blank ballots), a particularly stark dive when compared to the fact that Barak won 95 percent of the Arab vote in the direct election of 1999. The drop was a result of Palestinian Israelis' concerns not with the conflict itself but rather with their own status in Israel. Not only did the election follow the killing of 13 Arab citizens by Israeli police and Jewish rioters in October 2000, but it was widely seen as a rejection of both Barak himself and the Zionist left in Israel. Since Yitzhak Rabin's Labor government of 1992–1995 (considered the "Golden Age" of Jewish–Arab relations in Israel), the Arab community had become increasingly resentful of the neglect displayed toward it even by the Labor governments of Shimon Peres and Barak. Resources for the community were scaled back, their political demands were largely ignored, and issues of concern to them were lost as Israeli politics became focused on the conflict with the Palestinians, ongoing terrorist attacks, and debate over the settlements and the disposition of the WBG. There was a sense among the Arab community that it was no use participating in the election, even to vote for a Labor Prime Minister. The Arab voter turnout rate has been slow to recover, as voters have continued to use their nonparticipation as a form of protest.

Building on these frustrations, in 2006 several groups formed the Popular Committee for Boycotting the Knesset Elections. Comprising primarily academics, intellectuals, and a renewed Sons of the Village movement, it was supported by the northern faction of the Islamic Movement and received some sympathy from Balad and Ra'am–Ta'al, all of which emphasized the years of frustration and bitterness at official state neglect.

It is important to note that at the same time that Arab voters began to boycott or simply lose interest in Israeli elections, the turnout rate among Jewish voters also began to drop off. The entire voter turnout rate has fallen from the 80 percent range throughout much of the 1950s and 1960s and the high 70s percent range in the 1970s, 1980s, and 1990s. Israel may currently be in the middle of an upward trend, though, with the turnout rate rising from 64.9 percent in 2009 to 67.8 percent in 2013 and 72.3 percent in 2015. The Arab turnout rate has followed a similar pattern, rising from 53.4 percent in 2009 to 63.5 percent in 2015 (see Figure 7.3).

While Palestinian citizens have become more suspicious of the political process as a whole, they have at the same time increasingly voted for Arab parties over Jewish/Zionist parties. In 1999, 68.7 percent of the Arab vote went to Arab parties (Hadash, Ra'am, and Balad, and their subsequent manifestations). Though there was a small (4 percent) dip in support for these three parties in 2003, that percentage continued to rise to 71.9 percent in 2006, 81.9 percent in 2009, 77 percent in 2013, and about 80 percent in 2015 (see Figure 7.4). The significance of these percentages is more evident when the number of seats won by Arab parties since 1949 is examined. From 1949 to the 1970s, the non-Communist Arab parties (all of which were affiliated with Mapai/Labor) received up to two seats in every election,

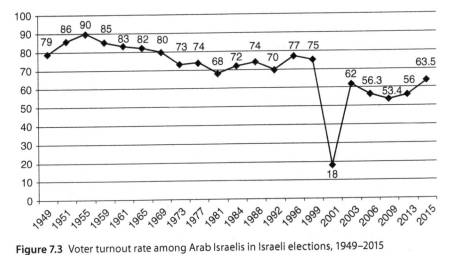

Figure 7.3 Voter turnout rate among Arab Israelis in Israeli elections, 1949–2015

SOURCES: Arik Rudnitzky, "Tel Aviv Notes 9, no. 7: Arab Politics in Israel: Pending Questions," Moshe Dayan Center, April 13, 2015; Ariel Ben Solomon, "Arab Israeli Voters 56% Turnout Defies Expectations," *Jerusalem Post*, January 25, 2013; Karin Tamar Schafferman, "Participation, Abstention and Boycott: Trends in Arab Voter Turnout in Israeli Elections," Israel Democracy Institute, April 21, 1999.

* The 2001 election was for Prime Minister only and was not a general election.

with one instance in which three mandates were secured. Yet once the Arab-dominated Communist party, Rakah, begin campaigning, it regularly won three to four seats. When Rakah merged into Hadash, it regularly received three to five seats. With the emergence of other, new independent parties, the total number of seats held by Arab parties in each Knesset from 1996 to 2013 was between eight and 11 (see Appendix B). In 2015 the Arab parties won 13 seats, their highest to date.

The raising of the electoral threshold to 3.25 percent in 2014 (see Chapter 8) was viewed as a backward step by many in the Arab community. In the 2013 election, Hadash and Balad both received less than 3 percent of the popular vote;

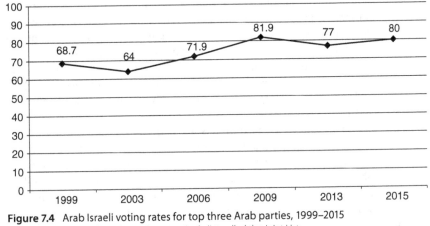

Figure 7.4 Arab Israeli voting rates for top three Arab parties, 1999–2015

* In 2015 the main parties ran together on a single list, called the Joint List.

Ra'am–Ta'al won 3.65 percent. Consequently the new threshold sparked concern that these parties would not obtain enough votes to enter the Knesset.

In addition to being passed with little active consultation with opposition parties, particularly the Arab parties, the new threshold was seen as the majority forcing the minority to adapt to its own preferences, rather than recognizing the special communal rights of the minority. For instance, the Association for Civil Rights in Israel (ACRI) and the Israel Democracy Institute argued that while raising the threshold makes sense as a way to cut down on the proliferation of small parties, it restricts the ability of the minority to represent itself and removes choice from Arab voters. ACRI and IDI have proposed instead an exemption for the Arab minority, a lower threshold, or a slower implementation of the threshold as a way to encourage greater Arab political participation. In addition to recognizing the collective rights of the minority, these approaches would also be more in line with the realities of Israeli politics, since none of the Arab parties has ever served in government and therefore has never destabilized the coalition.

When the threshold was raised, some observers argued that the Arab community would benefit in two ways. First, the higher threshold would force the Arab parties to cooperate closely, and perhaps even to merge, which would concentrate and therefore increase Arab political power. Second, a single Arab list could generate more interest and excitement among Arab voters, thereby increasing voter turnout. In the event, both predictions appear to have come true, as turnout rose to 63.5 percent, a rate not seen since 2003.

To speak of Arab participation in Israeli politics, then, is to speak of a community that remains only partially mobilized; is increasingly resentful and nationalist, demanding major changes to the character of the state; and has returned to the political arena through the electoral process.

SAYED KASHUA AS BAROMETER?

If Israelization, Palestinization, politicization, and Islamization are occurring at the same time, the process of Palestinization seems most prevalent in 2015 and will likely continue to be the major trend. It does not seem likely that more attention will be paid to the Arab minority in Israel until a peace agreement is finalized between Israel and the PA, and while right-wing or right-leaning parties continue to dominate the polls. But many in the Palestinian Israeli community seem to be coming to terms with the difficulty and complexity of their status within Israel. Arab parties continue to press issues of concern to the community, while levels of militancy and radicalism (as expressed in members' views about Israel as a Jewish state, for example) remain high.

The dilemma faced by the Palestinian Israeli community has been captured by prominent Arab Israeli author and journalist Sayed Kashua. Kashua, who is fluent in Hebrew, writes for the Israeli newspaper *Ha'aretz* and created the sitcom *Avoda Aravit* (Arab Labor), which is very popular among Jewish Israelis, even while it pokes fun at Jewish hegemony and racism (it also mocks the attitudes and politics of Arab Israelis). Kashua's books, columns, and television episodes highlight the dilemma in which Palestinian Israelis are caught: the Arab characters are un-anchored, drifting, uncertain—and sometimes even want to be like "the Jews." Yet his characters operate in an Israeli arena and even see themselves (as Kashua sees himself) as Israeli.

Kashua, then, represents an exciting and interesting new way of advancing Arab rights and identity within a hegemonic Jewish identity and politics. His efforts have focused on promoting an *Israeli* identity rather than an Arab identity, and the widespread recognition of his work has facilitated this.

Yet even Kashua has seemed to acknowledge that there are limitations beyond which the Arab minority cannot progress. Originally scheduled to take a one-year sabbatical in the United States, Kashua decided in the aftermath of the murder of Abu Khdeir that he could no longer remain in Israel. In an open letter, he wrote that he had long believed that his stories of the Arab experience, written in Hebrew, would one day turn Israeli Arabs "into equal citizens, almost like the Jews." But, evoking the Jewish experience of persecution, he continued,

> Twenty-five years of writing in Hebrew, and nothing has changed. Twenty-five years clutching at the hope, believing it is not possible that people can be so blind. Twenty-five years during which I had few reasons to be optimistic but continued to believe that one day this place in which both Jews and Arabs live together would be the one story where the story of the other is not denied. That one day the Israelis would stop denying the Nakba, the Occupation, and the suffering of the Palestinian people. That one day the Palestinians would be willing to forgive and together we would build a place that was worth living in.
>
> Twenty-five years that I am writing and knowing bitter criticism from both sides, but last week I gave up. Last week something inside of me broke. When Jewish youth parade through the city shouting "Death to the Arabs," and attack Arabs only because they are Arabs, I understood that I had lost my little war.[49]

SUMMARY

Thus, there are multiple trajectories in place regarding Palestinian citizens' attitudes toward and integration into the State of Israel. On the one hand, the state's attitude toward the Bedouin and the neglect of the right-wing or right-leaning governments of the 2000s indicate that the Arab community is deemed of little importance in Israel, which has helped lead to increased radicalization among its leadership and declining levels of identification with the state. Kashua's decision to leave Israel is anecdotal evidence of this trend. On the other hand, changes in the political arena, a willingness among the Arab Israeli public to maintain its connection to Israel, and some decline in hostile views in the Jewish and Arab sectors toward each other suggest there is political space to incorporate the Arab public into the state's political arena. Some increases in government resources channeled toward the community signify improvements in quality-of-life areas, which are bound to arrest negative attitudes toward the state.

Much will depend on the ability of the Arab political leadership and the community's activists to pry open space in the political arena to not only demand change, but force the Jewish majority to respond positively toward these activities. If Ghanem, Haklai, Jamal, Rekhess, and others are right, the community's mobilization is on an upward trend that shows no signs of reversing itself. The Jewish state will, then, have to account for the Arab public's demands one way or another.

Yet the loudest voices on both sides do not encourage such a process. Yisrael Beiteinu's Avigdor Liberman, the former Foreign Minister (2009–2015), called on Jewish Israelis to boycott Arab businesses during the 2014 Gaza war because some Palestinian citizens went on strike—a widely used tactic in Israeli politics—to protest the Israeli military campaign.[50] In October 2014, MK Zoabi said in an interview that that an Israeli fighter pilot "is no less a terrorist than a person who takes a knife and commits a beheading. . . . Both are armies of murderers, they have no boundaries and no red lines."[51] A conversation between Liberman and Zoabi, then, does not seem fruitful. A resolution of the Israeli–Palestinian conflict might well dampen these types of tension, as much of the motivation for the hostility and insecurity within each community would be removed.[52] But that may still be some time away.

KEYWORDS

Arab minority, Arab citizens of Israel, Palestinian Israeli, Israelization, Palestinization, Islamization, voter turnout, identity crisis, Sayed Kashua, ethno-nationalism, politics of indigeneity

NOTES

1. This excludes Arabs in east Jerusalem. Though Israel has annexed the entire city, most Palestinians in the eastern portion do not hold Israeli citizenship; instead, they have permanent residency status and can vote only in local—not national—elections. They therefore are not counted as part of the community's Israeli population. Though they are permitted to seek Israeli citizenship, most do not, as they do not want to recognize Israel's annexation of the area.

2. Two other moments of violence and clashes between Arab citizens and the state laid the groundwork for how Palestinian Israelis would view the state's role in the events of October 2000. At Kafr Qasim in October 1956, almost 50 Arab civilians were killed by Israel's Border Police. The military government had earlier imposed a curfew because of tensions and fears of fifth columns during the Suez Crisis. Any Arab caught breaking curfew, it was stipulated, would be shot. It is not clear whether the 50 slain Arab laborers returning from tending crops were aware of the curfew or if they simply did not obey it. The second event took place in March 1976 after the government published plans to expropriate 6,300 dunams of Arab-owned land in the Galilee (northern Israel). A series of protests erupted, which the state tried to quell with police and military units, tear gas, and threats. In the ensuing violence, six Arab citizens were killed. March 30 is now referred to as Land Day, and annual protests against Israeli expropriation of land are held on that day.

3. Dov Waxman, "A Dangerous Divide: The Deterioration of Jewish-Palestinian Relations in Israel," *Middle East Journal* 66 (2012): 11.

4. Cited in Elie Rekhess, "The Arab Minority in Israel: Reconsidering the '1948 Paradigm,'" *Israel Studies* 19 (2014): 190.

5. Waxman, "A Dangerous Divide," 12n.2. Scholars who use "Palestinian" also differ on specific characterizations. Oded Haklai uses the term "Palestinian Arab Citizens of Israel," while As'ad Ghanem uses "Palestinian-Arab minority in Israel." See Haklai, *Palestinian Ethnonationalism in Israel* (Philadelphia: University of Pennsylvania Press, 2011); and Ghanem, *The Palestinian-Arab Minority in Israel, 1948–2000* (Albany: SUNY Press, 2001).

6. Many of those who were displaced to the WBG during and after the war were then displaced again during the 1967 War. About 300,000 Palestinians were dislocated in 1967; of those, approximately 120,000 were refugees from the 1947–1949 War.

7. Sammy Smooha, *Index of Arab-Jewish Relations in Israel, 2004* (Israel: Jewish-Arab Center, University of Haifa, 2005), 130; Smooha, *Arab-Jewish Relations in Israel: Alienation and Rapprochement*, Peaceworks No. 67 (Washington, D.C.: United States Institute of Peace, 2010), 18.

8. Tamar Hermann, Ella Heller, Chanan Cohen, Gilad Be'ery, and Yuval Lebel, *The Israeli Democracy Index 2014* (Jerusalem: Israel Democracy Index, 2014), 59. The 2014 survey was conducted before the Israel–Hamas war that summer.

9. Smooha, *Index of Arab-Jewish Relations*, 130; Smooha, *Arab-Jewish Relations*, 18. The last figure also includes the category of "Palestinian Arab in Israel."

10. Sammy Smooha, *Still Playing by the Rules: Index of Arab-Jewish Relations in Israel, 2012* (Jerusalem: Israel Democracy Institute, 2013), 18.

11. Smooha, *Index of Arab-Jewish Relations*, 130.

12. Smooha, *Arab-Jewish Relations*, 18.

13. One dunam equals 1,000 square meters.

14. The official name is the Bill on the Arrangement of Bedouin Settlement in the Negev. It has also been called the Prawer-Begin Plan, after Likud member Benny Begin modified it in January 2013 in response to public criticism.

15. The plan includes provisions for the creation of nature reserves and military areas as well.

16. The state does recognize several official "minorities," which are based on religious—not national or ethnic—classification. These include Muslims, Christians, Druze, Bedouins, Circassians, and Aramaics.

17. Haklai, *Palestinian Ethnonationalism*, chapter 4; Ilan Peleg and Dov Waxman, *Israel's Palestinians: The Conflict Within* (Cambridge: Cambridge University Press, 2011), 50–52.

18. Ian Lustick, *Arabs in the Jewish State: Israel's Control of a National Minority* (Austin: University of Texas Press, 1980).

19. Haklai, *Palestinian Ethnonationalism*, 57–61.

20. For further discussion, see Adalah, *The Inequality Report: The Palestinian Arab Minority in Israel* (Haifa, Israel: Adalah, March 2011), http://adalah.org/upfiles/2011/Adalah_The_Inequality_Report_March_2011.pdf; and Dan Ben-David, ed., *State of the Nation Report: Society, Economy and Policy in Israel, 2013* (Jerusalem: Taub Center for Social Policy Studies in Israel, November 2013), http://taubcenter.org.il/tauborgilwp/wp-content/uploads/Taub-Center-State-of-the-Nation-Report-2013-ENG-8.pdf.

21. Peleg and Waxman, *Israel's Palestinians*, 53.

22. As'ad Ghanem, *The Palestinian-Arab Minority in Israel, 1948–2000* (Albany: SUNY Press, 2001).

23. The government passed an amended bill requiring only new non-Jewish citizens to take the oath.

24. The bill was amended to prevent rejection on the basis of "race, religion, nationality or physical handicap" and became law in March 2011. The law was later challenged in part on the basis that removing this clause would not prevent communities from enacting its provisions in practice, but it was upheld in September 2014 by the Supreme Court.

25. Amal Jamal, *Arab Minority Nationalism in Israel: The Politics of Indigeneity* (London: Routledge, 2011), 28–31.

26. Rekhess, "Arab Minority in Israel," 194–197.

27. Haklai, *Palestinian Ethnonationalism*, 1.

28. Cited in International Crisis Group, *Identity Crisis: Israel and Its Arab Citizens*, Middle East Report no. 25 (March 4, 2004), 9.

29. Smooha, *Index of Arab-Jewish Relations*, 129.

30. Smooha, *Still Playing by the Rules*, 16.

31. Elie Rekhess, "Islamization of Arab Identity in Israel: The Islamic Movement, 1972–1996," in *Muslim Minorities in Non-Muslim Majority Countries: The Islamic Movement in Israel as a Test Case*, ed. Elie Rekhess and Arik Rudnitzky (Tel Aviv: Konrad Adenauer Program for Jewish-Arab Cooperation, 2013), 54.

32. Lawrence Rubin, *Islamic Political Activism in Israel*, Analysis Paper No. 32 (Washington, D.C.: Brookings Institution, April 2014).

33. "Northern" and "southern" are useful shorthands, but Lawrence Rubin points out that the geographic terms were adopted only because the former's main base in Umm al-Fahm is a little north of the latter's headquarters in Kfar Qassem; Rubin, *Islamic Political Activism*, 4n.13.

34. Indeed, on the grounds that it regularly engages in incitement and therefore directly contributed to the spate of stabbings of Israeli Jews in the fall of 2015, in November that year the Netanyahu government declared the northern branch an illegal organization.

35. International Crisis Group, *Back to Basics: Israel's Arab Minority and the Israeli-Palestinian Conflict*, Middle East Report no. 119 (March 14, 2012), 12–13; Rekhess, "Arab Minority in Israel," 203–204.

36. Times of Israel Staff, "Netanyahu Apologizes to Arabs For Voter Turnout Remark," *Times of Israel*, March 23, 2015.

37. Smooha, *Still Playing by the Rules*, 26.

38. Hermann et al., *Israeli Democracy Index 2014*, 67; Tamar Hermann, Ella Heller, Nir Atmor, and Yuval Lebel, *The Israeli Democracy Index 2013* (Jerusalem: Israel Democracy Index, 2014), 53–54.

39. Smooha, *Still Playing by the Rules*, 20.

40. Hermann et al., *Israeli Democracy Index 2013*, 150; Hermann et al., *Israeli Democracy Index 2014*, 73.

41. Sikkuy, "Who's in Favor of Equality? Equality Between Arabs and Jews in Israel: Summary of an Opinion Survey," September 2011, http://www.sikkuy.org.il/wp-content/uploads/2013/12/shivion2011_english_abstract.pdf.

42. For more on these perceptions, see Hillel Frisch, *Israel's Security and Its Arab Citizens* (Cambridge: Cambridge University Press, 2011).

43. Smooha, *Still Playing by the Rules*, 12.

44. Jamal, *Arab Minority Nationalism*, 40.

45. Robert Cherry, "Increased Constructive Engagement Among Israeli Arabs: The Impact of Government Economic Initiatives," *Israel Studies* 19 (2014): 75–97.

46. Amal Jamal, "The Political Ethos of Palestinian Citizens of Israel: Critical Readings in the *Future Vision* Documents," *Israel Studies Forum* 23 (2008): 3–28.

47. Smooha, *Still Playing by the Rules*, 14.

48. International Crisis Group, *Back to Basics*, 10.

49. Sayed Kashua, "Why I Have to Leave Israel," *Observer*, July 19, 2014. http://www .theguardian.com/world/2014/jul/20/sayed-kashua-why-i-have-to-leave-israel.

50. Ariel Ben Solomon, "FM Liberman Calls for Boycott of Israeli Arab Businesses Who Strike for Gaza," *Jerusalem Post*, July 21, 2014.

51. *Haaretz* and Jonathan Lis, "MK Zoabi: Israeli Combat Pilots Are No Better Than Islamic State Beheaders," *Haaretz*, October 19, 2014.

52. Peleg and Waxman argue that the conflict is intricately tied to the activities and demands of the Arab minority in Israel. See Peleg and Waxman, *Israel's Palestinians*. On the politics and identity of Palestinian Israelis as part of the broader Palestinian nation, see Rashid Khalidi, *Palestinian Identity: The Construction of Modern National Consciousness* (New York: Columbia University Press, 1997); and Baruch Kimmerling and Joel S. Migdal, *The Palestinian People: A History* (Cambridge: Harvard University Press, 2003).

CHAPTER 8

❧

The Electoral System

Israel's electoral system was adopted at first for convenience sake—it was easy, in the middle of a war, to simply use the system that had been in place in the Yishuv. The system became permanent as politicians could not agree on what to change and what to change it into—although they did agree that the system should give as much voice to as wide a variety of groups within the polity as possible. In this sense, Israel is a hyper-democracy, if democracy is defined as the free competition between political parties representing different interests and segments of the population. However, this inclusiveness also embedded instabilities and weaknesses within the system that have plagued Israeli politics for many decades. Analysts and politicians have tried to address these problems by changing various elements of the electoral system. Some of these reforms have died in the legislative process, while some have been adopted and later reversed. No alteration has yet been implemented that has satisfied a critical mass of politicians and reformers.

As in any country, Israel's institutions, rules, and methods of voting have bounded the choices available to the electorate. In particular, the system of proportional representation has contributed to a proliferation of parties and electoral lists, which in turn has meant that no party or list has ever gotten a majority of seats (61 out of 120) in Israel's parliament, the Knesset. This has forced every government in Israel to be formed as a coalition of parties and lists, often making governing more difficult, as policies must be agreed to by several parties with divergent interests. Since 1949 Israel has had 34 governments, which means a new government every two years on average. From 1996 to 2015, Israel had seven general elections and one special election for Prime Minister only, leading to eight different governments. The regular tenure of a government is meant to be four years.

We begin this chapter with an outline of the development of the electoral system. The laws governing the conduct of elections, including their timing and the nature of the proportional representation system, follow. The process of participation—through a closed-list system built around a roster of candidates—is covered next. The chapter ends with a discussion of two electoral reforms that have had an effect on voting patterns: direct election for the Prime Minister and the raising of the electoral threshold.

THE DEVELOPMENT OF AN ELECTORAL SYSTEM

Israel's election laws are the product of four main developments: Jewish history in Europe, the development of the Zionist movement, adaptation to the British system, and the war into which Israel was born.

Alan Dowty writes that the Jewish experience in Europe forced the Jews to develop their own internal structures of governance.[1] Because they were viewed as outsiders to the national societies in which they lived—particularly in eastern Europe—they were constrained from full participation in national political life. Anti-Semitism also ensured that the Jews were excluded from the national political arena, while ongoing persecution and physical attacks forced the community to provide for its own protection. Most Jewish areas developed the *kehilla*, or community. As a form of political authority (populated primarily by men), the kehilla structured Jewish life in the absence of national authority. The kehilla governed aspects of taxation and resolution of disputes, and helped promote religious laws. The precise nature of kehilla governance varied across place and time, but it was normally of a consultative character, and by the eighteenth and nineteenth centuries in some places it was elected. By the time the Zionists set up communal institutions in the Yishuv, then, the Jewish community had experience with self-governance in the midst of a broader, and hostile, society.

Because it was subject to the authority of the non-Jewish states in which it operated, the Zionist movement adopted the voluntary character of the kehilla. The central institutions of the movement could only convince disparate communities to participate if each felt it could play a role in Zionist politics and governance. In addition, as a nationalist movement comprising Jews across the globe, early Zionist leaders accepted that constituencies were impractical. Elections based on proportional representation were considered the best way to achieve consensus and inclusivity among a globally dispersed population.

The Zionists also looked to Britain for support. As the preeminent world power at the beginning of the nineteenth century, London was involved in all major developments in global politics. It was given the Mandate for Palestine after World War I and thus directly controlled the territory in which the Zionists intended to establish their sovereignty. By the 1930s, too, many Zionists, such as Chaim Weizmann, leader of the British Zionists and later elder statesman of the movement, had established direct channels to British authorities. It seemed a natural progression to adapt the British parliamentary model to Zionist politics.

Finally, Israel's first leaders did not expect the Yishuv's electoral system to become the permanent Israeli system. But what had been a communal war between Jews and Arabs in Mandatory Palestine became an interstate war when Israel was established and a number of Arab state armies invaded. After the war was won, massive economic problems and the arrival of hundreds of thousands of immigrants from the Middle East and Europe meant that the state's priorities had to be development and absorption; there was little time to devote to detailed examination of how to change the political system. Under these conditions, disputes over what to replace the electoral system with quickly stalemated.

ELECTION LAWS

Israel does not have a written constitution but relies on a set of Basic Laws that have a higher legal status than regular laws. The electoral system is structured by the Basic Law: The Knesset, first passed in 1958, as well as by a series of election laws governing the electoral process. The Basic Law: The Knesset sets out the constitutional requirements for the conduct of elections and the right to vote. Section 4 states that "the Knesset shall be elected by general, national, direct, equal, secret and proportional elections, in accordance with the Knesset Elections Law." Most of these procedures govern other Western democracies as well; a proportional representation system operates only in some, such as Belgium, Germany, Poland, Italy, and Sweden. The other major difference from Western states is that Israel is not divided into separate voting districts; the entire country operates as a single constituency. This made sense given the small size of the population and the fact that the state's borders were never codified as a result of a lack of peace treaties at the end of the 1947–1949 War.

The Central Elections Committee (CEC) is a body composed of representatives of parties in the Knesset, chaired by a justice of the Supreme Court. It is formed by Members of Knesset after a general election for the purpose of conducting the following election; it therefore reflects the composition of the outgoing Knesset. This means the majority on the CEC comes from the majority in the Knesset. Its primary function is to ensure that elections are conducted freely and fairly, but another of its responsibilities is to approve or reject parties, lists, and candidates for the campaign. In 1984, the CEC banned *Kach* (Thus) from participating in future elections. Kach was a far-right party led by Rabbi Meir Kahane, founder of the Jewish Defense League in the United States, who had also served six months in an Israeli prison in 1980 for plotting "to commit a grave act of provocation on the Temple Mount." Because the party demanded that Arabs be stripped of their Israeli citizenship and prevented from marrying Jews, the CEC banned the party for incitement to racism. At the same time, the CEC disqualified the far-left Progressive List for Peace (PLP), a joint Jewish–Arab party, from running. The Supreme Court overturned both decisions, contending that the Basic Law: The Knesset had no provisions for banning parties on the basis of racism (Kach) or opposition to a Jewish state (the PLP, though it was unclear which of the party's actions or beliefs constituted that opposition). Kach won one seat in the 1984 election, and the PLP won two.

After a series of amendments, the Basic Law: The Knesset was brought into line with expectations about Israel as a Jewish and a democratic state, and to address both Jewish and Arab extremism. Section 7a of the Basic Law states that "a candidates' list shall not participate in elections to the Knesset . . . if the objects or actions . . . expressly or by implication, include one of the following:

1. negation of the existence of the State of Israel as a Jewish and democratic state;
2. incitement to racism;
3. support of armed struggle, by a hostile state or a terrorist organization, against the State of Israel."

The Basic Law: The Knesset is buttressed by the 1992 Parties Law, which includes the same stipulations for disqualification. This legislation is a little different from the Basic Law in that it can block registration of a party for "the rejection of Israel's *right* to exist as a Jewish and democratic state" (emphasis added). These two laws reflect the effort to set the boundaries of legitimate political discourse in a state trying to reconcile two types of identity (see Chapter 18).

The political makeup of the CEC also makes it a politicized body. With the rise of a neo-nationalist right in the late 2000s, the CEC used these laws to emphasize the Jewish facet of the state. At the behest of right-wing individuals on the committee, its focus has been almost completely on the Arab parties. In 2003 it voted to disqualify Balad and Ta'al from participating in the election at the same time it allowed Baruch Marzel, a former member of Kach, to run with a small far-right party. In 2009 the CEC voted to ban Balad and Ra'am–Ta'al, and in 2012 to disqualify Balad candidate Hanin Zoabi, from running. In 2015 it decided again to prohibit Zoabi and Marzel from the campaign. In each case, upon appeal the Supreme Court has overturned the CEC's ban.

Timing

Elections are to be held every four years, though they have been held both before and after that prescribed period. All of the elections in the 1990s, for instance, were held earlier than required. This can occur when the Knesset dissolves itself, usually because the government budget cannot be passed, because the coalition falls and cannot be replaced in the same Knesset, or because a majority of MKs decides that new elections are necessary. Alternatively, the Knesset can extend its mandate if specific circumstances warrant it. For example, in 1973 the election was pushed back from October to December because of the outbreak of the 1973 War.

Proportional Representation

The decision to rely on a proportional representation (PR) system entailed a clear trade-off. First-past-the-post systems, such as those used in Canada and the United States, usually produce stable governments, but they do not allow for as diverse representation. A PR system allows for more representation but makes governments more unstable. Israel is no exception to this general rule.

The entire country functions as a single district for voting purposes, and elections are conducted according to the rule of proportional representation. This means that parties and lists win an amount of seats in the Knesset directly related to the percentage of the popular vote they receive, so long as they pass a minimum vote threshold. A party that wins 20 percent of the vote, for example, will take roughly 20 percent of the seats in parliament. At first the vote threshold was set at 1 percent of the popular vote;[2] it was raised to 1.5 percent for the 1992 election, and then 2 percent for the 2006 election. In March 2014 it was increased to 3.25 percent.

Perfect proportionality does not, of course, exist, and so "excess" votes are allocated across the parties according to what is commonly called the d'Hondt system, but in Israel is known as the Bader–Ofer system after the two parliamentarians who proposed it (Yohanan Bader and Avraham Ofer). Surplus votes (votes for parties that pass the electoral threshold but do not add up to what is required for a full seat) are distributed according to a formula that favors parties that receive much greater numbers of votes over those that receive a smaller share, in recognition of their large gains in the election.

Since 1969 the law permits two lists to create "surplus" or "extra" vote agreements during an election, which allows them to share each other's surplus votes. First these votes are combined. If there are enough votes for only one seat, the party or list that won the greater amount of surplus votes will receive it. In the 2013 election, the following lists signed surplus agreements with each other: Labor and Yesh Atid; United Torah Judaism and Shas; Balad and Hadash; Bayit Yehudi and Likud–Beiteinu; and *Hatenua* and *Meretz*. In 2015 there were fewer such agreements, partly because there were fewer parties with a realistic chance to enter the Knesset, and partly because of ideological disputes. Surplus agreements were made between Likud and Bayit Yehudi; Yisrael Beiteinu and *Kulanu*; Zionist Union and Meretz; and United Torah Judaism and Shas. Votes that go to parties that do not cross the threshold are "wasted," because they are not allocated to any party.

PARTIES AND LISTS

Elections are contested by lists, or written slates of candidates. Chapter 9 discusses Israeli political parties in greater detail, but here Table 8.1 records the parties and lists that entered the Knesset as a result of the 2015 election. A list can be presented either by a political party or by a short-term electoral alliance between two or more parties. The latter is an agreement to run on a combined ticket for a specific election. It is not the same as an official merger, in which different parties fold into a single party. For example, in 1999, Labor ran on a list with *Gesher*, a small right-leaning party, and Meimad, a liberal Orthodox party, in an alliance called One Israel. In 2015 Labor and Hatenua ran on a joint ticket called the Zionist Union. The lists that are submitted to the Central Elections Committee must contain a ranked order of candidates. The big parties—those that are likely to do best in the polls—will include up to 120 candidates, marking 120 Knesset seats; smaller parties do not normally include that many slots.

Electoral lists are "closed"—voters must choose the entire slate, rather than individual candidates, and they cannot alter the order of or remove candidates' names from the list. The order that appears on the list determines which of a party's contenders will enter the Knesset. If a party wins 10 seats in the parliament, the first 10 names on the list will make it into the Knesset. Candidates who are placed near the top of the list, in what are termed "realistic" or "safe" positions, have a

Table 8.1 Parties/Lists in the Knesset, 2015

PARTY OR LIST	SEATS
Right-wing Camp	
Likud	30
Yisrael Beiteinu	6
Left-wing Camp	
Zionist Union[1]	24
Meretz	5
Arab Camp	
Joint List[2]	13
Religious Camp	
Bayit Yehudi	8
Shas	7
United Torah Judaism	6
Center	
Yesh Atid	11
Kulanu	10
Total	**120**

[1] The Zionist Union is an electoral alliance between Labor and Hatenua.
[2] The Joint List is an electoral alliance between Ra'am, Ta'al, Hadash, and Balad.

better chance of entering the Knesset than do those lower down. This can make the selection of candidates for a party's slate a fierce struggle in internal party elections and deliberations. The process can be even more competitive for electoral alliances. For their 2013 joint ticket, Likud and Yisrael Beiteinu had to agree on how to allocate the positions on the list and did so on the basis of each party's size and expected gains. The first spot belonged to the leader of Likud, Binyamin Netanyahu, while the second spot went to Yisrael Beiteinu head Avigdor Liberman. The rest of the first 10 spots were arranged as follows:

3: Likud
4: Yisrael Beiteinu
5: Likud
6: Likud
7: Yisrael Beiteinu
8: Likud
9: Likud
10: Yisrael Beiteinu

Each list is represented by a single Hebrew letter or combination of letters (up to four), which are often used as symbols of the party. The Labor Party has three letters that in Hebrew spell *Emet*, which means "truth." Voters enter a booth and select one piece of paper from a tray divided into boxes, each of which contains sheets of paper on which the letters symbolizing a different party or list are printed. That piece of paper is placed in an envelope, which is then put in a ballot box. Though perhaps more cumbersome than other forms of voting, this method makes accidental votes unlikely and the counting straightforward.

ELECTORAL REFORMS

While the electoral system allows for a wide representation of interests in the Knesset, the PR method combined with the low electoral threshold have made it difficult for parties to win a large enough plurality of seats to form a small coalition of parties—and no party has ever won a majority of seats. The closest any party or list has ever come to a majority was in 1969, when the Alignment, composed of Labor and Mapam, won 56 mandates. At only one other election has a list ever gotten over 50; otherwise, the highest number of seats has been in the 40s. Critics argue that this leads to coalition instability and a prioritization of politicking over good governance—and may even undermine democracy when, for example, voters' choices do not pass the threshold or are redistributed to other parties through the Bader–Ofer system. A number of electoral reforms have been proposed to address these concerns over the years, though only a few have ever been enacted by the Knesset.[3] Two in particular have had a major effect on the political system: the law for the direct election of the Prime Minister, and the raising of the electoral threshold.

Direct Election of the Prime Minister

The most significant reform to the electoral system was carried out between 1996 and 2001, when direct elections for Prime Minister took place alongside the regular elections for the Knesset.[4] Called the split-ticket or split-vote reform, this change reflected a widespread recognition that the political system had become too unstable as a result of the disproportionate power that small parties, particularly but not only the religious ones, wielded in coalition negotiations and subsequently around the Cabinet table. That it was later repealed indicates the widespread dissatisfaction with the effect of the reform and the recognition that more comprehensive changes were needed rather than piecemeal efforts in different areas.

Awareness of the instabilities built into the electoral system is longstanding, but the process of reform gained impetus as a result of problems in coalition building in the 1980s. The national unity government (NUG)[5] of 1984–1988 was formed because the big parties, Labor and Likud, wanted to avoid the demands of the small parties. A second NUG was built after the 1988 election, but it broke down by 1990 as a result of disagreement between Labor and Likud, and because Shimon Peres, the head of Labor, thought he could establish a Labor-led government without Likud. The quarrelsome nature of the subsequent negotiations, in which the religious parties played the two main parties off against each other, was too much for many observers. Several MKs pushed hard for electoral reform in order to avoid that kind of crass politics again, and many believed that direct elections for the Prime Minister would be a relatively easy reform to pass.

The bill was voted into law in March 1992, to come into effect at the next election. It served as an amendment to the Basic Law: The Government, though its second and third readings did not receive an absolute majority of 61 Knesset votes because many MKs did not show up. This is not unusual in either the Knesset or in other parliaments, but it was a foreshadowing of the law's lukewarm support. The new law stated simply that "the Prime Minister serves by virtue of his being elected in the national general elections, to be conducted on a direct, equal, and secret basis in compliance with The Election Law (The Knesset and The Prime Minister)" and followed that stipulation with specific rules regarding timing, eligibility, and the consequences of being unable to form a government. Under the new law, citizens were given two votes: one for the Knesset, based on the existing system of proportional representation, and one for Prime Minister, based on majoritarianism—the candidate had to receive more than half of the valid votes cast. If no one received the necessary amount of votes, a second round of voting between the top two vote-getters would be held.

The purpose of the law was to strengthen the executive by giving the Prime Minister a direct mandate from the people, to insert an element of more direct democracy into the electoral system, to remove the ability of the small parties to control the public agenda (or, as some critics put it, to blackmail the larger parties), and to rebuild public confidence in the political system. In addition, the law gave the Prime Minister the ability to dismiss the Knesset without its approval, even while the Knesset could still dissolve itself—what Arian, Nachmias, and Amir called a "balance of terror"[6]—in the hopes that this would force the parties in the Knesset to act more responsibly. The law was used in three elections: in 1996, 1999, and—a special election for Prime Minister only—2001. In each one a different Prime Minister was elected, and in many ways all three were referenda on the leadership of the incumbent. In this sense the law did increase accountability.

But for the most part the reform is widely considered to be a failure. The law had the opposite effect from what was intended: it weakened the Prime Minister vis-à-vis the parties and the Knesset. The impact was immediately obvious. The two largest parties, Labor and Likud, lost 10 seats in the 1996 election, and another 21 seats in 1999. Conversely, the size of the small sectarian parties grew. While this drop cannot be attributed solely to the electoral reform, it certainly played a role. First, the Prime Minister's party was weakened in the Knesset because voters understood they no longer had to vote for their preferred party if they wanted its leader to become Prime Minister. Second, the law strengthened smaller parties because voters could separate their preference for Prime Minister from their preference for a party. A citizen who wanted Binyamin Netanyahu to be Prime Minister but also wanted Shas to represent her interests in the Knesset could achieve both objectives at the same time. Third, the law changed to some extent the strategies of Likud and Labor, whose candidates were clearly the only real contenders for Prime Minister. Both parties focused extensively on their prime ministerial candidates, neglecting to some degree the race for the Knesset.[7] This contributed to the personalization of Israeli politics at the expense of issues.

In May 1998, a bill to repeal the direct election law passed its first reading (by a majority vote of 62–57; notably, an absolute majority had never voted *for* the direct elections bill), but it took another three years before it was successfully rescinded. Ariel Sharon, who won the special election for Prime Minister in February 2001, led the fight to annul the law. The last reading to implement the repeal passed by a vote of 72–37 in spring 2001, to come into effect at the next election.

Raising the Electoral Threshold

The second major reform has dealt with the electoral threshold—the percentage of the popular vote a list must receive in order to obtain seats in the Knesset. The number has been kept low in order to allow for as much representation of the population as possible. This has facilitated the participation of a large number of parties in elections, most of them representing narrow interests. It is normal for over 30 parties to contest elections, and for over 10 parties to gain entry into the legislature. The First Knesset (elected in 1949) and the Nineteenth Knesset (2013–2015) each included 12 parties. The Second Knesset (1951–1955), the Eleventh Knesset (1984–1988), the Twelfth Knesset (1988–1992), and the Fifteenth Knesset (1999–2003) each had 15 parties. The Twentieth Knesset (elected in 2015) has 10 parties or lists, one of which is a list that combines four parties (the Joint List), while another is a list that combines two parties (Zionist Union).

The low electoral threshold has facilitated the regular establishment of a fragmented Knesset and government. From 1951 to 1992, the threshold was 1 percent of the popular vote. That number was raised to 1.5 percent from 1992 to 2005, and after that to 2 percent. These increases had detractors, but opposition was overall muted.

The most recent increase, in March 2014, to 3.25 percent, on the other hand, was accompanied by fierce opposition. Opponents of the reform argued that those parties that did traditionally seek to play the big parties against each other—namely, the religious parties—were not the ones that would be affected by this increase, since they all regularly receive over 3.25 percent of the vote. Rather, the Arab parties would be the most affected. Of the three Arab parties in the Knesset at the time the reform was passed, two (Hadash and Balad) had received less than 3.25 percent of the popular vote in the 2013 election; only Ra'am–Ta'al had received more (see Table 8.2). This, critics continued, meant the new law was simply a way to undermine and constrain Arab representation in the parliament. They also contended that a higher threshold contradicts the Basic Law: The Knesset, which enshrines proportional representation.

Defenders of the law argued that other countries committed to a low threshold also have a higher minimum: Germany has a 5 percent threshold, while Norway and Sweden have a 4 percent threshold. They contended that the reform was necessary to ensure more genuine democracy. Just over 7 percent of the total vote in 2013 went to parties that did not pass the qualifying threshold, meaning that these citizens' votes were "wasted" and that they were not represented in the Knesset. A higher threshold would force these tiny parties to run as part of a larger whole, increasing the chance that their voters would obtain representation. Supporters noted that most of these wasted votes go to leftist parties of various types; if these

Table 8.2 Parties' and Lists' Percentage of the Popular Vote, 2013 and 2015 Elections

	2013			2015	
	PERCENTAGE	SEATS		PERCENTAGE	SEATS
Likud-Yisrael Beiteinu[1]	23.34	31	Likud	23.40	30
Yesh Atid	14.33	19	Zionist Union[2]	18.67	24
Labor	11.39	15	Joint List[3]	10.61	13
Bayit Yehudi	9.12	12	Yesh Atid	8.82	11
Shas	8.75	11	Kulanu	7.49	10
United Torah Judaism	5.16	7	Bayit Yehudi	6.74	8
Hatenua	4.99	6	Shas	5.74	7
Meretz	4.55	6	Yisrael Beiteinu	5.10	6
Ra'am-Ta'al[4]	3.65	4	United Torah Judaism	4.99	6
Hadash	2.99	4	Meretz	3.93	5
Balad	2.56	3			
Kadima	2.08	2			

[1] An electoral alliance between Likud and Yisrael Beiteinu.
[2] An electoral alliance between Labor and Hatenua.
[3] An electoral alliance between Ra'am, Ta'al, Hadash, and Balad.
[4] An electoral alliance between Ra'am and Ta'al.

Sources: Central Elections Committee, Final Official Results of the Elections to the 19th Knesset, http://www.knesset.gov.il/elections19/eng/list/results_eng.aspx; Central Elections Committee, Final Official Results of the Elections to the 20th Knesset, http://www.bechirot20.gov.il/election/English/kneset20/Pages/Results20_eng.aspx

votes could be channeled toward larger parties, it would strengthen the left-wing cluster against the right-wing camp in the Knesset. In the event, less than 5 percent of the 2015 vote went to parties that did not enter the Knesset. That percentage would have been even less, but the Shas party split, and a breakaway faction believed that it would pass the threshold if it ran separately; however, it only received 2.97 percent of the vote.

Finally, supporters insisted that the new threshold might have a positive effect on the Arab parties and Arab voters. In order to pass the threshold, these parties would have to cooperate—either in a combined list or a formal merger—thereby concentrating the Arab vote and leading to a larger, stronger list and more representation in the Knesset. Because the issue of Arab participation in the political system is fraught with concerns over majority–minority relations and questions about Israel's Jewish identity, organizations such as the Association for Civil Rights in Israel have suggested that if the threshold must be raised, then the Palestinian minority should have a lower threshold or be exempt from one altogether. This, such groups argue, would encourage greater participation and choice and is in line with systems in place in several European countries, such as Denmark, Poland, and Romania, that provide different thresholds for their minorities.[8] However, there has been little support for such measures in the Knesset. For their part, the

Arab parties did run together on a combined ticket in 2015 called the Joint List, and did increase their representation from 11 to 13 seats.

The issue of the setting of the electoral threshold has likely not been resolved. Ideas to raise it even higher have been floating around for many years, and there is an expectation among some that the 3.25 number is the beginning of a gradual increase over time. It is also widely recognized that the threshold is hardly the only structural problem of the political system and cannot by itself resolve the instabilities embedded therein.

SUMMARY

Israel's electoral system developed as a result of the Jewish experience in Europe and in the Yishuv. In many ways, then, it was a default option once Israel was established. Its election laws are also suited to Israel's complex society, and so while it has some similarities to the systems of other Western democracies, Israel's electoral structure contains a number of innovations.

Though many politicians and analysts have promoted reforms (David Ben-Gurion himself pushed early on for the establishment of a British-style parliamentary system), few have been carried out. There is great reluctance among many politicians to change something that has been in place for so long. Entrenched interests, particularly the smaller parties, are afraid that since most reforms are based on the assumption that there can be *too much* representation in the Knesset, they will be the ones who suffer most from any changes. Because reformers argue that many different elements of the system need to change, it is sometimes difficult to know where to begin. And, of course, there is competition among groups over different solutions. Finally, the negative experience of the direct election law has turned some people off from pursuing any more big changes.

Nonetheless, as evidenced by the recent raising of the electoral threshold, it is clear that there is interest in and a constituency for reform. At the very least, there is clearly a recognition that the system is not as effective as it could be. We should, then, expect electoral reform to remain on the public policy agenda.

KEYWORDS

electoral system, proportional representation, hyper-democracy, Central Elections Committee, competitive system, direct elections for Prime Minister, electoral threshold

NOTES

1. Alan Dowty, *The Jewish State: A Century Later*, updated ed. (Berkeley: University of California Press, 2001), 20–23.
2. Technically, the first general election that took place in Israel, in January 1949, was for a Constituent Assembly. It was structured by a very low electoral threshold of 0.8 percent. The next month the Constituent Assembly renamed itself the First Knesset. The first actual election to the Knesset occurred in 1951, by which time the threshold was already raised to 1 percent.

3. See Hanna and Abraham Diskin, "The Politics of Electoral Reform in Israel," *International Political Science Review* 16 (1995): 31–45; and Gideon Rahat, *The Politics of Regime Reform in Democracies: Israel in Comparative and Theoretical Perspective* (Albany: SUNY Press, 2008).

4. The law was modeled on an earlier reform at the municipal level, which saw mayors elected separately from their party's lists.

5. The term typically refers to a government composed of Likud and Labor, because they have usually been the largest parties and also sit on opposite ends of the political spectrum.

6. Asher Arian, David Nachmias, and Ruth Amir, *Executive Governance in Israel* (Houndmills, Basingstoke, Hampshire and New York: Palgrave, 2002), 7.

7. Ofer Kenig, "The 2003 Elections in Israel: Has the Return to the 'Old' System Reduced Party System Fragmentation?" *Israel Affairs* 11 (2005): 560–561.

8. Association for Civil Rights in Israel, "Position Paper on Raising the Electoral Threshold," September 29, 2013, http://www.acri.org.il/en/wp-content/uploads/2013/10/Electoral-Threshold-Position-Paper.pdf.

CHAPTER 9

꙼

Political Parties and the Party System

Political parties have long played a central role in Israeli politics—not just as organizations to articulate and promote specific political demands, but as vehicles for broader social, cultural, and educational development. This is the legacy of politics in the Yishuv era, when parties operated as self-contained communities for their members and were, as detailed in Chapter 3, movements more than simply political machines. In addition, during this period many parties emerged as a reflection of the multiple and varied streams and sub-streams of Zionism. The shift from a voluntary system to a compulsory one after 1948 helped entrench preexisting parties, as earning representation in the Knesset was now the only path to political power. At the same time, the independent ability of the parties to provide for their adherents declined as the Israeli state took over many of the activities the parties were once responsible for, while the expansion of civil society and, in the Arab sector, the growth of local governments as vehicles for resource distribution further diminished their influence.

The development and contemporary order of the Israeli party system can best be understood through three themes. First, the unstable structure of individual parties has contributed to a continuous series of splits and mergers among most of the parties that have existed in Israel's history. This instability has been facilitated by the low electoral threshold—the minimum percentage of the popular vote a party needs to enter the Knesset. Second, coexisting with this frequent reconstruction of individual parties has been a strong party system resting on four party camps, or clusters: left, right, religious, and Arab. Since the 1990s a somewhat vaguely defined fifth camp—the center—has emerged. Third, the dominance of the main left-wing and right-wing parties (Labor and Likud) until the mid-1990s ensured some measure of political predictability. But this began to change by the late 1990s, as these two parties contracted and a short-lived but serious challenge materialized from a third party, the centrist Kadima. While the two parties remained dominant in their respective clusters, a host of new parties, consistent challenges from the center, and a diffusion of the electorate's vote has diminished not only their representation in the Knesset, but also their ability to control the policy agenda.

This chapter explains the nature of the party system, focusing on the concept of the four clusters, and lays out the main parties in each one. All of these parties have emerged out of a long process of splits and mergers, breakups and reunions, and electoral alliances of varying lengths of time. It then discusses other types of party camps—centrists and special issue parties. It concludes with a typology of party organizations and a discussion of the process of leadership selection.

PARTY CLUSTERS

The party system today continues to rest on four main clusters, or camps—left, right, religious, and Arab. Each camp groups together several parties that share ideas about foreign policy, economic policy, ideology, and conceptualizations of Israeli identity, though they often still disagree over the best policies to address these issues. Two out of the four clusters (left and right) have a primary party at their center around which the other, smaller, ones orbit.

The four-cluster arrangement is not a perfect division. Beginning in the 1990s, as Labor and Likud moved closer to each other on some issues (agreeing, for example, on a free market economy and general acceptance of the idea of a Palestinian state), the center point of the political spectrum shifted, making it easier for parties to straddle the middle. New parties emerged that shared ideas with more than one cluster, blurring the lines between them. Nevertheless, the categorization is still useful for analytical and descriptive purposes, since parties within each cluster tend to gravitate toward one another during the bargaining leading up to the formation of coalition governments and votes on legislation. We can identify a number of ideas and policy priorities that tie the parties together within each cluster.

LEFTIST PARTIES

Left-wing parties in Israel are defined by their socialist character, that is, the belief that government should be a major player in the economy, should regulate economic activity, and should oversee a broad safety net for society composed of various welfare services, such as pensions, health care, and unemployment insurance. They were not distinguished from other parties on the basis of foreign policy in Israel's first few decades. Indeed, while most of the leftist factions were more pragmatic on the issue of partitioning the Land of Israel than the right-wing parties, some did believe that all of the territory belonged to Israel and actively supported settlements after 1967. Others, including the dominant Mapai, were quite hawkish and advocated for the type of aggressive, even militarist, foreign policy often associated today with right-wing parties.

The Six-Day War and the capture of east Jerusalem and the West Bank aroused nationalist sentiments across the political spectrum, leading even leftist groups that had advocated for dividing the land to argue for holding on to portions of the West Bank and all of Jerusalem. Not until the 1980s and early 1990s did these preferences decline within the cluster, and by the 2000s the remaining leftist parties were unambiguously calling for the establishment of a Palestinian state that would include almost all of the West Bank and Gaza Strip (with land swaps often being proposed to compensate the Palestinian state for the remaining territory that Israel would retain). In addition to a willingness to remove some or all settlements in the occupied territories, left-wing parties are now also known for being more open to negotiation with the Palestinians and supportive of an independent Palestinian state in the WBG in the near term—what is sometimes referred to as a "dovish" foreign policy.

The party at the core of the left-wing cluster is the Labor Party. This party has been around in one form or another since 1930, when Mapai was formed (see Chapter 3), though its consolidation took a number of years.[1] The dominant party in the political system until 1977, it remained a contender for power through the 1980s and the early 1990s, always winning over 40 seats in the Knesset (except for the 1988 election, when it received 39). Its fortunes began to decline in the 1996 election, when it won only 34 seats—its worst showing since 1977. The party continued to fall at the polls, receiving 26 seats in 1999 (as part of an alliance with two other parties), 19 in 2003 and 2006, 13 in 2009, and 15 in 2013. In 2015 it won 24 seats as part of the Zionist Union, a joint ticket with Hatenua—a party that itself had lured away Labor MKs when it was established in 2012.

One major reason for Labor's decline was party infighting as contenders for leadership repeatedly challenged each other. In the beginning Labor had an undisputed leader in David Ben-Gurion, and the party was strong enough that it consistently won a plurality of Knesset seats. But a series of events beginning in 1954 undercut the party, causing it considerable damage and haunting it for years afterward. This was the Lavon Affair, which lasted from 1954 through the early 1960s. In 1953, Ben-Gurion retired from politics and was replaced as Prime Minister by Moshe Sharett. Pinhas Lavon succeeded Ben-Gurion as Defense Minister. By the next year rumors began swirling about a plot by Israeli intelligence to disrupt Egyptian–American relations. It was said that Israel had helped a handful of Egyptian Jews try to blow up a number of Egyptian and American buildings in Cairo in hopes that Washington would blame the attacks on Egyptian radicals, which in turn would convince the United States that Egypt was too unstable to be a reliable ally. Thirteen members of the group involved in this plot were caught, and two were executed. Lavon proclaimed that he had not authorized the operation, but in the face of testimony from two of the party's "young Turks," Shimon Peres and Moshe Dayan, and pressure from party leaders, he was forced to resign. Ben-Gurion returned to replace him, and eventually replaced Sharett as well.

Five years later Lavon came forward claiming he had evidence that proved his innocence.[2] Unwilling to revisit the issue, Ben-Gurion decided not to consider Lavon's information. Lavon then went public, going directly to the Knesset Foreign Affairs Committee. Ben-Gurion convened an inquiry, which found the evidence to be inconclusive. Further efforts by party leaders and senior officials to deal with the matter were resisted by Ben-Gurion. After the 1961 election, these tensions could no longer be contained, and the party split along factional and generational lines. Ben-Gurion, who had led the party for decades and was considered the founding father of the country, left in 1963, taking a younger generation of officials with him, including Peres and Dayan, to form *Rafi* (an acronym for Israeli Workers List). Rafi won 10 seats in the 1965 election, largely on the strength of Ben-Gurion's and the young Turks' name recognition. The party later joined the Labor-led government (though Ben-Gurion stayed out) and eventually merged back into Labor.

By then the foundations for a Labor loss were already in place, and in 1977 the party was defeated at the polls. For the first time in the country's history, Labor did not form the government; a right-wing party, Likud, did (see the following section). Though Labor's share of Knesset seats did not drop all that much in the 1980s, Likud remain dominant.

Labor rebounded in the 1992 election, winning 44 seats to Likud's 32, mostly on the strength of the appeal of its leader, Yitzhak Rabin, complaints about the Likud government's management of the economy, and frustration at Likud leader Yitzhak Shamir's obsessive focus on settlements. But the murder of Rabin in 1995 by an Orthodox Jew who opposed his policies toward the Palestinians was a blow from which the party never recovered. Since then the party has been convulsed by internecine struggles, leading to the regular replacement of its leader. The constant change at the top has undermined its ability to set coherent policy and made it look feckless to the public. Between 1995 and 2015 the party had seven leaders,[3] two of whom were elected twice; the longest tenure was about four years, with most lasting only two. This changeability also made it easier for Likud to buy the support of specific Labor leaders and bring them into a Likud-led government as junior partners, undermining the party's ability to serve as a serious and viable alternative. For example, in January 2011, while Labor served in a Likud government, a number of Labor MKs agitated for the party to leave the coalition. Labor leader Ehud Barak, who was Defense Minister under Prime Minister Binyamin Netanyahu, did not want to leave the government. Rather than drop out of the coalition and maintain the unity of the party, Barak and four other MKs resigned from Labor and formed a new party, *Atzmaut* (Independence), for the sake of remaining in the government. This left Labor with a rump eight-seat caucus in the Knesset. Atzmaut dissolved itself before the 2013 election.

The 2000s were particularly difficult times for Labor for other reasons as well, especially as it moved away from its "traditional" economic and foreign policy agendas. The need to tame hyperinflation in the 1980s first prompted Labor to shift away from its commitment to a state-run economy in an effort to cut back on government expenditures. By the 1990s, Labor had all but given up its socialist agenda in favor of supporting a market-oriented economy. This made it harder for the party to distinguish itself on economic policy from Likud.

In the mid-2000s the party seemed to be inching its way back to its socialist origins with the election of Amir Peretz as party chairman (November 2005–June 2007). Peretz had been head of the Histadrut, Israel's giant labor federation, and in that position had often called for general strikes to improve conditions and pay for workers in different areas. In September 2011, Shelly Yacimovich, a former journalist and Labor parliamentarian, was elected leader of the party and upheld its focus on social and economic issues, particularly in the aftermath of the social justice protests that erupted throughout Israel in July 2011. She also recruited several high-profile Labor candidates who were known for their left-wing positions on such issues.[4] The party's 2013 political platform made no mention of foreign policy, the peace process, or settlements.

The concentration on socio-economic conditions had a negative effect on Labor's electoral fortunes, because it undermined its claim to be the premier party representing the peace camp. By the time Labor leader Yitzhak Rabin signed the Oslo Accords on September 13, 1993, the party had been moving in the direction of negotiation with the PLO and tolerance for the idea of an end to Israeli control in the West Bank for at least a decade. The Oslo process, and Likud's fierce struggle against it, solidified Labor as the party of negotiation and Palestinian independence, particularly as the Israeli public became more tolerant of these positions.[5]

But under the leadership of Peretz and Yacimovich, the party shifted away from these issues. Yacimovich, in particular, pulled Labor so far away from a discussion of foreign affairs during the 2013 election campaign that the party lost several Knesset seats from its traditional base to parties that did talk about foreign policy and the peace process: Meretz and Hatenua. At the same time, Likud's opposition to a Palestinian state has been diminishing, bringing it closer to Labor. A backlash against Yacimovich's silence on foreign affairs (along with criticisms that she was too authoritarian) contributed to the move to eject her from the leadership position. Isaac Herzog was elected chairman in November 2013 in part on his promise to reorient Labor back toward the peace process. Yet he has not distinguished the party from Likud when it comes to relations with the Palestinians all that much either. Even as he has criticized Likud leader Netanyahu, he has also publicly supported many of the Netanyahu government's foreign policies, without presenting alternate ideas. While Labor has moved closer to Likud, smaller parties within the cluster have maintained their ideological purity and policy differences and thus have been able to siphon off votes from Labor. For instance, during the 2014 Gaza war, Herzog defended the Prime Minister's decisions, while Zehava Gal-On, of the smaller leftist party Meretz, actively criticized the government for preferring violence over peace.

In addition to Labor, other socialist parties were formed during the Yishuv period and continued into the state era. In January 1948, a few months before the state was proclaimed, several small Marxist parties merged into Mapam, a Hebrew acronym for United Workers Party. Considerably to the left of Labor, Mapam adopted a strong pro-Soviet, even pro-Stalin, position into the early 1950s. It maintained a commitment to socialist values and government intervention in the economy even when Labor began to drift from the same commitment in the 1980s and 1990s. It did well in the 1949 election, winning 19 seats and becoming the second-largest party after Mapai; subsequently, its appeal declined, and, except when it joined an electoral alliance with Labor, it never achieved so many seats again. In 1992 Mapam aligned with three other small parties to form Meretz (a Hebrew acronym that also translates to "vigor"); a few years later the merger was formalized, and the independent parties disappeared.

Meretz remains the only political alternative to Labor on the Jewish left. The party defines itself as social-democratic, supports a clear separation between religion and state, and advocates for a renewed peace process and independent Palestinian state. Though the party has a small, devoted following and can expand its appeal on socio-economic issues and on its opposition to settlements, without a strong Labor, there is little chance Meretz can join the government. It is too ideological for any of the right-wing parties on most of the major issues, with perhaps the exception of the separation of religion and state. Its electoral fortunes have generally declined since the early 1990s, in part because centrist parties have drawn away some of its support. In 1992 it won 12 seats in parliament; in 1996, nine; and in 1999, 10. In the 2000s it never won more than six seats, with its lowest showing in 2009, when it ran as part of a joint list, New Movement–Meretz, and only received three mandates. In 2015 it won five seats.

RIGHTIST PARTIES

While the left-wing cluster served as the anchor of the political system from 1948 to 1977, the right-wing camp assumed dominance thereafter and has maintained it ever since. From 1948 until the formation of Likud in 1973, the right in Israel was divided into several small parties according to issue. Some, like Herut, focused more on issues of identity and foreign policy and held to maximal demands for the borders of the Jewish state. These parties emphasized an aggressive security policy. Others, such as the Liberal Party, focused on economic policy, promoting a free market system and working to scale back government involvement in the economy (though some factions were more conciliatory toward Labor). Both sets of parties shared a secular orientation with the left-wing parties but were broadly seen as more sympathetic to the demands of the religious communities and less fervently secular than their leftist counterparts.

Those that focused on identity placed greater emphasis on Jewish nationalism and the Land of Israel either for historical or for biblical reasons (indeed, they were often referred to, and liked to call themselves, the "national camp"). They were also generally suspicious of the Christian world and mistrusted both the Arabs and the West. Herut leader Menachem Begin, for example, often referred in his speeches on foreign policy to the Holocaust, which for him served as Israel's orientation point. These differences from the left-wing parties became starker after 1967, when Israel captured the West Bank and eastern Jerusalem and began expanding the Jewish population in those areas, and particularly by the 1980s as Labor and other left-wing parties drifted toward a more dovish foreign policy.

Likud is the largest party in the rightist cluster, putting it at the center of the right-wing universe.[6] It has also served as a catchall party to challenge Labor, because it has generally merged parties with economic priorities, parties with a more hawkish bent in foreign policy, and parties with a vaguer policy agenda but a clear opposition to the dominant left-wing parties. Its core faction, Herut (Freedom), emerged out of the Revisionist Zionist movement during the Yishuv period. As such, it long held a maximalist interpretation of the Balfour Declaration and the Palestine Mandate, rejecting any division of the biblical Land of Israel. Though Herut was never a serious challenge to Labor, it was an attractive political home for many voters who appreciated its ideological agenda.

Other rightist parties that were more concerned with economic policy included the General Zionists. Originally founded in 1922, this was a catchall party composed of several nonaffiliated centrist, free enterprise Zionist groups. Its policy platform was focused on promoting free market capitalism within Israel, in direct contrast to the socialism that Mapai represented. The party peaked at 20 seats in the Knesset in 1951, but fell to 13 and then to eight seats in the following elections. In 1961 it merged with the Progressive Party, another small economically right party, to form the Liberal Party. The Liberals and Herut each won 17 seats in the 1961 election, spurring both to realize they could not hope to challenge Labor's dominance on their own. In 1965 they formed a joint list called *Gahal* (the Hebrew acronym for Herut–Liberal Bloc), which won 26 seats in both 1965 and 1969. The unification process among the right continued thereafter, culminating with the establishment of the Likud (which means "consolidation") in 1973. From that point on Likud has been the dominant party on the right and the only serious challenger to Labor for the ability to form the government, except for the 2006–2009 period, when Kadima briefly became a major player.

Within Likud, the Liberals and Herut initially dominated, with the former's economic policy and the latter's priorities regarding the West Bank and Gaza, settlements, and a hawkish foreign policy becoming the official platform. Herut had been somewhat of a populist party, which—despite its commitments to free enterprise—necessitated some government intervention in the economy. For a time this led to clashes with the Liberals, but by the 1990s, with the ascendance of Binyamin Netanyahu within the party, economic populism was no longer prominent.

The major shift within Likud occurred after the death of Begin in 1983, though it did not become apparent until the 2000s. Begin had rejected recognition of the Arab community as deserving of special minority rights. For Begin, Israel was—indeed, had to be—a Jewish state. Yet he shared with the founder of Revisionist Zionism, Vladimir Ze'ev Jabotinsky, a commitment to classical liberal ideas of individual civil rights. He certainly emphasized a more tribal division of Israel into two communities—Jewish and Arab, but with greater recognition for the Jewish majority—but he believed sincerely that Israel's Arab citizens should be accorded political rights and not be purposely marginalized (though that is what occurred in practice as Begin focused on foreign policy and the settlement enterprise).

Under Begin's leadership, Likud was nationalist and maximalist, but it was not chauvinist. He bequeathed to Likud the necessary political space so that by the 1990s a crop of "Likud princes" had emerged within the party who were committed to a liberal policy of tolerance toward Palestinian citizens of Israel. This group (many of whom were the children of the founders of Herut) included his son Benny Begin, Dan Meridor, Ehud Olmert, and Reuven Rivlin (elected as President of the state in 2014). Though the party remained attached to the concept of the Land of Israel, it gradually came to accept that some limitations on Israel's ability to hold on to all of it were inevitable. Begin's agreement to evacuate Jewish settlements in the Sinai was the precursor to this acceptance, but after the Oslo process began, Likud—reluctantly and grudgingly, to be sure—did not overturn the Accords and did implement some of the subsequent agreements to redeploy from parts of the West Bank. By the beginning of the 2000s, most MKs of the party had come to accept that some form of Palestinian state was likely, though they argued the timing of it should be subject to changes in Palestinian policy and attitudes. Over the course of the 2000s, though, the party moved away from the pragmatism that marked it in the late 1990s and became more ideological as a result of generational changes, a renewed emphasis on Jewish nationalist identity, and the deeply felt insecurity and mistrust generated by the Second Intifada and continuing rocket attacks on Israeli civilians.

The November 2012 primaries to determine the order of candidates on Likud's election list were an important landmark in this process. Most of the princes, with the exception of Rivlin, were either ousted or pushed down on the list by the party membership and were replaced by a cohort of younger, more radical candidates who are actively committed to full Israel sovereignty over the West Bank, are intolerant of even Jewish critics of the state, and do not think the Arab minority should be given equal communal rights in the Jewish state. Their preference, reflected in the bills they have promoted in the government and in the Knesset, is to elevate the Jewish identity of the state at the expense of Arab minority rights.[7] This group includes Gideon Sa'ar,[8] Danny Danon, Ze'ev Elkin, Tzipi Hotovely, Yariv Levin, Miri Regev, and Moshe Feiglin.[9] The 2015 primary returned some of these candidates to higher spots (Regev, for instance, won fifth place), and others to nearby slots (Danon, for example, was moved from sixth to tenth place).

Under the influence of the new nationalists, the party has served as a constraint on Prime Minister Netanyahu's policymaking, particularly in foreign affairs. A pragmatic opportunist, Netanyahu has given indications that he is prepared to recognize some form of Palestinian self-determination in the West Bank.[10] Yet even this position is constantly challenged by the radicals, which has led to a contest for control over Likud's governing bodies (described later).

Beginning in the 1980s, a number of smaller, far-right parties were established to represent the old rightist opposition to any reduction in Israeli control over the territories. It was a Likud government that signed a peace treaty with Egypt that necessitated Israeli withdrawal from the Sinai, including the Jewish settlements there, and Likud leaders in the 2000s came to accept the idea of a Palestinian state in the WBG. *Tehiya* (Revival), *Tzomet* (Crossroads), Kach, *Moledet* (Homeland), and *Ichud Leumi* (National Union) won a handful of seats in this period, with the single largest win being Tzomet's eight seats in 1992.[11] Eventually these parties were forced to run or merge with each other in various elections or risk dropping below the electoral threshold. None of them was able to seriously challenge Likud's position, but they were able to draw away votes from it.

At the same time, the emergence of Shas (a religious party) in the 1980s, a string of centrist parties populated by right-leaning MKs in the 1990s and 2000s, and Yisrael Beiteinu in 2006 combined to weaken Likud, contributing to the party's poor showing in 1999 (when it won only 19 seats) and 2006 (12 seats). The establishment of Kadima siphoned off both Knesset members and voters from Likud, undermining it for the next two election cycles. The appearance of centrist or center-right parties in 2013 also contributed to a general decline in strength. That year Likud ran on a joint ticket with Yisrael Beiteinu, winning a total of 31 seats, 20 of which belonged to Likud and 11 to Yisrael Beiteinu. It was an uncomfortable alliance, and the two reverted to their independent status in July 2014. In 2015 the party seemingly bounced back, winning 30 seats on its own, largely at the expense of the other right-wing parties.

Two other parties that have played an important role within the right-wing camp are *Yisrael B'aliyah* (loosely translated as Israel for Immigration) and Yisrael

Beiteinu. Yisrael B'aliyah was formed in 1996 by prominent former Soviet refusenik Natan Sharansky. It won seven seats in the 1996 election, six in 1999, and two in 2003. After that it folded into Likud. Yisrael Beiteinu was established as a replacement for Yisrael B'aliyah in 1999. A nationalist party that has campaigned to the right of Likud, it sees the Arab minority as a threat to the Jewish character of the state. Party leader Avigdor Liberman, for example, has long promoted a plan to exchange pieces of Israeli territory with a significant concentration of Arabs to an independent Palestinian state in return for annexing large settlement blocs in the West Bank. Under his plan, the Arabs to be moved will not have the option of remaining Israeli citizens. When Labor MK Raleb Majadele, an Arab Muslim, became Science and Technology Minister in 2007—the first Muslim to join the government—a Yisrael Beiteinu MK called it a "blow to Zionism."[12] But unlike Likud, the party supports withdrawing from parts of the West Bank and Gaza. Yisrael Beiteinu won only four seats in its first year, ran on a joint ticket with a smaller right-wing party in 2003 and won only seven seats, then peeled away and jumped to 11 seats in 2006 and 15 in 2009. It ran on a joint ticket with Likud in 2013; the list won 31 seats, with 20 going to Likud and 11 to Yisrael Beiteinu. In 2015 it dropped to six seats.

Because both their leaders and their voter base are immigrants from the former Soviet Union (FSU), both Yisrael B'aliyah and Yisrael Beiteinu are commonly referred to as "Russian parties" or immigrant lists. But apart from aiming to reduce haredi Jewish control over personal status issues, their policy platforms have not generally prioritized issues important to the Russian community.[13] They have adopted more general right-wing positions on economic and foreign policy similar to those held by Likud. This made it easy, for example, for Yisrael Beiteinu to run with Likud in 2013.

RELIGIOUS PARTIES

Today the religious cluster contains two haredi (ultra-Orthodox) lists (United Torah Judaism, which is an alliance between two factions, and Shas) and one Religious Zionist party, Bayit Yehudi.

To understand the role of religious parties in Israel, it is important to understand the religious conceptualization of Jewish history. Its modern arc is divided into two broad periods: exile and redemption. Exile refers to the destruction of the Jewish Temple in 70 CE and the dispersal of the Jews across the world; redemption is the period in which the Jews will return to the Land of Israel and rebuild their Temple. It is at this point that the religious parties diverge. Haredi parties are non-Zionist and believe that human hands cannot make the period of exile end; that, they contend, will happen when the Messiah returns through God's own plan. Religious Zionists believe that the State of Israel is a messianic, redemptive vehicle even if it has been created by human hands. Indeed, it is imperative that humans continue the process of redemption, since this is—in their interpretation—part of God's plan.

All of the religious parties share a commitment to a prominent role for Judaism in public life. A secondary priority is to obtain state resources for their communities and supporters, which for the haredi parties means funds for their education systems and social welfare programs, and for Religious Zionists entails subsidies to continue the settlement enterprise.

Nevertheless, the religious parties are not the same. Each represents a different ideological, religious, and ethnic segment of Israeli society. This makes it more difficult to identify a core party in the religious camp today. For a long time it was the National Religious Party (commonly known by its Hebrew acronym Mafdal), which frequently served in Labor's coalition and, after 1977, helped to tip coalition bargaining in favor of Likud. But by the 1980s the NRP's status was challenged by Shas, and by the 1990s it had declined so much from its previous position that it was winning only a handful of seats in elections. The party continued to fade throughout the 2000s as it broke apart under the stress of factional infighting, and in 2008 it was absorbed into Bayit Yehudi.

A newer version of Bayit Yehudi won 12 seats in 2013 but declined to eight in 2015 as many voters shifted to Likud. The party is a good example of the difficulty of placing some parties in specific clusters but can be roughly located in the overlap between the rightist and the religious camps (see Figure 9.1). Composed primarily of Religious Zionists, with a strong base in settler communities in the West Bank, it has under the leadership of Naftali Bennett (who won the party leadership race

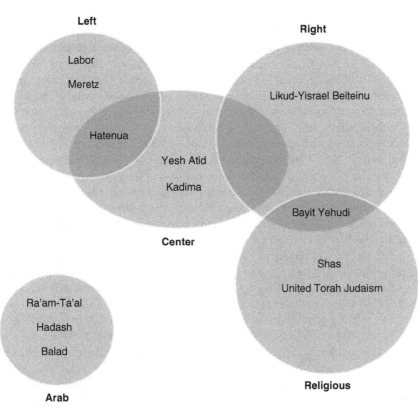

Figure 9.1 Party camps in Israel after the 2013 election

in November 2012) worked hard to appeal to the English-speaking community and to nonreligious Zionist Jews by advocating for the Jewish middle class and reinvigorating Jewish identity. Ayelet Shaked, a prominent secular woman in the party, has helped promote this image, as has Bennett's own public persona—he lives in a Tel Aviv suburb rather than the West Bank and talks often about economic policy. The party's 2013 platform declared the party's mission to be "to restore the Jewish-Zionist essence to the State of Israel and its people" and to settle "all parts of the state"— including Judea, Samaria, and the Jordan Valley.

The party takes a hard line on policy toward the Palestinians. During the 2014 Gaza war Bennett both publicly and in government discussions pressed for a broader invasion of Gaza to destroy Hamas. The party actively supports the expansion of settlements, and Bennett has promoted a plan to annex 60 percent of the West Bank where Jewish settlements are located and to give Palestinians who live there autonomy. This attachment to the Land of Israel and to support for the state has helped divide the religious camp. For instance, while many Religious Zionists do not believe in giving up any settlements, former Chief Rabbi Ovadia Yosef, spiritual guide to Shas, once proclaimed that withdrawing from biblical lands is permissible if it would help save lives. The cluster also split during the coalition negotiations after the 2013 election, when Bennett successfully blocked the haredi parties from joining the government, and subsequently when Bayit Yehudi worked with a secular party, Yesh Atid, to make conscription compulsory for the haredi community.

The non-Zionist haredim are represented by United Torah Judaism and Shas. UTJ emerged as a result of a series of splits and mergers between haredi parties. In the first decades of Israel's existence, the haredi community was represented by Agudat Yisrael and its socialist counterpart, *Poalei Agudat Yisrael* (Agudat Yisrael Workers). The party contained both Hasidic Jews—Jews who follow a more mystical-spiritual practice of religion—and haredi followers of the Lithuanian tradition, which focuses more on Talmud study as the path to holiness. Tensions over how to divide party positions between the two groups, underlain by theological differences, boiled over. In 1988, Rabbi Eliezer Shach, one of Agudat Yisrael's most prominent Ashkenazi rabbis, took his Lithuanian faction out of the party and formed *Degel HaTorah* (Banner of the Torah) to exclude Hasidic representation. The party did poorly in the 1988 election, winning only two seats. After that, the two parties patched up their differences and agreed to run on a joint list, UTJ. The list has consistently won between four and seven seats ever since.

Agudat Yisrael also split along ethnic and ideological lines, facilitated by personal antipathy between the party's rabbinical leaders. Because the party had long been dominated by Ashkenazi Jews, Mizrachi Jews had often felt marginalized. In 1984, under pressure from growing discontent, Rabbi Shach encouraged Ovadia Yosef to lead a faction of Mizrachi rabbis out of Agudat Yisrael to form a new party, Shas (the acronym for Sephardi Torah Guardians). Yosef became the party's spiritual leader; for all intents and purposes, his decisions were final. Because Shas was led by Mizrachim, it was immediately able to claim representation of the Sephardi and Mizrachi community, even those who were not haredi. The party won four seats in the 1984 election and six in 1988 and in 1992. By the mid-1990s Shas was able to produce results for its voters by successfully pitting Labor and

Likud against each other in bids for its support. Riding a wave of popular support, the party won 10 seats in 1996 and 17 in 1999—more than the NRP had ever gotten. By the 2000s its support had dropped a little as a number of smaller parties that straddled the right-wing and religious camps were established to compete for its voters. From 2003 to 2013 Shas won either 11 or 12 seats.

In 2015 the party fell to seven seats, mostly as a result of an internal struggle for control. In the 1990s Aryeh Deri, a brilliant young rabbi and a favorite of Ovadia Yosef, had become the political head of the party and played a critical role in its electoral success. In 2000 Deri was convicted of accepting bribes while in office and sentenced to three years in prison (he served 22 months). Deri was known to be charismatic and tolerant, and he had worked to spread the party's appeal beyond the Mizrachi religious community. In his absence Yosef appointed Eli Yishai party leader. Yishai had a very different personality than Deri and became known for his inflammatory statements about Palestinians, African migrants, and others. He took a hard line on foreign policy and the peace process, bringing him much closer to Likud's position than Deri had been. In 2013 Deri returned to politics. Unwilling to eject Yishai, Yosef decided to split the leadership of the party between the two and another Shas MK, Ariel Atias. This divided the party into two camps.

When Yosef died in October 2013, the two leaders engaged in an open contest. When Deri appeared to gain the upper hand at the end of 2014, Yishai announced he was leaving Shas to form a new party. He subsequently created the *Yachad* (Together) list with a small far-right party composed of hardline nationalists and former disciples of Meir Kahane. In the 2015 election Yachad did not pass the electoral threshold, but it did siphon off a considerable number of votes from Shas. Combined with a dent in the party's allure as a result of the absence of Yosef, this caused Shas to drop to seven seats. The last time the party received such a low number of mandates was in 1992.

Another interesting development within Shas has been the effort to expand the role of women in the party. An attempt to place women on the electoral list was blocked, but Yosef's daughter Adina Bar-Shalom and Deri's wife, Yaffa Deri, are currently heading an advisory council within Shas to address this and other issues.

This move within Shas was part of a larger effort by a number of haredi women to play a more direct role in politics. In 2015, for the first time, a party led by and for haredi women was established. Called *B'zchutan: Haredi Women Making a Change*, its focus was on issues of concern to haredi women, such as support for single mothers, spousal abuse, and help in obtaining divorce in the face of rabbinical opposition. The party received only 1,802 votes in the election, not enough to pass the threshold. It is not clear how effective these efforts will be in the near term, but they have certainly helped bring attention to the status of women in the haredi political world.

ARAB PARTIES

The nature of political representation in the Arab sector has changed over time. In the first years of the state, the Arab community was viewed primarily as a potential fifth column and was subjected to military administration until 1966.

The community was also unfamiliar with and suspicious of the new Jewish state and its democratic practices. At the same time, Labor governments were interested in facilitating some Arab presence in the political arena. The Labor Party thus established a series of "satellite" parties—parties composed of Palestinian Israelis that ostensibly represented Arab interests but in reality mostly followed Labor's lead rather than taking an independent line. It was not until the mid-1960s that a prominent independent Arab party emerged, and not until the 1980s and 1990s that more competitive communal politics developed. By then a younger generation of Arab citizens, better educated and more comfortable with the Israeli political system than their forebears, were mobilized, leading to the establishment of a number of independent Arab parties, all non- or anti-Zionist and committed to enhancing the status of their ethno-national community.

In 1965 the Israeli Communist Party split over the question of recognizing the State of Israel as a Jewish state. The Arab members of the party left to form Rakah, though a few Jewish politicians joined them. This opened the door to an independent Arab presence at the national political level.[14] In the next three elections Rakah won three or four seats, eventually merging with a number of small far-left parties into Hadash, in which it remains the primary force. Hadash is commonly referred to as an Arab party, though it does have a tiny number of Jewish members and one Jewish MK. The party advocates for a redistribution of resources to ensure equality between Jewish and Arab citizens, in keeping with its Marxist-socialist worldview, though its rhetoric and pronouncements have increasingly been cast in terms of Palestinian nationalism. Up until 2015, the party regularly took between three and five seats in elections.

As the Palestinian community in Israel became increasingly politicized, the independent parties it established began to promote a more assertive and confident political agenda. Today three more such parties have emerged. They share a commitment to ending discrimination against Palestinian citizens of Israel, an equal distribution of government resources to both the Jewish and the Arab sectors, and more autonomy for their communities. And they have adopted a more nationalist politics, calling for full communal rights for the Arab sector on the basis of its status as an indigenous minority. Taken together, these aims translate into an anti-Zionist agenda.

In 1996 Ra'am was established, comprising the Arab Democratic Party and some elements of the Islamic Movement. The party performed moderately well in the election that year, winning four seats, a number that increased to five in 1999 but dropped to two in 2003. After its poor showing that year, it joined a list with Ta'al, which won four seats in each of the next elections (2006, 2009, 2013). The list represents the religious and nationalist segments of the Arab community in Israel. Its most prominent leader, Ahmad Tibi (a former advisor to the Palestinian Authority), best represents the conflicted feelings about Israel held by many Arabs. He is known for his fiery rhetoric against racism and discrimination in the Israeli state and has publicly flirted with anti-Zionism, but he does not call for an end to Israel. He is also known for his commitment to democratic norms and his awareness of the Jewish position on Jewish sovereignty. His 2010 Knesset speech marking the Holocaust, for example, is widely considered to have been particularly moving; President Reuven Rivlin said it was "one of the best speeches [about the

Holocaust] he has ever heard in the plenum."[15] In January 2015, Ra'am–Ta'al broke apart its alliance and reverted to two independent parties.

The other Arab party in Israeli politics is Balad, which is considered to be the most radical and nationalist of the cluster. It explicitly supports a single state in Israel-Palestine, without priority given to either its Jewish or its Arab citizens. Its previous leader, Azmi Bishara, was accused of consorting with and giving comfort to Israel's enemies when he visited Lebanon and had contact with Hezbollah; he has since moved to Qatar to escape prosecution in Israel. Bishara ran for Prime Minister in 1999, before pulling out and throwing his support to Ehud Barak at the last minute.

The role of the Arab parties in Israeli politics is complicated. On the one hand, their nationalist agenda is in many ways a necessary corrective to decades of marginalization, and their argument that working within a Zionist framework of politics cannot provide the necessary rights the community deserves is strong. On the other hand, their strident rhetoric and support for elevating the Arab minority to equal status with the Jewish majority, which would entail changes to the Jewish character of the state—for example, replacing Jewish symbols on the flag and the coat of arms—is seen as threatening by most of the Jewish-Zionist parties, particularly those of the right wing.

There have been occasions when the Arab parties have cooperated with the Jewish parties. Soon after Labor Prime Minister Yitzhak Rabin signed the Oslo Accords in 1993, Shas left the coalition, leaving the government with less than 61 votes in the Knesset. But Rabin's government was propped up from the outside by votes from the two Arab parties, Hadash and the Arab Democratic Party, which ensured that the opposition could not pass a no-confidence vote to bring down the government.

As discussed in Chapter 7, the raising of the electoral threshold in 2014 to 3.25 percent prompted all four parties (Hadash, Ra'am, Ta'al, and Balad) to cooperate. In January 2015 they agreed to run together on a single list, called the Joint List (commonly called the Joint Arab List in English). This is the first time all of Israel's major Arab parties have campaigned on the same ticket, and it took a series of intense negotiations for the parties to hammer out a program and division of power that satisfied each of them. But despite the alliance, the differences between the parties remain. While Ayman Odeh, the leader of Hadash and head of the Joint List, has worked to ease Jewish concerns about the party's challenge to Israel's Jewish character, Balad MK Jamal Zahalka has said that "the fact that Balad supports a framework of equality for all citizens, and the fact that our vision did not make it into the political program of the list, does not prevent us from believing in a bi-national state. . . . I believe that the relevance of the two-state solution is fading, and that the moment for a one-state solution has yet to come."[16] The list contributed to an increase in the Arab parties' representation in the Knesset, from a combined total of 11 seats in 2013 to 13 in 2015.

CENTER OR "THIRD" PARTIES

Centrist parties exist as a separate category but do not form a primary cluster in the Israeli political system. This is because while there have been several of them over time, none have lasted more than two elections, with the exception of Kadima and the first incarnation of Shinui. But Kadima received only two seats in the January 2013 election and did not run in the 2015 election. For its part, Shinui entered three different Knessets from 1981 through 1988 with two to three seats only. Centrist parties' primary purpose has been to serve as vehicles for the promotion of an individual's political ambitions, to represent a "white knight" out to save the Israeli political system from itself, or to embody the country's fear of a set of circumstances that existing parties seem unable to resolve. But none have worked to build a country-wide organization or sustained communal or grassroots support; without these, no party can last in the highly competitive system of Israeli politics against parties whose roots lie in the Yishuv period and therefore have developed powerful party machineries and cultivated sets of committed voters. Center parties also tend to make grandiose promises and create large expectations. When they are unable to fulfill them, their credibility is undermined. Most do not survive more than a single election.

Centrist or third parties can be identified as such not only because they promote themselves that way, but also because they all claim to represent the middle of the political system, a center point on the left–right spectrum between Labor and Likud. More often than not their policy platforms are vague. They tend to call for change, particularly to the normal conduct of politics and the structure of the electoral and political systems. Sometimes their economic policy is a mixture of socialism and capitalism, and their foreign policy—especially toward the Palestinians and regarding settlements in the West Bank—is generally framed by vague rhetoric setting out hardline positions with a willingness to negotiate; in short, they represent indifference. These positions are attractive to a critical mass of Israeli voters who are suspicious of Labor or Likud on economic or security grounds. Until the 2010s, center parties rarely won enough seats to tilt the balance of power between Labor and Likud.

The first centrist party was the Democratic Movement for Change (sometimes known as *Dash*, its Hebrew acronym). The DMC was meant to challenge Labor's dominance, but it drew votes from both the right and the left. Although it promoted electoral, constitutional, and political reforms, it was less clear on economic and security issues. Formed in time to compete in the 1977 election, it won 15 seats, mostly at the expense of Labor, but only a year later the party's internal divisions broke it apart.

The DMC's successor was Shinui, originally formed in 1978. Unlike most centrist parties, it did have a firm political agenda. It held to a staunchly secular position, arguing that religion should be completely separated from the state, and was dovish on policy toward the Palestinians and the peace process while in the economic sphere advocating a strict free market economy. It managed to win a handful of seats throughout the 1980s until its merger into Meretz in 1992. A breakaway faction split off from Meretz in 1997, reconstituting itself as Shinui and taking six seats in the 1999 election. This revived Shinui unexpectedly won big in 2003, garnering 15 seats to become the third-largest party in the Knesset, and joined the Likud government. The party splintered into several factions before the 2006 election, none of them exceeding the 2 percent threshold then required for representation in parliament.

Other parties followed. In 1996 *HaDerekh HaShlishit* (The Third Way) was established by popular former IDF General Avigdor Kahalani and won four seats, but disappeared in 1999. That year another well-liked former General, Yitzhak Mordechai, led *Mifleget HaMerkaz* (The Center Party) to six seats. The party also attracted other prominent personalities, including Dan Meridor, former IDF Chief of Staff Amnon Lipkin-Shahak, Yitzhak Rabin's daughter Dalia Rabin-Pelossof, and former negotiator of the Oslo Accords Uri Savir. Indeed, there was considerable excitement at the time over the party, especially in response to Mordechai's decision to run for Prime Minister in the direct elections (he later dropped out). The party failed to have an impact, however, and internecine struggles broke it apart before the next election.

The most important third party is Kadima, and that may be because it was established specifically to serve as a governing party rather than a balancing party.[17] It was formed in November 2005 by Prime Minister Ariel Sharon, in the aftermath of the withdrawal from Gaza and four small settlements in the northern West Bank in summer 2005. Sharon had, in a surprise move—he had previously said that "the fate of Netzarim [in Gaza] is the fate of Tel Aviv"[18]— managed to get Knesset approval for the removal of all Israeli soldiers and civilians from Gaza by bringing Labor into the coalition. The move was deeply unpopular within Likud, and Netanyahu began planning to unseat Sharon. When it became clear that Sharon could not get past Likud's party institutions to mobilize support for the next phase of his plan—disengagement from elsewhere in the West Bank—he resigned from Likud and formed Kadima as a vehicle to complete his policy.

The electorate and the media were galvanized. What made Kadima even more exciting was that it was being driven by Sharon—a war hero—and included major figures from both Labor (Shimon Peres and Haim Ramon) and Likud (Ehud Olmert, Tzipi Livni, and Tzachi Hanegbi) as well as other prominent individuals who had not previously been involved in politics (Avi Dichter).[19] It was widely believed that Kadima represented the greatest challenge to the party system since 1977, and that its impact could well rival the political earthquake of that year; some observers started calling its founding a "big bang." Polls at the same time suggested it would get over 30 seats in the next elections; one survey even indicated it could win 42, something no party had done since Labor won 44 seats in 1992 under Rabin's leadership.

Though it did not do as well as polling suggested, the party was still the big winner in 2006, even after Sharon had been incapacitated by a massive stroke, taking 29 seats in the Knesset to Labor's 19 and Likud's 12. Ehud Olmert, Sharon's second in command, succeeded him and became Prime Minister. He began negotiations with the Palestinian Authority at the same time he continued working on Sharon's disengagement plan. But in 2008 Olmert was forced to resign from the leadership under the shadow of a corruption investigation into his political activities. (He was later convicted on different charges and sentenced to six years in prison.) Tzipi Livni won the leadership but was unable to maintain the coalition government, prompting early elections in 2009. At the polls, Kadima won 28 seats to Likud's 27. However, it became clear after the election that Likud's Netanyahu had more support in the Knesset than Livni did. Netanyahu became Prime Minister, and Kadima was left out of the coalition. In the aftermath of its failed policies, the costly and unpopular 2006 war in Lebanon, vicious internal fighting, and poor leadership, Kadima's support all but disappeared by the 2013 election. The party, then under Shaul Mofaz's chairmanship, barely made it into the Knesset, winning only two seats. It was gone by the 2015 election.

Kadima's success is all the more notable for its briefness and the magnitude of its collapse. When it formed the government in 2006, it was the first time a party other than Labor or Likud had done so. It appeared, then, as though the party system really had been realigned. But like other third parties, Kadima had no organization; it had coasted to victory in 2006 on the strength of its leaders and its single-minded focus on the disengagement plan, which was popular among voters at the time. In the end Kadima collapsed because of the same weaknesses that struck all of the smaller centrist parties that came before it.

The 2013 election featured two new centrist parties: Hatenua and Yesh Atid. Hatenua was established by Tzipi Livni, a former Kadima leader and Foreign Minister, for the sole purpose of pushing peace negotiations with the Palestinians forward. Because Amir Peretz was in third place on its electoral slate, the party also advocated for social justice. It won six seats that year. Yesh Atid is led by newcomer Yair Lapid, son of the former head of Shinui. Lapid put together an impressive electoral list, drawing on a wide range of representation of Israeli society, including an Orthodox rabbi, former security officers, legal scholars, and social justice activists. If Kadima made waves with its entrance to the political scene in 2006, Yesh Atid did the same in 2013. The party won 19 seats, making it the second largest in the Knesset. Lapid purposely drew up a policy program that kept within the Israeli consensus on foreign affairs and the peace process, advocated major changes to the privileges afforded the haredi communities (such as child allowances and the right to avoid the military draft), and promised to focus on rebuilding Israel's middle class. In this sense, Yesh Atid does represent a genuine centrist or third party, though one that is closer to the right rather than the left camp.

In 2015, however, neither of these two parties did as well as they previously had. Livni formed an alliance with Labor, and they ran together as the Zionist Union, winning 24 seats. It is difficult to know whether its voters were choosing Labor or Hatenua, or were simply pleased that the two were working together given the similarities between them on foreign policy and the fact that some members of Hatenua came originally from Labor. For its part, Yesh Atid dropped from 19 to 11 seats, an unsurprising decrease given the history of centrist parties. Still, 11 seats is a strong showing for a centrist party's second election.

Yesh Atid might have gotten even more seats but for the formation of yet another center party in time for the 2015 election, *Kulanu* (All of Us). Created by former Likudnik Moshe Kahlon, the party focused its messaging on the same issues Yesh Atid had in 2013: addressing the rising cost of living and helping the middle and working classes. Kahlon himself is very popular. As Minister of Communications during Netanyahu's second government (2009–2013), he broke open the wireless industry to allow more companies to compete, bringing down prices in the mobile phone arena. As a Mizrachi he is also seen as a champion of that community, and he is more liberal on domestic issues, such as reducing haredi control over personal status issues. On foreign policy he has generally been in step with Likud, taking a hard line on the peace process. In his 2015 campaign he downplayed his opposition to this process, but indifference is a better description of his foreign policy. Like Lapid, Kahlon put together a notable roster of candidates, including former ambassador to the United States Michael Oren. Kulanu won 10 seats in 2015.

Figure 9.1 depicts these four main clusters, plus the centrist camp, in the context of the 2013 election. Figure 9.2 does the same for the 2015 vote. These diagrams demonstrate the intersecting issues that can make it more difficult to place certain parties, particularly the centrist ones, on the political map. In 2013, for example, Hatenua fit into the overlapping area between the left-wing camp and the centrist camp because its sole focus was a negotiated solution to the end of the Israeli–Palestinian conflict, even if that included a Palestinian state—a goal that has long been a Labor Party objective, but not a Likud objective. In 2015, Yesh Atid and Kulanu sat at the juncture of the center and the right-wing camps, because while both advocate for government action to ease the rising cost of living, they are also closer to Likud on foreign policy.

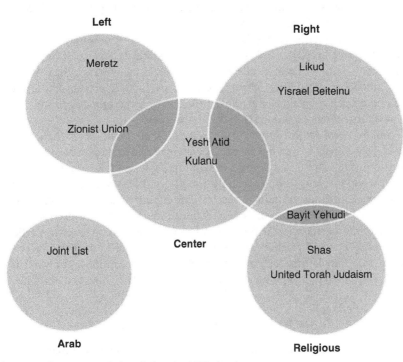

Figure 9.2 Party camps in Israel after the 2015 election

ETHNIC OR SPECIAL ISSUE PARTIES

Despite being an immigrant society, ethnic or special interest parties have largely been missing from Israeli politics. This is for two reasons. First, there were almost no such parties in the Yishuv, and since the Israeli political system was inherited directly from the Yishuv, it was harder for ethnic or special interest parties to access the political arena after the state was established. Second, many bigger parties in the four clusters claim to speak for these communities or interests. For example, Russian and FSU voters are represented in parties whose ideological and political agenda places them within the right-wing cluster, the Arab parties form their own cluster, and Mizrachi voters have turned out in larger numbers for an explicitly haredi political party (Shas).

Nevertheless, there have been a handful of special interest parties in Israel history. In addition to operating outside of the four main camps, they all share the distinction of having lasted no more than two elections, and most lasted only one. The first elections in Israel, in 1949, brought three special parties into the Knesset, two of which ran explicitly on an ethnic ticket. *Sephardim and Edot Mizrachi* (Sephardim and Oriental Communities) represented the Sephardi and Mizrachi Jews who were living in Palestine before the establishment of Israel; the Yemenite Association represented Yemenite Jews; and the Women's International Zionist Organization (WIZO), a nongovernmental organization founded in 1920 to advance social justice and the status of women among Jews in the diaspora, represented Zionist women as well as more general causes. The most successful special interest party, and the big surprise of the 2006 election, was *Gil* (the Hebrew acronym for Pensioners of Israel to the Knesset). By that year, voters were clearly feeling the impact of the economic slowdown, the sense of insecurity that followed the onslaught of the Second Intifada, and major cuts to transfer payments and social welfare allowances. Gil was, in many ways, a form of protest vote. Although it joined Ehud Olmert's government (2006–2009), it had little impact on economic policy. Factional infighting broke the party apart soon after, and none of its constituent parts was able to get back into the Knesset.

The first real radical protest party was *Ha'olam Hazeh–Koah Hadash* (This World–New Force). Driven by one man, Uri Avnery, the party won one seat in 1965 and two in 1969. But it had no base of support, possessed few resources, and was considered too far left at a time when the Israeli electorate was on the verge of turning to Likud. The most prominent special interest party was *Tami* (an acronym for Movement for the Heritage of Israel). Founded in 1981 by a former member of Mafdal, it was the first effort to break away from the dominant Ashkenazi parties to represent religious Mizrachim. As such, it was a precursor to the more successful Shas. In 1981 it took three seats in parliament, but only one in 1984—by which time Shas had emerged on the political scene. After that election it merged into Likud.

PARTY ORGANIZATION

All of Israel's parties are governed by an elite of party officials. For many of these parties, internal practices are rooted in the Yishuv period, when party leaders had complete control over internal developments. These leaders decided on party rules and policy platforms and chose other leaders and electoral lists on the basis of their own deliberations. In many instances, a single long-serving and popular leader played the major role in these decisions. This was the case with David Ben-Gurion in Labor until 1963 and with Menachem Begin in Likud until his death in 1983.

The oligarchic structure of early Israeli parties eventually came under pressure by lower-level party members, officials from younger and upcoming generations, and, as part of their demand to open up the entire political system, the electorate. One outcome was an expansion of civil society (see Chapter 11); another was a set of internal party reforms within the secular parties that opened them up to wider debate, including the chance for members to select candidates for the electoral list. The religious parties remained under the control of rabbinical councils until Bayit Yehudi opened up its selection process in the 2010s. United Torah Judaism and Shas remain closed.

The secular Zionist parties (and the NRP, when it existed) are organized hierarchically. At the bottom of the pyramid is the mass membership, which elects delegates to the tiers above it, often through party conventions. The most important of these upper-level institutions is the Central Committee, which in turn selects an executive and a secretariat to govern the daily activities of the party. Often divided according to faction, ideology, or support for one party leader over another, these committees tend to be powerful bodies. Labor and Likud have a Central Committee of between 3,000 and 4,000 members (the precise numbers have varied over time). Others, such as the NRP and Meretz, have had between several hundred and a thousand delegates to their Central Committees.

Key policy issues are debated in the Central Committee, which also establishes party constitutions. This makes for intense competition for positions in this body. Likud in particular has been convulsed by disputes within the institution, which have sometimes had profound effects on the party. For example, it was the Central Committee's opposition to Ariel Sharon's West Bank disengagement plan that prompted Sharon to break from Likud and establish Kadima. This weakened Likud in the 2006 election cycle and resulted in the party dropping to 12 seats, facilitating Kadima's formation of the government.

Though Binyamin Netanyahu led the opposition within Likud to Sharon's plan, he himself has faced rebellion in the party and efforts to constrain him through the Central Committee. As his opponents are fond of repeating, even though Netanyahu accepted the principle of two states in a 2009 speech,[20] none of the party's institutions have ever voted to accept the idea.

The struggle between Netanyahu and his rivals grew more intense after the November 2012 primaries. The nationalist hardliners within the party were opposed to Netanyahu's participation in peace talks led by U.S. Secretary of State John Kerry in 2013–2014 and worked to block him in the party institutions. The Central Committee became a key battleground for that dispute. In 2013 Danny Danon was elected chairman of the Committee and by December had proposed a number of changes to the party's constitution that both constrained Netanyahu's policymaking and threatened his position as leader if he blocked party resolutions. One of the stipulations of the amendments, for instance, was that a leader would be automatically removed if he went against any Central Committee resolution—an addition meant to tie Netanyahu's hands in peace talks. Ironically, in 2002 the Committee had—at the behest of Netanyahu—formally rejected a Palestinian state in the WBG. Netanyahu managed to fend off these challenges by obtaining support for his efforts in the broader party membership and by using other party institutions, such as the Likud court, which had been created to resolve disputes among other party agencies. In May 2014 an agreement was brokered that stipulated that the chair of the Central Committee could not propose changes to the party's constitution without the party leader's support. This left Netanyahu—and whoever comes after him—with enormous power to shape or reject constitutional provisions.

The haredi parties (UTJ and Shas) are governed by a council of rabbis (usually referred to as the Council of Sages) and do not have any other party organization to speak of.[21] The councils make all of the party decisions (though in Shas, Ovadia Yosef long dominated this process), which are simply accepted by their constituents because of the commitment to follow rabbinical instructions and rulings. The Arab parties are small, a condition not conducive to a large, active membership, and they, too, are governed by small committees. But in the case of Balad and Hadash, the committee process has been quite democratic, with party members participating fully in decision-making procedures.

Leadership Selection

As in any parliamentary system, the position of party leader is important because of the critical role party leaders play in the political arena. Only leaders of the biggest parties (so far only Labor, Likud, and Kadima) have a chance at becoming the head of government, while those who immediately follow the leader on a party list may become ministers in the government if the party joins the coalition. The manner in which a leader is selected can also be an indicator of how democratic the party is. For example, questions of succession decided by a single leader mean there is little debate about the successor's qualifications.[22]

In the past, parties often selected as party chiefs compromise candidates who would be acceptable to the different factions. Contemporary Israeli parties can be divided into two rough categories: those that select leaders on the basis of a democratic procedure through one of the party's internal bodies, and those that rely on a single individual—the top political or spiritual leader—to decide who is placed where on the electoral list.

In the first category are Labor, Likud, Meretz, Kadima, and Bayit Yehudi. The first three underwent a process of opening up over time that focused on changing the body responsible for selecting the leader and the electoral slate. For Labor this process began with the top officials, often those in the Central Committee. By the late 1970s the election process had been moved to the party convention, which contained close to 3,000 party delegates. In 1992 Labor was the first major party to move toward primaries, which entailed a voting process by the entire party membership.[23] After Rabin won the primary contest against Shimon Peres and then led Labor to victory in the general election, the sense was that the primary system worked and should be institutionalized. Likud and Meretz followed suit. Likud reverted to a selection process run through the Central Committee between 1999 and 2009, and then shifted back to the primary system. Meretz has moved away from primaries as well and now uses a convention—attended by delegates chosen by the membership—to select its candidates and leaders. Hadash follows the same method.

For its part, Kadima's slate was first created largely by its founder, Ariel Sharon. When he fell into a coma soon after the party's establishment, Ehud Olmert—widely seen as Sharon's deputy—was declared the new leader by default. In 2008 the party used primaries to determine its electoral slate. When Bayit Yehudi transitioned from its first version established in 2008, to its current one, it held a registration drive to bring in new members and then a primary in November 2012 to determine the party leader (which Naftali Bennett won) and the electoral slate. But the party might be reverting to a less democratic process. In September 2014, at Bennett's insistence, a party convention voted to change the party constitution. The new rules give Bennett, as leader, considerable power over placement of candidates on the electoral slate, allowing him to choose one out of every five candidates, and the decision over who can become a minister in the government is his alone.[24] Such a position of power can also backfire on a leader, however. In 2015, as part of his continuing effort to broaden the party's appeal, Bennett appointed a popular former soccer star, Eli Ohana, to the electoral list. Fierce opposition broke out, because soccer is usually played on Saturdays, the day of rest according to Jewish law, and Ohana had supported disengagement from Gaza. Both of these points were an affront to Religious Zionist sensibilities. Ohana later agreed to forgo the appointment.

In the second category of parties—those in which decisions are made by a single leader—are Shas, Yisrael Beiteinu, Yesh Atid, and Kulanu. While he was alive, Rabbi Ovadia Yosef was formally Shas's spiritual leader, but he was popular and respected enough to run Shas according to his own preferences. He exercised almost sole authority in party matters. Party regulations included a clause that stated, "[t]he party sees the council of sages under the leadership of . . . Rabbi Ovadia Yosef . . . as the superior religious, biblical, ideological and political authority in the Land of Israel."[25]

Yisrael Beiteinu has an official party committee that appoints candidates to its list. But it is headed by Avigdor Liberman, who for all intents and purposes decides who goes where; neither the committee nor the party challenge his decisions. In fact, it is not clear whether the party would survive without Liberman. Finally, Yesh Atid and Kulanu were founded as political vehicles for the personal ambitions of their leaders. As such, both Lapid and Kahlon have selected the party slates.

The importance of leadership selection is both reflective and constitutive of another development in Israeli politics: the personalization of parties. In the past, when the political system was more ideological, party policies were the factors that mattered most for the electorate, even though many parties were clearly identified by their leaders. Over time, as Israeli politics has become increasingly "Americanized" through the use of American campaign methods, the importation of American political operatives to run campaigns, and the growing importance of the media in transmitting messages and framing issues and candidates, so too have party leaders become more important. The constant replacement of Labor leaders has contributed to the idea that leaders, rather than the party or its policies, matter for elections. The direct elections for Prime Minister, the establishment of several centrist parties—Kadima, Yesh Atid, Hatenua, and Kulanu—as channels to political power for individuals, and the strident rhetoric of some Arab party leaders have all pushed this development forward through a focus on what the leaders do and say.

SUMMARY

Though this chapter divides Israeli parties into four main camps, it has become increasingly difficult to identify clear boundaries among them. Their positions on issues frequently overlap, and the competition for the same voters sometimes draws parties in different clusters closer together. Notably missing from this discussion, too, are any parties specifically representing the Ethiopian community, Reform or Conservative Judaism, or American or British Jewish immigrants—all of which are small but growing segments of Israeli society. That none of these have created their own political party may speak to their small size or lack of broader appeal, but it also speaks to the nature of the party system itself. The only new parties that have been able to form are those that have split off from an existing party or those that have been broad enough to claim the political center. Special interest or sectarian parties have not fit easily into this system.

At the same time, the continuing predominance of the cluster system—even while individual parties within each camp undergo changes to their structures—serves as a disincentive for parties that do not fit into any of the four existing camps to participate in politics. This is evidenced by the weak staying power of the centrist parties. While their short-term success indicates there is an electorate out there interested in supporting them, they do not have the voter loyalty that the cluster parties do. The continuing dominance of economic and security concerns and of issues of religion and state in elections provides a further constraint on special parties (see Chapter 10).

Nonetheless, the centrist parties are the biggest "wild cards," because they pop up right before an election is held and claim to speak for the Israeli center. That group (discussed in the next chapter) has been big enough to garner these parties anywhere from six to 20 or more seats. They can disrupt an election and cause the major parties to lose Knesset seats as well as siphon off votes from the smaller sectarian parties. While they remain for the foreseeable future a permanent part of the political landscape, it does not seem that they can shift the foundations of the party system, with its deep roots in the parliamentary activity of the Yishuv.

KEYWORDS

party system, party camps, Labor, Likud, leftwing camp, rightwing camp, religious camp, Arab camp, centrist parties, leadership selection

NOTES

1. Yonathan Shapiro, *The Formative Years of the Israeli Labour Party: The Organization of Power, 1919–1930* (London: Sage Publications, 1976). Most of the main socialist Zionist parties and movements eventually joined the merger.

2. The information he provided did, at the very least, raise questions about the accusation put forward against him, particularly the testimony from other security officials.

3. Shimon Peres (1995–1997, 2003–2005), Ehud Barak (1997–2001, 2007–2011), Binyamin Ben-Eliezer (2001–2002), Amram Mitzna (2002–2003), Amir Peretz (2005–2007), Shelly Yacimovich (2011–2013), and Isaac Herzog (2013–present). Party rules make this constant cycling of leaders easier: if Labor does not win an election, internal elections for the party's leader must be held within 14 months.

4. This included Itzik Shmuli and Stav Shaffir, leaders of the 2011 protests; Mickey Rosenthal, an investigative journalist; and Hili Tropper, who had received praise for his work with high school dropouts.

5. Asher Arian, *Security Threatened: Surveying Israeli Opinion on Peace and War* (Cambridge: Cambridge University Press, 1995); Mira M. Sucharov, *The International Self: Psychoanalysis and the Search for Israeli-Palestinian Peace* (Albany: SUNY Press, 2005).

6. The name Likud will be used to refer to the party's prior manifestations as well, including Herut and Gahal.

7. See, for example, Elisheva Goldberg, "Likud: The Party of Annexation," *Daily Beast*, November 27, 2012, http://www.thedailybeast.com/articles/2012/11/27/likud-the-party-of-annexation.html.

8. Sa'ar was considered by some to be more pragmatic than the rest of the cohort. In September 2014 he announced his intent to resign (more specifically, to take a "time out") after that year's Jewish high holidays.

9. Some of them were already MKs, but the 2012 primaries raised all of them to more realistic positions on the electoral list. Feiglin left the party in 2015.

10. Brent E. Sasley, "The Domestic Politics of Israeli Peacemaking," *Foreign Policy*, July 22, 2013, http://mideastafrica.foreignpolicy.com/posts/2013/07/22/the_domestic_politics_of_israeli_peacemaking; Ben Birnbaum and Amir Tibon, "The Explosive, Inside Story of How John Kerry Built an Israel-Palestine Peace Plan—and Watched It Crumble," *New Republic*, July 20, 2014, http://www.newrepublic.com/article/118751/how-israel-palestine-peace-deal-died.

11. In 2006 Ichud Leumi ran on a joint ticket with the National Religious Party and won nine seats.

12. BBC, "Israel Names First Arab Minister," January 12, 2007. http://news.bbc.co.uk/2/hi/middle_east/6254691.stm.

13. As Chapter 4 discussed, personal status in Israel is subject to each religious community's religious laws. In the Jewish sector, those issues fall under haredi authority. Because many of the hundreds of thousands of FSU immigrants either were not Jewish by halachic standards or brought relatives with them who were Christian, their status as Jews entitled to the same benefits as those who have been able to prove their Jewishness has been subject to questioning by religious authorities. Two of the parties' biggest issues have been a less demanding conversion process and civil marriage.

14. Haklai, *Palestinian Ethnonationalism*, 74–81.

15. Jonathan Lis, "Arab MK Slams Holocaust Denial, Wins Praise from Jewish Colleagues," *Haaretz*, January 27, 2010.

16. Orly Noy, "'A Palestinian State Isn't the Solution, but It's a Step in the Right Direction': Meet MK Jamal Zahalka," *+972*, February 5, 2015, http://972mag.com/a-palestinian-state-isnt-the-solution-but-its-a-step-in-the-right-direction-meet-mk-jamal-zahalka/102266/.

17. Thanks to Shmuel Rosner for this insight.

18. Cited in Scott Wilson, "After 38 Years, Gaza Settlers Gone," *Washington Post*, August 23, 2005, http://www.washingtonpost.com/archive/politics/2005/08/23/after-38-years-gaza-settlers-gone/b347e45e-d949-46ad-b8a3-273f453071a2/.

19. Survey data indicate that Kadima voters ranked themselves close to the middle of the left–right spectrum. Asher Arian and Michal Shamir, "A Decade Later, the World Had Changed, the Cleavage Structure Remained," *Party Politics* 14 (2008): 701.

20. Binyamin Netanyahu, "Address by PM Netanyahu at Bar-Ilan University," June 14, 2009, http://mfa.gov.il/MFA/PressRoom/2009/Pages/Address_PM_Netanyahu_Bar-Ilan_University_14-Jun-2009.aspx.

21. The two factions in UTJ, Agudat Yisrael and Degel HaTorah, have their own rabbinical councils as well.

22. However, there may also be costs associated with an open selection process. See Ofer Kenig, "Democratizing Party Leadership Selection in Israel: A Balance Sheet," *Israel Studies Forum* 24 (2009): 62–81.

23. The DMC was the first party to utilize primaries, in 1977.

24. For more details on the primary selection process across the parties, see Ofer Kenig and Assaf Shapira, "Primary Season in Israel," Israel Democracy Institute, December 4, 2012, http://en.idi.org.il/analysis/articles/primary-season-in-israel/.

25. Cited in Ofer Kenig and Gideon Rahat, "Selecting Party Leaders in Israel," in *The Selection of Political Party Leaders in Contemporary Parliamentary Democracies: A Comparative Study*, ed. Jean-Benoit Pilet and William P. Cross (London: Routledge, 2014), 208.

CHAPTER 10

⚘

Voting Patterns

It is commonly assumed that Israeli elections are all about foreign policy and national security, especially the peace process with the Palestinians. In recent years American analysts have focused on Iran and relations with the United States as the deciding factors in elections and in coalition negotiations. It is certainly true that foreign affairs plays an important role in voters' considerations, and policy regarding the occupied territories has become particularly salient since the 1980s. Nevertheless, Israeli elections are fought over other issues as well, and sometimes these concerns predominate.

The overarching story of Israeli elections from 1949 to 2015 is one of a shift in power from the left (led by Labor) to the right (led by Likud). This trajectory was the result of multiple factors, including the growth of the marginalized Mizrachi population in Israel and its "rebellion" against Labor hegemony (and Likud leader Menachem Begin's ability to tap into this ethno-class resentment), the conquest of the West Bank and other territories in 1967, the shock of the 1973 War, the failure of the Oslo process in the 1990s, the onset of the Second Intifada in 2000, and the rocket attacks on Israel from Hezbollah in the north and Hamas in the south throughout the 2000s. From 1948 to 1977 the political system was dominated by the Labor Party. From 1977 through 2015, Likud achieved a preferential position, but not dominance, in elections, with Labor often coming in a close second. In 1981, for example, Labor won 47 seats to Likud's 48, and in 1984 even beat Likud 44 to 41 seats.[1]

We begin this chapter with a discussion of the four main issue-areas Israeli elections are fought over: security and foreign policy; social-economic conditions; the place of religion in Israel, or the Jewish character of the state; and the meaning of Zionism and the importance of the West Bank for Israel's identity. A description of demographic factors and a discussion of voter turnout rates follow. The chapter then traces, in broad outline, the major trends in electoral outcomes, beginning with the period of Labor hegemony that ended when Likud won the 1977 election, ushering in a period of genuine multiparty competition.

FOUR MAIN ISSUES

Sometimes transitory or sudden domestic or external events can influence electoral outcomes. As a result of a Hamas terror campaign that year, the 1996 election for Prime Minister resulted in a narrow victory for Binyamin Netanyahu of Likud by 30,000 votes (about 1 percent of the popular vote). The 2009 election was influenced by two military confrontations during the government's term, with Hezbollah in July 2006 and with Hamas in December 2008–January 2009. Other elections have been conditioned by the appearance of third parties. For instance, Likud's victory in 1977 was partially a result of the appearance of the Democratic Movement for Change, which won 15 seats, many at the expense of Labor. In 2013 first-time parties Yesh Atid and Hatenua campaigned on issues traditionally associated with Labor and siphoned off some votes that would otherwise have gone to it. Individual leaders of parties are also important in campaigning. Between 20 and 30 percent of the electorate regularly indicates that candidates are important factors in their choice, but the extent to which this translates directly into votes is not clear.

Apart from these unforeseen developments, Israeli voting patterns are, and have always been, heavily conditioned by ideology—and Israelis perceive that to be the case as well. This tendency stems from the period of the Yishuv, when most members of the community belonged to political parties and movements that represented particular ideological strains of Zionism. The shift from a voluntary to a compulsory political system after 1948 did not change these patterns.

Security and Foreign Policy

Israel's longstanding threat environment, continuing terrorism, and the onset of the peace process since the early 1990s have made security issues and foreign affairs prominent concerns for voters. Indeed, Michal Shamir and Asher Arian contend that the Israeli–Palestinian conflict has "locked" other issues out of electoral competition, even though in public opinion surveys respondents claim that other issues—such as economic concerns—are important to them.[2] These scholars note that it is "impossible to achieve significant and long-term standing in the Israeli party system and the Israeli electorate without providing a rallying-cry and at least alluding to some stance regarding . . . security and the territories."[3]

To a large degree security is understood by Israelis in terms of peace with the Arabs, a strong military, and good relations with other countries. In 1969, the first year of the Israel National Election Study (INES), a poll conducted prior to the election asked Jewish citizens what they considered the most basic problem for Israel today.[4] The top two responses were "peace in the area" (56.8 percent) and "military strength" (12.4 percent). Asked what the second most important problem was, 22.1 percent said "military strength," 17.9 percent said "economic independence," and 15.5 percent said "peace in the area." In 1974, to the same questions, 42.3 percent said "peace" was the most important problem, while 41.7 percent said "security" was (though it is not clear what difference respondents saw between the two). By the 1990s and 2000s, security was also understood in the context of relations with the Palestinians in the West Bank and Gaza (WBG), including the need for and likelihood of a peace deal and the establishment of a Palestinian state.

In other surveys, peace and security have continued to be among the top concerns, but other issues—particularly social and economic conditions—have also become important. Though the 2013 INES survey did not ask respondents to rank the most important problem facing Israel, it did ask (in a preelection survey) what issue would most influence their vote. Israelis identified the top issue influencing their vote as security and terror (56.4 percent), corruption (53.2), peace and the territories (52.1 percent), the economy (46.4 percent), social policies (42.5 percent), and the Iranian threat (35.2 percent).

Good relations with the United States, Israel's main ally in world politics, are a fundamental concern of voters. But it would be a mistake to assume that Israeli voters care more about the American–Israeli relationship than other issues. In 1992, for example, Washington and Jerusalem had a bitter public fight over $10 billion in loan guarantees for Israel's development. President George H. W. Bush did not want these guarantees to be used for development of settlements, while Prime Minister Yitzhak Shamir insisted they would be. During his election campaign Labor leader Yitzhak Rabin argued that if elected he would improve relations with the United States. Though Labor won 44 seats in the election and Likud 32—a decisive outcome—dissatisfaction with Shamir's management of the country's relationship with the United States was only one small piece of the explanation for Likud's loss. Rather, a host of domestic political and social changes and widespread discontent with Shamir's governing were responsible for the changeover.

In the contemporary period, while President Barack Obama and Prime Minister Binyamin Netanyahu have had a number of public spats, and public opinion surveys regularly show that Israelis harbor suspicions of Obama's commitment to Israeli security and well-being, there is little evidence that Israelis would base their vote on this issue. In 2013 39.2 percent of respondents to an INES survey disagreed, to some degree or another, and 57 percent agreed that "Israel should do what is best for its security, even at the price of a confrontation with the American administration." This suggests that Israeli governments have some leeway to "confront" Washington, even if there are costs involved.

The most discussed issue related to American–Israeli relations in 2015 was Obama's push for a deal with Iran over its nuclear program. A poll conducted about a month before the election found that only 21 percent of Israelis trusted Obama to prevent Iran from obtaining a nuclear weapon; 72 percent did not trust him to do so. But the same poll found that only 10 percent of likely voters listed the Iranian threat as the most important issue in the election—48 percent said economic issues were more important, and 19 percent said relations with the Palestinians were.[5]

Other interstate relations have mattered at other times. For example, in the 1950s and 1960s questions about Israel's relationship to Germany in the aftermath of the Holocaust were important public issues in elections of that period.[6]

Social-Economic Conditions

The problems Israelis identify as the country's most important have routinely alternated between security/foreign affairs and socio-economic concerns; indeed, these two issue-areas historically have largely determined whether Israelis think things are going well for the country or not.

In the 1969 INES, very few Israelis identified the economy as the most important problem facing Israel, but some did identify it as the second most important (17.9 percent) or the third most important (17.6 percent) problem. In 1977, the year Likud came to power, in large part as a result of Mizrachi voters' rebellion against Labor, 38.3 percent said the economy was the main problem the government had to take care of, 24.6 percent said security, 13.3 percent said social inequality, 9.2 percent said peace, and 4.6 percent said education. In 1984, in response to the same question 50.4 percent of respondents said the economy, and 28.5 percent said security. These figures do change according to circumstance. In 1988, almost a year after the beginning of the First Intifada, the main problem that Jewish Israelis wanted the government to take care of was security, cited by 32.3 percent of respondents; the Palestinian issue/occupied territories, cited by 16.4 percent; the economy, cited by 13.4 percent; uprising in occupied territories, cited by 12.9 percent; and peace (solving the Arab–Israeli conflict), cited by 5.7 percent.

Security continues to be a baseline concern for Israelis, while some voters will always remain with the same party for ideological reasons. But in the 2010s social and economic issues have reinserted themselves onto the electoral agenda. The 2011 social justice protests (see Chapter 15), which continued into the middle of 2012, had the biggest effect on the 2013 election. Beginning in July and August 2011, thousands of Israelis protested in the streets of Tel Aviv and other cities across the country against the high cost of living in Israel, including high food and housing costs, and high levels of poverty.

In the 2013 election, three of the top four vote-getting parties focused their campaigns either exclusively or primarily on social and economic issues (Likud–Yisrael Beiteinu, which won the election, did not speak much to these issues). Yesh Atid's success was largely the result of its promises to "ease the burden" on the middle class and to end privileges for the haredi community; a brand-new party, it won 19 seats. Labor leader Shelly Yacimovich refused at first to talk about the occupation, settlements, or the peace process—all issues that had come to be associated with the party—and focused only on social and economic conditions. Labor won 15 seats, two more than its previous showing. This mediocre outcome was widely blamed on Yacimovich's emphasis on the economy rather than the peace process, which probably cost the party a handful of seats. Bayit Yehudi, although at its core a Religious Zionist party, focused heavily on social and economic issues and won 12 seats, up from seven in 2009. It did well in cities populated by middle-class and working-class Israelis and Israelis working in the high-tech industry, including Rishon LeZion, Petah Tikvah, Netanya, and Ra'anana. In a postelection survey, INES asked respondents what they thought the election had been about; by a wide margin, respondents placed social and economic issues at the top (see Table 10.1). All of this took place at a time when multiple security issues—relations with the Palestinians in the West Bank and Gaza, a November 2012 war with Hamas, the development of the Iranian nuclear program, and public quarrels between Netanyahu and Obama—were ongoing.

Table 10.1 INES Postelection Survey, 2013

"ALL IN ALL, IN YOUR OPINION, WHAT WERE THE ELECTIONS ABOUT?"	PERCENTAGE
Social protests on housing and cost of living	40
Equality of burden for army service	23.7
The leadership and performance of Netanyahu as Prime Minister	11.9
Don't know	8.5
Security threats	8.1
Policy issues related to the Palestinian state and the Golan Heights	5.9
Attacking Iran	1.9
Total	**100**

Source: INES Election Study 2013, http://www.ines.tau.ac.il/2013.html.

The results of the 2015 election indicate that these same concerns predominated. In addition to numerous polls citing social and economic issues (particularly the high cost of living) as being of greatest importance to citizens, the center parties Yesh Atid and Kulanu together won 21 seats. Their campaigns focused almost solely on reducing the burden on the middle class and addressing economic inequalities (Yesh Atid's leader, Yair Lapid, also tied these priorities to the need to reduce the Orthodox community's privileges and exceptions in government expenditures and military service). Likud's increase from 20 to 30 seats was not about economic issues, but nor was it about foreign or security policy. The party did not present a platform, and while Netanyahu spoke often about the Iranian threat, he used for the most part bland, boilerplate language about improving conditions for Israelis. Likud's windfall came at the expense of other right-wing and religious parties, particularly Yisrael Beiteinu and Bayit Yehudi, and appears to have stemmed from domestic concerns about the undermining of the Jewish character of the state rather than from foreign policy fears. Indeed, leaders of those parties consistently took a more aggressive, hardline position in security affairs than did Netanyahu.

Religion

Israel was founded by secular Zionists. Though they frequently referred to major events in Jewish history and drew upon the biblical claim to the land itself, they interpreted that history and those claims as emphasizing Jewish power and self-determination, rather than divine will or religious inspiration. But partly because there was always a significant presence of Orthodox and ultra-Orthodox Jews in Israeli life, and partly because Judaism itself was an inseparable part of Jewish peoplehood, questions about the role of religion in political and social life were (and remain) ever-present. And because the Status Quo Agreement between David Ben-Gurion and Agudat Yisrael enshrined the notion that religion would be given priority in certain areas of public life, these specific questions are tied up in a broader idea of what it means to be a Jewish state.

There has always been a significant minority in favor of a greater role for religion in the public and private spheres. In 1969, when the INES asked Jewish Israelis whether they agreed that laws of marriage and divorce should be under the Rabbinate's exclusive jurisdiction, 37.6 percent "absolutely" agreed, 17.9 percent agreed, 17.9 percent expressed reservations, and 17.6 percent "absolutely" disagreed. Results did not differ widely in later surveys (or using slightly differently phrased questions), indicating the presence of a core group of supporters for the status quo.

At the same time, high levels of support for these issues represent Israelis' perception of Israel as a Jewish state in the abstract. Just under a majority of Israelis self-identify as secular. Israeli Jews want Israel to remain a Jewish state, but not necessarily a state governed by Orthodox Judaism. Their definition of Jewish state is thus different from a religious interpretation of the term. A stark example of this distinction is found in the increase in recent years in the number of stores selling Christmas trees in Israel, as Israelis have associated what is clearly a non-Jewish symbol not with another religion but simply as a kind of cultural artifact. Further data from the 2013 INES survey confirm that many Israelis place an emphasis on Jewishness rather than Judaism the religion. When asked whether civil marriage should be instituted alongside religious marriage, about two-thirds (66.6 percent) said yes. When asked whether they would be willing to see the government spend more or less on religious schools and institutions, only 17.7 percent thought the government should spend more, while 63.2 percent thought it should spend less (16.5 percent wanted the current level to remain in place). Finally, public opinion polls during the 2013 election campaign show that the positions of Yair Lapid and Naftali Bennett in support of both reducing government funding for haredi communities and absorbing haredi men into the military draft were very popular among the electorate.

A different way to understand trends on this issue is to look at how well religious parties have performed in elections (see Figure 10.1). In 1949, four religious parties cooperated on a single list for the election and won 16 seats. These parties continued to do about as well, give or take a seat or two, until 1981. In 1984, the arrival of Shas siphoned off some support from the Ashkenazi haredi parties. But because Shas did increasingly well at the polls, the overall number of seats that went to the religious parties remained high. As Shas declined slightly into the 2000s, a rejuvenated NRP in the form of Bayit Yehudi made up the difference. In all, the religious parties have won above 20 seats in every election since 1996, except in 2009, when they received only 19.

There is clearly a core constituency for the religious parties. But in addition, Shas and Bayit Yehudi have drawn votes from conservative and non-Orthodox Jews who appreciate what they represent. Many Shas supporters vote for the party for ethno-class reasons: Shas explicitly claims to represent the long-marginalized Mizrachi Jews and provides for many of its less well-off constituents' needs. For example, it runs a network of schools open to anyone. Some of Bayit Yehudi's support has come from secular nationalists who like the party's emphasis on settlement in the West

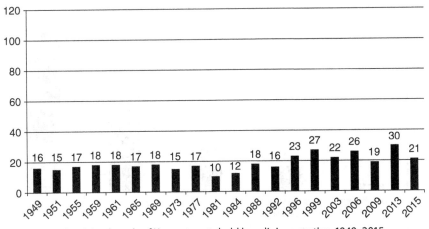

Figure 10.1 Combined totals of Knesset seats held by religious parties, 1949–2015
SOURCES: Israel Knesset website, http://www.knesset.gov.il/description/eng/eng_mimshal_res.htm; Central
Elections Committee website, http://www.bechirot20.gov.il/election/English/kneset20/Pages/Results20_
eng.aspx.

* In 2006, the NRP ran on a joint list with a far-right secular nationalist party, winning nine seats.

** In 2009 and 2013, Bayit Yehudi incorporated small far-right secular nationalist factions.

Bank, or citizens who support its efforts to reduce the government's dependence on haredi political support and financial payouts to the haredi community. Others prefer its focus on expanding economic opportunities for Israeli citizens. In other words, while many Israelis still consider religion to be an important determinant of their voting behavior, the line between strictly religious parties and other groups within Israeli society has become increasingly blurred.

Such conclusions are bolstered by a 2014 Israel Democracy Institute survey of the national religious community in Israel that found that more Israeli Jews identify with this constituency than previously thought. While levels of religiosity are generally higher for the national religious community than for other Israeli Jews, members of the former are not necessarily committed either to settlements or to Israeli sovereignty over the West Bank (though some certainly are). Rather, those who do identify as part of the community share a number of other characteristics, including a tendency to vote for right-wing parties and a staunch commitment to Jewish nationalism. Figure 10.2 highlights the extent of Jewish Israeli identification as national religious: 45 percent of Jewish Israelis feel affiliated to this community to one degree or another.

A third approach to understanding the importance of religion as a motivator for political action is to examine how Israeli Jews perceive their own identity. According to the IDI's 2013 Democracy Index, just under a majority of Israeli Jews self-identify as "secular" (49.1 percent), while the size of various religious sectors of Jewish society is much smaller: 15.1 percent see themselves as "traditional religious," and 13 percent as "traditional nonreligious" ("traditional religious" are closer to the Orthodox in their social conservatism and religious observance, while "traditional nonreligious" are closer to secular groups on these practices). Among Jews, 9.4 percent identify as haredi, 9 percent as national religious, and

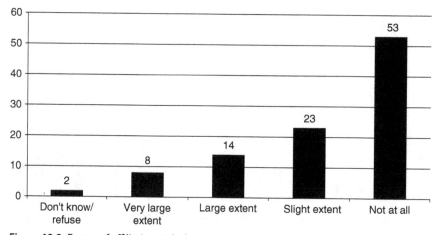

Figure 10.2 Extent of affiliation with the national religious camp among total Israeli Jewish population, 2014 SOURCE: Tamar Hermann, Gilad Be'ery, Ella Heller, Chanan Cohen, Yuval Lebel, Hanan Mozes, and Kalman Neuman, *The National-Religious Sector in Israel 2014: Main Findings* (Jerusalem: Israel Democracy Institute, 2014), 2, http://en.idi.org.il/media/3863902/Madad-Z-English_WEB.pdf.

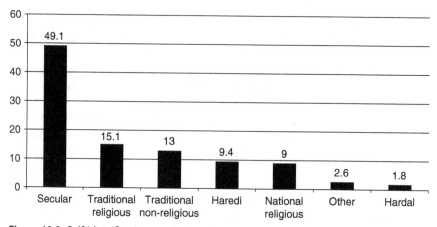

Figure 10.3 Self-identification among Israeli Jews, 2013 SOURCE: Israel Democracy Institute, *Israeli Democracy Index 2013*, 179, http://en.idi.org.il/media/2720081/Democracy%20Index%20English%20 2013.pdf.

1.8 percent as ultra-Orthodox-national religious (sometimes shorted to *hardal*, a combination of haredi and *dati leumi*, or national religious) (see Figure 10.3). Thus, an important minority—about one-third of Jewish Israelis—indicates that religion is an important element of public life.[7]

Zionism and the West Bank

Zionism as a motivator for voting behavior refers here to the place of Judea and Samaria as the biblical and historical heartland of the Jewish people in conceptions of Israeli identity.[8] There is some overlap between this category and the previous one, but the former issue is about the place of halacha (Jewish law) in public life rather than the relevance for Zionism of settlements and Israeli sovereignty over the West Bank.[9] This stance is often referred to as a commitment to "Greater Israel."

Differentiating between what the West Bank means for Zionism and what it means for Israel's security is also difficult, though not impossible. In many early INES surveys, Israeli Jews expressed the desire to hold on to the West Bank and Gaza because they believed that relinquishing this region would undermine Israel's security. In the early 1970s, slight majorities or pluralities were willing to give up an unspecified, but small, part of the territories. Attitudes began to turn against that position by the time Likud came to power in 1977. That year, only 6.8 percent of Israeli Jews were prepared to give up all of the West Bank in return for a peace agreement; 7.1 percent said they would give back "almost all of it," 21.1 percent "a part of it," 22.2 percent "a small part of it," and 40.6 percent "nothing at all" (definitions of these terms were not explicated).[10]

Later on, the Oslo process had a clear impact on public opinion. Once the government agreed to withdraw from parts of the WBG and to contemplate the establishment of an independent Palestinian government there, attitudes became more supportive. Before the 1996 election, at a time when Hamas suicide bombings were still wracking the country, INES asked Israelis whether they supported the Oslo Accords or not. A clear majority of Israelis (62.7 percent) supported the agreement, while 37.3 percent objected to them. Support for an agreement that incorporated a Palestinian state continued to remain high, so that by 2009 Likud leader Binyamin Netanyahu was able to declare, in a speech at Bar-Ilan University, support for "a demilitarized Palestinian state . . . alongside the Jewish state"—provided certain requirements were first met.[11] In other words, by the end of the first decade of the twenty-first century, for most (but certainly not all) Israelis and their representatives, a willingness to leave most of the West Bank had become an accepted part of the political discourse.

Today, a clear majority of Israelis, even among Israeli Jews, favor withdrawing from most of the West Bank outside of the main settlement blocs in return for a peace treaty and a final end to the conflict with the Palestinians. Before the 2013 election, INES asked Israelis whether "Israel should consent or not consent to the establishment of a Palestinian state in Judea, Samaria, and the Gaza Strip under the framework of a permanent agreement." A majority (57.2 percent) said Israel should consent, while 35.9 percent said it should not. The specific details of an agreement—what it would entail—do change the answers. Asked about withdrawing from settlements, a plurality (43.8 percent) was willing to evacuate "small and isolated settlements," while 31.5 percent said there should be no evacuation at all. Just over 19 percent was willing to withdraw from all the settlements.

The survey also asked whether, in the event of an agreement, Israel should return or continue to occupy Arab neighborhoods of Jerusalem, even at the expense of an agreement. This is one of the more sensitive issues for Jewish Israelis, and one that they have been least willing to contemplate. Yet 42.8 percent said Israel should return these areas to the Arab community, while 50.6 percent wanted

Israel to continue to occupy them. These differences fit with longstanding evidence that most Israelis remain suspicious of the Palestinians' ultimate intentions, are skeptical an agreement with them can be made, and are hesitant about some of the details of such an agreement. For example, in the April 2014 Peace Index produced by the Israel Democracy Institute, while a clear majority (64.6 percent) of Israelis were in favor of peace talks, a similar majority (69.7 percent) did not believe that negotiations would lead to peace "in the coming years." A similar result was found in the April 2015 Index: 69.2 percent of Israelis said they did not believe "moderately" or "at all" that negotiations between Israel and the Palestinian Authority would lead to peace in the coming years, although 61.1 percent were "strongly" or "moderately" in favor of such talks. Subsequent surveys repeat this pattern.

DEMOGRAPHIC FACTORS

Israelis' voting patterns are conditioned by the same demographic factors that influence voters in other countries: age, levels of education and income, place of residence (urban or rural area), and ethnicity.[12] Some general observations can be made. Ethnicity is an important factor, particularly since 1977. Mizrachi citizens tend to vote for parties in the right-wing camp, while Ashkenazi citizens—particularly older, wealthier, well-educated ones—generally vote for the left or the center-left. Labor's base remains solidly Ashkenazi. From the early 1990s to the late 2000s, Russian citizens were not closely identified with any one party. In the direct elections for Prime Minister, their vote alternated between Likud and Labor leaders. Yisrael B'Aliyah and Yisrael Beiteinu did capture much of the Russian vote in the late 1990s and early 2000s, but part of this may be explained by the introduction of direct elections for Prime Minister, in which voters were able to split their vote. In the 2010s it is less clear whether support for Yisrael Beiteinu is due to the ethnicity of its voters or to its position on political-security issues. On the other hand, ethnonational identity is strongly correlated with voting behavior, with Arab voters opting for Arab parties in increasing numbers.

Those who identify as more religiously observant are more likely to vote for Likud. Younger Israelis gravitate toward the centrist parties, but in the late 2000s the right-wing parties also increased their appeal to young voters on nationalist grounds. Gender does not seem to have a strong correlation with voting patterns: men and women are divided according to ideology and other demographic factors (for example, a Mizrachi woman is still more likely to vote for Likud than Labor). Though class differences are relevant, as mentioned previously, they are closely correlated with ethnicity (Mizrachim versus Ashkenazim). In addition, economic factors played an important role in voter decisions in the 2013 and 2015 elections.

One final demographic factor to account for is place of residence in Israel versus residence in West Bank settlements. As would be expected, Israelis within the Green Line vote for different parties on the basis of the motivations set out previously. Within the West Bank, though, voters lean toward the religious and right-wing parties, particularly Bayit Yehudi and Likud. Labor has done very well in the settlements in the Jordan Valley, perhaps because of its history as the patron of these "security settlements" and because of these communities' collectivist origins. Likud comes in a close second in these places. In the main settlement blocs—those close to the Green Line and considered likely to be annexed to Israel in the event of a final peace deal—Bayit Yehudi dominates, especially in Gush Etzion. In settlements with a high concentration of haredim, United Torah Judaism predominates.

VOTER TURNOUT

Turnout rates in Israel used to be among the highest of any Western democracy. This is because Israelis are highly politicized—rates of newspaper readership (or consumption of electronic media) and discussion of politics, among other indicators, have regularly been high. The threat environment, which necessitated a compulsory draft, kept public policy issues in the public eye. The percentage of Israelis turning out to vote was, until 1999, in the high 70s and into the 80s. The highest turnout was in 1949, at 86.9 percent. Since the 1999 election that rate has steadily declined, from 78.7 percent that year to 64.7 percent in 2009 (the 2001 election for Prime Minister had the lowest turnout rate in Israeli history, at 62.3 percent, in part because of the Arab boycott). In 2013 and 2015 turnout began to rise, to about 68 percent and then to 72 percent (see Figure 10.4). As already discussed in Chapter 7, turnout among Arab voters has fallen even more sharply, as a result of protest, but also out of community members' distrust and despair that they can be fairly represented in the system, though it, too, rose in 2015.

The Israeli decline reflects a general worldwide trend, but a comparison of countries in the OECD shows that rates still remain relatively high among other developed states, with Israel ranking in seventeenth place in voter turnout (see Table 10.2).

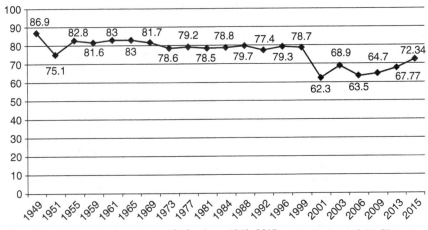

Figure 10.4 Voter turnout rate, Israeli elections, 1949–2015   SOURCE: Knesset website, "Knesset Election Results," http://www.knesset.gov.il/description/eng/eng_mimshal_res.htm.

* The election in 2001 was a special direct election for the Prime Minister only.

Table 10.2 Voter Turnout Rates in OECD and Other Countries (Most Recent Election)

		TURNOUT (%)			TURNOUT (%)
1.	Australia	93	19.	Finland	69
2.	Luxembourg	91	20.	Spain	69
3.	Belgium	89	21.	United States	68
4.	Denmark	88	22.	United Kingdom	66
5.	Turkey	88	23.	Russia	65
6.	Sweden	86	24.	Estonia	64
7.	Iceland	81	25.	Greece	64
8.	France	80	26.	Mexico	63
9.	Brazil	79	27.	Hungary	62
10.	Norway	78	28.	Canada	61
11.	New Zealand	77	29.	Czech Republic	59
12.	Korea	76	30.	Slovak Republic	59
13.	Austria	75	31.	Portugal	58
14.	Italy	75	32.	Poland	55
15.	Netherlands	75	33.	Japan	53
16.	Germany	72	34.	Slovenia	52
17.	**Israel**	**72**	35.	Chile	49
18.	Ireland	70	36.	Switzerland	49

Source: OECD, "Voter Turnout," *Better Life Index 2015*, http://stats.oecd.org/Index.aspx?DataSet Code=BLI#
* Israel's 2015 election had not been incorporated into the database yet; the authors inserted it here.

This decline has been attributed to general voter apathy, which is not uncommon in other countries, though some communities (such as settlers and haredim) have continued to vote at high rates. It is unusual for Israel, however, where studies indicate that not voting for political reasons (i.e., to make a point about politics or in response to poor choice among parties) has been infrequent, except among the Arab population. Some have contended that young people's alienation from the state has affected the overall turnout rate, which might reconcile the growing population with the larger percentage of nonvoters. It may be that the Second Intifada, which began in September 2000, had a dampening effect on voter interest: Israelis became more concerned with personal security and disillusioned by the government's inability to quell the violence, and therefore became mistrustful of politics in general. At the same time, growing concern with the rising price of consumer goods and housing, culminating in the 2011 social justice protests, may have generated a simmering anger not only among the younger generation, but also among some older Israelis, particularly those with children. Data from the Taub Center, for instance, show that in the period before the protests, the cost of living in general, and the cost of housing in particular, had driven more Israelis to move back in with their parents—and that many Israelis had not moved out at all. This shift may coincide with the decline of Israel's collectivist ethos and the rise of a more individual-oriented society that exhibits less interest in communal and public affairs.

Lamentations on the rupturing of Israeli democracy may be premature, though—at least if the measurement of such a break is electoral participation. As noted, the turnout rate has increased in both the 2013 and the 2015 elections. Israelis may be recovering from the aftermath of the Second Intifada. The appearance of Hatenua, which emphasized a need to resolve the Israeli–Palestinian conflict, and of Yesh Atid and Kulanu, which focused on social and economic issues and assembled diverse lists of candidates, may have also generated a sense of newness and change.

ELECTORAL TRENDS

Finally, it is worth looking at broad electoral trends in Israel over time. We can identify three patterns in party support. In the beginning the political system was marked by Labor hegemony. After 1977 a competitive system emerged, but one in which the right increasingly did better even as the two major parties declined. In the 2000s the phenomenon of the center became important, tipping the balance of power in favor of the right.

Labor Hegemony

Asher Arian, drawing on Maurice Duverger, argued that from 1948 to 1977 Israel had a "dominant party system."[13] By this he meant that Mapai/Labor not only consistently won a plurality of votes in national elections but was so closely identified with the state that one was often viewed as inseparable from the other. As the party in charge of government, Labor guided the new country through its first five wars, the absorption of hundreds of thousands of new immigrants within the space of only a few years, and the consolidation of the state as a functioning polity.

By 1948 it was inevitable that the Labor Zionist movement would become the controlling force in the new state, given its dominance in both the World Zionist Organization and the Yishuv. The movement's control of Yishuv institutions also meant that officials and members of the various socialist parties already had experience in a "civil service," so that once the state was established they were the only ones with the qualifications to run the state machinery. Labor Zionism's collectivist and nationalist ideology held appeal for groups even outside the movement. Its focus on pioneering and voluntarism gave it a community-wide significance that others could support, providing it with greater relative weight in national institutions.

After 1948 this pattern continued. The Labor Party won a plurality in all of the state's elections until 1977, typically taking between 40 and 50 seats in the Knesset. It received 56 mandates in 1969, and 51 in 1973. The closest another party came to catching up to it was in 1973, when the newly formed Likud took 39 seats. By this time Labor's hegemony was fading, although it took one more election to make its decline obvious. Because Labor always served as the dominant party in the coalition, it was able to shape the state's priorities and policies in accordance with its own preferences.

A Likud-Dominated Competitive System

Israelis refer to the election on May 17, 1977, as a *mahapach* (a revolution or upheaval). For the first time since the founding of the state, a nonsocialist party won a plurality of seats, with Likud taking 43 seats to Labor's 32. With the support of the National Religious Party and the Democratic Movement for Change, Likud was able to put together a majority coalition in the Knesset and form the government.

The elections did not completely overturn the party balance in the Knesset. Likud's 43 seats were only four more than it had won in 1973, though Labor's drop from 51 seats in 1973 to 32 in 1977 was significant and represented the party's poorest showing to date. The seats won by the two parties remained close in the 1980s as well. Of greater importance was Likud's success in pulling the support of other parties from Labor to form the government.

Labor's slump was also the result of a convergence of broader social and political processes that had been building for some time, catalyzed by the shock of the 1973 War. The party had been in power so long that while its legitimacy was not questioned, its dynamism and creativity were. By the mid-1970s, the population of Mizrachim had overtaken the Ashkenazim. The former group's experience at the hands of the Ashkenazi Jews who formed the bulk of the labor movement—and therefore of the government and the state—was one of marginalization and discrimination. Widespread discontent, buttressed by a number of political scandals among Labor's leaders, had made the public receptive to a different party.

Likud's political legitimacy had been steadily growing since the 1967 War. Although the party's leadership was composed of Ashkenazim, the chairman, Menachem Begin, managed to portray himself and the party as committed to the Mizrachim. Begin also had a more "common touch" than Labor's leaders, who were viewed as elitist. It helped that the Mizrachi community tended to be more traditional and conservative in religious and social practices; on these markers, too, Begin compared favorably to Labor leaders, who were often viewed as less respectful of Judaism.

Other economic and social problems were attributed to Labor, including a decline in immigration, growing unemployment and inflation, and increasing agitation among labor unions. The Lavon Affair split the party, prompting even its long-time leader, Prime Minister David Ben-Gurion, to defect. Finally, the trauma of the 1973 War (Egypt and Syria's surprise attack, the failure to stop the Arab assault in its first days, and the widespread fear that Israel might be overrun) undid all of the prestige that Labor had accumulated as a result of winning the 1948, 1956, and 1967 wars. Labor's failures in the war also channeled what had been a growing frustration with its settlement policy. A new generation of Religious Zionists had by the early 1970s been pushing for settlements in the biblical and historical heartland of the Jewish people, Judea and Samaria. They argued that settling the West Bank was simply a continuation of the Zionist enterprise. Though it did build a handful of settlements, Labor resisted the pressure to open up the territories to large-scale expansion. The Religious Zionists and the secular nationalists who now saw their ancient kingdom open before them believed Labor to be blocking the Zionist project.[14]

After 1977 the political arena was dominated by Labor and Likud. At first they continued to win the lion's share of Knesset seats, always coming in first or second place in the elections. Though both remain at the core of their respective camps, their share of the total vote—represented by their total seats in the Knesset—has declined over time as other parties both within and outside of their clusters have challenged them and drawn away voters. The 2015 election gave the two parties a bump—together they reached 49 seats, a significant increase over the previous three elections—but it is not yet clear whether this is an anomaly or not (see Figure 10.5).

This decline has had multiple effects on Israeli politics. First, although it is a reflection of changing voter preferences, it also contributes to the perception that the era of Labor and Likud has passed. Other options may be available now—indeed, they increasingly *are* available in the form of centrist parties. Though they do not normally last more than a single election, the mere appearance of such parties is enough to upset the balance of power between the two former big parties. Second, it demonstrates the fragmentation of the electorate. Smaller, sectoral parties are doing better at the same time that larger centrist parties have emerged. Indeed, in addition to their decreasing absolute number of seats, Labor and Likud are no longer assured of being the largest two parties in the Israeli political constellation (see Table 10.3). Third, it makes coalition governing more difficult. Certainly, in the past, coalitions have been composed of parties with different agendas. But because of the decline of the big parties, other parties are now able to assert themselves more effectively, making governance a more delicate balance. The 2013–2015 government, led by Likud, had trouble balancing those parties that actively promoted or supported peace talks with the Palestinians (Hatenua, Yesh Atid) with those that opposed such talks (Bayit Yehudi, factions in Likud).

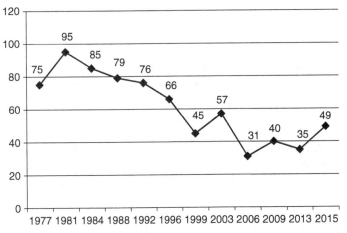

Figure 10.5 Labor and Likud's share of Knesset seats, 1977–2015

* Results for the 2013 election include the 20 seats apportioned to Likud as part of its electoral alliance with Yisrael Beiteinu.

** Results for the 2015 election include the 19 seats apportioned to Labor as part of its electoral alliance with Hatenua (Zionist Union).

Table 10.3 Combined Totals of Knesset Seats of the Two Largest
Lists, 1981–2015

ELECTION	NUMBER OF SEATS	TWO LARGEST LISTS
1981	95	Likud, Labor
1984	85	Labor, Likud
1988	79	Likud, Labor
1992	76	Labor, Likud
1996	66	Labor, Likud
1999	45	Labor, Likud
2003	57	Likud, Labor
2006	48	Kadima, Labor
2009	55	Kadima, Likud
2013	50	Likud–Yisrael Beiteinu, Yesh Atid
2015	54	Likud, Zionist Union

* "Labor" is used, for convenience sake, to refer to all versions of its lists.

It walked a similar line on issues related to religion in the public sphere, including civil and same-sex marriage, as Yisrael Beiteinu and Hatenua on the one hand and Bayit Yehudi on the other locked horns over these issues.

Finally, though both have been diminished, the decline of the big parties has affected Labor more than Likud. In addition, more parties on the right and on the center-right have appeared. Even though Likud may lose support to these parties, they are either still within the right-wing camp or closer to Likud on several key issues. The religious parties have also come to prefer Likud over Labor. All of this has made it difficult for Labor to obtain a majority of votes in the Knesset to form a government.

The Rise of the Center

Though ideology has declined from being the primary indicator of voter behavior, it remains an important influence on voting patterns. A breakdown of Jewish Israelis' self-identification on the political spectrum (on political-security issues) shows that the rightist camp is much stronger than the leftist camp, which corresponds to the trend in electoral outcomes discussed previously. The political right—which corresponds to the right-wing cluster—comprises just under a majority of Jewish Israelis (49.8 percent), while the political left—which can be expected to vote for parties in the left-wing camp—has the support of only 16.1 percent of Israeli Jews (see Figure 10.6). The IDI study on the national religious community (see Figure 10.2) reinforces these findings.

A related phenomenon is the appearance of the Israeli center. This is not a new development (see Chapter 9), but in the 2000s these parties have come to play a bigger role in electoral outcomes. It is thanks to these centrist voters that Kadima won the government in 2006—the first time that a party other than Labor or Likud became the senior coalition partner. They are also responsible for the rise of Yesh

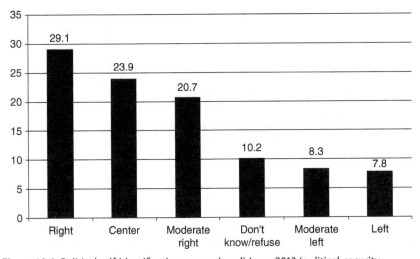

Figure 10.6 Political self-identification among Israeli Jews, 2013 (political-security issues) SOURCE: Israel Democracy Institute, Israeli Democracy Index 2013, 180, http://en.idi.org.il/media/2720081/Democracy%20Index%20English%202013.pdf.

Atid, Hatenua, and Kulanu—parties that drew support away from Labor and Likud in 2013 and 2015.

The percentage of those who place themselves in the center on political-security issues is 23.9. This fits with most analyses that locate between one-quarter and one-third of Jewish Israeli voters toward the center of the political spectrum. Pollsters have identified these voters as mostly Ashkenazi, secular, middle class, and urban. Because they are in the center, they can support a moderate-left or a moderate-right party. They are not floating, in the sense that they move from one end of the spectrum to the other and back; rather, they remain in the center.

But they do tend to lean right, meaning that they might also be called "soft right" voters, and parties that are established on their votes might be called center-right. These voters share elements of both rightist and leftist positions on the peace process: they support a Palestinian state and would be willing to dismantle settlements in return for a peace agreement, but they do not trust the Palestinians in light of several outbreaks of violence, beginning with the Hamas terror campaign in the mid-1990s; they are skeptical about Palestinian intentions toward the Jewish state; and they are pessimistic about the chances for a peace agreement. Because of their skepticism and pessimism on security issues, they are willing to ignore the Israeli–Palestinian conflict to support center-right parties whose foreign policies they can tolerate and whose economic policies they actively support. Alternatively, they can move a little further right toward Likud, as happened in 2015. Finally, they tend to move more firmly into the right-wing camp when violence between Israelis and Palestinians intensifies.

At the same time, because these centrist voters continue to identify as Zionists and support Israel's existence as a Jewish state (with an Arab minority), they have come to see the left as a little too non-Zionist. Radicalization on the vocal far left, including the emergence of post-Zionism and the promotion of solutions to the Israeli–Palestinian conflict that underline human rights rather than security concerns (see Chapter 18), has colored their views of the left in general. In the meantime, the right has successfully defined Zionism as pride in the Jewish state—something centrist voters can easily accept. For example, Bayit Yehudi's 2013 platform was titled *Because Israel Is Our Jewish Home*, and the party declared it would "act to strengthen the Jewish nature of the state" and "fight against those who attempt to transform Israel into 'a state of its citizens,'" that is, a state devoid of its specific Jewish identity. Under these conditions, centrist voters see the right or center-right as their best choice.

SUMMARY

The Israeli electoral system was relatively stable until the 2000s. The issues that mattered most to the electorate, as well as the usual demographic factors that play a role in any country's elections, were best addressed through the two big parties, Labor and Likud. These two parties dominated the electoral process. A series of domestic and external developments undermined their position at the top of the electoral hierarchy, though, and there is little indication that this trend will—or can—be reversed any time soon. Much will depend on whether Labor, especially, can rebuild itself and regenerate its appeal. Whether or not it does, we can expect the center to determine the balance of power in the Knesset for the near future.

KEYWORDS

elections, voter turnout, voting issues, security and foreign affairs, social and economic issues, religion and state, Zionism, social justice, Labor hegemony, competitive party system, demography, ethno-class voting

NOTES

1. From 1984 to 1988 the two parties sat in a national unity government, rotating the prime ministership. In 1988 they formed another NUG, but Likud was the senior partner.
2. Michal Shamir and Asher Arian, "Introduction," in *The Elections in Israel: 2009*, ed. Asher Arian and Michal Shamir (New York: Transaction, 2011), 13.
3. Asher Arian and Michal Shamir, "A Decade Later, the World Had Changed, the Cleavage Structure Remained: Israel 1996–2006," *Party Politics* 14 (2008): 689.
4. All references to the Israel National Election Studies are taken from its website, http://www.ines.tau.ac.il/.
5. Stephan Miller, "3 in 4 Israelis Don't Trust Obama to Keep Iran from Nukes," *Times of Israel*, February 11, 2015, http://www.timesofisrael.com/3-in-4-israelis-dont-trust-obama-to-keep-iran-from-nukes/#!.
6. Michael Brecher, *The Foreign Policy System of Israel: Setting, Images, Process* (New Haven, CT: Yale University Press, 1972), 122–126.

7. These findings are different from the study on the national religious community cited previously. In that study, researchers looked not just at levels of religiosity, but also at broader political attitudes and sociological factors to broaden the definition of "national religious."

8. After it was captured in 1967, the Israeli government officially named the territory Judea and Samaria to evoke the ancient kingdoms in the area. This is the term used in much of the public conversation in Israel; outside of the country the predominant term is West Bank.

9. Until 2005 the Gaza Strip was part of this consideration. Since the withdrawal that summer, few people in Israel have suggested a return to Israeli control over the area, although in the 2014 war, several prominent right-wing politicians, such as Naftali Bennett and Avigdor Liberman, did suggest that the Israeli military should reoccupy Gaza for the purpose of destroying Hamas for good.

10. There were four waves of surveys that year. Results are taken from the first wave; similar results were found in the other three.

11. These included recognition of Israel as a Jewish state, attention to Israel's security needs, and demilitarization of the Palestinian entity.

12. See Asher Arian, *Politics in Israel: The Second Republic*, 2nd ed. (Washington, D.C.: CQ Press, 2005), 243–253.

13. Ibid., 123.

14. Gershom Gorenberg, *The Accidental Empire: Israel and the Birth of the Settlements, 1967-1977* (New York: Times Books, 2006); Brent E. Sasley and Mira Sucharov, "Resettling the West Bank Settlers," *International Journal* 13 (2011): 1004–1006; Idith Zertal and Akiva Eldar, *Lords of the Land: The War Over Israel's Settlements in the Occupied Territories, 1967-2007*, trans. Vivian Eden (New York: Nation Books, 2007).

⚓

CHAPTER 11

Interest Groups and Political Protest

Israeli citizens participate in politics outside of the parties and elections to the Knesset in several ways. One is through interest group activity, which in any country is structured and shaped by the primary political institutions of that country—the specific type of political system (e.g., democracy or autocracy); the boundaries of the judicial, legislative, and executive branches of government; the role played by political parties; and society's political culture. Because the Israeli political system was, for most of the country's existence, heavily structured and regulated by political parties, most associational groups were organized through specific parties, and therefore were relatively weak. Indeed, several parties were directly tied to specific interest groups. Organized labor, for example, was represented by the Histadrut, which was identified with Mapai/ Labor; for most of its history, the Histadrut's top leaders came from that party. *Gush Emunim*, which promotes settlements in the West Bank, is aligned with the Religious Zionist parties.

If interest groups are meant to be different from political parties and to serve as an alternate form of democratic participation, then this longstanding arrangement was detrimental to Israeli democracy and pluralism in the early decades of the state. Though some interest groups have long operated outside the party structure—for example, the Manufacturers' Association—it was the 1973 War and the breakdown of the party system in the 1980s that really opened up space for more independent group activity. The beginning of Israeli–Palestinian peace talks in the 1990s and greater awareness of inequality between Jewish and Arab citizens have either raised the profile of existing organizations or facilitated the emergence of new ones dedicated to these issues.

We define an *interest group* here as an organization that works to influence public policy, usually on specific issues, but without seeking political office. Interest groups are part of *civil society*, which serves as a buffer between the state and society, mediating between and connecting the two. Civil society comprises a multitude of types of organizations, including professional associations, social groups, unions, religious movements, clubs, and more. *Political protest* is another form of popular participation, a way to shape the political process from outside the bodies and agencies in which decisions and laws are made.

This chapter first discusses the nature of access in the Israeli political system and the manner in which it has changed over time from a relatively closed system to an open one. To give some sense of the range of interest groups, their activities, and their varying levels of success in the Israeli political system, the chapter then looks at four main types of interest groups that operate in domestic and in foreign affairs: organized labor, the security network, peace groups, and the settler movement. It then briefly describes several others that fall outside these categories. It ends with an examination of political protest in Israel—an activity that Israelis have increasingly used to articulate their demands.

CHANGING ACCESS IN THE ISRAELI POLITICAL SYSTEM

The American political system is considered the most penetrated in the world—that is, it has multiple access points to the decision-making process, including Congress, the presidency, the courts, and the civil service that implements decisions and laws. By contrast, the Israeli political system was for a long time relatively closed, and so activity has been much more constrained. Stemming from their development in the Yishuv, Israeli political parties controlled all decision-making processes.[1] The collectivist political culture reinforced the state's dominant role in political, social, and economic life. Heavy regulation of interest groups was the norm. To this end the state denied or slowed down its consent to operate to those groups it deemed inappropriate on ideological grounds or for activities it felt should be conducted only by the state. The bulk of the groups in existence at this time were business oriented or religious in nature, though there were also a significant number of professional associations.

The party and electoral systems reinforced these restrictions. As discussed in Chapter 8, proportional representation has led to a proliferation of parties both running in elections and winning representation in the Knesset. This allows for special or single-interest parties to be formed quickly, which in turn has facilitated the appearance of small parties representing very specific issues obtaining a small number of seats in one election and then disappearing in the next election. Examples include Gil in the 2006 election and far-right parties like Moledet and Tzomet in the 1980s and 1990s. The relative ease with which a group of individuals can form a political party and compete in elections serves as a disincentive for the formation of formal, long-term lobbying organizations. The continued use of the closed-list system further narrows access. Candidates are chosen by party leaders or by party primaries, and so depend for their place on the electoral list not on interest groups that provide funding and mobilization but on party operatives (as in Labor and Likud) or religious leaders (as in Shas or United Torah Judaism).

Over time, Israeli society became frustrated with the heavy presence of the parties in social and economic life. The country no longer seemed to live at the edge of the precipice in security terms, and a consumer-based economy was developing. The slide from a collectivist culture to a more individualist ethos prompted

Israelis to feel frustrated at their inability to influence the political process. This contributed to the expansion of civil society groups and a greater willingness to use protest as a form of pressure.[2]

The period of the 1960s through the 1980s marked an important change, leading to an expansion of interest group and civil society activity. In this era strong economic growth brought with it an availability of consumer goods that heralded a shift within the population from a socialist to a more materialist ethos. As Israel became increasingly plugged into the global economy, there was an expansion of business groups, which increased the lobbying pressure on the government.[3] In the political arena, the end of Labor hegemony in 1977, the increasingly competitive nature of the system from 1977 to the 2000s, and the emergence of new sectarian parties in the 1980s all broke down the traditional role of the party as the main vehicle for advancing a policy agenda and providing services for constituents. Some efforts to fill these gaps—such as protest movements from the Mizrachi and Arab communities and among women—contributed to the legitimacy of interest group activity. The Association for Civil Rights in Israel was founded in this period. Finally, the 1973 War facilitated the emergence of two prominent but opposing movements: one promoting settlements in and Israeli sovereignty over the West Bank and Gaza, called Gush Emunim (Bloc of the Faithful); and another proposing a peace settlement with the Arab states that would entail withdrawing from these territories, called *Shalom Achshav* (Peace Now).

During the 1980s and 1990s society continued to prosper as the state-run economy was transformed into a free market economy. The polity matured, and a more assertive population emerged. These trends converged and enhanced the process, begun in the previous period, of opening up the political system to an autonomous and active civil society. An activist Supreme Court opened the door for litigation to become a more favored (and successful) tactic by many interest groups and nongovernmental organizations, which in turn facilitated a more activist agenda among these groups as well.

In the 2010s, political parties sought to rejuvenate the state's power to condition the existence of civil societal groups on specific ideological principles. Members of Likud, Yisrael Beiteinu, and Bayit Yehudi—supported by interest groups such as *Im Tirzu* and NGO Monitor—worked to constrain what they have called far-left, anti-Zionist Israeli organizations from operating freely—groups like the New Israel Fund, B'Tselem, and several Arab civil society organizations. For example, in summer 2013 MK Ayelet Shaked of Bayit Yehudi proposed a bill that, among other stipulations, would raise the tax that organizations would have to pay on any funding they receive from foreign sources if the organization or its members call for boycott, divestment, or sanctions against Israel or deny Israel's existence as a Jewish and democratic state.[4] Because many of these groups receive support from European governments and funding agencies, and because they often cooperate with outside organizations to provide information on Israeli activity in the West Bank, the right-wing parties and interest groups that champion such an initiative claim that harmful foreign interests are influencing developments in Israel. In response, the left-wing and human rights groups that would be most affected by the law argue that Israeli democracy is being undermined because alternate voices are being silenced, and that the funds that rightist groups receive from abroad (from private organizations and individuals) are not being subjected to the same constraints.

Though the system has opened up and there has been a proliferation of interest groups and civil society actors, access to decision-making remains circumscribed. Most interest and civil society groups identify with a particular point on the ideological spectrum or with one of the four main party camps. Specific parties, then, are automatic sites for interaction and lobbying. For example, it is common to count the number of MKs who are settlers, rabbis, kibbutzniks, and former generals or security officials. The weight of their numbers serves as a vehicle for their group's interests. These MKs also act as liaisons between the party and the Knesset on the one hand and their communities on the other, smoothing the way for the transmission of ideas and policies and for reconciliation in the aftermath of major policy disputes.

At the same time, Israeli political culture is marked by high levels of informality, and it is considered normal for a citizen to simply call up a friend or acquaintance and ask to be introduced to someone else. The small population, the (near) universal nature of the military draft, and the lingering sense of community that still blankets much of Israeli society (although the Jewish and Arab sectors are relatively self-contained in this respect) make for a "who you know" type of system that in Hebrew is called *protekzia.*

There has not been a comprehensive, large-N study on Israeli interest groups in several years, but close attention was paid to their activity in the early 1990s. Yael Yishai, who has done most of the comparative work on Israeli interest group politics, found in one study that the most prominent method adopted by interest groups in lobbying was direct contact with government bureaucrats and ministers, either through personal interaction or through formal contact.[5] In part, this was because many of these individuals had served in a specific party or government post in the past, or had operated in the same ethnic, religious, military, or other circles as a key decision-maker.

INTEREST GROUPS

Interest group and civil society activity was first structured by the Ottoman Law of Societies (1909), which Israel—distracted by many other problems—simply left in place. In 1954 a new law to govern interest groups was proposed, but though it passed its first reading in the Knesset, it proved too controversial and few MKs considered it important enough to fight for. It died in the legislative process. It was not until 1980 that a revised law was introduced and passed, the *Amutot* Law (Law of Associations). This law stipulates the requirements that must be met for an organization to officially register with the state. The legislation is intrusive, because it sets out what would otherwise be rules the group would set for itself, such as those regulating membership, the structure of meetings, and board requirements. Existing provisions also make it easy for the state to shut down an organization. Noteworthy, too, is the specific restriction on registration with the state (which itself is another form of supervision) that stipulates that an association "shall not be registered if any of its objects negates the existence or democratic character of the State of Israel."[6] Thus, although the number of civil society groups has grown over the years and their spheres of activity have broadened, the lingering remnants of a heavy state presence have remained, in theory giving the state considerable authority over what is meant to be a zone of autonomous group activity.

Organized Labor

Until the 1980s, organized labor, anchored by the Histadrut, was the most powerful interest group operating in Israeli politics. Because it was so closely connected to the dominant party, Labor, which in turn controlled the government and the state bureaucracy, it was able to transmit and refract socialist-collectivist ideas about Israeli life. It also played a major role in the economy. Much of its power stemmed from its ability to bargain on behalf of workers, using tactics including the threat of strikes.

Formed in 1920, the Histadrut was at first a giant federation of unions that had workers' committees in most industries and sectors of the economy. Later it became a major player in the Israeli economy through direct ownership and operation of and investment in critical institutions like health care insurance, pension funds, one of Israel's largest construction firms, *Solel Boneh,* and one of the country's major banks, *Bank HaPoalim* (The Workers Bank). Its primary purpose, though, has remained to improve the working conditions and wages of state and other employees. It also often supports non-Histadrut unions in their struggle against owners.

Because it was founded by socialist Zionists, and because of its size, the Histadrut also became a major instrument of patronage for Labor governments, giving them considerable control over the Israeli economy. But power ran both ways. Histadrut chairmen could influence the party and the government, either by calling for massive strikes in various areas or by mobilizing its members for different activities in support of government policy.

However, the Histadrut's supremacy began to decline in the 1980s and 1990s. The Likud governments of the late 1970s and early 1980s sought to nationalize some of the organization's enterprises, and the effort to control runaway inflation in the mid-1980s by reducing government expenditures, spearheaded by Labor head Shimon Peres, broke policy taboos and public expectations about the Histadrut's power. It lost one of its most important enterprises, *Kupat Cholim Clalit* (the General Sick Fund, essentially a health insurance company) in 1995 when the state passed a new National Health Insurance Law. Likud Finance Minister Binyamin Netanyahu's relentless privatization drive in the early 2000s further weakened the organization's power as major corporations were sold off and industries were made more competitive. The Histadrut's decline is highlighted by the falling off of its membership numbers. According to one study, "up until the mid-1980s, [the Histadrut's] enterprises produced a quarter of the country's output, employed around a quarter of the country's workforce, and accounted for almost a third of Israel's industrial investment."[7] In 1988 it had 1.5 million members and accounted for 80 percent of the employed working force. By the early 2000s that number had fallen to about 300,000, and some estimates put its current membership at several hundred thousand.

At the same time, the Histadrut has been challenged in recent years by an alternate labor union, *Koach LaOvdim* (translated as Power to the Workers, but also known as the Democratic Workers' Organization). Founded in 2007, Koach LaOvdim was a reaction to the perceived entrenchment of interests in the Histadrut that undermined a focus on workers' rights. Its claim to be an alternative organization lies in its "democratic constitution," which puts decisions about organizational policy in the hands of the membership. Koach LaOvdim is small but has been successful, and it represents a move toward plurality in an area long dominated by the state, the Labor Party, and the Histadrut.

But as the largest labor federation with deep roots in the Israeli economy, the Histadrut still retains some power. This is particularly evident in its ability to call for large-scale strikes in certain sectors. For example, in March 2007, the Histadrut called a general strike in order to protest nonpayment of wages to municipal workers including garbage collectors and employees at banks, electricity providers, and phone companies. The strike lasted about eight hours. In January 2013, the Histadrut launched a strike of its dock-workers over what were perceived as inadequate salaries and to break up the power of a small set of owners that controlled the sector, slowing down shipping activity. In fall 2013, in January 2014, and in March 2014 the Histadrut threatened to have its dock-workers at the ports in Ashdod and Haifa go on strike again over concerns about the effects that two private ports would have on laborers at state-owned ports. And in spring 2014, staff at the Foreign Ministry—supported closely by the Histadrut—went on a 10-day strike to protest unsatisfactory working conditions and wages, which led to the shutting down of Israel's embassies abroad and the rescheduling of the visit of Pope Francis.

The Histadrut also retains branches in many sectors of the economy. As well, many unions in the public sector have a loose, informal relationship with the Histadrut that either side can activate when necessary. Finally, Israel has seen a dramatic increase in both the number of new unions and the membership of existing ones in recent years, driven by what one report has called "union fever."[8] The issues that drove voters in the 2013 and 2015 elections (see Chapter 10) are the same ones prompting the expansion of unions: rising costs of living, economic inequality, and job and pension security. Some of these voters are joining Koach LaOvdim, but most are connecting with the Histadrut.

The Security Network

Some analysts consider the security network to be the strongest interest group in Israel. Primarily an informal set of connections between individuals and agencies, it is also the most diverse. Indeed, there is considerable disagreement within it on key issues, particularly at the strategic level. Gabriel Sheffer and Oren Barak define Israel's security network as

> first, acting and former members of the state's large and powerful security sector, particularly the military, that is, the Israel Defense Forces (IDF); second, former lower-ranking security personnel, also mainly from the army; third, influential actors operating within various civilian spheres (politics, the economy, and civil society), including politicians, bureaucrats, wealthy private entrepreneurs, academics, and journalists.[9]

The third category of individuals can be qualified to include former military and intelligence officials who, having retired from active service, have moved into different sectors of Israeli life. The defense industry is also sometimes considered an element of the network.

These individuals and agencies share a set of conceptual frameworks and policy priorities, including an autonomous military and an expectation of primacy in government decision-making regarding both foreign affairs and certain domestic issues, such as the government budget. Though they are military and security officials, they do not necessarily prioritize the use of force over diplomacy. In the aftermath of the 1993 Oslo Accords, for example, the IDF leadership tended to support negotiations with the Palestinians over military confrontation. Similarly, many serving and former officials argue that the Joint Comprehensive Plan of Action signed in July 2015 by the P5+1 (the United States, Russia, China, France, the United Kingdom, and Germany) and Tehran to prevent the development of Iranian nuclear weapons is not perfect but it does delay the possibility of Iran producing a nuclear weapon, which avoids the need for a strike against Iran's nuclear facilities.

The security network's influence stems from the close association of the military with the development of the state itself. In addition to the obvious factor that Israel was born into a state of war and had to endure a continuing siege after the end of the first Arab–Israeli War, the military's importance expanded because it was one of the few institutions capable of developing the state in the early years. Thus the IDF was given specific civilian functions to perform. These included:

1. Education of new immigrants, particularly Mizrachim. The IDF not only inculcated (socialist) Zionist values in these new recruits but also taught them Hebrew.
2. Absorption of new immigrants. Given the rapid expansion of the population immediately after 1948, there was a pressing need to house, clothe, and feed the new immigrants. By having many of them enter the military, the state bought time to build housing and other infrastructure, and in the meantime the immediate needs of the immigrants could be fulfilled.
3. Settlement expansion within the Green Line. The IDF used its *Nahal* (Youth Pioneer Fighting) Corps to establish agricultural communities around the country, often close to the state's borders, to serve as a first line of defense against invasion.
4. Dual development of technology and skills. The need to remain ahead of its enemies in qualitative terms has engendered a dynamic creativity in military officers, researchers, and developers. The skills and training that officers receive are transferable to civilian activity. Many of Israel's advances in biomedical technology, for example, have been made by former IDF members who started their own companies after leaving service. Unit 8200, a large sigint (signal intelligence) agency, serves as an incubator for civilian high-tech development. At the same time, the security agencies serve as an avenue for socio-economic mobility. Veterans are entitled to a number of social and medical benefits that others are not. Furthermore,

many companies are reluctant to hire those who have not served. In 2014, for example, a number of Arabs and Jews were fired from Israel Railways when the company decided that only military veterans could do its security-related work.

The security network's influence is both direct and indirect. First, because some of its members are serving officials of state institutions (the IDF and the intelligence agencies), they directly participate in governmental policymaking and so can insert their preferences and demands into the decision-making process.[10] Second, because Israel is still threatened by surrounding states and nonstate actors and engages in military confrontation regularly, much of its foreign affairs is tied to security affairs. As such, there is a real need for these individuals' expertise, particularly in tactical planning. Third, former security officers frequently move from defense to politics, occupying top spots in various political parties and, when the party joins the government, serving as key ministers. They bring with them their connections to former colleagues in the military, as well as their expertise, which fosters a sense of proprietorship over policymaking regarding security and foreign affairs and keeps security issues at the top of the policy agenda. Sheffer and Barak calculate that since 1984, between 10 and 16 percent of parliamentarians have had significant security backgrounds.[11]

Fourth, former defense officials occupy leadership positions in the private sector, in the economy, in prominent research institutes, and elsewhere in what is referred to as their "second careers." They carry authority on the basis of their former positions within the military and security agencies. The repeated circulation of shared ideas about the importance of security matters and their authority to pronounce on them, about procurement of military items, and about the budget for the IDF and other security agencies—for example through participation in research centers like the Institute for National Security Studies and a series of security conferences bringing together academics, former analysts, and current military officers, such as the annual Herzliya Conference—is thus reinforced at both the public and the governmental level. Finally, there is little public dissent regarding the security network's role in policymaking. The Israeli population still tends to view the country as threatened, and therefore accepts a more activist security framework as necessary. There is, for example, considerable public tolerance for a large military budget.

Peace Groups

Coexisting alongside the security network are groups broadly referred to as "peace" organizations. These are groups that argue for "dovish" policies: less reliance on the use of force in and a negotiated settlement to the conflict with both the Arab states and the Palestinians. They argue that Israel is occupying the West Bank[12] and that the best way to resolve the conflict is by ending that occupation and evacuating most of the settlements. Peace groups normally recognize that by this point, at least some settlements—the so-called "consensus" settlements, or the main blocs—will likely be annexed by Israel in return for land swaps from Israeli territory. Therefore they tend to be firm supporters of the two-state solution. But although peace groups share this agenda, there is some diversity among them.

The most prominent, Peace Now, was formed in 1978 by reserve officers and soldiers when the Egypt–Israel peace talks appeared to be faltering, in part over the future disposition of the West Bank. In a public letter, the group argued that it was better to give up the notion of Greater Israel than to undermine the Jewish and democratic character of the state and its normalization in the Middle East. Despite its roots, however, today the organization is not identified as a security-oriented one. Its primary method of influencing government policy is by working through the outside array of forces—namely, public opinion. This includes organizing public rallies on specific events and government policies, as well as working with opinion leaders, politicians, foreign visitors, and others to provide analysis, trips through the West Bank, and information sessions. The group also cooperates with different political parties, providing information on settlement activity, and testifies to various government agencies.

Another group is the Council for Peace and Security (CPS). Founded in 1988 and composed primarily of former security and military officers, this group uses its security expertise and links to the security network to promote dovish policies. For example, in 2002 the government began construction on the security barrier— a complex of concrete blocks, electrified fences, monitors, and open, sandy spaces over which passage would be obvious. Designed to stop the wave of Palestinian terrorists coming from the West Bank into Israel, this wall ran along the Green Line but looped into the West Bank to protect Jewish settlements there.[13] Many Palestinian villages, towns, and agricultural lands were caught up in the web of the barrier and were cut off from each other or divided. In 2004, as the barrier was being constructed around Mevasseret Zion (a Jewish city in Israel), it cut the nearby West Bank Palestinian village of Beit Surik off from the villagers' farmland. Citizens of Mevasseret Zion mobilized to make sure this did not happen, enlisting the aid of the CPS. When the case was brought before the High Court of Justice, the CPS was recognized as a "friend of the court," and its testimony helped convince the court to rule that the barrier had to be rerouted in that area.[14]

A third prominent peace group, no longer in existence, was Four Mothers. This organization's specific purpose was to push for an end to the Israeli occupation of the "security belt" in south Lebanon—a narrow strip about 10 kilometers wide that Israel retained after its invasion in 1982. Immobilized in the zone, the IDF was subjected to continuous guerilla attacks by Hezbollah. Over the course of the occupation 256 soldiers were killed in combat—an average of about 20 per year (excluding accidents). On February 4, 1997, two military helicopters crashed over the zone, killing 73 soldiers. Four women, whose sons were serving in the security belt, were galvanized into action and formed a movement to pressure the government to withdraw, performing outreach and organizing protests. Under Ehud Barak, Israel did evacuate all its soldiers in May 2000, and the United Nations soon afterward certified it no longer occupied any part of Lebanon. The movement dissolved itself soon after.

Though these groups do have some direct connections to policymakers and political parties, they tend to operate like "regular" interest groups. That is, they seek to change public and government attitudes through lobbying, provision of information, and shaping public opinion through media work and public protests. Other peace-oriented research institutes, such as the Peres Center for Peace and the Economic Cooperation Foundation, have been founded or led by individuals who have participated actively in informal or track-two peace negotiations and continue to promote these ideas in the same manner.

A common tactic used by all such groups has been to demonstrate the costs to the Israeli public of occupation of territories outside the 1949 armistice lines, especially the West Bank. Peace Now's current campaign is meant to show citizens that while their cost of living is rising, the government has been giving the settlements in the West Bank subsidies, thereby decreasing the cost of living for settlers. A second prominent tactic has been to organize protests and rallies. Although there was broad initial public support for the invasion of Lebanon in 1982, the population soon sensed the mission had gone off course. The massacres at the Sabra and Shatilla refugee camps tipped the scales against the war, facilitating the success of Peace Now's rallies.[15] At one demonstration an estimated 400,000 people, equal to about 10 percent of the country's population, gathered in Tel Aviv. Peace Now's efforts led to the creation of other antiwar groups that shared its anti-settlement and anti-occupation agenda, including Mothers Against Silence, the Committee Against the War in Lebanon, and *Yesh Gvul* (There Is a Limit).

If changes in government policy are the measure by which to judge the success of these groups, then the peace groups have had only limited impact. The withdrawal from settlements in Sinai in the early 1980s and from Gaza in 2005 were carried out in response to the decisions of individual government leaders who already believed withdrawal was in the national interest, without having been pushed by peace groups. Nevertheless, these groups do keep the issue of settlements and occupation on the public agenda.

The Settler Movement

Working in opposition to peace groups is the settler movement. The leaders of this movement are Religious Zionists or secular nationalists who deeply believe that the West Bank is the Jewish people's biblical and historical homeland and should remain so today as part of a Greater Israel. Their goal is to expand the number of settlements across the West Bank to both stay connected to the land and to create "facts on the ground" that will make it harder for any government to withdraw. But many settlers are not as ideological as these leaders and move to the territory for wider, greener spaces and cheaper housing; Peace Now estimates that about 31 percent of settlers fall into this category, while 29 percent are haredi, many of whom share the former's nonideological goals.

The settlement movement was created as a result of the 1967 War. Although many on the right did not fully accept the armistice borders established in 1949, they could not actively press for Israel to expand beyond them. The capture of the West Bank during the Six-Day War opened up the area and catalyzed what had been a slow process of radicalization among the younger generation. At first, the Labor government restricted expansion to "security settlements," although it allowed the formation of some on the basis of religious conviction (in Hebron) or historical attachment (Kfar Etzion). Still, the movement remained amorphous and unorganized until the 1973 War and Likud's ascent to power in 1977. At that time national religious and secular nationalists believed that Israel's poor performance at the start of the war was a consequence of the stagnation of the Zionist project. In response, in early 1974 a number of young Religious Zionists resolved to become more organized and established Gush Emunim as something like a youth movement within the NRP.

Gush Emunim became the lead group of the settler movement through its settlement arm, *Amana*, but it operated via the NRP for most of its early existence. There was a constant tension between it and the "old guard" (or moderates) of the party. The youth of Gush, strongly influenced by the ideas of Rabbi Zvi Yehuda Kook, wanted to take a more active, even aggressive, role in promoting settlements and did not care about participating in politics. The leaders of the party wanted to be more circumspect and to work through coalition governments.[16] This seemed easier to do when Menachem Begin and Likud won the 1977 election, but even then Gush became impatient with Begin, particularly after his decision to evacuate settlements in Sinai as part of the peace treaty with Egypt, a move that Gush saw as a betrayal. Scenes of violence in opposition to the evacuation order were particularly poignant at Yamit in northern Sinai, where residents of the settlement physically resisted removal and supporters came from outside the area to defend them.

Today Gush is no longer active, though former members and subgroups within it—such as Amana—continue to operate. Its political work has largely been taken over by the *Yesha* Council (the Hebrew acronym for Judea, Samaria, and Gaza). Individual leaders and heads of national religious yeshivot have also sprung up throughout the settlements and Israel to coordinate activity.

The settler movement operates on multiple fronts. First, it participates directly in the political process through the existence of national religious parties (previously the NRP, but today Bayit Yehudi) and individuals in other parties (particularly Likud and Yisrael Beiteinu). Second, it seeks to shape public opinion by demonstrating the importance of the West Bank to Jewish history and identity, although it has been less successful in this aim. Third, it seeks to create "facts on the ground" by expanding settlements even without the government's permission. A faction within the movement, sometimes called "hilltop youth," has been particularly active on this front. These youths spread out from existing settlements to the high ground of the West Bank and set up small, makeshift camps there (known as outposts) to claim them as a new settlement or as a new neighborhood of an existing one. Once these settlements have been established, the government feels obligated to support the settlers and so runs electricity and plumbing lines to these "illegal outposts." Fourth, settlers and their supporters have penetrated the government, taking up key positions in the bureaucracy and the military.[17] This allows them to both block implementation of decisions to evacuate settlements and to directly support the founding, expansion, and protection of settlements through concrete action—such as the decision to provide materials for building roads or the approval of tenders for construction in the West Bank. The issue of settlement expansion is also related to the dynamics of the Israeli–Palestinian conflict. Israel's governments have been reluctant to unilaterally remove settlements in the absence of a peace treaty because of deep suspicion of Palestinian intentions.

There have always been tensions between different groups within the settler movement, particularly over methods of settlement promotion. The moderate-radical disagreement of the 1960s and 1970s within the NRP was an early example of this. The hilltop youth of today clash with the Yesha Council and other settlers over how active and aggressive they should be. Some of the radicals have adopted violent tactics, including attacks against Palestinians in the West Bank and against army bases in advance of expected forced evacuations. Additionally, they have launched what are called "price tag" operations—assaults on Palestinians and their property in the West Bank meant to dissuade the Israeli government from halting settlement growth or carrying out efforts to dismantle settlements by demonstrating the consequences of such actions.

The settler movement remains one of the most successful of Israel's interest groups. Since 1972, the number of settlers in the West Bank (excluding east Jerusalem) has increased from 2,000 to about 350,000. Not only have the number of settlements and the number of settlers continued to rise since the 1970s, but few governments have had the political will to remove them from the West Bank.

Other Groups and Movements

There are many other civil society groups operating within the political system that deserve some mention. Some are smaller and weaker, while others have been able to effect considerable legal and political change. Religious movements are an important feature of associational life in Israel. Most obvious among them are the haredi communities discussed in Chapter 6. Much of the power of the haredim comes from their role in the political system through specific parties such as United Torah Judaism and Shas. In addition to haredi and Orthodox groups, the Masorti (Conservative) and Reform movements also operate in Israel. Though these denominations make up the bulk of American Jewry, they are small in Israel. In 2013, an Israel Democracy Institute poll found that only 7.1 percent of Israeli Jews identify as either Reform or Conservative. Because of this, their success is limited. Most Jewish Israelis associate religion with Orthodox interpretations or prefer not to associate with organized religion at all. Nevertheless, the Reform and Conservative movements have played an important role in getting some issues on the public agenda and in helping individuals navigate the complex and slow-moving Israeli bureaucracy. They have also had some small successes through their educational and lobbying efforts in expanding available space for non-Orthodox religious practices. Other organizations not tied to specific denominations, such as Hiddush, seek to limit the implementation of religious rules in the public sphere.

Another important grouping is composed of organizations focused on human rights or Arab rights. Examples of the former category include the New Israel Fund, the Association for Civil Rights in Israel, and Rabbis for Human Rights, as well as several that focus specifically on Israeli policy in the West Bank, such as B'Tselem, Breaking the Silence, and Yesh Din. Examples of groups concerned more specifically with the rights and quality of life of Arab citizens include Adalah, Mossawa, and Sikkuy. Organizations lobbying on this issue-area have expanded since the 1980s, at the onset of the "constitutional revolution" in Israel, a period that saw an expansion of legal understanding of civil and political rights in the absence of a specific constitutional document. A more activist Supreme Court under President Aharon Barak facilitated this effort (see Chapter 14).

Not surprisingly, these organizations' activity has also become highly politicized, as, beginning in 2009, a succession of right-wing governments comprising several neo-nationalists has produced a series of bills these groups deem antidemocratic, illiberal, and anti-Arab. For their part, right-leaning parties and organizations accuse the Arab rights groups of trying to undermine the Jewish character of the state (which, given their calls for an end to the distinction between Jewish and Arab citizens, is not wholly inaccurate) and the human rights groups as being far out of the Israeli mainstream. Thus the struggle over these issues is now viewed as a political contest between left and right.

A final interest group that deserves mention is diaspora Jewry—populations of Jews who live outside of Israel, the largest and strongest community of which is in the United States. It may seem strange to include noncitizens of Israel in a discussion of Israeli associational life, but the connection many diaspora Jews feel to Israel is deeply embedded in their communal consciousness. As such, they have long participated in supporting Israel through philanthropy, advocacy work in their home countries, and tourism.[18] As well, because Israel is the only Jewish state and an important element of diaspora Jewish identity, this group has long felt it necessary to try to influence Israeli policy when it touches on questions of identity that encompass what it means to be Jewish—for example, on questions of how to define Jewishness, civil marriage, and religious pluralism in Israel.

At the same time, though Israelis tend to neglect the ideas of American and diaspora Jewry, Israel's leaders have sometimes turned to U.S. Jews for help. In August 2013 Justice Minister Tzipi Livni appointed Ruth Gavison, one of Israel's most prominent legal scholars, to prepare a report on how a constitution might address the question of Israel's character as a Jewish and democratic state, partly in response to efforts by members of Likud, Yisrael Beiteinu, and Bayit Yehudi to privilege Israel's Jewish identity over other elements, such as its democratic foundation, in a Basic Law. Gavison then asked the Jewish People Policy Institute to prepare a report on what Jews outside of Israel think about how best to maintain Israel as a Jewish and democratic state. The report found that among diaspora Jews, "the dominant view was unmistakable: the desire to see an Israel that is both Jewish and democratic, and the assumption that such a combination is certainly possible, despite the tensions involved."[19] This suggests that diaspora Jews are likely to continue trying to influence Israeli policy when deemed necessary.

Though we have divided civil society groups into different categories, there is some overlap between them. For instance, Arab rights groups and organizations focused on the occupation have much in common. This raises the question of whether the domestic and foreign spheres can be completely separated, particularly when it comes to the West Bank and questions about the applicability of Israeli law. Though no government has formally annexed any part of the West Bank apart from east Jerusalem and, through the expansion of the city's municipal boundaries, the immediate area around it, Israeli law does apply in Israeli settlements. Most of the rest of the territory, including places where Palestinians live, is subject to Israeli military law under the Civil Administration, which is part of the Defense Ministry. It does not seem that a clear separation is possible, which complicates the advocacy work of these groups.

Constraints on interest groups exist in Israel, as they do in many other countries. Marginalized populations tend to be underrepresented, the security situation often takes precedence over other considerations, and the unresolved question of how to maintain a Jewish and democratic polity complicates associational groups' legal and political efforts. But it is also clear that Israel has a vibrant civil societal life, with many groups operating in a variety of different issue-areas.

POLITICAL PROTEST

A final form of participation is political protest. Protests are a direct form of citizen pressure. Gadi Wolfsfeld has contended that protests arrived late to Israel, in the early 1970s, but since then have been used regularly by Israelis to try to influence policymakers.[20]

The 1973 War facilitated the emergence of public protest as a viable alternative to the political party. In October of that year Egypt and Syria achieved strategic surprise in a coordinated attack on Israel. In the first days of the war the Israeli military was pushed back, which posed what many believed to be an existential threat to the country. The IDF recovered and won the war, but at great cost. Confidence in the Labor Party, already shaky because of growing discontent with its long years of rule, was shattered. Labor was able to win the December 1973 election, but it lost seats. After the election, a lone soldier, Motti Ashkenazi, began a one-man protest outside the Prime Minister's office. Word spread, and hundreds of people soon joined him. Under pressure the government appointed the Agranat Commission to investigate the causes of the war's failures. First released in April 1974, the commission's report held several senior military and security officers liable but left the political leadership (Prime Minister Golda Meir and Defense Minister Moshe Dayan) largely free from responsibility. This engendered further protests, and Meir eventually resigned.

Public rallies at first focused on very narrow issues of concern to small segments of the population. The Black Panthers, named after the American group, organized a number of demonstrations in the early 1970s to protest discrimination against Mizrachi Jews; the highest turnout may have been several thousand. That same decade saw the emergence of the Young Couples protests. Anticipating the 2011 social justice protests, these demonstrations were meant to raise awareness of the high cost of housing, which was prohibitive for young, newly married couples. Turnout was typically between 200 and 300 individuals. Israel's Arab citizens have been protesting on and off since the 1970s as well, an ongoing effort that culminated in the protests of 2000, which turned into riots and direct clashes with Jewish citizens and police. Each year, on March 30, Arab Israelis march to commemorate the events of that day in 1976 (see Chapter 7) and to protest the Israeli state's land expropriation policies and other forms of discrimination.

Peace Now's protests against the invasion of Lebanon have already been mentioned. The Israeli withdrawal from most of Lebanon after 1982 is attributed in part to the widespread public opposition to the campaign. Settlers and their supporters have also held several rallies over the years against plans to dismantle settlements. The haredi population of Israel regularly protests the opening of roads through their neighborhoods on Shabbat, archaeological digs at sites they consider sacred, immodest advertising at bus stops, and women praying loudly and from the Torah at the Western Wall. Tens of thousands came out regularly over the course of 2013 and 2014 against the imposition of a draft on the community (similar numbers came out in rallies in New York, which has a significant haredi population as well). In 2014 and 2015 several haredi men were arrested for avoiding conscription, which prompted further protests. Haredi protesters have typically blocked streets and sometimes have hurled garbage and rocks at police and trespassers. In April and May 2015, a few thousand Ethiopian Israelis, with some support from other citizens, marched in Jerusalem and Tel Aviv to raise awareness of police brutality and institutionalized racism against the community.

The other major protest activity in recent years was the series of demonstrations concerning social justice that began in July 2011, sometimes referred to as the housing protests. Pitching tents in the middle of trendy Rothschild Boulevard in Tel Aviv, young Israelis protested the high cost of housing, the high cost of living more generally, and the free market policies of the Netanyahu government. One of the primary issues highlighted was the excessive price of cottage cheese, which exemplified these problems. The young protestors were soon joined by many others, and the demonstrations spread to other cities where younger generations felt trapped by poverty. Hundreds of thousands of Israelis came out over the course of the rest of the year. In September 2011 an estimated 450,000 Israelis rallied across the country, though the protests petered out by the middle of 2012.

Public protests have helped put specific items on the policy agenda, but they have not often led to direct changes in government policy. The Black Panther, Palestinian Israeli, and social justice protests, for example, have prompted the government to create committees or commissions of inquiry to look into the issues of concern and propose recommendations for addressing them. But typically these recommendations have not been enacted, or have only been partially enacted. The 1973 War and its aftermath dislodged the Black Panthers' concerns from the government agenda. The continuation of the Second Intifada and subsequent military confrontations with Hezbollah and Hamas shifted the government's concern toward security matters, and the Or Commission's recommendations regarding Arab Israelis were mostly disregarded. The Trajtenberg Committee's recommendations on improving social and economic conditions were opposed by various parties and groups, and very few of them have been implemented.

It has also been difficult for protestors to sustain their momentum and public interest, except perhaps in the case of the haredi protests. This may be because the government has often promised to look into the issues (regardless of whether it resolves them), but it seems to also be due to an underlying apathy among the population. It is not clear what has driven this apathy. It may be that the shift toward an individualist political culture away from the collectivist ethos has engendered greater concern among people with their own problems rather than public affairs. Uri Ben-Eliezer makes a strong argument against the efficacy of interest group activity and public protest as a result of Israel's lingering collectivist and statist political culture.[21]

SUMMARY

This chapter has noted the relatively closed nature of the Israeli political system. Over the years the decision-making system has opened up, and as civil society has expanded a plethora of interest groups have gained access to the system. Some groups have had success in the political and judicial arenas, and the Israeli public has been able to change policy through protest. Still, while these activities have become legitimate means of political participation, the public's ability to effect change is still largely mediated by the political parties. In this sense, Israel is no different from other democratic countries where citizens protest. In the face of a government determined to ignore an issue or to focus on another, more compelling, concern, citizens might push public opinion in a different direction in the long term, but they have less of a direct influence over immediate policy.

KEYWORDS

interest groups, civil society, access, lobbying, organized labor, security network, peace groups, settler movement, political protest

NOTES

1. See Asher Arian, *Politics in Israel: The Second Republic*, 2nd ed. (Washington, D.C.: CQ Press, 2005), 317–319; Paula Kabalo, "Constructing Civil Society: Citizen Associations in Israel in the 1950s," *Nonprofit and Voluntary Sector Quarterly* 35 (2006): 161–182; Yael Yishai, "Civil Society in Transition: Interest Politics in Israel," *Annals of the American Academy of Political and Social Science* 555 (1998): 147–162; Yael Yishai, *Land of Paradoxes: Interest Politics in Israel* (Albany: State University of New York Press, 1991).

2. Gadi Wolfsfeld, *The Politics of Provocation: Participation and Protest in Israel* (Albany: SUNY Press, 1988); Yaron Ezrahi, *Rubber Bullets: Power and Conscience in Modern Israel* (Berkeley: University of California Press, 1997).

3. See, for example, Gershon Shafir and Yoav Peled, *Being Israeli: The Dynamics of Multiple Citizenship* (Cambridge: Cambridge University Press, 2002), chapter 9.

4. The condition that a group cannot deny Israel's existence as "Jewish and democratic" was removed in December 2013 by the Ministerial Committee for Legislative Affairs.

5. Yael Yishai, "Interest Groups and Bureaucrats in a Party-Democracy: The Case of Israel," *Public Administration* 70 (1992): 269–285. See also Yishai, "Civil Society in Transition"; idem, "Bringing Society Back In: Post-Cartel Parties in Israel," *Party Politics* 7 (2001): 667–687; and idem, "Civil Society and Democracy," *Voluntas: International Journal of Voluntary and Nonprofit Organizations* 13 (2002): 215–234.

6. The language was in reaction to fears that some Arab organizations were pushing for an end to the Jewish character of the state, and that some religious groups were pushing for the imposition of halachic rules over democratic decision-making.

7. Yair Zalmanovitch, "Transitions in Israel's Policymaking Network," *Annals of the American Academy of Political and Social Science* 555 (1998): 195.

8. Hila Weissberg, Haim Bior, and Tali Heruti-Sover, "Labor of Love: Israelis Get Organized, Flock to Union in Record Numbers," *Haaretz*, June 5, 2013.

9. Gabriel Sheffer and Oren Barak, *Israel's Security Networks: A Theoretical and Comparative Perspective* (Cambridge: Cambridge University Press, 2013), 2.

10. Charles D. Freilich, *Zion's Dilemmas: How Israel Makes National Security Policy* (Ithaca, NY: Cornell University Press, 2012).

11. Sheffer and Barak, *Israel's Security Networks*, 51.

12. Gaza is often considered a separate, more complex, problem because Hamas—which refuses to renounce violence or recognize Israel's existence—rules there, and because Israel does not technically occupy it but does maintain a land and sea blockade against it.

13. Critics argue it was also a land grab to ensure the settlements it protected could not be dismantled in case of a final peace treaty.

14. Oded Löwenheim, *The Politics of the Trail: Reflexive Mountain Biking Along the Frontier of Jerusalem* (Ann Arbor: University of Michigan Press, 2014), 105.

15. Sabra and Shatilla are two Palestinian refugee camps in Lebanon. In September 1982, during the course of its invasion, Israel worked with Maronite Christians to root out the Palestine Liberation Organization and to reconstitute the government of Lebanon. When the recently elected President Bashir Gemayel was assassinated, his followers blamed Palestinians. They invaded the two camps, which were within the area that Israel controlled, and over the course of about three days killed several hundred civilians. An Israeli commission of inquiry found that although Israel did not participate in the attacks, it was "indirectly responsible" for them because Israeli forces had allowed the Maronite forces into the camps and should have anticipated what happened next.

16. Kook had been promoting messianic ideas of a religious nationalist revival even before 1967, spurring many of his followers to "seize the moment" after the war. Yossi Klein Halevi, *Like Dreamers: The Story of the Israeli Paratroopers Who Reunited Jerusalem and Divided a Nation* (New York: HarperCollins, 2013).

17. Oded Haklai, "Religious-Nationalist Mobilization and State Penetration: Lessons from Jewish Settlers' Activism in Israel and the West Bank," *Comparative Political Studies* 40 (2007): 713–739.

18. Theodore Sasson, *The New American Zionism* (New York: New York University Press, 2013).

19. For the full report, see Jewish People Policy Institute, *Jewish and Democratic: Perspectives from World Jewry*, 2014, http://jppi.org.il/uploads/jewish_and_democratic-eng.pdf.

20. Wolfsfeld, *Politics of Provocation*. The first major protests broke out in Wadi Salib, a poor neighborhood of Haifa populated by North African immigrants, in 1959. These turned quickly into riots, which shocked the public consciousness but did bring widespread attention to the discrimination against the Mizrachi population.

21. Uri Ben-Eliezer, "The Meaning of Political Participation in a Nonliberal Democracy: The Israeli Experience," *Comparative Politics* 25 (1993): 397–412.

CHAPTER 12

✦

The Knesset

I srael's legislative body is the Knesset (Assembly), which has the duty of passing the laws of the state. The character of the Knesset reflects the state's multiparty system and proportional representation electoral system. In principle it is the focal point of the governmental structure, especially since the government (i.e., the Cabinet) must be approved by the Knesset and is responsible to it. Moreover, the Knesset does have the power to bring down the government, even if that power has been attenuated by the requirement for a constructive vote of non-confidence.

In this chapter we compare the 120-member Knesset to other parliaments, stressing the relationship between the Knesset and the government. As in other parliamentary systems, the executive power is not separate from the legislative power, because the executive (the Cabinet or government) is voted in and can be brought down by the legislature. In technical terms it is responsible to the legislative body. The chapter then examines the effect of the electoral system on the Knesset; the members of the body; how the Knesset operates in the Israeli system; the legislative process, including committee work; and the relationship between the Knesset and the government.

STRUCTURE OF THE KNESSET

The basic structure of Israel's system of government is similar to that of other parliamentary democracies, especially those in Europe. However, there are some important differences. One is that Israel has a unicameral legislature, whereas other countries, such as the United States, Canada, Britain, France, Italy, and Germany, have bicameral legislatures. Another is the nature of the proportional representation electoral system based on a single national constituency. Few European countries have a voting system quite like Israel's, though Slovakia, the Netherlands, and Russia do have one statewide constituency, albeit with higher electoral thresholds for the inclusion of parties in the parliament. A third is that for traditional and structural reasons, Israel's electoral system is generally multiparty, producing an unusually large number of parties contesting elections as well as winning Knesset

---

BOX 12.1

Knesset Facts 2015

Members	120
Number of Knessets Since 1949	20
Term of a Knesset	4 years (appx.)
Presidium	Speaker plus several Deputy Speakers
Permanent Committees	12
Number of Parties/Lists	10
Dual Role	Legislature and Constituent Assembly
Site	Jerusalem

---

seats. This, in turn, has made it virtually impossible for the government to be formed by a single party; all governments are coalitions, usually led by the largest party in the parliament. In fact, Israel has never had a single-party majority government.

A major point of contention for reformers, who are generally concerned with managing a system that is divided among so many parties, is the relatively low threshold of vote proportion required in order for a party to gain representation in the Knesset. The threshold, set at 0.8 percent of the total vote for elections to the Constituent Assembly in 1949, was raised to 1 percent for the 1951 election to the Knesset, to 1.5 percent for the 1992 election, and to 2 percent for the 2006 election. Such low thresholds encouraged the splintering of parties and contributed to the large number of parties running for office and being elected. A significant increase in the threshold, to 3.25 percent, was adopted in 2014 after a proposal for 5 percent provoked intense opposition. Despite the final figure being lower than the proposal, several parties, notably the Arab parties, remain strongly opposed to the change, charging that it is an attempt to exclude them from the Knesset. The latest reform compelled the four Arab parties to run on a combined list (the Joint List) in order to get over the threshold in the 2015 election. A newly formed right-of-center Jewish party, Yachad, missed crossing the threshold in that election but would have passed the 2 percent threshold.

In recent elections it has been common for over 30 parties to compete, with 10 or more gaining seats in the legislature. The multiplicity of parties, some of them rather small, exacerbates the problem of forming and maintaining a government. All of these various factors contribute to a situation that makes governing Israel a challenge. In fact, in the 2013 election, Likud and Yisrael Beiteinu ran together on a joint list and won the most votes (23.34 percent) and therefore the most seats (31), though their total constituted barely a quarter of the seats in the Knesset. By mid-2014 the two parties had dissolved their alliance and decided to sit separately in the Knesset. Likud alone won 23.40 percent of the vote and 30 seats in 2015, making it the largest party in the parliament and able to dominate the new coalition, while Yisrael Beiteinu shrank to only six seats. Table 12.1 sets out the current makeup of the Knesset.

Table 12.1 Current Knesset by Party/List, Party/List Leader, and Seat Allocation, 2015

PARTY/LIST	LEADER	SEATS
Likud*	Binyamin Netanyahu	30
Zionist Union	Isaac Herzog	24
Joint List	Ayman Odeh	13
Yesh Atid	Yair Lapid	11
Kulanu*	Moshe Kahlon	10
Bayit Yehudi*	Naftali Bennett	8
Shas*	Aryeh Deri	7
United Torah Judaism*	Menachem Moses	6
Yisrael Beiteinu	Avigdor Liberman	6
Meretz	Zahava Gal-On	5
Total		**120**

* Indicates a party that is in the government.

Given all its flaws, the electoral system has been controversial since the early days of statehood. Even David Ben-Gurion, considered the founder of Israel, reportedly had doubts about the way the system was working but lacked the support necessary to make changes.[1] Yet despite the fact that reformers have been seeking a way to improve the system for decades, no solution is on the horizon, especially as an attempt during the 1990s failed.

Like so many other parliamentary systems, Israel has experienced a trend toward executive dominance during the past several decades.[2] This trend has been reinforced by the power of the political parties, which have been central players in politics since before the creation of the state. In fact, the government tends to dominate the legislative process, using the parties in the coalition to keep individual members of Knesset in line. This has diminished the importance of the individual members in the legislative process, leading many of them to focus on activities in which they have greater autonomy, such as constituency service,[3] promoting pet causes, or engaging in debates outside parliament on public issues. MKs from parties that are perennially outside the coalition, notably the Arab parties, seek to maintain a high profile outside of the Knesset in order to publicize the needs of their community. Good examples of Arab MKs who have become well known outside the Knesset are Ahmad Tibi (Ta'al), Haneen Zoabi (Balad), and the former MK Azmi Bishara (Balad). Bishara in fact ran a high-profile campaign for Prime Minister in the 1999 direct election but withdrew at the last minute.

Despite the intent of Israel's founders to adopt a constitution soon after independence, that goal has not been achieved yet. Nor is there any indication when the process of adopting one will be completed. The First Knesset was elected as a Constituent Assembly in 1949, charged with the task of producing a constitution, but soon after the election it became simultaneously a legislative body (the First Knesset). However, it quickly became apparent that the necessary consensus could not be achieved on matters such as individual rights and the place of religion in the state. Consequently that Knesset made two decisions: to adopt a series of Basic Laws piecemeal and to transfer to succeeding Knessets the status of constituent assembly. This meant that any later Knesset could adopt part or all of a constitution. The result has been that over the years 15 Basic Laws have been enacted and in some cases later amended or, in three cases, even repealed. The most recent, adopted in 2014, requires a super-majority in the Knesset or a national referendum if any peace treaty proposes to relinquish territory that is under Israeli sovereignty. It is widely understood that eventually all of the Basic Laws will be brought together as parts of a constitution, though there is no sense of when that might be (see Chapter 14). Until that process is complete, each Basic Law (such as the Basic Law: The Knesset) must stand on its own. Moreover, Basic Laws may be amended by a majority of voting Knesset members, though certain Basic Laws (The Knesset, Human Liberty and Dignity, Freedom of Occupation, and the Government) require an absolute majority (61 votes) for amendment.

LEGAL ASPECTS

Israel has universal suffrage: any citizen aged 18 and over who is in the country or in settlements in the West Bank on election day is eligible to vote. Any citizen who is at least 21 may be a candidate for the Knesset, with certain types of officials and officeholders excluded. A Knesset is elected for a term of about four years, with the next election scheduled for the third Tuesday of the Hebrew month of *Heshvan* (a month in the fall) four years later. As in other parliamentary systems, however, there are events that can lead to new elections being held earlier than the date prescribed by law. In Israel that typically occurs when a coalition government falls apart because one or more parties leave and the major parties agree that no new coalition can be established. At that point the Knesset will usually be asked to pass a bill setting a date for an early election. In December 2014 Prime Minister Binyamin Netanyahu, frustrated by two of his coalition partners, fired their party leaders from their ministerial posts, thus precipitating the 2015 election.

Historically the key elements in the election process are the parties, the cornerstones of the political system. However, there was an attempt during the 1990s to modify the electoral system so that it would not be entirely about parties. That reform introduced the direct election of the Prime Minister, described in Chapter 8. However, it proved to be a failure after only a few years and was repealed. Hence the electoral system today is much as it was at the beginning of statehood, except that the vote threshold for inclusion in the Knesset is substantially higher (3.25 percent compared to 0.8 percent).

Since MKs are dependent on their party for their place on its list (even when the parties hold primaries), they do not enjoy much autonomy with regard to Knesset business. Although factions do sometimes break away from a party, normally discipline is strictly enforced and the consequences of challenging it are quite significant, especially if the MK wants to have a realistic spot on his or her party's list in the next election. But there are occasions, usually not on top-priority bills, when an individual member bucks party or coalition discipline. The punishment for such action is up to the party leader and can range from denial of speaking opportunities to relegation to a lower spot on the party's list in the next election. MKs are rarely thrown out of a party, especially one that is part of the governing coalition, because that would weaken the party's place in the government. This means that there are few surprises when votes are taken in the Knesset. There may be lots of maneuvering behind the scenes as legislation is being developed or is working its way through the Cabinet, but once it comes to the floor of the Plenum, as the full Knesset is known, individual MKs have little leeway in the vast majority of cases.

KNESSET MEMBERS

After an election, the number of seats allocated to each party is determined according to a formula that is written into the law so that a party receives a number of seats very close to its proportion of the popular vote. The equivalence cannot be exact because there are no fractional seats. If a party is entitled to 25 seats, for example, the first 25 people on its electoral list become MKs. Should one of them resign or die during the term of that Knesset, the next person on the list becomes an MK. Hence there are no by-elections, and the party composition of the parliament cannot change unless sitting Knesset members switch parties.

A major issue for MKs is that they do not represent geographic constituencies and therefore are not individually accountable to voters. Rather, they are accountable to their parties, which selected them to run, gave them a realistic spot on the party's election list, and provide them with resources that facilitate their job performance. Proposals for electing at least some of the legislators, perhaps as many as half, from geographic districts (with the rest elected nationally, as done presently) have been around for years but have never garnered sufficient support to become serious options. Other options might be to elect all MKs from constituencies, which is unlikely, or to have multimember constituencies with proportional elections.

One interesting point is that the size of the Knesset has been fixed at 120 members since the creation of the state, and that number has not changed, despite a more than tenfold growth in population. During that same period, the lower houses of legislatures in some larger countries, such as the United States, Britain, and Canada, have grown in size to reflect population growth. There has been little discussion of doing so in Israel, perhaps because of the symbolism of a body that notionally contains a *minyan* (the traditional requirement of 10 participants in a prayer service) from each of the biblical 12 tribes.

In place of accountability to constituents within a district, Knesset members do represent interests within that portion of the electorate that voted for their party, and insofar as those interests can have an impact on the party list for the next election, members do have to worry about keeping them happy. They can and do communicate with such constituents and can be persuaded to take up the various causes that the interests hope to pursue. In the early days of the state, Mapai members often represented part of the kibbutz movement or organized labor. Today, many Bayit Yehudi members are known to represent the interests of the West Bank settlers and have been quite vocal in that regard since entering the government in

2013. But ultimately it is not the individual MK who formulates major policy proposals, but the party leadership or bureaucrats. Members do introduce private members' bills; many are put forth each year, and some of them do pass, but they tend not to deal with central policy issues. Moreover, most MKs aspire to advancement in the party and perhaps eventually a ministerial position. Fulfilling such aspirations generally requires following directions from those higher in the party and the parliamentary delegation. As a result, the incentive system discourages individual members from initiating major policy changes.

The relatively unimportant role of individual MKs in shaping legislation, which is the main responsibility of the Knesset, leads many to focus on their relationship with members of the public, called constituency service. While the constituents served do not necessarily live in a well-defined geographic area, they are aware of which MKs are most likely to be responsive to their needs (presumably backbenchers or more junior members of the party for which they voted).

In addition, MKs can play a public role by speaking out on or espousing various issues and causes outside the Knesset. For example, Stav Shaffir, who came to the Labor Party from the 2011 protest movement, has been active in speaking and writing about social and economic issues, particularly government funding for West Bank settlements. Miri Regev in Likud has spoken publicly several times about her opposition to the presence of African migrants in the country. Even party leaders resort to this tactic: Bayit Yehudi leader Naftali Bennett, Hatenua head Tzipi Livni, and Yesh Atid leader Yair Lapid have all been very active on Facebook, posting declarations on their walls regarding government policy on issues from peace talks to economic policy. These activities outside the Knesset itself can have an important impact on an MK's performance in party primaries in advance of the next election and thus his or her position on the party's list. An MK who is trying to work his or her way up within the party's Knesset delegation needs to be attentive to the possibilities stemming from these outside activities for advancing a political career.

Knesset members enjoy a number of privileges and immunities that are considered vital to the proper exercise of their duties. Most prominent among these is immunity from criminal prosecution while serving as a member, except when caught in the act of committing a crime or betraying the state. Thus members have immunity for what they say and do in the Knesset and are protected in their outside actions as well. Such immunity ends when one is no longer an MK. However, it is not uncommon for members to be the target of criminal investigations. In such cases the Attorney General can ask the Knesset to lift the member's immunity so that he or she can be prosecuted. The House Committee and the full Knesset must approve the request before immunity is lifted, and only a majority vote for that action is required. After immunity is lifted the individual can be prosecuted in the ordinary criminal process. If convicted and sentenced to a prison term of at least one year, the MK can be removed from office by a two-thirds vote in the Knesset. There have been several occasions when an MK's immunity was lifted. During the mid-1980s Shmuel Flatto-Sharon lost his immunity when France demanded that he be extradited to face criminal charges. One of the best-known examples is the case of Shas leader Aryeh Deri, who served in the Cabinet. When corruption charges were brought against him during the late 1990s his immunity was lifted so that he could be prosecuted and eventually convicted. And in 2014, in a most unusual move, MK Haneen Zoabi had her speaking and other privileges suspended for six months by the Knesset Ethics Committee because of her involvement in external activities that were considered incitement. However, her right to vote was not affected, nor was she subject to criminal charges.

Aside from immunity to prosecution, the most important privilege enjoyed by MKs is the freedom to express themselves as they see fit. This has led to freewheeling debates on the floor of the Plenum. Not only is the member who has the floor protected, but very often other members will heckle the speaker, frequently leading to a rowdy and boisterous atmosphere. The practice of heckling and interrupting speakers has become one of the hallmarks of Knesset debates and has not enhanced the reputation of the body. Sometimes members have to be removed from the chamber because of such disruptions. The unruly atmosphere has also facilitated other antics. In 2013, for example, Meir Porush of United Torah Judaism handcuffed himself to the Knesset podium to emphasize his opposition to the haredi draft law.

Individual Knesset members who are not in the Cabinet do have opportunities to influence the legislative process, but even these are constrained. One is through the practice of Question Time, in which an MK can pose a question to a minister. But since ministers are not required to respond on the spot, as is the case in Britain and Canada, much of the drama of challenging the policies of the government is lost. Sometimes the answers are returned weeks later. Backbench members can also introduce Motions to Add to the Agenda, which is a way of forcing the government to address an issue that it would prefer not to address. However, if the government is determined to defeat the motion it can usually do so. Finally, the Knesset does have the power of investigation, usually through the committees. This process provides individual members with another opportunity to put the government on the spot, though this option may not be available if the committee chair is close to the Prime Minister. Despite the availability of these various options, the government can usually overcome such challenges by using its majority.

One of the more embarrassing aspects of politics in the Knesset is the frequency with which members or small factions have defected from the party through which they were elected. When that happens, the defectors may join one of the other existing factions, may form a new party, or may simply sit as independents. In the past potential defectors were enticed by offers of ministerial posts to join the government side, but that practice has been discouraged by amendments to the Basic Law: The Government that rule out the practice, imposing sanctions on those who engage in it. The most significant punishment for such behavior is the barring of such MKs from becoming ministers during the term of the present Knesset. Even so, party splits continue to take place. A high-profile example from a time before the current rules were in place occurred when Moshe Dayan, a stalwart of Labor, defied his party in 1977 by agreeing to become Likud Prime Minister Menachem Begin's Minister of Foreign Affairs. He did not switch parties, but his Labor colleagues saw his move as a betrayal nonetheless, given the decades of enmity between Labor and Likud (and their predecessor parties). Hence he was expelled from Labor and sat as an independent MK while serving as Foreign Minister. Another example was the break in the Labor Party's Knesset delegation in 2011, when the party split over whether to remain in the Likud-led government or not. Most of the party's MKs abandoned the party leader, Minister of Defense Ehud Barak, who wanted to stay in the government. The five MKs who left with him sat as an independent party and adopted the name Atzmaut; it did not contest the 2013 election. Nevertheless, Barak was able to remain in his office through the vehicle of his new party until the new government was formed after the election. There have also been instances in which parties have merged to form a new party (e.g., Herut and the Liberals joined to form Gahal in 1966 and then merged with smaller parties in 1973 to form Likud) or have agreed to run together in an election on a joint list (e.g., Likud and Yisrael Beiteinu in 2013; Ra'am, Ta'al, Balad, and Hadash in 2015; and Labor and Hatenua in 2015).

FUNCTIONS AND POWERS OF THE KNESSET

In principle the Knesset has full legislative powers, thereby setting policy for the state. In practice, however, much power has been delegated to the government, acting as a collective executive. In particular, the government has full powers in the areas of foreign affairs, security, and war and peace. It is the government that decides when to deploy military forces or to go to war. When there is a peace treaty or agreement it is the government that carries out the negotiations, although approval of the Knesset is generally required for the signing of such documents. In part this is the result of historical circumstance. The conventional military threat the country endured from 1948 until at least the 1970s, and the increase in terrorist attacks after that, required an expedited decision-making process and heightened secrecy. Most politicians and the public accepted the need for less public debate in order to maintain security, though by the 1980s and 1990s a general dissatisfaction with such procedures was increasingly felt. During the Gaza war of 2014 decision-making authority was delegated to an eight-member diplomatic and security cabinet. That body formally made the key policy decisions throughout the conflict. After several weeks of the fighting some MKs began to complain that they and the rest of the Knesset membership were being kept in the dark. However, the operation of the security cabinet was not affected by these complaints.

On domestic matters, passage of laws by the Knesset is generally required. However, the government, through the Ministerial Committee on Legislation, dominates the legislative process, with the vast majority of government bills being passed into law. The governing coalition generally determines the content of such bills and then guides the legislation through the Knesset, making adjustments as necessary. The Knesset does provide a forum for criticism of government policies and is a focal point for national debate about political priorities and how to achieve them.

The Knesset possesses some specific powers. For example, it elects the President of the state and the state comptroller, each for a term of seven years. Whereas the presidency is largely a symbolic office, the comptroller has real power to investigate any aspect of government activity and make public reports. Consequently it is a highly sensitive position. Furthermore the comptroller is accountable to the Knesset rather than to the government, thereby reinforcing the significance of the post.

Despite the fact that an outside observer attending a Knesset session might gain the impression of a chaotic atmosphere, the body is really quite well organized. The key person is the Speaker, who retains considerable authority in regulating the debates. There are also several Deputy Speakers who assist the Speaker and sometimes preside over the body themselves. Together the Speaker and Deputy Speakers constitute the Presidium, which runs the Knesset. Among their powers are the requirement that they approve the tabling of private members' bills and motions for the agenda. These are two devices that give backbenchers some measure of independence from the government, though the latter does dominate Knesset proceedings. Another body that deals with private members' bills and motions for the agenda is the House Committee, one of the standing committees of the Knesset. That committee allocates the number of private members' bills and motions for the agenda that each party can bring forward during the year. Thus the combination of the Presidium and the House Committee substantially controls the flow of nongovernment business.

One other committee, the Arrangements Committee, should be mentioned here. This committee only operates at the beginning of a new Knesset, that is, after a general election. Its task is to organize the new Knesset, after which it dissolves. Among its responsibilities is the allocation of committee seats to the parties that are represented in the legislature, usually in proportion to the number of seats that each party holds in the Knesset. It also recommends specific MKs to chair committees (usually ratifying choices agreed upon in the coalition negotiations for a new government), seating arrangements in the Plenum, and assignment of the various rooms and offices in the Knesset building.

The Legislative Process

The Knesset convenes annually for two sessions of about four months each. This leaves members with considerable time to service their constituents and to engage in other activities that are not strictly lawmaking. When they are in session, the technical aspects of the legislative process are similar in many respects to those employed in other parliamentary systems. In particular, bills must go through three readings and be approved by a majority of those voting at each stage before they are considered passed. Because of the predictability of outcomes, it is not unusual for bills to pass with fewer than 50 votes. After passage several signatures are required, notably from the Speaker, the Prime Minister, and the President, before the bill is officially enacted. But these signatures are not substantive; no one has the power to veto a bill. In effect, once a bill passes the requisite three readings in the Knesset, it will become law.

One way in which Knesset practice departs from that of legislative bodies elsewhere is that there is no quorum requirement. The only other country with a similar system but no quorum is Sweden. As a result sessions are often poorly attended, even when votes on relatively important issues are taken. As with many aspects of Knesset business, this can be attributed to the strictly enforced party discipline that substantially guarantees the outcome of votes on the floor and even in committees. Because the electoral system emphasizes parties rather than individuals, legislative practice reflects the same calculation.

The most important bills introduced are government bills; they are sent to the Knesset after being approved by a majority in the Cabinet, which means many of the political struggles regarding the content of bills are carried out in that body. Votes are taken there to resolve contentious issues, and once a bill emerges from the government it is expected that the members of the coalition in the Knesset will vote for it. Since normally the coalition has a majority in the Knesset, passage is usually assured. Consequently, the Knesset adopts the vast majority of government bills. There are some cases, however, in which debate in the Knesset or its committees might lead to changes in bills proposed by the government. Thus party leaders in the coalition have to assess the political costs of a controversial bill before deciding whether to accept amendments to it.

Generally the first reading of a bill is pro forma, after which the bill goes to the appropriate committee. Committees can take a considerable amount of time to examine a bill, as will be discussed in the next section. They can and do hold hearings and entertain amendments. Once the committee has completed its work the bill is returned to the Plenum for the second reading. That is the key point in the process; bills that pass the second reading often proceed directly to the third reading and completion of the legislative process. If the bill has been reported out with amendments or extensive revisions, the minister managing the bill may recall it and take it back to the government for further consideration to determine whether the amendments are acceptable. At that point the government has to decide whether to accept the changes, make alternate changes, or withdraw the bill altogether. If it wants to continue with the bill it sends it back to the Knesset for the second reading. Amended government bills are usually held for about a week between the second and third readings.

During the debates on the floor of the Plenum the leadership of the various parties determines the allocation of speaking time to their respective members. This results in speeches that tend not to be overly lengthy. Given that the outcome of most votes can be anticipated, much of the speaking time, especially by a bill's opponents, is devoted to various forms of posturing—a common tactic in any parliamentary democracy.

Private members' bills in principle follow essentially the same pattern as government bills (though they do undergo a preliminary reading before the first reading). Nevertheless, the process is very tightly controlled in a manner that prevents the majority of such bills from moving through the Knesset, and only a very small percentage make it into law. The private bills are screened and their numbers limited by the Presidium and the House Committee. Those that are permitted to move ahead generally do not have the backing of the government, which means that their passage is hardly assured. Indeed, whips for the coalition parties may well get their members to oppose particular bills. Nevertheless the number of private members' bills that have passed has increased in recent years. In fact, in the Sixteenth Knesset (2003–2005), nearly as many private members' bills as government bills passed, and that pattern has persisted ever since.

The increase in private members' bills is due to weaknesses in the parties, increasingly inconsistent coalition discipline, and the value such bills offer to MKs without high-profile positions to attract attention. Many deal with social issues such as housing. Most such bills never clear the preliminary hurdles and thus are not taken up by a committee. Those that do progress benefit from cooperation between backbenchers from both the coalition and the opposition, though on occasion a minister may decide to get behind such a bill. Ultimately, as noted, most private members' bills are defeated, and even those that pass are subject to enforcement by government departments under the authority of a minister.[4]

Committees

There are 12 standing or permanent committees in the Knesset, along with a small number of special committees (see Table 12.2). Most of the legislative work of the body is carried out in the standing committees. Normally MKs are given seats on one or two committees, but occasionally they are placed on three. The committees have no regular staff assigned to them and are often dependent on ministerial staff, a practice that only accentuates the weakness of the Knesset compared to the government. Chairmanships are often a matter of negotiation between the parties comprising the coalition, although a few chairmanships of less important committees are usually given to opposition parties. Because the coalition controls the business of the Knesset, the ability of a chair from the opposition to wield significant influence is very small.

A committee does have flexibility to modify a bill, but there is no assurance that amendments will remain part of the bill that is ultimately passed. Committees can even initiate bills that eventually are adopted, but those are few in number. Within the committees the coalition representatives keep a close eye on the progress of bills and strive to avoid amendments that will prove embarrassing for the government. Nevertheless, committees do on occasion act independently, leaving matters to be

Table 12.2 Knesset Committees

STANDING COMMITTEES	COMMITTEES ON PARTICULAR MATTERS
House	Drug and Alcohol Abuse
Finance	Rights of the Child
Economic Affairs	Public Petitions
Foreign Affairs and Defense	Ethics
Internal Affairs and Environment	
Constitution, Law, and Justice	
Immigration, Absorption, and Diaspora Affairs	
Education, Culture, and Sports	
Labor, Welfare, and Health	
State Control	
Status of Women and Gender Equality	
Science and Technology	

resolved after they have reported out the bill. It is hardly surprising that members generally do not regard committee assignments or even chairmanships very highly; posts in the Cabinet are much more highly prized. Once a party knows its seat allocation for a given committee the leadership parcels out the specific assignments. However, the ebb and flow of parliamentary politics over the years does not encourage the degree of specialization found in U.S. congressional committees, for example. For opposition parties, though, leadership or membership of a particular committee can be a way to increase their profile or focus attention on a specific public policy issue. After the 2015 election, for instance, the Joint List tried to trade its allocated seats on the Foreign Affairs and Defense Committee in return for more seats on the Finance Committee.

In addition to the standing committees, there are also special committees on particular matters. These committees, which focus on particularly urgent public policy issues, are not regarded as permanent and do not usually have a time limit placed on their operation (although they sometimes can become a standing committee, such as the Committee on the Status of Women). For example, currently there are four special committees dealing with issues such as drug and alcohol abuse and the rights of children. Different Knessets can also strike Parliamentary Inquiry Committees, which are appointed to examine a specific issue within a limited time period and submit a report on how the country should respond. The Seventeenth Knesset (2006–2009) established the Inquiry Committee on the Absorption of Ethiopian Immigrants in Israel, while the Eighteenth Knesset (2009–2013) created the Inquiry Committee on the Integration of Arab Employees in the Public Sector. Because these inquiries take testimony from a variety of individuals and groups, they can construct careful policy recommendations, but it is up to the government to accept or reject these proposals.

RELATIONSHIP TO THE GOVERNMENT

The government must retain the confidence of the Knesset in order to remain in power. Given that the government is always a coalition of several parties, its tenure cannot be taken for granted. Indeed, the breaking up of coalitions is the main source of governments falling and can lead to early elections. This has occurred often, particularly since 1996. Non-confidence motions have been common in the Knesset, but they rarely result in a government being brought down. That process became even more difficult with the adoption of a true constructive vote of non-confidence requirement in 2014 (see Chapter 13). When a government falls it is usually because one or more parties (or even parts of parties) have withdrawn from the coalition. In that eventuality the Prime Minister can try to cobble together a new coalition based on a new coalition agreement. The new government might even consist of the same parties as the old one. David Ben-Gurion did this during Israel's early years, but that practice is less common now.

Theoretically, if a government resigns, the President could ask a different party leader to try to form a government without holding an election, but that would be unusual. The more typical approach would be to make some modifications to the composition of the coalition and then install the new government.

Of course, if the party that dropped out left the coalition with 61 seats or more, it could simply continue in power. Alternatively, opposition parties could provide the necessary support to the coalition if it lost its majority. When Yitzhak Rabin was Prime Minister during the early 1990s, he lost his majority after signing the Oslo Accords with the Palestine Liberation Organization's Yasser Arafat. Although he was left with only 57 seats in the coalition, he continued to govern because Arab parties refused to support any motion of non-confidence, which meant that his 57 seats were always enough to keep his government in power. During the 2013–2014 peace talks between Israel and the Palestinian Authority, when Bayit Yehudi as well as members of the Prime Minister's own Likud party threatened the government with a vote of non-confidence if peace talks went too far and Israel agreed to divide Jerusalem, the Labor Party, under both Shelly Yacimovich and her successor Isaac Herzog, publicly stated its willingness to provide a "safety net" to the government in order to ensure it retained a Knesset majority and could continue with the talks or pass a treaty that resulted from them.

Until the Thirteenth Knesset, elected in June 1992, the government could be brought down by a simple non-confidence vote in the Knesset. One case involved Prime Minister David Ben-Gurion, who lost a vote on education policy in 1951 that was not formally a non-confidence motion. Even so, he decided to resign, but he was able to form a new government without an election. One vote of non-confidence that succeeded brought down the national unity government of Prime Minister Yitzhak Shamir (Likud) in 1990 when the Labor Party, led by Shimon Peres, dropped out of the government and joined the opposition. (This became known as the "stinky trick" that led to demands for reform that were eventually realized in 1992.) Peres anticipated that he would be able to form a new government, with himself as Prime Minister. Instead, he was outfoxed by Shamir, who formed a government without Labor. Since then non-confidence motions have been common but have generally failed. Governments are brought down not by such votes, but rather by the withdrawal or expulsion of one or more parties from the coalition, which may lead to early elections, as in 2014–2015. Such elections can only be held if the Knesset passes a law to that effect, which means that most of the parties have to agree.

No-confidence motions have generally become a technique used by opposition parties to annoy the government. As a result they have occurred with considerable frequency. During the Eleventh Knesset (1984–1988) there were 165 such votes. There were even more (240) in the Sixteenth Knesset (2003–2005). The 2014 changes in the law, however, have made it more difficult to defeat the government and therefore are likely to discourage non-confidence votes in the future.

Since 2001, the Basic Law: The Government has required what is known as a constructive vote of non-confidence. That means that at least 61 Knesset members must be prepared to vote for such a motion, and the motion must specify who the new Prime Minister will be. In 2014 a further amendment was made to this law that requires that the entire new government and its policies be named in the motion. This provision makes it difficult for opposition members to reach agreement. Since the 2001 change in the law no non-confidence motion has been successful.

The instability caused by Israel's dependence on coalition governments has resulted in governments often being vulnerable. Prime Minister Binyamin Netanyahu's 2015 government was the thirty-fourth in Israel's 67-year history to that time, meaning that, on average, governments have lasted for about two years. During the same period there have been 20 Knessets. Israelis might want to see more continuity in their governments, but elected officials have learned to navigate the system and provide greater steadiness than would appear at first blush.

The rules of the electoral system and the norms of alliance building between parties can also lead to changes in the Knesset after an election. Likud and Yisrael Beiteinu's 2013 electoral alliance won 31 seats in total—20 for Likud and 11 for Yisrael Beiteinu. In 2014 they dissolved their partnership—but because the electoral list had alternated between members of Likud and members of Yisrael Beiteinu, when two Likud members left the Knesset their seats were filled by Yisrael Beiteinu members, leaving Likud with only 18 seats while Yisrael Beiteinu increased to 13, a factor that weakened the Prime Minister's hand and made early elections more likely.

SUMMARY

In terms of operation and the legislative process, the Knesset is similar to other parliaments but has had to face the complexity of an electoral system that produces a relatively large number of parties in the legislature. As a result, few Knessets last for their full term. Nevertheless, the Knesset has provided opportunities for most parts of society to be represented. Members rarely achieve much power in their own right, unless elevated to the Cabinet, but they do perform a number of functions outside the parliament, especially in terms of constituency service. Within the Knesset there is frequent vigorous debate over bills and the government's policies, though it is increasingly difficult to bring the government down through a non-confidence vote.

KEYWORDS

Knesset, parliamentary system, legislative politics, electoral threshold, non-confidence vote, executive power

NOTES

1. Anita Shapira, *Israel: A History* (Waltham, MA: Brandeis University Press, 2012), 190.
2. See Asher Arian, David Nachmias, and Ruth Amir, *Executive Governance in Israel* (Houndmills, Basingstoke, Hampshire and New York: Palgrave, 2002).
3. The term "constituency service" might seem strange here because there are no electoral constituencies in Israel. Nevertheless, MKs do service functional constituencies, that is, groups of people bound by shared interests that are meaningful to the MK and his or her party. However, the people served do not necessarily live in the same geographic area.
4. Itzhak Galnoor, private communication, May 29, 2015.

CHAPTER 13

⚓

The Government

Israel's Cabinet, commonly known as the government, is the focal point of the Israeli political system. It is a collective executive, which is typical of parliamentary systems. Once a coalition has been formed, the Cabinet is selected by the Prime Minister, presented by him to the Knesset, and then approved by a minimum of 61 votes. Subsequently it is formally responsible to the Knesset and in principle can be rejected by that body through a non-confidence vote. Whereas the Knesset sits symbolically at the center of governmental activity and is the body that represents the country's electorate, it is in the government that policies are formed and decisions made.

As in most parliamentary systems, the executive is technically chosen by the parliament and is responsible to it. But in Israeli practice, given that no party has ever held a majority of Knesset seats, the Cabinet is formed through negotiations between the various parties that are represented in the Knesset. Those negotiations involve both questions of policy and the determination of which specific Cabinet posts a coalition party will receive. Israel is similar to other parliamentary democracies in that the trend for decades has been toward an increasing concentration of power in the executive at the expense of the legislature, though the government's exercise of executive power is probably more extensive than in other countries because of the prominence of security issues.

Once a government is installed, its component parties maintain discipline over their Knesset members, thereby guaranteeing that nearly all of the legislation that the government proposes to the Knesset is passed. Moreover, as long as the coalition of parties that have formed the government sticks together, the government cannot be defeated in the Knesset. Nevertheless, there are ways to bring a government down. This is evidenced by both the fairly frequent changes of government during the country's history (34 governments during 67 years of statehood through 2015) and the difficulty of maintaining multiparty coalitions when 10 or more parties are represented in the Knesset; taken in combination, these factors in turn have led Israel to be regarded as a relatively unstable system. Yet we would argue that despite the vagaries of the multiparty system, Israel has a reasonably stable political process that does enable coalitions to govern, if not always as well or as effectively as some might wish. This was particularly the case between 1948 and 1977, during the period of Labor hegemony.

Clearly Israel's system is not nearly as neatly structured as a parliamentary system that produces majority governments, such as those in Canada or Britain. But multiparty coalitions are common in many other democratic countries, which means that Israel's challenges are not unique. Countries like Italy, Belgium, Greece, and the Netherlands come to mind in this regard, as does France under the Fourth Republic, though the latter did remedy its problems by significantly modifying its system in the Fifth Republic. What does set Israel apart, however, is the fractious nature of its politics, as well as the complications brought about by political discourse being carried out simultaneously in three dimensions (socio-economic, security, and religion) and the ornery nature of parties with narrow, and often conflicting, agendas. On the other hand, the realities of coalition building serve to help bridge the gaps between a complex and diverse society and a political system that facilitates governance.

In this chapter we first examine the place of the government at the center of the political system. Next we look at the formation and then the running of government, including how and why governments fall apart before the expiration of the Knesset to which they are responsible. We then examine the government's relations with the Knesset. The chapter ends with a discussion of the role of the President in the Israeli system.

THE GOVERNMENT AT THE CENTER OF THE SYSTEM

The government is headed by the Prime Minister (PM), who is usually the leader of the party with the largest representation in the Knesset. Table 13.1 lists Israel's Prime Ministers, from statehood to the present. However, leaving aside national unity governments (when the two main parties jointly form a government), there has been one occasion when a party other than the largest party has had the best chance to form a government and its leader has been designated to try to do so. This occurred in the aftermath of the 2009 election, which produced 28 seats for Kadima and 27 for Likud. However, the President, after consulting with the parties in the Knesset, realized that Likud's Binyamin Netanyahu was more likely to succeed in putting together a coalition than Kadima's Tzipi Livni, because more parties in the Knesset, representing a majority of the seats, supported Netanyahu than supported Livni. Netanyahu was thus given the opportunity and became Prime Minister.

Since Israeli Prime Ministers always head coalition governments, they generally have less clout than a Prime Minister heading a government in which the PM's party has a majority of seats in the legislative body. Nonetheless Israeli Prime Ministers clearly do lead and may even dominate the government, particularly on security issues. Yet they are always vulnerable to demands from parties in the coalition who are backed by implicit, or even explicit, threats of withdrawing from the government. As a result, Prime Ministers often try to build a coalition larger than the minimum necessary (61 of the 120 Knesset seats) in order to

Table 13.1 Prime Ministers of Israel, 1948–2015

YEARS	PRIME MINISTER	PARTY/LIST
1948–1954	David Ben-Gurion	Mapai
1954–1955	Moshe Sharett	Mapai
1955–1963	David Ben-Gurion	Mapai
1963–1969	Levi Eshkol	Alignment (Labor)
1969–1974	Golda Meir	Alignment (Labor)
1974–1977	Yitzhak Rabin	Alignment (Labor)
1977–1983	Menachem Begin	Likud
1983–1984	Yitzhak Shamir	Likud
1984–1986	Shimon Peres	Alignment (Labor)
1986–1992	Yitzhak Shamir	Likud
1992–1995	Yitzhak Rabin	Labor
1995–1996	Shimon Peres	Labor
1996–1999	Binyamin Netanyahu	Likud
1999–2001	Ehud Barak	One Israel/Labor
2001–2006	Ariel Sharon	Likud, Kadima
2006–2009	Ehud Olmert	Kadima
2009–present	Binyamin Netanyahu	Likud

give themselves a cushion should a small party threaten to leave the government over some matter of principle or even personality. But too large a coalition can also prove hard to manage. Consequently, the ideal size of an Israeli coalition is probably between about 63 and 75 seats, except in the case of unity governments. The coalition formed in 2015, which contains only the minimum 61 seats, is unusual.

Constitutional law, as embodied in the Basic Law: The Government, does give the PM the power to resign, thereby bringing about the resignation of the government; the power to request from the President dissolution of the Knesset, thereby forcing new elections; and the power to appoint and dismiss ministers. None of these steps would be taken lightly by a Prime Minister, because any of them could prove to be inimical to his or her interests and those of his or her party. Consequently, a key component of a PM's power is his or her ability to negotiate with coalition colleagues, both during the period of the formation of a government and during the tenure of the government. In other words, the negotiating process necessary to hold a government together never ends. The skill set required to be Prime Minister is therefore quite formidable indeed.

One of the realities of Israeli politics is the presence of a multitude of small parties. Since 1949 the range of lists contesting an election has been between 14 and 33, with a move toward the upper end of the range in recent years. Between 10 and 15 of those succeed in winning Knesset seats. Moreover, the share of the Knesset seats obtained by the two largest parties has declined sharply since reaching a high point of 95 seats in the 1981 election.

The dispersion of power among the parties in the Knesset since then has greatly increased the difficulty of forming and maintaining coalitions and has given small parties considerable leverage with regard to legislation and policy. Religious parties have been particularly adept at utilizing such leverage. Broad popular dissatisfaction with this situation led to a push for electoral and governmental reform around 1990. Not surprisingly, there were disputes about the proper direction for change even among the reformers. The main result was a substantial change in the electoral system that was adopted in 1992 and took effect with the 1996 election. In that election and in 1999 voters had two votes, one for a candidate to be Prime Minister and the other for a party for the Knesset. The idea behind the reform, known as the direct election of the Prime Minister, was to strengthen that office by giving its incumbent more power relative to the parties in the Knesset compared to the previous system. The reform was backed and promoted by a number of law professors and gained broad support in order to pass the Knesset as a new Basic Law on the Government. Interestingly, political science professors generally opposed the initiative for reasons that became clear within a few years (see Chapter 8).

The new structure, while certainly well intentioned, proved to be awkward because of the inherent contradiction between the electoral mandate for the individual Prime Minister and his subsequent dependence on the Knesset's confidence. This made governing more difficult, as Prime Ministers Binyamin Netanyahu and Ehud Barak found out in 1999 and 2000, respectively, when they encountered challenges over relations with the Palestinians and especially the collapse of the Camp David peace initiative, among other issues. Netanyahu chose to go to an early election, which he lost, while Barak resigned and sought a renewed mandate in the 2001 special election for Prime Minister (which was available under that system), in which he was defeated by Ariel Sharon of Likud. Interestingly, in both elections, the incumbent lost by what were unprecedented vote margins compared to previous Knesset elections. In 1999, Barak defeated Netanyahu by 56 percent to about 44 percent. In 2001, Sharon defeated Barak by an even larger margin, 62 percent to 37 percent.

One of Sharon's first actions as PM was to initiate the repeal of the direct election procedure, substituting a new Basic Law: The Government. The new law essentially restored the status quo ante, with some minor tweaking. Voters again would cast only one vote, for a party. But one difference compared to the pre-1996 system is that a Prime Minister and government can only be defeated in the Knesset by a quasi-constructive vote of non-confidence, which requires 61 votes and the inclusion of the name of the Knesset member to be asked to form a new government if the motion succeeds. In principle this added some stability to the system, but non-confidence votes were never a serious threat anyway; only one has succeeded in Israel's history, in 1990. Rather, the problem remains the threat of one or more parties withdrawing from the government unless their demands are met.

A further reform of the non-confidence procedure was adopted in 2014. Not only must a new Prime Minister be named in the non-confidence motion, but the members of the Cabinet, with their portfolios and the specifications of the policies of the replacement government, must also be part of the motion. The requirement of at least 61 votes for the motion to pass remains in force, and such a vote results directly in the formation of the new government. The new procedure makes it nearly impossible for a government to be brought down.[1] Whether it will also reduce the credibility of threats by parties to leave the coalition remains unclear in the aftermath of the adoption of the new policy.

In sum, the Prime Minister's power rests on several considerations: the fact that he organized the government and his party is usually the largest in the Knesset; his skill at shaping the government's agenda and moving it forward; his ability to negotiate continuously with coalition partners to keep his government together; and his ability to bring down the government if it becomes unmanageable because of partisan rivalries. Certainly he is weaker than the leader of a party that alone holds a parliamentary majority, but nevertheless he remains the dominant player in the Israeli system. As a result, different eras in Israeli history are associated with the Prime Minister of the day, much as Americans mark their historical eras by their Presidents. Some of the Prime Ministers who have stood out include David Ben-Gurion (1948–1953 and 1955–1963), arguably the architect of the political system; Menachem Begin (1977–1983), who broke the dominance of Labor and opened up new policy directions; Yitzhak Rabin (1974–1977 and 1992–1995), who presided over the Oslo breakthrough in relations with the Palestinians; and Ariel Sharon (2001–2006), who led the struggle to contain the Second Intifada and then pushed through the dramatic disengagement from the Gaza Strip. All of them clearly dominated their governments.

POWERS OF THE GOVERNMENT

On paper the government's powers are substantial, allowing for a very strong executive. Its effectiveness, however, is a function of the ability of its members to work together to produce policies and laws. To start, legislation that requires Knesset passage, especially bills dealing with major policies, is usually shaped in the government. The parties in the government negotiate over proposed bills and even vote on matters relating to the bills. These votes are not part of the public record, though differences between the parties about legislative proposals often leak to the media. Bills that originate in the government are considered first by the Ministerial Committee on Legislation before going to the full Cabinet. Sharp differences are common in both bodies, but once a majority of the Cabinet has approved it, a bill goes forward with the full support of the government. Cabinet solidarity is an important feature of the system, though parties or individuals do dissent occasionally. As a result the coalition parties generally are able to hold the members of their Knesset factions in line, which means that government bills are almost always passed by the Knesset.

In addition to its role with respect to legislation, the government has primary responsibility for national security, military affairs, and intelligence and security services. Officials of the various organizations may appear before the Knesset Committee on Foreign Affairs and Defense, but they are not responsible to the Knesset. Rather they are appointed by, are responsible to, and can be removed by the government. Therefore it is within the government that decisions are made on military action and tasks assigned to the security and intelligence services. Indeed, it is the government that has the power to commit the country to war and to make peace. Theoretically it is not necessary to put a peace treaty to a vote in the Knesset, though governments have done so. Legal changes adopted in 2014 do require a national referendum or a supermajority of MKs if sovereign Israeli territory is to be relinquished as part of a peace agreement.

Though the entire Cabinet must vote on major security matters, the real day-to-day decisions, even during periods of armed conflict, are made in the Ministerial Committee on Defense (sometimes called the Diplomatic and Security Cabinet). Composed normally of between seven to nine top ministers (although it contained 12 members in Netanyahu's 2015 government), this inner cabinet is meant to cut down on political debates and decision-making paralysis.[2] As was apparent during the 2015 coalition negotiations, because the PM can appoint more ministers to the Security Cabinet, it has also become another way to balance out party demands within the government. Decisions made in this forum are normally "rubber stamped" by the full Cabinet if such approval is required. Given the centrality of security issues in Israeli history, service on such a body is highly valued among Cabinet members. Prime Ministers might also choose to rely on less formal bodies or small groups of advisors or trusted colleagues, sometimes called "kitchen cabinets" (the term comes from Golda Meir's tenure, when she held discussions on security issues around her kitchen table). Such groupings are entirely informal; they have no legal authority to make decisions. Finally, a PM who feels strongly about a particular policy can rely primarily on one or two Cabinet ministers to make decisions. For example, in the 2014 Gaza war, Prime Minister Netanyahu and Defense Minister Moshe Ya'alon (both from Likud) made most of the decisions about the direction of the war themselves; discussions in the Security Cabinet and the full Cabinet were often about the specific choices these two made, though sometimes ministers who disagreed tried to argue in favor of another policy.

Besides its control over foreign affairs and security issues, the government exercises a number of significant powers, usually on its own, but in some cases with Knesset approval. These include broad emergency powers; the ability to reorganize the structure of the government, including ministries and other governmental bodies; and the authority to delegate some of its powers to a minister or civil servants. In addition, the government has various residual powers: it can do anything not specifically prohibited or assigned to another authority. It may also establish direct relationships with Knesset committees in order to deal with problems within a committee's jurisdiction. Finally, ministers of the government enjoy considerable power over legislation concerning their departments and are traditionally given broad discretion over how their departments are administered. They also wield substantial authority to make regulations that govern the application of statutes as a result of the manner in which bills are handled.

Creative use of these formal powers, coupled with the general supervision of legislation, make the government a potent force in Israeli politics. However, as with any other aspect of governing Israel, the success of a government is dependent on its ability to maintain a coalition and make the necessary compromises for the passage of executive decisions.

FORMING A GOVERNMENT

Although there are formal rules for forming a government that must be followed, in the end success depends much more on political and negotiating skills than on following rules. After a general election there is an elaborate process of putting together a new government, though it should be stressed that Israel is never without a government. Whatever the circumstances that require the formation of a new government, the existing government remains in place with full powers until the new one takes the reins. Generally such a caretaker government does not undertake major initiatives—although one contrary example did provoke considerable controversy. In late 2000 Prime Minister Barak resigned because he did not have a majority in the Knesset, which automatically triggered the resignation of the government as well. Yet during the interim period between his resignation and the special election of a new Prime Minister (which was then the procedure) Barak continued negotiations with the Palestinian Authority at Taba, Egypt, over a possible peace agreement and offered significant concessions as part of those negotiations. As it turned out, the negotiations failed to produce an agreement, but questions remain about the propriety of conducting such a process with a caretaker government in place. It is not clear either that had he signed an agreement he would have had the necessary votes in the Knesset to approve the treaty.

In general, after an election the President, performing one of his few specific duties, consults with representatives of all the factions in the new Knesset in order to ascertain which member of that body is most likely to be able to form a government. Usually, but not necessarily, that person will be the leader of the Knesset's largest faction. The President then gives that MK a mandate to try to form a government. The mandate runs for 28 days and may be renewed for as much as another 14. In 2013 Netanyahu took virtually all of the 42 allotted days before he succeeded in his task, and in 2015 he only completed formation of his government less than two hours before the final deadline. During the bargaining period the designated MK negotiates with potential partners about the policies that a new government will pursue. Usually each party will establish a negotiating team for this purpose, but inevitably the prospective Prime Minister him or herself has to get involved directly. In this process he or she faces both an arithmetical constraint—at least 61 of the 120 MKs must support the proposed government—and political constraints regarding how well the main party can work with others and how well prospective coalition partners can work with each other, that is, how well they can manage opposing ideologies.

Normally the main opposition party will not be seen as a viable coalition partner unless a national unity government is deemed to be necessary. Removing members of the leading opposition party from the calculations greatly reduces the possible pool of government supporters. Furthermore, no government as yet has included any Arab parties in a coalition, because they do not support the primary objectives of the state. Typically the Arab parties have controlled about 10 seats, which further reduces the number of MKs that might join the coalition. For example, after the 2013 election, Likud–Yisrael Beiteinu won 31 seats. Labor, with 15 seats, was seen as the main opposition party and reaffirmed its intent to remain in that camp while the coalition negotiations were underway. The more left-wing Meretz party, with six seats, did not want to join a Netanyahu government and was not seen as a possibility by Likud anyway; nor were the Arab parties, with 11 seats, viewed as viable partners. This left the prospective Prime Minister, Netanyahu, the task of forming a government with 61 of the 88 seats remaining after Labor, Meretz, and the three Arab parties were discounted. Yesh Atid had 19 seats, more than Labor, and made it clear that it was interested in joining the coalition, but its leader, Yair Lapid, stipulated that he would not join a government that included the two haredi parties, Shas (11 seats) and United Torah Judaism (7 seats). That left Netanyahu with only 70 seats, representing five parties, to work with. He finally cobbled together a coalition representing 68 of those 70 seats and including three parties in addition to his own—Yesh Atid, Bayit Yehudi, and Hatenua (he left Kadima out of the government; see Table 13.2). His only other option would have been to build a coalition around the two haredi parties while losing Yesh Atid. However, Lapid and Naftali Bennett, of Bayit Yehudi, backed him into a corner by proclaiming that they would either join a coalition together or neither would join. So in effect Netanyahu had no choice, because there was no other way to find the requisite 61 seats.

The 2015 negotiations were simpler in some respects and more complicated in others. With 30 seats compared to the 24 held by the Zionist Union (a joint list of Labor and Hatenua), Likud won a decisive victory. Moreover, there appeared to be a clear majority of seats in the hands of parties that preferred a right-of-center government, the Zionist Union rejected any suggestions of a unity government, and Yesh Atid (11 seats) was unwilling to join a Likud-led coalition. That should have made it easy for Netanyahu to form a government. But because he needed nearly all the remaining potential partners in order to reach the 61-seat mark, those parties raised the stakes with excessive demands. The result was protracted

Table 13.2 Parties and Lists in the Knesset and the Government, 2013

PARTY/LIST	SEATS
Likud–Yisrael Beiteinu[1]	31
Yesh Atid[1]	19
Labor Party	15
Bayit Yehudi[1]	12
Shas	11
United Torah Judaism	7
Hatenua[1]	6
Meretz	6
Ra'am–Ta'al	4
Hadash	4
Balad	3
Kadima	2
Total	**120**

[1] Indicates a party in the government.

negotiations and surprisingly significant concessions by Netanyahu and Likud. The situation was further complicated when Avigdor Liberman pulled Yisrael Be-iteinu out of the picture only two days before the negotiation deadline. That in-creased the bargaining power of the remaining parties, especially regarding preferred ministerial posts, because Netanyahu needed each of them to reach the minimum 61 seats. After further concessions, he put together a coalition of Likud (30 seats), Kulanu (10), Bayit Yehudi (8), Shas (7), and United Torah Judaism (6). But in the process he angered some of his own Likud MKs, who felt that he had given away too many choice ministries, leaving less desirable options for his own party colleagues (see Table 13.3).

Once the arithmetical and political constraints are factored in, the hard bar-gaining begins. Typically there is considerable public grandstanding by party lead-ers as they try to extract the best deal in private negotiations. The issues before the negotiators concern the program of the new government. What policies will it pursue? What legislation will it propose? What will be its view about peace nego-tiations with the Palestinians? What are its views about the relationship of religion and the state? Often each prospective party will have a particular policy agenda, with one or two signature pieces of legislation they are set on. Moreover, even though a tentative agreement may be reached between two parties, another possi-ble coalition party may find part of that agreement to be unacceptable. As a result the negotiating process is protracted and often will appear to be on the verge of failing. In practice, however, agreement is usually reached because the alternative is either a new election or having the President give another MK (presumably the leading alternative to the first choice) the mandate to form a government. Parties must balance out, then, how far they can push their demands with their worries that a new election might lead to a drop in seats and therefore a weakening of their bargaining power. To date, the first MK to receive the mandate has usually

Table 13.3 Government of Israel, November 15, 2015

PARTY/LIST	KNESSET SEATS	MINISTERS
Likud	30	11[1]
Kulanu	10	2
Bayit Yehudi	8	3
Shas	7	2
United Torah Judaism	6	1[2]
Other	0	1[3]
Total	**61**	**20**

[1] In addition to being Prime Minister, Binyamin Netanyahu holds four other ministries; they are not counted here.
[2] United Torah Judaism as a matter of policy declined to take ministerial posts until 2015. It also holds a Deputy Minister position. The other Deputy Ministers are from Likud (4), Shas (2), and Bayit Yehudi (1).
[3] The Minister of Environmental Protection, Avi Gabai, is not a Member of Knesset and is not identified with a party.

succeeded in cobbling together a coalition. The exceptions were Yitzhak Shamir after the 1984 election and Shimon Peres after the government lost a vote of non-confidence in 1990. The incentives to reach agreement are high: no prospective PM relishes sitting in the opposition instead, and the various parties that are invited to negotiate would also much prefer to be in government and gain the benefits of running ministries for their parties.

After an agreement has been reached, it is written up, signed by the leaders of all parties in the new coalition, and published. That document represents the program and priorities of the new government and is a guide to what can be expected over the next four years. Subsequent breaches of the coalition agreement can lead to one or more parties leaving the coalition. Once there is a signed coalition agreement in place, the new Prime Minister presents his government to the Knesset, which must approve it with at least 61 votes. At that point the government takes power, replacing the prior government. Normally the coalition will have at least 61 members, so Knesset approval is really a formality. Indeed, Netanyahu's fourth government, in 2015, was installed by the bare-minimum 61–59 vote.

National unity governments, in which the two largest parties, usually Labor and Likud, work together, may have large coalitions. These governments are not common, but there have been several over the years. The first was in 1967, when there was widespread support for the idea of unity in the face of the crisis leading up to the Six-Day War. The second occurred after the 1984 election, which produced close outcomes for both Likud (41 seats) and Labor (44 seats) and made it impossible for either party to set up a government without the other, particularly in light of the economic crisis that gripped Israel at the time. The two parties agreed to share power over the next four years, rotating the premiership. Similarly, the 1988 election led to a virtual tie between the two parties, with Likud winning 40 seats to Labor's 39. Labor agreed to join the coalition without a rotation at the top. And after the 2001 special election for Prime Minister, the victor, Ariel Sharon of Likud, was stuck with the Knesset elected in 1999 that was dominated by Labor and had to put together a Cabinet that included both Likud and Labor, as well as other parties. In 2009 Netanyahu invited Labor to join his new government and offered the defense portfolio to Labor's Ehud Barak. Although part of Labor left the government in 2011, Barak remained as Defense Minister until the 2013 election.

There are a few fairly obscure situations that can necessitate the formation of a new government without an election. For example, if a PM dies or resigns without recommending a new election the President can ask another MK to attempt to form a government. Or, as mentioned previously, the opposition can mount a constructive vote of non-confidence, which now requires specification of the entire Cabinet and its policies.

If a Prime Minister resigns, dies, or is incapacitated, then the government is considered to have resigned. That is what happened after Prime Minister Sharon's 2006 stroke, after the assassination of Prime Minister Yitzhak Rabin in 1995, and after the death of Prime Minister Levi Eshkol in 1969. In such cases the President consults with the party representatives, as would be done after an election, and then selects an MK—even, in the case of a resignation, the outgoing PM—to try to form a government. When David Ben-Gurion was Prime Minister he would sometimes resign in response to internal coalition problems and then proceed to form a new government. On occasion the new government turned out to be the same as the old one. When Prime Minister Ehud Olmert was forced to resign in 2008 because of corruption accusations, his Kadima party selected Tzipi Livni as its new leader. However, she was unable to form a government, which necessitated the 2009 election. The failure of the government to get the Knesset to pass the annual budget within a specified time limit also brings about the automatic resignation of the government.

The Knesset does have the power to dissolve itself and move for a new election, but that does not happen unless the government decides that such a move is necessary. For example, if the existing coalition is not working well and there is no alternative, that is the route to an early election. In practice all the major parties have to agree to pass a law that moves up the election date. Otherwise a Knesset's term is fixed by law, and no election is necessary until that term, approximately four years in duration, expires.

MAINTAINING AND RUNNING A GOVERNMENT

One of the most challenging aspects of Israel's political system is maintaining a government, which essentially means holding the coalition together. During recent decades coalitions have often involved five or six parties. In some cases one or more middle-sized parties will hold enough seats to pull out and deprive the government of its majority. And if that majority is slim, even a party with three to five seats can leave the coalition without a majority in the Knesset. Consequently, losing a majority is the major way in which governments fall. Given the nature of Israeli coalitions, that is a constant threat, virtually from the moment that a new government is established. During the first 29 years of statehood, when Mapai/Labor always led the government, the problem was less acute than it has been since then, but coalition problems did materialize on occasion even during those early years.

Since 1977 the situation has been more volatile because of the frequent presence in the Knesset of a realistic alternative to the leading party. For example, in mid-2013, less than three months after the government was installed, Yesh Atid's Yair Lapid was already threatening to take his 19 seats out of the coalition if his demands on certain policies were not met. In fact, a quip that made the rounds at the time was that there had never been a Yesh Atid policy that Lapid had not threatened to resign over if it were not enacted. Therefore a major requirement for a successful Prime Minister is the ability to placate the various factions and continually negotiate with them to keep the government intact. If a party in the coalition does withdraw, the PM can try to entice a replacement party to join the government, but he of course would have to pay a price for that move in terms of giving the new party some things that it wants, such as new policies, new legislation, and desirable ministries. Even so, the new party's priorities might be at odds with those of existing coalition partners. Alternatively, the PM might ascertain that it really is not possible to construct a new governing coalition, in which case a new election is probably the only alternative. Sometimes the decision to go to new elections is precipitated not by an actual withdrawal from the coalition but rather by the determination by the PM that one or more parties are making political life impossible by their demands or difficulties in working together. Friction between Netanyahu and coalition partners Lapid and Livni was a major factor in the breakdown of the government in 2014.

The reality is that parties that can find some leverage in the political situation are likely to use it to their advantage, which can lead to unseemly deals to keep the various parties satisfied. Of course, the incentives do not work in only one direction. Parties have much to gain from remaining in the government. One of the reasons for this, going back to the early years of Israeli statehood, is that parties have extensive leeway in running their departments—that is why the allocation of portfolios is so important during the coalition negotiations. Parties often have their eyes on particular ministries because they perceive that controlling those ministries means that they can deliver the goods to their (functional) constituencies or more readily fulfill campaign promises. For example, religious parties usually seek to control the Ministry of Religious Affairs (today, Religious Services) and sometimes the Ministry of the Interior. A party that includes a significant settler presence might seek the Housing Ministry. A left-of-center party might seek the ministry that controls social welfare. And a free market–oriented party might want to have either the Finance or the Economy Ministry.

The most sought-after ministries are normally Defense and Finance. Given the strategic situation, a PM generally wants to keep Defense in safe hands, preferably those of a trusted ally from the PM's own party, though in the past some PMs have kept the Defense Ministry for themselves. On any military matter the Defense Minister will be a key decision-maker. Finance, while prestigious and powerful, is also potentially dangerous, because the minister often has to make unpopular decisions that affect all citizens, typically concerning taxation. It was widely believed in 2013 that Yair Lapid was reluctant to take on this ministry because the country's economic problems were so severe that he feared damaging his own reputation if unable to succeed at the post. Foreign Affairs carries some prestige but usually not much power.

Generally new ministerial positions can be created easily and often are formed to enable the PM to reward a close ally. A 2014 law limited the Cabinet size to 18 ministers and four Deputy Ministers besides the PM, and eliminated ministers without portfolios. Such changes will undoubtedly affect the PM's ability to reward colleagues with ministerial posts. Indeed, Netanyahu found the new rules too constraining as he attempted to form a coalition after the 2015 election. In order to accommodate all of his coalition partners he had to go beyond the limits of the new law. As a result his coalition suspended application of the law until the next Knesset in a 61–59 vote in May 2015. The new Cabinet contained 20 ministers besides the PM and eight Deputy Ministers (see Table 13.4).

Leaders of middle-sized to large parties in the coalition will usually seek the major ministries regardless of other considerations. For example, Ben-Gurion usually took the Defense portfolio while serving as PM. Undoubtedly there were a number of reasons for that, but one was to ensure that he personally controlled it. Sometimes such calculations produce unlikely results, such as when Labor leader

Table 13.4 Distribution of Government Ministries, November 15, 2015

MINISTRY[1]	PARTY/LIST HOLDING THE MINISTRY
Prime Minister[2]	Likud
Agriculture and Rural Development	Bayit Yehudi
Communications	Likud
Construction and Housing	Kulanu
Culture and Sport	Likud
Defense	Likud
Development of the Negev and the Galil	Shas
Diaspora Affairs	Bayit Yehudi
Economy	Likud
Education	Bayit Yehudi
Environmental Protection	Non-MK[3]
Finance	Kulanu
Foreign Affairs	Likud
Health	UTJ
Immigration and Absorption	Likud
Information	Likud
Intelligence and Atomic Energy	Likud
Internal Affairs	Likud
Jerusalem Affairs and Heritage	Likud
Justice	Bayit Yehudi
National Infrastructure, Energy, and Water	Likud
Public Security	Likud
Regional Cooperation	Likud
Religious Services	Shas
Science, Technology, and Space	Likud
Social Equality	Likud
Strategic Affairs	Likud
Tourism	Likud
Transportation and Road Safety	Likud
Welfare and Social Services	Likud

[1] The government has 20 ministers besides the Prime Minister. Ministers may be responsible for more than one ministry.
[2] The Prime Minister holds four other portfolios, reserving them for possible changes in the composition of the governing coalition.
[3] The Minister of Environmental Protection is not an MK and is not identified with a party in the coalition.

Amir Peretz accepted the Defense portfolio in 2007 as one of the key party leaders in the coalition, despite his lack of expertise in defense. Similarly Avigdor Lieberman demanded and received the Foreign Affairs portfolio for himself as head of the second-largest party in Netanyahu's 2009 government, even though he had relatively little relevant experience in international affairs. The upshot of all this is that governments are constructed not only to control a majority of the Knesset seats but also to satisfy the needs of the various parties (and their leaders) that join the coalition. This is very different from the American system, in which the heads of departments can be chosen for their expertise or qualifications from the private sphere or other areas and do not need to come from the Congress or even a specific party.

Prime Ministers do have a lot of cards to play in this never-ending game. As the leader of the largest party in the government, the PM will ensure that his or her party will have the most ministers, and he or she is the person who can remove as well as appoint a minister. Furthermore, he has also negotiated the coalition agreement with the participating parties. Smart Prime Ministers will think several moves ahead as they negotiate the agreement and assign portfolios. Still, there are always unanticipated events that can throw off the best-made plans. Therefore, every government will sooner or later face challenges to its continuation in office, whether they are due to policy disputes, personality clashes, externally generated crises, or even scandals. For example, the 1954 Lavon Affair haunted Ben-Gurion's Mapai governments for years after the event (see Chapter 9). The effects of relations with the Palestinian Authority, especially over terrorism and the peace process, have been particularly problematic for Labor governments ever since 1993.[3] And Likud has struggled since 1996 to balance some factions' desire to become more centrist, or more open to the idea of a Palestinian state, and elements within the party that represent settlers who live in areas that the Palestinians demand be part of such a state. So instability stemming from difficulties within the major party can also undermine a coalition. Finally, the PM has leverage over the coalition partners because if they make life too difficult within the government, he can probably force a new election in one way or another, as happened in 2014.

RELATIONS WITH THE KNESSET

In principle, the Knesset installs a government with a vote of confidence and can defeat it as well. But in practice, the government dominates the legislative and governmental process and controls most of the formal Knesset votes. The Knesset's major formal responsibility is to vote on legislation, an area in which the government has been especially powerful. In more recent years, however, the proportion of bills passed that originated as private members' bills has become comparable to the proportion of government bills passed. Nevertheless, most important legislation is shaped within the government, not in the Knesset, and goes through considerable deliberation in the Cabinet first. When preparing legislation, ministers know that if the parties within the government can be satisfied, it does not matter what the opposition parties think or do. Opposition MKs can make a lot of noise and perhaps embarrass the government, but they normally cannot defeat a bill. The opposition can also try to embarrass the government through investigations or hearings, but normally such actions are not decisive. And with the constructive vote of non-confidence now on the books it is extremely difficult for the Knesset to bring down the government.

Once the government has approved a bill and sent it to the Knesset, party discipline is enforced strictly, and thus almost all government bills are passed into law. Even if amendments are proposed by the relevant Knesset committee, they have to be approved by the government before they can be incorporated into the bill that will come to a final Knesset vote. (This provision does not apply to private members' bills.)

For example, in 2014 three bills (to conscript the haredim, to create a Basic Law mandating a referendum on any peace deal that includes relinquishing sovereign Israeli territory, and to raise the electoral threshold) were written with little input from the opposition parties. These parties, led by Isaac Herzog of Labor and including the haredi and Arab parties, argued that such consultation was necessary given the long-term implications of these bills. When the government did not oblige, the opposition parties boycotted the Knesset debate of the bills, even holding an alternate session in an antechamber. Despite media and public attention, they could not prevent any of the bills from becoming law.

The Knesset does have a tool available in the vote of non-confidence. These votes have been quite common and are a regular feature of Knesset sessions; however, they also do not matter because they are simply a routine part of the Knesset process. Indeed, even before the introduction of the constructive vote of non-confidence, only once was a government brought down by passage of a non-confidence motion. That was in 1990, when Labor's Shimon Peres broke up a national unity government in the mistaken expectation that he could form and lead a narrower coalition afterward. Instead it was Likud's Yitzhak Shamir who formed the narrower government. Since then no non-confidence motion has succeeded. In practice, only defections from the coalition, not non-confidence votes, can bring down the government—and those happen within the government, not in the Knesset.

THE PRESIDENT OF THE STATE

The President is the ceremonial head of state, analogous to the monarch in a constitutional monarchy or the President in republics such as Germany or Italy. He (there has never been a woman in the position) is not part of the government and has few formal powers. The most prominent of these is to oversee the process of forming a government and, in particular, to give a mandate to a Knesset member to attempt to form a government. In practice, the President actually has limited discretion in awarding the mandate. Arguably, the pardon power, which is his exclusively, is more consequential. Presidents have exercised this power from time to time, sometimes controversially, especially when the criminal had been convicted on a terrorism charge. On occasion the government has agreed to a substantial prisoner release in order to free one or more Israelis held by hostile groups. The President has little choice but to cooperate with the government on such matters. Presidents must also sign all bills passed by the Knesset into law but have no discretion over their passage. Still, the presidency is often seen as a prominent position, given the visibility of the office and the fact that several Presidents have reached the office after years of service to the country. See Table 13.5 for a list of Israeli Presidents.

Presidents are elected by the Knesset by secret ballot for a seven-year term, which may not be renewed. Normally an absolute majority of 61 is required to

Table 13.5 Presidents of Israel, 1948–2015

YEARS	PRESIDENT
1948–1952	Chaim Weizmann
1952–1963	Yitzhak Ben-Zvi
1963–1973	Zalman Shazar
1973–1978	Efraim Katzir
1978–1983	Yitzhak Navon
1983–1993	Haim Herzog
1993–2000	Ezer Weizman
2000–2007	Moshe Katzav
2007–2014	Shimon Peres
2014–present	Reuven Rivlin

produce a victor. However, if voting goes to a third or later ballot, only a simple majority of those voting is required. The candidate with the least number of votes is dropped. Most successful candidates have been politicians such as Knesset members, but people with no political background have been candidates as well. Ephraim Katzir, elected in 1973, came from academia. Originally, Presidents were elected for renewable five-year terms, and several did serve two terms. However, when the Basic Law: The President of the State was adopted in 1964, the change to a single seven-year term was made. This helped to avoid a situation in which a President who contemplated reelection might be influenced in his actions by political considerations.

Most Presidents have limited their roles to what is prescribed in the Basic Law: The President of the State. However, some Presidents have used their informal power as head of state and a highly visible and respected figure to pronounce on important political issues. Ezer Weizman (1993–2000) and Shimon Peres (2007–2014) were both unusually active in engaging in diplomacy and speaking their minds on a number of occasions, including during appearances abroad, often in a manner that was not entirely consistent with the policies of the government. This was particularly the case on issues related to foreign policy and the peace process.

Peres's activist presidency surely represented a departure from the norm and was thanks to his strong personality and experience as both an MK and Prime Minister. In addition, the government during most of his presidency was led by Likud Prime Minister and Peres's previous competitor Binyamin Netanyahu. Another example of how Peres raised the profile of the presidency was the establishment of the President's Conference, which he chaired annually for several years. The conventions brought world-class speakers to Israel and became a focal point of Israel's interaction with the outside world. They have since been discontinued but were very popular while they lasted. Peres's experience is unlikely to be repeated by those who come after him.

A President does have an opportunity to be a moral force, but since most of those elected to the post have been politicians for many years, the opportunity to exercise moral leadership is minimal. At times this capacity is undermined by the individuals in office. Peres's two immediate predecessors were forced to resign under embarrassing circumstances. Ezer Weizman was under criminal investigation in 2000 when he decided to resign, though he was never charged criminally. The next President, Moshe Katsav, was investigated on charges of rape and obstruction of justice. When he was indicted in 2007, shortly before his term was about to end, he resigned. Subsequently he was convicted and sentenced to a prison term.

Israel's President in 2015 is Reuven ("Rubi") Rivlin, a veteran Likud MK, who holds political views sharply different from those of Peres (Rivlin is an opponent of an independent Palestinian state) but is less likely to try to promote his own views while in his current position. Nevertheless, he has already used the office to pronounce on critical public policy issues, particularly those regarding the Arab minority. In October 2014, at a memorial for the 1956 Kfar Kassem massacre, Rivlin stated that Israel was the Jewish homeland, but that Israeli Jews must understand Israeli Arabs will never be able to feel the same and cannot be forced to. He also reinforced this community's concern over discriminatory state practices, noting that "we must state plainly—the Israeli Arab population has suffered for years from discrimination in budget allocation, education, infrastructure. . . . This is another obstacle on the road to building trust between us. A barrier which we must overcome."[4] Rivlin has also publicly criticized Prime Minister Netanyahu on both domestic and foreign policy on several occasions. Rivlin cannot, as noted, influence government policy, but sometimes Presidents can help shape public attitudes.

SUMMARY

The consequences for the political system of the manner in which the government has evolved over the years are several: there is strong pressure throughout the system to maintain party discipline; small parties have undue leverage and can extort concessions from the larger parties; larger parties may be reluctant to act because of fear of offending smaller members of the coalition; and coalitions are vulnerable to breaking up at any time. Yet despite these concerns, Israeli governments have had their successes over the years and have experienced greater stability than one might expect. How the reforms of 2014 will affect the functioning of the government will only become clear over time, but at this writing it can be said that the Israeli cabinet system, though far from perfect, has managed to function in a manner that is acceptable to most Israelis. The major reform of the 1990s, the direct election of the Prime Minister, which was the culmination of years of criticism, was rather quickly recognized as a failure. Since the return to the previous system in 2001 there has been little appetite to undertake any other major reforms. The most important changes since then include the establishment of the constructive vote of non-confidence (introduced in 2001 and modified in 2014) and the increase in the vote threshold to 3.25 percent in 2014. As a result of the latter change, the 2015 election was closely scrutinized, as discussed in Chapter 8. A key question to keep in mind is how the higher threshold will affect the functioning of the Knesset and the government.

CHAPTER 14

⚜

The Judiciary and the Development of Constitutional Law

One of the most interesting aspects of the Israeli political system is the way in which the judiciary has evolved over the years. At the outset the courts were mainly concerned with deciding conventional cases. But over the past two decades the Supreme Court has increasingly turned to the use of judicial review, thereby making the judicial branch a significant factor in politics. This chapter looks at the development of the judicial system, the structure of the state and religious court systems, the role of the Attorney General, the use of Basic Laws as the building blocks of a constitution, and the creation of a body of constitutional law through the use of judicial review.

THE JUDICIAL SYSTEM

Israel's independent judicial branch strives to be impartial in comparison to the overtly political branches, the Knesset and the government. Nevertheless it often deals with highly charged political issues and is often accused by right-of-center groups of tilting toward the left, while left-wing groups sometimes accuse it of elevating Jewish identity and permissive security considerations over human rights and civil liberties. The preeminent body in the judiciary is the Supreme Court, which exercises appellate jurisdiction but also sits as a High Court of Justice (HCJ) and exercises original jurisdiction. This dual role for the Court gives it greater power than a more conventional appellate court possesses. The High Court of Justice in particular is often willing to rule against the government on controversial issues. And because access to the legal system through the HCJ is relatively easy, it has become the focus of numerous challenges to government policy.

Theoretically, laws passed by the Knesset have the highest ranking in the legal system because of the idea of parliamentary supremacy. In practice, however, the Supreme Court has become increasingly assertive over the years regarding its role and even began to exercise judicial review to a modest extent about 20 years ago. This initiative, led by the President of the Supreme Court, Aharon Barak (1995–2006), is all the more remarkable because Israel has yet to adopt a constitution. In fact, after statehood was achieved, Israelis anticipated that the Constituent Assembly elected in 1949, and quickly transformed into the First Knesset, would write a constitution in relatively short order. No constitution was produced, but Israel does have a series of Basic Laws that are meant to be the building blocks of one, even though numerous political considerations have delayed the completion of the project for decades. The ability of the Court to consider what amounts to the constitutionality of laws distinguishes Israel from most other parliamentary democracies. Though some do have constitutional courts, since the Barak era Israel's Court has been more activist than high courts in comparable systems.

The court system in general is designed to operate independently of mundane political concerns and to act as a check on possible excesses from the legislature, the government, or the bureaucracy. In order to maximize judicial independence judges are selected by a special committee, as specified in the Basic Law: The Judiciary, with a substantial professional as well as political component. Once appointed, a judge serves for life, until mandatory retirement at age 70.

Sources of Law

The law that judges must interpret has several sources, reflecting the history of the land both before and after 1948. The laws of the Ottoman Empire, which ruled the territory for some 400 years, remain relevant in certain areas of the legal system, especially those regarding land titles, even though the Ottoman Civil Code was finally repealed in 1984. Following termination of Ottoman rule, Britain's Mandate for Palestine governed the country from 1922 to 1948 and enacted quite a number of laws. As well, common law precedents from Britain were incorporated into local practice.[1] When the provisional government of Israel took over in 1948 it decided, by adopting the Law and Administration Ordinance, that those laws would remain in force until it had an opportunity to review all of the statutes on the books. Eventually some British laws were repealed, while others have remained in force to the present. For example, a law giving the government emergency powers was enacted by the Mandatory government during the 1940s and still applies today.

Without doubt, British laws, and not only those specifically adopted in the Mandate, have had a profound influence on the Israeli legal system. Following British practice at the time of independence, there was no provision for the courts to strike down a law on constitutional grounds, not least because there was no constitution. One of the major shifts in Israeli jurisprudence was the eventual assumption by the Supreme Court of precisely that power, utilizing the Basic Laws that have come into effect piecemeal since 1958. That proved to be a highly controversial move that is still debated. Over the years, the Supreme Court has followed developments in the jurisprudence of the American and Canadian Supreme Courts as well as in that of various European courts and has cited precedents from those bodies.

As time has progressed since 1948, the Knesset has legislated over a wide range of subjects, making the positive law of the state the primary source of law. Some critics contend that laws adopted by the Knesset should not simply reflect the will of that body, but should also reflect elements of what has come to be known as

Mishpat Ivri (Hebrew Law), or law rooted in the Jewish tradition. That has never been the predominant view, however, and Israeli laws are similar to those passed in other developed democratic states in that they generally have a secular basis.

STRUCTURE OF THE COURT SYSTEM

Aside from the purely local municipal courts, there are three levels in the national judicial system. The lower courts are known as Magistrates Courts. They deal with civil cases in which the money at stake is below a certain threshold, currently 1 million shekels (about $255,000), and criminal cases in which the possible prison term is less than four years. The mid-level District Courts exercise both original and appellate jurisdiction. They can hear appeals from the Magistrates Courts and also hold both civil and criminal trials in which the matters at stake exceed the limits set for the lower courts. All trials in Israel are held before a judge (occasionally more than one); there are no juries. Finally, the highest level of the judiciary is the Supreme Court, which handles appeals from the District Courts.

The Supreme Court has 15 members, but cases are normally decided by panels of three or five members. Very important cases may warrant larger panels. The position of President of the Supreme Court is an important one, not only because of the formal powers attached to that position but also because of the ability of the President to shape the direction of the judiciary, both through intellectual leadership on matters before the Court and through influential involvement in all judicial appointments. Aharon Barak, who held that post from 1995 to 2006, exemplifies the potential inherent in the position, combined with a unique ability to convert that potential into truly significant influence on the direction of the judicial system. It should be noted, however, that the position is filled on the basis of seniority; when it becomes vacant the justice with the greatest seniority becomes President. Since the judge with the greatest seniority is often not far from the retirement age, tenures as President tend to be short. Barak, who was appointed to the Court at a relatively young age, was an exception who enjoyed a much longer than usual tenure.

In an effort to reduce the impact of politics on the judicial branch all judicial appointments are chosen by a Judges' Election Committee, the composition of which is specified by law. The nine members include the President of the Court and two other justices, the Minister of Justice and another minister selected by the government, two Knesset members elected by the Knesset, and two practicing lawyers selected by the Bar Association. The Supreme Court President is in a position to influence the selection of all judges, including colleagues on the Supreme Court. Barak was particularly adept in this regard, which only enhanced his influence on the intellectual direction of the Supreme Court during his tenure. The President of the State formally appoints judges chosen by the Committee.

The High Court of Justice, which consists of the Supreme Court justices technically operating separately, exercises original jurisdiction over a number of types of cases. Theoretically, as outlined in the Basic Law: The Judiciary, its main task is to "hear matters in which it deems it necessary to grant relief for the sake of justice." This is a broad mandate that gives the HCJ great leeway both in terms of taking cases and in rendering decisions. Essentially, any petitioner can attempt to find an approach that will enable the HCJ to weigh government actions against independent standards of fairness and justice. Examples of issues that may come before the HCJ include allegations of arbitrary behavior by government officials, mistreatment of prisoners, unlawful detention, and government action that infringes on individual rights. Over the years many petitioners in the HCJ have fared well in claims against unjust government decisions. Thus the HCJ, through its decisions, accentuates the independence of the judiciary. In effect it has become the arbiter of what civil liberties mean in the Israeli context.

Without an entrenched bill of rights and with a presumption of parliamentary supremacy, the challenges facing the Court have been formidable. These conditions have compelled the Court to be quite creative in dealing with the various cases brought before it. The fact that the country constantly faces security threats has meant that the Court is frequently called upon to weigh public safety against individual liberty. Its record in this regard is not consistent. Generally, on the big issues involving security, such as the basic legitimacy of the security fence or the detention of people who are deemed security threats, it has upheld the government's position, but there have been numerous cases in which government claims were rejected and individual claims, including on occasion those of Palestinians from the West Bank, were upheld. It should be noted that Palestinians in the territories do not normally participate in the Israeli civilian court system because they do not live in Israel and are not citizens of the state. However, they do have access to the HCJ, which they have not hesitated to use.

THE RELIGIOUS COURT SYSTEM

Operating separately from the general court system is the religious court system, which dates back to the Ottoman period and the millet system and was formally legislated by Britain in 1922. Each religious community is entitled to its own court that decides matters of personal status for its adherents according to its own religious laws and practices. There are several Muslim religious courts as well as a Muslim Appeals Court. In addition, there are courts for Roman Catholics, Protestants, Greek Orthodox, Melkites, Maronites, and Druze.

The most prominent of the religious courts for Jews are the rabbinical courts. There are several such courts in different parts of the country, as well as a Grand Rabbinical Court of Appeals. Generally the losing party does not have the option of appealing further to the secular courts, certainly not on substance, but there are occasional appeals on procedural or jurisdictional grounds. The rabbinical courts have authority over all Jews in the country on matters concerning marriage, divorce, conversion, and burial. These courts are run by rabbinical judges who base their decisions on halacha, rather than the laws passed by the Knesset.

A key problem is that the rabbinical courts are controlled by Orthodox or, in recent years, even haredi rabbis, while most of the population is not Orthodox, thereby leading to conflict and controversy when courts insist on traditional Jewish legal principles and definitions in cases in which one or both parties are not Orthodox. Haredi rabbis are likely to be especially strict in their interpretation of halacha. This has antagonized non-Orthodox Israeli Jews (mainly secular, but also Conservative, Reform, and Reconstructionist Jews), including recent immigrant communities, such as Russians and Ethiopians, whose commitment to observance is less strict, and who find the judges to be too rigid and out of touch with the modern world. Non-Orthodox movements, which have large followings in North America, have been the most vocal about their adherents' frustration with the manner in which rabbinical court judges apply halacha in, for example, divorce cases or when a convert wants to marry. Another oft-cited issue concerns judges' refusal to marry a *kohen* (a man descended from the priesthood that traces its roots back to the biblical Aaron, brother of Moses) and a divorcee on the grounds that such a union is halachically impermissible. Reform and Conservative Jews are not very numerous in Israel, which has translated into less sympathy in the political and judicial arenas for their practices. Indeed, the only religious parties in the Knesset are Orthodox or haredi, which means that any claims for recognition of non-Orthodox positions are likely to get short shrift there.

In fact, friction is more likely to occur in matters concerning secular Israelis, who constitute most of the non-Orthodox Jews. It is they who encounter problems from what many regard as an unfeeling and rigid religious court system, particularly when they want to marry. A number of incidents over the years have led to calls for major reforms of the religious court system, particularly when a party with a decidedly secular orientation plays a significant role in the government coalition. Such was the case with Shinui after the 2003 election and Yesh Atid after the 2013 election. Religious parties, especially haredi parties such as Shas and United Torah Judaism, strive to be in the coalition specifically to prevent secular parties from moving too fast and too far with reforms. For the most part they have been successful (though notably not during 2013–2014, when they were not in the government). This has prompted secular Jews to find creative outlets for addressing their nonreligious needs. For example, many of them find the rabbinate's traditional wedding ceremonies to be not very meaningful, and indeed restrictive; a trip to Cyprus or some other country for a civil ceremony is enough for them. Israel does recognize such foreign marriages for civil purposes, even if the rabbinate does not recognize them at all.

One result of dissatisfaction with the rabbinical courts' control over personal status issues is the increasing agitation for civil marriage and for a nonreligious path to divorce, but such proposals have attracted insufficient support to pass the Knesset. Partly this is because traditionally religious parties have usually been necessary for coalition purposes, so the larger parties have been reluctant to antagonize them. Furthermore, the haredi parties that vigorously oppose any changes of this sort have used their influence in various governments to prevent liberalization. The resulting situation leaves many secular Jewish Israelis alienated from the system and questioning its legitimacy.

With the establishment of a government in 2013 that included no haredi parties and in which the second-largest party, Yesh Atid, had a decidedly secularist outlook, there were renewed expectations that some changes in personal status laws might be achieved. One specific change was the 2013 passage of the so-called "Tzohar law," named after a group of modern Orthodox rabbis that promoted it and persuaded the various parties in the government to back it. The new law loosened the procedures for getting married by enabling prospective brides and grooms to choose any marriage registrar and local rabbi in the country, replacing the previous procedure that restricted them to the registrar and rabbi in the districts in which they lived. Overly zealous application of halachic rules to determine eligibility for religious marriage by some registrars and local rabbis had been a source of frustration to many secular Israelis. Such people, who did not want to submit to the authorities in their own districts, had to either marry outside the country or choose to live together without marriage. The objective of the Tzohar law was to provide them with an opportunity to locate rabbinical authorities who might operate from a more lenient perspective than those in their own district.

Even with the relaxation of the marriage procedures as a result of the Tzohar law, reformers continue to promote an ambitious agenda. Their main objectives are to create procedures for civil marriage and divorce, independent of the religious court system. The attempt to adopt such measures could create intense conflict within society and would be fought bitterly by religious opponents of the measures on the grounds that such policies would undermine the unity of the Jewish people. Any proposed changes would also have implications for Israeli policy that gives each religious community autonomy over its personal status affairs. With haredi parties joining the coalition after the 2015 election, the fate of the Tzohar law is in question, as they are working to repeal it. In the meantime the Chief Rabbinate has taken steps to circumvent the law, avoiding implementation. Other measures adopted during the 2013–2014 period, such as conscription of haredim and improvements in conversion procedures, might also be reversed.

THE ATTORNEY GENERAL

An independent part of the judicial system is the post of Attorney General. Unlike the similarly named post in other countries, where the appointments are overtly political and the position is usually part of the Cabinet, in Israel the Attorney General, though appointed by the government to be its legal advisor, strives to be intensely independent. He or she heads the legal part of the executive branch and is tasked with protecting the rule of law and the public interest when threatened by government action. Thus the Attorney General is often called upon to express an opinion as to the legality of a proposed action and to advise the government, especially the Justice Minister.

When the post is vacant, a high-level committee of five members recommends nominees. The members include a retired Supreme Court judge, a former Justice Minister or Attorney General, an MK, a practicing attorney, and a law professor. Usually the committee provides the Minister of Justice with a list of suitable candidates, and the minister then chooses one. The appointment is subject to approval by the government. In addition to advising the government and the Justice Minister in particular, the Attorney General heads the state's prosecution service and represents the government in court. Perhaps the Attorney General's most sensitive task is to evaluate criminal accusations against prominent politicians and government officials and then decide whether to charge such individuals formally and prosecute them, though when a decision is made to prosecute, the ultimate determination of guilt or innocence lies with judges. MKs, Ministers, and even Prime Ministers and Presidents have faced investigations and even criminal charges at various times in the history of the state. Obviously an Attorney General must handle such cases wisely and with utmost delicacy.

One example of the Attorney General's interaction with the political echelon was the case of MK Avigdor Liberman (Yisrael Beiteinu), who served as Foreign Minister under Prime Minister Binyamin Netanyahu both before and after his 2013 trial. Accusations of corruption had swirled around Liberman for years until Attorney General Yehuda Weinstein decided in 2012 to prosecute him on one particular charge. Ultimately the judges acquitted Liberman at his trial, but Weinstein faced severe criticism from some quarters, particularly from those on the left end of the political spectrum, that he had bungled the prosecution, thereby allowing Liberman to escape punishment. Defenders of Weinstein's position have noted that the Attorney General may have felt there was insufficient evidence to prosecute Liberman on other charges.

BASIC LAWS: A CONSTITUTION IN THE MAKING?

From the beginning of statehood in 1948 the founders intended for the state to have a written constitution. This was clearly demonstrated by the first national election in the country, in 1949, to a Constituent Assembly (later designated also as the First Knesset), and their optimism that a constitution could be produced quickly. However, it soon became apparent that the task would be extremely complex and could not be rushed. Moreover, Ben-Gurion, the dominant political figure during the early years of statehood, found the British model attractive and was skeptical about adopting a written constitution because he feared that if the Supreme Court had the power of judicial review it would "restrict the parliamentary government."[2] Among the most important issues that made writing a constitution too divisive were the relationship between religion and the state and the specification of civil liberties. Consequently, the Knesset decided to put aside the constitution project and instead to concentrate on the adoption of certain foundational statutes, which came to be known in English as Basic Laws. Even that task proved formidable; the first Basic Law (on the Knesset) was adopted only in 1958, and the process has yet to be completed. The Knesset has adopted 15 Basic Laws over the years; three have been repealed. The most recent, requiring a national referendum or a supermajority of MKs to approve the relinquishing of sovereign Israeli territory in any peace treaty, was passed in 2014 (see Appendix E). It is generally understood that there is more to be done in the arena of foundational lawmaking, notably in terms of individual rights.

The reason that the task has proved so nettlesome is that religious parties often have reservations about the impact of human rights principles on religious practice. Such reservations have stymied those who want to complete the process of adopting a constitution. A second area of controversy and difficulty is finding an accepted, and effective, balance between Israel as a Jewish and a democratic state (see Chapter 18). A third dilemma requires balancing ever-present security concerns with individual rights, which has since the 2010s also become a political battle between left and right. Finally, the concept of equality has not been defined adequately in the Basic Laws. As a result, much of the definition of civil liberties necessarily comes from case law rather than legislative enactments. Menachem Hofnung, a leading scholar on law and politics, has pointed out other roadblocks to completing the constitution, including the unwillingness of the religious parties to agree that "the people are the source of authority" and the reluctance of Arab citizens to agree to a constitutional designation of Israel as a Jewish state.[3]

The lengthy delay in completing the constitutional project has been frustrating for the Supreme Court, especially since it came under the leadership of Aharon Barak. This frustration eventually led the Court to begin to treat the Basic Laws as if they were a constitution. In so doing the Court introduced and implemented the practice of judicial review to an unprecedented extent. Predictably, the utilization of this tool produced an outcry from some parties in the Knesset because it undermined the principle of legislative supremacy and the responsibility of elected representatives for the creation of laws. Nevertheless Barak was successful. At his retirement in 2006 he left the Court much more powerful than it had ever been. Generally civil libertarians were pleased with the Barak Court's performance, while many legislators, as well as conservative and religious groups, were not.

Even though Basic Laws are intended to define the powers of the various governmental bodies as well as the values of the state, aside from their titles they are not different from other laws in principle because most can be amended by a simple majority of voting Knesset members (a few have more stringent requirements for amendment, such as an absolute majority of 61 votes). Nevertheless, in practice they are regarded as having some sort of special status, even if they have been amended frequently, as in the case of the Basic Law: The Government.

Generally, once enacted, Basic Laws remain on the books, with amendments making improvements on the margin. A more ambitious change to the Basic Law: The Government took place in 1992 when the Knesset decided to establish direct election of the Prime Minister. The reform was soon shown to be improvident and was repealed in 2001. Since the elected officials could not agree on how to replace the direct election procedure, the default option was for the country to simply return to the pre-1992 practice. Thus the direct election Basic Law was on the books for only nine years and covered two general elections and one special election for Prime Minister.

The expectation is that eventually the process of passing Basic Laws will be complete, though there is no clear time frame for this. At that point they can be codified as a constitution and entrenched. It is not yet clear what entrenchment would entail, but presumably some kind of special majority of the Knesset would be required. There are not too many other options.

INTERPRETING THE CONSTITUTION

Despite the presumption of parliamentary supremacy in the Israeli system, the long delays in the process of completing the constitution created an opening for the Supreme Court to step in and begin to treat the Basic Laws as if they were a constitution. As early as 1969 the Court had struck down a law that was contrary to the Basic Law: The Knesset. In the Bergman case, which involved public financing of election campaigns, the Court set a very limited precedent for judicial review by invalidating a provision of the relevant statute. The decision was highly technical, was reversed by subsequent Knesset action, and only hinted at the use of judicial review.

The process begun in the Bergman case, however, was revitalized about 25 years later. Led by the Court's President Barak, during the 1990s, the judges brought about a veritable constitutional revolution, using two Basic Laws, on Human Dignity and Liberty (1992) and on Freedom of Occupation (1994), as the cornerstone for their reasoning. For all intents and purposes Israel thus became a constitutional democracy when the Court, in *United Mizrachi Bank plc v. Migdal Cooperative Village* (1995) held that the judiciary may exercise substantive judicial review regarding the constitutionality of a law if a law conflicts with a Basic Law. Essentially this gave the Court the power to declare acts of the Knesset unconstitutional, even though that power has been used sparingly since 1995. Arguably Barak's initiative was even more daring than U.S. Chief Justice John Marshall's decision in *Marbury v. Madison* (1803). Whereas Marshall could rely on the concept of an entrenched constitution as a higher law, Barak had to make a greater intellectual leap, given a system in which the Basic Laws are barely entrenched, if at all. Indeed, he used the fact that the 1992 and 1994 Basic Laws were entrenched, unlike most of the other Basic Laws, to justify the decision. The ruling clearly demonstrated the supremacy of Basic Laws over ordinary statutes, thereby limiting the power of the legislature. Moreover the Court reaffirmed the position that each Knesset is empowered to add to the constitution, meaning that the continuity of the Knesset as a Constituent Assembly has not been broken.[4]

The result of the Court's actions in effect has given all the Basic Laws supreme normative status, even though a non-entrenched one can still be amended or repealed by a small ordinary Knesset majority.[5] The acquisition of this power by the Court has been controversial because some of the political parties are concerned about the judiciary gaining an advantage over the Knesset. This has led to tension and threats of ameliorative legislation, though the Knesset has not followed through with any definitive action. On the other hand, realization by the legislators of the Court's judicial review powers may deter the Knesset from adopting new Basic Laws. Indeed, since the *Mizrachi Bank* decision in 1995, the only Basic Laws that have been passed have abolished the direct election of the Prime Minister and clarified the powers of the government (2001) and have required a national referendum or Knesset supermajority on a peace agreement with the Palestinians (2014). But activity in the area of human rights, the major remaining gap in the constitutional process, has not been significant.

When Ayelet Shaked of Bayit Yehudi was appointed Justice Minister in 2015 there was a widespread expectation that she would act on her publicly declared objective to restore a greater balance between the Knesset and the Court—in other words, to rein in the practice of judicial review to a certain extent. It is likely that the issue of the proper role of the judiciary will be a concern of the coalition established in 2015, though Moshe Kahlon of Kulanu has been firm in his opposition to

Shaked's agenda. Without his party's support, the government will be unable to change the judicial system.

Despite the challenges of protecting individual rights in the absence of a formal constitution, the High Court of Justice has addressed human rights issues in a number of cases[6] since 1995, often coming to a conclusion different from what the government wanted. For example, in 1995 the HCJ heard a case from an Arab citizen, Aadal Ka'adan, who contended that rules preventing Arabs from building a home on state land allocated to the Jewish Agency were discriminatory. In *Aadal Ka'adan et al. v. Israel Lands Administration et al.* (1995) the Court held that allocating land to Jews only amounted to illegal discrimination and ordered the Jewish Agency to consider Ka'adan's application. In another case involving Arab citizens and Palestinians from the territories, *Adalah Legal Centre for Arab Minority Rights in Israel et al. v. Minister of the Interior et al.* (2006), the HCJ was narrowly divided on the question of whether provisions of the Citizenship and Entry into Israel Law of 2003 were unconstitutional violations of the rights to human dignity and equality. The issue concerned whether the Palestinian spouse of an Arab Israeli was entitled to enter and live in Israel under the law. A majority of six judges upheld the prohibition of entry by the authorities, while five judges vigorously dissented on the grounds that basic human rights had been abridged.

Other cases that have arisen involve the route of the security fence separating Israel and Israeli settlements from West Bank Palestinians that was erected beginning in 2004 after the Second Intifada's waves of terrorism. In *Beit Sourik Village Council v. Government of Israel and Commander of IDF Forces in the West Bank* (2004), the HCJ considered orders to confiscate land on which a portion of the fence would be built. In light of standards of proportionality established earlier, several orders for land confiscation were canceled. In another case, *Judgment on the Fence Surrounding Alfei Menashe* (2005), in response to a petition from five Palestinian villages near the West Bank settlement of Alfei Menashe, the Court ordered the state to reconsider the route of the barrier and to investigate "security alternatives" in order to reduce the injury to the interests of the residents of the villages. It held that the military commander must balance, according to the standard of proportionality, security-military concerns against the human rights of the Arab residents. A similar ruling was made in 2007, when the Court ordered the military to reroute the barrier so that it would not cut the residents of Bil'in, in the West Bank, off from their farmlands.

Thus, noncitizens of Israel have gained access to Israel's judicial system. While some argue that this is a positive development for human rights, others contend that it really represents the application of Israeli law across the West Bank—nonsovereign Israeli territory. These legal issues, then, may have implications for foreign policy and domestic political struggles.

The sensitive question of torture of security prisoners was addressed in *Public Committee against Torture v. State of Israel* (1999). In this case the HCJ found that democracies must accept limitations on their actions in order to respect human rights: "Preserving the Rule of Law and recognition of an individual's liberty constitutes an important component in its understanding of security." The Court attempted to balance state needs involving security against individual rights and concluded that while the Knesset could allow physical measures in interrogation of terrorism suspects, such techniques must conform to the Basic Law: Human Dignity and Liberty. It specifically banned several techniques that had been used in various situations, including shaking, the frog crouch, and sleep deprivation, and rejected the necessity defense as authority for the use of such practices. The impact of the decision was to prohibit the "use of liberty infringing physical means during interrogation of suspects suspected of hostile terrorist activities." The only physical actions that can be used during an interrogation are those that are inherently necessary and are fair and reasonable, though critics contend that even these methods constitute torture and also need to be banned.

Actions during military operations have also fallen within the purview of the HCJ. In *Physicians for Human Rights et al. v. Commander of IDF Forces in the Gaza Strip* (2004), the Court found that such actions must conform to international humanitarian law. This gave judicial support to the need to protect the civilian population in a combat zone.

The cases mentioned here, while certainly not exhaustive, do demonstrate some of the issues that come before the HCJ and are indicative of its methodology in resolving such matters. In the larger picture, Israel's independent judiciary is an important counterweight to the political branches of government. The unusual features of the HCJ system give petitioners—including Palestinian noncitizens in the West Bank—an exceptional opportunity to address alleged wrongs perpetrated by the government in an expeditious manner. As a result, while Israel has yet to conclude the writing of its constitution, it has a de facto constitutional order and a judicial system that is prepared to act within that context.

SUMMARY

In this chapter we have examined many aspects of the Israeli judicial branch, including the structures of both the state and the religious court systems. Israeli courts are fiercely independent, a trait that often leads to dissatisfaction with decisions both by some Knesset members and by sections of the general public. The Supreme Court, which also sits as the High Court of Justice, has greatly expanded its role over the years, especially under the leadership of President Aharon Barak. In particular, it has innovated in the use of judicial review, despite the country's lack of a written constitution. The Basic Laws have been employed by the Court as part of the constitutional order, a precedent that has had implications for the cases it hears and the kinds of rulings it makes. Civil liberties cases have been particularly thorny, as the Court, sitting as the High Court of Justice, has tried to balance several concerns at once. Because of this, it cannot satisfy all segments of society.

KEYWORDS

Supreme Court, High Court of Justice, judicial practice, Basic Laws, constitutional development, religious versus civil law, judicial activism, Attorney General

NOTES

1. In the English system, precedents based on decisions by judges have accumulated over centuries together constitute what is known as the common law. Another type of law is statutory law, that which is enacted by legislatures. Finally, constitutional law takes precedence over other types of law.
2. Anita Shapira, *Ben-Gurion* (New Haven, CT: Yale University Press, 2014), 190.
3. Menachem Hofnung, personal communication, July 15, 2013.
4. Suzie Navot, *The Constitutional Law of Israel* (New York: Kluwer Law International, 2007), 36.
5. Navot, *Constitutional Law of Israel*, 50.
6. The cases mentioned are reported in unpublished course materials edited by Lorraine Weinrib, Aharon Barak, and Dieter Grimm, Constitutional Courts and Constitutional Rights, Faculty of Law, University of Toronto, Fall 2010.

CHAPTER 15

⋏

Political Economy

Israel's economy has undergone a substantial transformation from the early days of statehood, when government involvement was very high, to the present situation, with its emphasis on free enterprise and substantially reduced state intervention. Although security and defense have traditionally been the main areas of government concerns, the economy also ranks quite high on both the government and the citizenry's list of priorities. Robust economic growth has been a key factor in the country's development. Despite the inevitable ups and downs that any developing country faces, Israel's economic growth, with the attendant societal benefits, has enabled it to move from being a relatively poor country that was heavily reliant on the agricultural sector to joining the group of highly developed countries that make up the Organisation for Economic Co-operation and Development (OECD).

Despite numerous crises and challenges along the way, including periods of slow growth and recession; hyperinflation; a systemic banking meltdown; the necessity of fighting several wars, with the resultant needs of a large defense sector; and the long-running threat of terrorism on the home front, Israel is able to rank very well on some key economic indicators, such as gross domestic product (GDP) growth and unemployment (see Table 15.1). Moreover, inflation has been under control for over 20 years, and the currency, the New Israeli Shekel, is stable. As well, Israel ranked 19 out of 187 countries on the United Nations Human Development Index in 2014. Still, not every forecast is rosy. The country faces systemic labor force problems, its GDP per capita remains in the lower tier of the OECD countries, its economic inequality is among the highest in the OECD, and its middle class feels squeezed, especially by high housing prices. These issues led to widespread protests, centered in Tel Aviv, during the summer of 2011 and affected the 2013 election results. Nevertheless, the Israeli economy is clearly a maturing one, having moved from its traditional emphasis on agricultural products to a service economy that stresses high-technology ventures. In the manufacturing sector, the country also exhibits particular strength in a number of defense industries.

To better illustrate the country's current economic situation we begin this chapter, as we have elsewhere, with the process of economic development in the

Table 15.1 Comparison of Various Economic Indicators, Israel and OECD Average

	ISRAEL	OECD AVERAGE
GDP Per Capita, 2013 (USD)	32,505	35,922
Employment Rate, 2014 (%)	67.8	65.7
Unemployment Rate, 2014 (%)	6.2	7.3
Labor Force Participation Rate, 2013 (%)	74.7	74.2
Debt to GDP Ratio, 2012 (%)	79.8	108.7

Source: OECD.

Yishuv. In the early years of the state, the government played a major role in creating and running the national economy. After Likud came to power in 1977 there was a distinct shift toward a free market economy, the subject of the next section. Despite phenomenal growth, several structural weaknesses are embedded in the Israeli economic system; we discuss these in the last section.

IDEAS ABOUT ECONOMIC DEVELOPMENT IN THE YISHUV

During the period of intense Zionist immigration early in the twentieth century, newcomers were often steered toward occupations that involved working the land, even though few had had any relevant agricultural experience in Europe. This was particularly true for the immigrants of the First and, especially Second, Aliyot, who tended to be ideological and oriented toward a worldview that emphasized the importance of the land. Members of the First Aliya were less committed to Zionism as a political project and less enamored of socialism, though, which at times led to conflict with members of the Second Aliya. The Third Aliya and later aliyot were less ideological, more urban, and more oriented toward the free market.

The prevalent Zionist idea early in the twentieth century was that part of the process of transforming immigrants into "new Jews" meant that the immigrants had to be directed away from their former occupations and encouraged to work the land, thereby acquiring a much stronger connection to the traditional homeland than would otherwise have been the case. The idea of working the land was even romanticized, especially in the context of kibbutzim (socialist agricultural communities that abjured private property and fostered communal living) and moshavim (cooperative agricultural ventures based on private ownership with many aspects of agricultural work carried out in common).[1] Even though residents of kibbutzim and moshavim never constituted more than a small percentage of the population of the Yishuv, the idea of farming in the communal context resonated strongly among the Jews of Palestine during the Mandate, especially because of the influence of thinkers, like A. D. Gordon, who stressed the intrinsic value of Hebrew labor.

A STATE(IST) ECONOMY

In general, policies during the Yishuv era were tilted toward the agricultural sector, while industrial or manufacturing undertakings were largely dominated by the Histadrut. Nevertheless, the Jewish economy, stimulated by several waves of immigration, grew at a rapid pace throughout the Mandate period. However, once the state was declared and faced general war in 1948, defense had the largest claim on resources, which were further stretched by the massive aliya of Mizrachi Jews from North Africa and the Middle East and Ashkenazi Jews who had survived the Holocaust in Europe. Once the War of Independence had ended and society had begun to absorb the immigrants, economic growth resumed at a rapid clip. On balance, Israel has found that despite the initial costs of absorbing immigrants, the longer-term effects of immigration on the economy are quite positive.

Certainly immigration stimulated demand, but the government itself played a significant role in directing the economy during the crucial years of the 1950s. As social democrats, the governing Mapai party engaged in a considerable amount of planning, which led to the government and the Histadrut controlling major parts of the economy. Sectors such as transportation, communications, and defense were particularly emphasized. Moreover, land ownership was largely in the hands of two agencies closely connected to the government—the Jewish National Fund and the Israel Land Authority, which managed state lands for Israel under the doctrine of "perpetual property for the Jewish People." (Though the economy has shifted toward a free market system, this principle regarding land has remained intact, with state agencies still owning about 93 percent of the land.) The result was an economic system that neatly represented the ideals of social democracy, including social welfare policies. Although the governing party took pride in its economic accomplishments, its insistence on its own centrality and its responsibility to determine what the economy needed proved in the end to be a source of inefficiency, producing a sclerotic economic system. It took nearly four decades before a major overhaul and redirection of the economy could be enacted.

For the entire period that Mapai/Labor dominated the political system (1948–1977), the tight alliance between that party and the Histadrut, as well as the socialist ideology of the leadership, contributed to a preference for economic planning and government-run monopolies, subsidies for a large variety of consumer goods, and little support for a manufacturing sector outside of direct or indirect government control. Since the government tended to determine what citizens wanted and needed, the economy in those days frequently experienced rapid growth but was not yet fully meeting the needs of consumers. The reality was that citizens had relatively few choices with regard to consumer goods, the media were tightly controlled to exclude private outlets, and technological innovation was constrained.

In actuality, economic life was closely connected to politics, society, and culture. Labor's leadership looked to examples from western European countries for inspiration but lacked the Europeans' already-established industrial sector. Much of the industrial growth that the government encouraged was carried out through the various enterprises associated with the Histadrut, including banking and construction. Moreover, the unions that were part of the labor federation were in a position to influence government policy and to obtain various favors from the government. Patronage was also deeply embedded in the economic system.

Increasing demand, driven by immigration, served as a powerful stimulant to economic growth, but the existence of a large public sector proved to be an impediment. Even so, the country achieved about 10 percent annual GDP growth between 1954 and 1965. During that period the Histadrut played the major role in the industrial sector, dominating the military industries, communications, consumer products, and transportation, although the Histadrut companies were not particularly effective economically. Eventually the country did face a recession, in 1966–1967, followed by a resumption of growth. But after the 1973 War Israel faced many of the same problems as Western countries: sluggish growth and increasing inflation.

LIKUD AND THE FREE MARKET

The primary political factor affecting the economy was that for nearly 30 years there was no credible alternative to Mapai-dominated governments. The more left-wing Mapam party, which finished second in the 1949 election, faded and was never a threat to Mapai. The main intellectual opposition came from Menachem Begin's Herut party, which did have a free market ideological commitment but tended to focus its energies on defense, security, and foreign affairs. The effect of this orientation was that Herut was never able to challenge Mapai's dominant position in the government. The possibility of change first appeared in 1965 when the Gahal electoral alliance of Herut and the Liberals was formed. However, the major shift did not occur until the 1977 election, which was won by Likud and was not fought primarily on economic issues but nonetheless had profound economic implications.

The Likud victory ushered in a prolonged period of economic transition, though the process proved difficult and did have its negative aspects. Begin, who preferred to work on foreign policy and security issues, including the peace negotiations with Egypt, left economic matters to the Liberal faction of Likud. The result was a loosening of government control over the economy, a process that proved to be more difficult than anticipated. The resultant difficulties, including the inability of the government to move quickly to a capitalist framework, engendered hyperinflation in the early 1980s, the worst that the country has experienced to date. It was only after the establishment of a national unity government—a partnership between Labor and Likud—following the 1984 election that the government was able to begin bringing inflation under control with an economic stabilization program. Part of the process involved replacing the shekel, the currency introduced by Likud after 1977, with a new devalued shekel (the New Israeli Shekel). Another major governmental intervention was the nationalization of the banks during a severe banking crisis.

Although the inflation and currency problems were the most visible indications of economic change, the most important development was the inauguration of a process to encourage private enterprise. That process took many years, but by the time it was underway by the late 1980s, Labor, despite its ongoing membership in the Socialist International, had recognized that Israel's future economic success depended on a vibrant free enterprise system. As a result Labor did not protest as government or Histadrut enterprises were spun off into private hands. In political terms, this helped bring Labor and Likud closer together on economic policy, making it harder for the two parties to distinguish themselves from each other. This convergence marked the beginning of a decisive shift to private enterprise and free markets, a shift that the Labor Party never reversed.

Once Labor returned to power in the 1992 election, it too continued to focus on security and foreign affairs, specifically the Oslo peace process, and allowed the economic transformation to continue. The period from 1996 to 2006, which featured alternating governments of Likud and Labor, saw some inconsistencies in policy, but on balance the direction set during the 1980s continued apace. Furthermore, the prospect of peace made this a period of robust economic growth. Discussions about integrating Israel into the regional economy were promoted, and as Turkey and Israel began to cooperate in military-security affairs, trade between the two also began to expand.

By 2003, when Likud returned to power under Prime Minister Ariel Sharon, the country was receptive to further economic reforms. As Finance Minister, Binyamin Netanyahu completed the process that had begun some two decades earlier, clearing the way for substantial economic expansion driven by an invigorated private sector that was dominated by world-class technology start-up companies. Some examples of key companies privatized during this period include *Bank Hapoalim* and *Bank Leumi*, El Al Israel Airlines, *Zim* (the major Israeli shipping company), and the telecommunications company *Bezeq*.

As a result, during the first decade of the twenty-first century Israel became renowned for its economic climate and the quality of its new technology companies, many of which were acquired by large Western, mainly American, corporations. In 2011, for example, Israel had the highest percentage of GDP devoted to civilian research and development of any OECD country, at 4.4 percent. Several American corporations, such as Google, IBM, and Intel, established research and development centers in the country. The Israeli public was also increasingly happy with the availability of more high-end consumer goods.

By the time that Likud returned to power in 2009 (after the Kadima interlude), with Netanyahu as Prime Minister, there was little dissent within the political class regarding the country's economic direction and orientation. However, the massive street protests in Tel Aviv during the summer of 2011 demonstrated that there were still those whom economic growth had left behind, as well as larger questions about the individual effects of macro-level growth. The catalysts for the protests were the shortage of affordable housing, especially for young families, and the cost of living in general, but most of the demands were for reforms within the context of a decidedly capitalistic system. Tables 15.2 and 15.3 put Israel's growth and development in a comparative and a historical framework.

Table 15.2 Israeli GDP Growth, 2004–2014

	2004	2005	2006	2007	2008	2009	2010	2011	2012	2013	2014
GDP (%)	4.9	4.9	5.8	5.9	4.5	1.2	5.7	4.6	3.4	3.6	2.8

Sources: Israel Ministry of Finance, Central Bureau of Statistics, and OECD.

Table 15.3 Historical Comparison of Various Economic Indicators, 1948 and 2014

	1948	2014
GDP (USD)	1.98 billion	295 billion
Per Capita GDP (USD)	2,181	33,000
Per Capita Consumption (USD)	2,455	20,600
Population	806,000	8.25 million

STRUCTURAL WEAKNESSES

The modern Israeli economy has many positive aspects, with perhaps the most noteworthy being the way in which it performed during the worldwide economic crisis that began in 2007–2008. During a period in which many of the world's top economies were mired in recession and plagued by high unemployment rates for years afterward, Israel experienced a very short period of recession and then resumed economic growth at rates considerably above those of most OECD economies, even though the country was now more integrated into the global economy than ever before. In addition, unemployment remained fairly low because of the continued high pace of economic activity.

Moreover, surprising developments in the energy area provided grounds for increasing economic optimism. For decades a standard Israeli joke, made famous by Prime Minister Golda Meir, was that Moses had led the children of Israel through 40 years of wandering in the wilderness and had finally stopped in the one place in the Middle East that had no oil. Indeed, the Israeli economy had always been dependent on oil and gas imports, which was the source of many problems and challenges. But during the past decade Israel has discovered massive reserves of gas under the Mediterranean Sea as well as exploitable shale oil deposits onshore. The first gas from the new fields became available in 2013 with the expectation that within the foreseeable future Israel will become an energy exporter and will no longer be dependent on unreliable suppliers for its energy needs. These natural resource discoveries probably rival the transformation to a free enterprise economy as the country's most important economic development. Already gas deals have been signed with Egypt and Jordan, and Israel has been cooperating with Greece and Cyprus to expand its Mediterranean sales.

Despite many economic accomplishments, Israel still faces some serious economic challenges, both external and internal. Among them are threatened and real boycotts. Israel was first subjected to a boycott by the Arab world in 1948, with some other Muslim countries joining in later. In more recent years anti-Israel activists in Europe and North America have attempted to get their fellow citizens to join in the Boycott, Divestment, and Sanctions (BDS) movement, which is potentially much more serious. BDS calls for the application of these economic tactics against Israel until the country ends "its occupation and colonization" of all Arab lands conquered in 1967; recognizes full equality for Palestinian citizens of Israel; and promotes the right of Palestinian refugees to return to their homes within

Israel. Thus the movement makes no distinction between Israeli control over the West Bank and Israel's sovereign existence within the Green Line, and therefore its proposals are anathema to the entire range of Zionist Israelis. Although some of the impetus for the BDS initiative stems from anti-Zionism or opposition to the existence of Israel, other participants claim to be motivated solely by objections to Israel's presence and settlement activity in territories that came under Israeli control during the Six-Day War in 1967.

As yet, the BDS effort has not had a consequential effect, aside from some impact on British and American college campuses. Several musicians and entertainers have canceled their tours in or refused to come to Israel, and a few economic enterprises have also claimed they would divest their assets from the country. But unless other *countries* begin to restrict trade, or put legal restraints on companies headquartered within their borders, it does not seem likely that BDS could alter Israel's economy, precisely because it makes no distinction between Israel itself—a legally recognized member of the international system—and its presence in the West Bank. The one area in which BDS has been more successful, at least in creating a climate of acceptance for its ideas, is in facilitating boycotts of products from West Bank settlements. Even apart from BDS efforts, in 2015 the European Union (EU) established a labeling regime that would mark products from settlements as distinct from products from within the Green Line. Though only about 0.7 percent of Israel's exports to the European Union come from the West Bank, east Jerusalem, and the Golan Heights, such a plan sets a major precedent and highlights the link between economic policy and foreign policy.

Another economic issue, an internal one, is policy toward guest or foreign workers. In 2015 there were over 200,000 Asians, Africans, and eastern Europeans in Israel, perhaps half of them legally, who have come seeking work or asylum. The demand for such workers increased sharply after the Palestinian intifadas in the late 1980s and early 2000s. Prior to those events, Israel had offered jobs to many Palestinians from the West Bank and Gaza. Though border closures were increasingly regular, if of short duration, after 1987, a series of terror offensives gave particular impetus to the shutting down of crossing points and the establishment of a permit regime that made it difficult, if not unlikely, for Palestinians to enter Israel for work. The country's decision to replace the Palestinian laborers thereby opened up opportunities for overseas workers. Such workers are not seen as potential immigrants, but many have worked in Israel for years without becoming fully part of the society. Additionally, many have started families in Israel, raising questions about the country's moral and legal obligations to their children in the face of economic necessity. These workers remain essential for the economy, but no resolution of the problem of their status is on the horizon. In order to avoid reliance on guest workers or others without permanent resident status, Israel has had to find manpower either among those permanently residing in the state or among Palestinians from the territories who can commute to work daily. The former solution depends on expanding the labor force while the latter depends on improving relationships with the Palestinians. By 2015 the situation with the Palestinians had improved to the extent that thousands of workers were allowed to cross the separation barrier daily in order to go to work.

Finally, despite its economic advances, Israel continues to have a high poverty rate, as well as one of the largest OECD disparities between wealthy and poor. During the years of Labor dominance the manifold features of the welfare state helped to combat severe poverty. Since then, however, many of those protections have been eliminated or diminished. Furthermore, poverty is concentrated in two important sectors of the population, Arabs and haredim. Members of these two sectors are least likely to receive the quality of education found in the state schools, normally are excused from army service (which serves to provide job skills and access to employment), and have among the highest birthrates in Israeli society. The percentage of each group below the poverty line in 2013, according to the Bank of Israel, was 52.1 for haredim and 47.4 for Arab Israelis. Even excluding those two groups, the poverty rate was 16.9 percent, the worst of any OECD country, with the exception of the United States.[2]

Perhaps the two issues that were most prominent in the dramatic 2011 street protests were housing and inequality, though the price of consumer goods, exemplified by the cost of cottage cheese, received more publicity. The problem with housing is that the prices of apartments (few Israeli housing units are stand-alone dwellings) are extremely high relative to incomes. One reason for this situation is the scarcity of land in the areas in the center of the country, where most people want to live. A second is the absence of government building programs at affordable levels, aside from subsidized housing in settlements in the West Bank. A third is the demand for second homes among non-Israeli Jews, especially in Jerusalem and to a lesser extent in Tel Aviv and its environs. The result is that a young couple starting out cannot afford to buy an apartment unless parents provide substantial assistance. Though the issue has become more prominent as a result of the 2011 protests, the "young couples" protests of the 1970s first drew some attention to the issue; since then, the problem has only been exacerbated. Indeed, such aid has become a family issue as young people plan their marriages. In June 2013, the financial paper *Calcalist* published a survey that found that 87 percent of Israeli parents gave their children—those living on their own—regular financial aid every month and/or provided a large amount of start-up funds to help them. Another recent estimate found that it takes 11 years of salary to purchase a small apartment. As well, high taxes make car prices about double what they are in the United States. Taken together, the heavy burden of consumer costs is one of the reasons for many Israelis' lack of economic advancement.

The other major issue motivating the 2011 protesters was inequality. During the past two decades some Israelis have become exceedingly rich as a result of their involvement in high-tech companies that have been sold to foreign corporations. Furthermore, a relatively small number of companies dominate the market for consumer goods, and many of these companies are controlled by a handful of very wealthy families that exercise great economic power. As a result middle- and lower-class Israelis face high prices for the consumer goods that they need even though their incomes are inadequate to support what should be an achievable lifestyle. Political conflict over these socioeconomic issues is generally muted because of the precedence of military, security, and foreign policy issues. Indeed, one of the main reasons why Shelly Yacimovich did not significantly improve Labor's showing in

2013, despite widespread dissatisfaction with incumbent Binyamin Netanyahu, was the widespread feeling in the party that she had emphasized socioeconomic issues almost exclusively, moving her party too far away from matters such as the peace process with the Palestinians. Still, survey data indicate that social and economic issues are high on the public agenda and do play a role in electoral outcomes (see Chapter 10).

Another key economic issue facing Israel is labor force participation. Two important segments of the population, the Arabs and the haredim, are severely underrepresented in the labor force, albeit for diverse reasons. That underrepresentation is a drag on the economy with broad social implications. Most notable is that neither group can be fully integrated into the larger society. Although there has been some recognition of the need for integration, efforts to bring about change have been inadequate and have been stymied by the complexity of the two groups' relations with the mainstream of Israeli society. In addition, of the non-haredi Jewish population, Ashkenazim tend to be better educated than Mizrachim and as a result are also likely to have better and higher-paying jobs. As a consequence of these groups' underrepresentation and underemployment, Israel's labor force participation rate was 74.7 percent in 2013, about the average of the OECD countries, even though the employment rate was above the OECD average. In 2011, over 52 percent of haredi men and 42.3 percent of haredi women were not employed. Interestingly, between 1979 and 2011 the unemployment rate among haredi men rose substantially, while the rate among haredi women dropped, reflecting government policies that have increased financial support to men engaged in kollel study.[3]

The low labor force participation rates of the haredim and Arabs create serious problems for the economy and are closely related to political considerations. Pushing the haredim into the workforce, for example, would require cutting down on government subsidies to the community and forcing its members out of the yeshiva and places of study. This is seen by some as a direct infringement by the state on religious requirements and a violation of the 1947 Status Quo Agreement between David Ben-Gurion and Agudat Yisrael. For this reason, the haredi parties have vociferously opposed such moves, and their usual pivotal role in coalition bargaining has made the realization of such efforts difficult. But if participation rates in these two groups could be increased there would be a salutary impact on economic output and economic growth over the longer run. As well, to the extent that members of these two groups are able to obtain employment, they will be less dependent on the government. Indeed, their situation has direct implications for the high poverty levels in the country: their underemployment requires greater social spending, such as welfare, which is one of the factors that keep Israeli taxes high. Thus, there is a double cost to the society: high taxes lead to economic inefficiency and suppressed economic output, while the affected families are consigned to a lower standard of living than would be the case if working-age family members were gainfully employed.

The problems of the haredim are twofold: large family sizes and limited education. The Israeli government cannot do much about the first factor, and has great difficulty addressing the second. Having large numbers of children, often six to twelve in a family, is seen as a religious imperative among this group, and thus government intervention regarding family planning is not likely to have much of an impact on this practice. The opposition to a general education, though not explicitly a religious matter, is closely tied to the social norms of the haredi community, which stress Torah education above secular studies, especially for boys. It is also connected to the controversial issue of indefinite draft deferments for haredi men who are involved in religious study. These men avoid military service by engaging in Torah learning throughout young adulthood. That choice is detrimental to them, because they miss out on the opportunities that may be produced by army service and fail to acquire the knowledge and skills needed to find gainful employment in contemporary society. In addition haredi women are at best prepared for very limited careers in the working world. The result is that haredi families are often consigned to poverty. The cost of these choices to the haredi community and to the larger Israeli society is substantial. There has been some change in recent years, but it has been quite gradual. Some haredi women have begun working, a development that has been spurred by the opening of technical colleges that cater to a haredi clientele. Men have also begun to seek training and then employment, a change that will be accelerated if the conscription law for haredim passed in 2014 is implemented.

One recent estimate placed the cost to the government of haredi education, including higher religious education, at about $2 billion per year.[4] Since the low earners in the haredi community pay little income tax, such spending amounts to a transfer payment to the haredim funded by the workers in the larger society. A major reason why the government is willing to fund such payments is because of the leverage that haredi political parties have been able to exercise over the years through their participation in governing coalitions. Even though a 2008 law, strenuously promoted by Shas, exempted the haredi school systems from teaching the state's core curriculum, the government continues to fund those schools at 60 percent of the funding level of state schools. On a broader level, the state's continued willingness to fund school systems that do not prepare their students for life in a modern economy is emblematic of the problems that face the political system. The government knows that the graduates of those schools will be a drag on the economy, yet it supports the perpetuation of such a situation.

Another minority sector that has lagged behind the rest of the country in terms of economic development is the Arab community, largely as a consequence of the focus on building a Jewish state. Many Arab Israelis live in their own communities and interact minimally with the Jewish majority. The fact that they do not enter the army also inhibits their economic integration. In addition, the political parties that represent the Arab sector of the country generally adhere to an anti-Zionist posture. In practice this has meant that the Zionist parties that have formed governments over the years have generally not considered any of the Arab parties as candidates to join coalitions. Since government expenditures are largely determined within Cabinet deliberations, it is not surprising that communities in the Arab sector have not been funded as well as those in the rest of the country. It should be noted, however, that policy under the 1992–1996 Labor government was an exception to this generalization, as some progress was made toward closing the gap. Another explanation of the Arab community's poor economic performance is that "the Arab parties have failed to represent the true concerns of their constituency, paying too much attention to the Israel-Palestinian conflict while abandoning domestic problems."[5]

The chronic underfunding of this sector has had a cumulative effect on economic development among Arab Israelis. The government has long been aware of the disparities between Jews and Arabs, and has been especially sensitive about the subject since the report of the Or Commission in 2003 (see Chapter 7). As a result, there have been some improvements, but the Arab community remains beset with poverty (just under 50 percent fall below the poverty line) and unemployment (about 8 percent are unemployed) and falls short of its potential educationally. Clearly, much economic potential among the Arabs of Israel remains untapped, further complicating efforts to spread economic opportunity throughout the entire Israeli population.

One other political issue has had significant economic implications. Since 1967's Six-Day War Israel has controlled territory with significant strategic and historical importance, particularly the West Bank, which the government refers to by the historical names of Judea and Samaria. Governments of both the left and the right have encouraged Israelis to settle in the territories, primarily to strengthen the country's claims in negotiations with the Palestinians. Some governments have been more supportive of the settlements than others, so the intensity of building and expansion has varied over the years. The most rapid growth in the number of settlements took place during the Begin years, from 1977 to 1983. The priority assigned by various governments to the construction of settlements and the expansion of housing within settlements has imposed economic costs on the country. This, of course, represents a political choice, but one with economic consequences.

One estimate of the cost of building beyond the Green Line was about $8 billion between 1979 and 2008, the period of most of the growth in such communities.[6] There are other economic costs attached to the settlement enterprise, including security, the construction of infrastructure, and subsidies. At the same time, Likud governments during this period—particularly when Ariel Sharon was in the Cabinet—made a conscious effort to entice nonideological settlers to move to the West Bank by providing cheaper housing, lower taxes, and more open space. Although the policy of expanding Jewish communities beyond the Green Line is controversial in Israeli politics, little emphasis has been put on the economic aspect of this effort in the political debates until now. The 2011 social justice protests drew some attention to the occupation, because activists and peace groups argued that the presence of settlers, and of the Israel Defense Forces to guard them, meant that government expenditures flowed to the West Bank instead of helping Israeli citizens within the Green Line. In fact, Peace Now has created a new campaign to emphasize the economic costs of the settlements to make them a political issue and build support for withdrawing from them. In the Knesset Labor MK Stav Shaffir has made exposure of and reduction in settlement funding one of her priorities. Furthermore, if a peace agreement with the Palestinians can be reached, there will undoubtedly be economic costs to relocating Israelis from the parts of the West

Bank that will be turned over to the Palestinians. It is difficult to put a number on such costs in advance of any agreement, though one point of reference is the Gaza disengagement in 2005. That cost the government about 8 billion shekels, well over $2 billion, and represents a far smaller figure than would be involved in a possible West Bank disengagement.

SUMMARY

It is clear that a number of the economic challenges that Israel confronts today have a political dimension. Even though Israel has done remarkably well economically since independence, it could do even better if it could find a way to overcome some of these challenges. Paul Rivlin, a close analyst of Israel's economic development, has identified five major challenges to Israeli economic growth. They include bringing the haredim into a more mainstream education system and then into the workforce; integrating the Arab community so that its members can participate fully in society, especially in terms of employment; resolving the conflict with the Palestinians so that expenditures associated with holding disputed territory can be removed from the budget and the threat of boycotts can be neutralized; bringing defense expenditures under control; and strengthening the cultural dimension of Israeli life in order to foster greater societal cohesion.[7] Actually, defense expenditures had been declining for several years, dipping down to 5.6 percent of GDP in 2012, but then began to rise to over 6 percent again the following year in order to deal with changing threats.

All of these points bear some relationship to the state of the political system. Thus there is a direct connection between economic outcomes and the way in which the political process is carried out. The government formed in 2013 continued the policies to which its leader, Netanyahu, has long been committed. It did take steps to provide incentives, backed by coercion, to get haredim to seek gainful employment and made efforts, though not always successful, to bring down the budget deficit while confronting the need for higher defense spending in the wake of the 2014 war against Hamas. However, the presence of two haredi parties in the government formed in 2015 raises doubt as to whether there will be continuity with some of the innovations of the previous government. Economic policies are likely to continue to be subject to the buffeting of political winds as they shift direction in future elections and governmental policymaking.

KEYWORDS

political economy, statism, socialism, capitalism, economic development, consumer goods, defense burden, hyperinflation, poverty, wealth disparity, haredi unemployment, Arab unemployment

NOTES

1. S. Ilan Troen, *Imagining Zion: Dreams, Designs, and Realities in a Century of Jewish Settlement* (New Haven, CT: Yale University Press, 2003), 15–26.

2. *Globes*, "Flug: Haredim Now Poorer Than Arabs," January 15, 2015, http://www.globes .co.il/en/article-flug-haredim-now-poorer-than-arabs-1001001226; Dan Ben-David, *A Picture of the Nation: Israel's Society and Economy in Figures 2014* (Jerusalem: Taub Center for Social Policy Studies in Israel, May 2014), 36–37, http://www.israel-braingain .org.il/Uploads/Attachments/6675/a_picture_of_the_nation_2014_eng_taub.pdf.

3. Ben-David, *Picture of the Nation*, 78.

4. Paul Rivlin, *The Israeli Economy from the Foundation of the State through the 21st Century* (New York: Cambridge University Press, 2011), 180.

5. Aviad Rubin, Doron Navot, and As'ad Ghanem, "The 2013 Israeli General Election: Travails of the Former King," *Middle East Journal* 68 (2014): 263. See also Chapter 10.

6. Rivlin, *Israeli Economy*, 152.

7. Ibid.

CHAPTER 16

⌁

The Israeli–Palestinian Conflict

Any study of Israeli politics needs to devote some attention to foreign affairs and national security because they are usually at or near the top of the public policy agenda and occupy a dominant place in the public conversation. As of this writing two major issues facing Israel are the still-unresolved conflict with the Palestinians and the potential threat from a nuclear Iran. This chapter explores the political nature of Israeli decision-making as regards the Arab–Israeli conflict and its subset, the Israeli–Palestinian conflict. It does not provide a detailed chronology or analysis of the conflict.[1] Rather, it discusses the four factors that matter most for understanding Israeli policy toward the Palestinians and the broader Arab and Muslim world.

The first factor is Israel's external security environment, particularly the consistent hostility and threat from the Arab states and Iran and nonstate actors such as Hamas and Hezbollah. The importance of security considerations has been so great that observers often speak of Israeli security policy, rather than foreign policy. An old quip has it that the Defense Ministry makes foreign policy, while the Foreign Ministry sells it. Second is the domestic political contest between the left and the right, traditionally represented by Labor and Likud, over the best approach to deal with these external threats. The two parties switched back and forth as senior coalition partners between 1981 and 2006, which led to different government priorities. By the late 1990s these differences had converged into a shared willingness to engage with the Palestinian leadership and consider an independent Palestinian state in the West Bank and Gaza Strip, but the parties disagreed over timetables and the specifics of a possible agreement. After Kadima's brief period of success Likud returned to power in 2009. The third factor is the defense establishment's prominent role in governmental decision-making. Because it is comprised of various military and intelligence agencies and officials, the consequence has been an emphasis on military concerns in all aspects of foreign policy, including policy toward the Palestinians. Finally, public opinion has reflected a "creeping dovishness" since the 1990s as Israelis have gone through a process of reassessing long-held assumptions about their adversaries[2] (although this outlook has become more suspicious and even militant since the 2000s—a "creeping non-dovishness," in Ehud Eiran's words[3]). This has had some effect on policy, creating opportunities for and imposing restraints on policymaking. The public's perception of threats to the country has also mattered for electoral outcomes as the electorate has turned to Likud or Labor depending on conditions during a given election.

THREE LEVELS OF THREAT PERCEPTION

We begin this chapter with an explanation of the three levels of threat perceived by Israel. All three levels intersect in the political arena and help shape Israelis' attitudes and priorities regarding policy toward various issues such as the peace process, the settlements, and war. First is the personal level. Threats to individual Israelis come from paramilitary and terrorist groups (such as factions within the Palestine Liberation Organization [PLO], Hamas, Hezbollah, Palestinian Islamic Jihad [PIJ], and the Popular Resistance Committees) and target lone Israelis or small groups of citizens. The consequences of this type of threat have been terrible: from the onset of the Second Intifada in September 2000 through 2014, 1,250 Israelis (including military personnel) were killed in terrorist attacks. In the 2000s, rocket attacks from Hamas and the PIJ in Gaza and from Hezbollah in Lebanon have frequently forced Israelis within the increasing range of the rockets to hide in bomb shelters, sometimes for long periods of time, disrupting life. Despite the high casualty toll, threats to individual Israelis are insufficient to defeat the state, but particularly when these attacks are concentrated and continuous, they can result in widespread fear, frustration, demoralization, and disruption of normal life, psychologically scarring individuals and society.[4] This is, in fact, one of the goals of terrorist activity—to make life so intolerable for civilians that some will consider emigrating.

The second type of threat is at the collective level. These are threats to the state itself—its territorial integrity, ability to look after its citizens, security, and survival. These threats can only come from other states. Defense of borders and industrial and population centers, as well as political independence, are the major concerns here, and all of them have been threatened in a number of wars, including those in 1947–1949, 1967, and 1973. Israel's last interstate war was in 1973; since then its wars have been against nonstate actors who cannot threaten the country's existence. In the 2000s Israel's major concern in this regard has been Iran and its nuclear program, which is widely believed to be oriented toward construction of a nuclear weapons arsenal.

The third threat level is the symbolic level. The threat here is to the identity and purpose of the country. The founders of Israel wanted not just to reestablish Jewish sovereignty but to create a new Jewish identity—the "new Jew," or what Max Nordau called "muscular Judaism." The Zionist movement represented a complete break from the past. In the Zionist conceptualization, where the old Jews were European, religious, pale, weak, and bent, the new Jews were Zionist, secular, tanned from the Middle Eastern sun, strong, and tall. The new Jews would not let themselves be bullied and killed but would fight back. Collective memories have had a profound effect on modern Israel, casting contemporary threats to Israel as shadows of past atrocities and attacks against Jewish communities throughout history. Prime Minister Binyamin Netanyahu, for example, has regularly accused Iranian leaders of threatening a new Holocaust and has called Iran's Supreme Leader a modern-day Hitler.

ISRAEL'S THREAT ENVIRONMENT

By almost any measurement, Israel is the strongest military power in the region. In quantitative terms it does not necessarily have more military manpower or armaments than its neighbors, and certainly not if those resources are combined. But, as a 2010 Center for Strategic and International Studies report comparing Israel and Syria stated, "the balance of force quality . . . decisively favors Israel and vastly offsets the balance in numbers."[5] Israel has an enormous technological advantage driven by a continuous supply of human capital and creativity, manifested in a well-regarded domestic defense industry. Israel is protected by a multilayered missile and rocket defense system (Iron Dome, Iron Beam, David's Sling, and the Arrow system), and it is the only regional power with a nuclear arsenal, including second-strike capability.[6] All of this is underlined by a close alliance with the United States, which includes about $3 billion of regular military aid per year. In addition, the quality of Israel's military officers and enlisted personnel is much higher than those of its enemies.

Despite these advantages, Israel's consistent emphasis on security concerns stems from both real threats to its security and from collective memories of centuries of persecution of Jewish populations around the world—what Alan Dowty has summed up as "the filter of security."[7] These Jewish-Zionist-Israeli memories begin with the destruction of the First and Second Temples and the end of Jewish sovereignty in the Land of Israel in 70 CE, when the Romans destroyed the last Jewish kingdom there. Though there is some debate among historians, archaeologists, and biblical scholars about the accuracy and specifics of these events, they have been memorialized and mythologized in Jewish religious rituals. This commemoration includes the solemn three-week period beginning on the seventeenth of *Tammuz* in the Jewish calendar, which marks the start of the destruction of the Second Temple, and ending on *Tisha b'Av* (the ninth of *Av*), a day of mourning and fasting. Jewish liturgy and prayers also feature multiple references to the rebuilding of Jerusalem. Most early Zionist leaders came out of the eastern European milieu, where Orthodox interpretations of Judaism were prevalent, and so would have been very familiar with these commandments and memories. They carried this legacy into the Zionist movement and worked to appropriate these events and memories to support and inspire the nascent movement.

Later events reinforced this shared experience of loss of sovereignty and insecurity. Decades of harassment, expulsion, forced ghettoization, and pogroms in Europe throughout the medieval and modern periods culminated in the Holocaust, when about 6 million Jews were murdered in horrifically cruel ways. The Nazis and their allies throughout Europe sought to clear entire areas of Jews. The Zionist community in Ottoman and Mandatory Palestine faced a series of threats from the local Arab population, which opposed the effort to establish a Jewish homeland there. Simmering resentment was punctuated by Arab riots against and massacres of the

Jewish population, leading to the murder of scores of Jews and the destruction of property (in particular, in 1920, 1929, and from 1936 to 1939).

Finally, on the day after Israel's independence was proclaimed, the nascent state was invaded by five Arab armies bent on eliminating it. Though Israel not only survived the attack but prevailed and in the process conquered more territory than had been allotted to it under the 1947 U.N. Partition Plan, the war ended with armistice agreements, not peace treaties. Since that war, Israel has continued to face unrelenting hostility, antagonism, and a refusal to recognize its existence from most of its regional neighbors (with the exceptions of Egypt and Jordan, which signed peace treaties with Israel in 1979 and 1994), and has endured the outbreak of several wars, border skirmishes, and terrorist attacks. In short, a sense of protracted siege has long marked Israel's position in the region.

Contemporary security concerns include threats at all three levels of perception. The biggest threat is perceived to come from Iran, whether it finally acquires nuclear weapons or not.[8] This sense of Iran as the major strategic threat was evident as early as the 1990s, even as the interstate element of the Arab–Israeli conflict wound down, Israel improved its relationships with major states around the world (including Russia, China, India, and Turkey), and the United States came to the Middle East in 1991 to force Iraq (an unrelenting enemy of Israel until then) out of Kuwait—destroying Iraq's military capability in the process.

Contemporary military threats also come from Hezbollah, Hamas, and a set of smaller jihadist movements like Palestinian Islamic Jihad and fragmented al-Qaeda groups active in the Syrian civil war. These groups cannot destroy the Israeli state or diminish its ability to look after its citizens, but they can harm Israelis and provoke fear throughout society through terrorist attacks, such as firing rockets over the Lebanese and Gaza borders, kidnapping soldiers, and individual attacks on lone soldiers waiting at bus stops or small crowds of civilians on Israeli streets. In October and November 2015, Israelis were subjected to a wave of random stabbings (65 by the middle of November) by individual Palestinians that killed 14 people and wounded 167. The digging of tunnels from Gaza through which terrorists can move under the border into Israel heightens these fears. There is also some sense that the Arab uprisings that began in 2011 have created additional instability around Israel. The Hosni Mubarak regime in Egypt that had maintained the peace treaty with Israel was removed from power, while the Syrian civil war has spilled over into the Golan Heights and facilitated the spread of the Islamic State. The antagonistic relationship between Israel and Turkey under its Islamist governments further exacerbates this sense of isolation.

Another strategic issue that is currently shaping Israeli threat perception is the global effort to delegitimize both the Israeli state and the right of the Jewish people to self-determination. This effort emerged in the United Nations, where the number of General Assembly or Human Rights Council resolutions on Israel has consistently remained far higher than the number of resolutions on all other countries combined, and, since 2005, through the Boycott, Divestment, and Sanctions movement. As noted in the previous chapter, the BDS movement does not have the ability to bring the Israeli economy down, but by calling into question Israel's right to exist even within the pre-1967 borders, it reinvigorates Jewish-Zionist collective memories of the past, when Jews were kept in a state of perpetual uncertainty in the countries in which they lived and denied a series of political, civil, and religious rights. The movement is also connected in the public mind with the Hamas Charter (1988), which classifies all of Mandatory Palestine as an Islamic *wakf* (trust) and proclaims that "in order to face the usurpation of Palestine by the Jews, we have no escape from raising the banner of Jihad." There is no room for a Jewish state under these stipulations.

These genuine threats to Israel and to Israelis, combined with the haunting memories of past Jewish traumas, have made Israelis overtly suspicious of the Palestinians' intentions. The political right has emphasized these worries, but even parties in the center and on the left have expressed concerns. The Israel Democracy Institute's (IDI) August 2014 Peace Index asked citizens whether they agreed with the statement "The world is against us." Among respondents, 27.6 percent said, "I'm sure it's true," while 32.6 percent said, "I think it's true." Only 35.9 percent did not think the statement was true or were sure it's not true. In May 2014, before the outbreak of the war with Hamas, the Peace Index asked Israelis how they would define the level of military-security risk to Israel. There were differences between the Jewish and the Arab communities, but overall 22.6 percent defined it as very high, 40.4 percent as moderately high, 20.5 percent as moderately low, and 11.7 percent as low.

HAWKS AND DOVES IN THE POLITICAL SYSTEM

The threat environment has been refracted by the domestic political competition between the right and the left in Israel, often conceptualized as a contest between hawks (those suspicious of Palestinian intentions and therefore skeptical about making concessions and more likely to resort to force) and doves (those who are more optimistic about Palestinian intentions and therefore more willing to negotiate and cede territory to achieve peace, and less willing to resort to force). Chapter 9 divided the Israeli party system into four clusters, including a left and a right camp. For most of Israel's early years the hawkish–dovish continuum did not fit neatly onto the left–right political spectrum. Though the right, represented by Herut/Gahal/Likud, was clearly hawkish, Mapai/Labor on the left was itself divided into hawkish and dovish factions. Labor also pursued an aggressive military policy of preemptive war and retaliatory strikes.

For most of the period of Labor hegemony (1948–1977), disagreements between Labor and Likud on security issues were moot because the de facto eastern border of the state was the Green Line. Most of Labor's leaders in this period—such as David Ben-Gurion, Golda Meir, and Yitzhak Rabin—held hawkish positions regarding Israel's foreign and security policies. When the rest of Jerusalem—including the Old City and the Western Wall—and the West Bank were captured, Labor leaders were caught up in the emotional excitement and nationalist sentiments that were aroused by the reconnection with the heart of biblical and historical Jewish kingdoms. This made Labor's tolerance of the 1949 armistice borders untenable. The government soon annexed all of Jerusalem and made Judea and Samaria the official name of the West Bank, evoking the ancient Jewish kingdoms in the area and the historical nomenclature that was even used by the British during the Mandate. Some Labor leaders, such as Yigal Allon, Yisrael Galili, and

Shimon Peres, actively supported establishing Jewish settlements in the area, but even those who did not—like Rabin—were reluctant to oppose outright their construction and normally gave retroactive support to sites established by private groups. Still, most of these settlements were concentrated in areas considered important for defense. The period of Likud government (1977–1984) was marked by an expansion of settlement activity: in its first term (1977–1981), the number of settlements nearly doubled from 27 in the previous 10 years to 50. Likud also built new neighborhoods in Jerusalem, tied them all to Israel proper through a network of roads and electrical grids, and placed many in areas of heavy Arab concentration, along the spine of the West Bank.

The division of the political parties into hawks and doves really only became relevant in the 1980s, when control over the territories became an important electoral issue. Likud did not consider territorial withdrawal to be either feasible (out of security concerns) or desirable, but it was Menachem Begin of Likud who put the issue of Palestinian autonomy in the West Bank and Gaza into formal terms, by letting the Camp David Accords with Egypt (1978) contain a reference to "the legitimate right of the Palestinian peoples and their just requirements," to be achieved through the establishment of autonomy for the people in the WBG who would nonetheless remain under Israeli sovereignty. (Begin purposely left out any reference to national rights.) Nevertheless, it was the Labor Party that became the dovish party in the public mind, mostly because Likud governments continued to expand the settlements and rely on nationalist rhetoric. In addition, Labor was committed to giving up some parts of the WBG in return for peace treaties. By the mid-1980s Labor's position was "defensible borders based on territorial compromise." Likud's commitment to withdrawal was, at best, vague.

Elections in the 1990s and early 2000s led to an alternation of Likud and Labor as the leading government party (see Table 13.1 in Chapter 13). In 1993 Labor signed the Oslo Accords with the PLO, which marked the party as not only supporting territorial withdrawal but also being open to an independent Palestinian state in the WBG (though this position was not formalized until 1996, when opposition to a Palestinian state was purposely omitted from the party's policy platform). The Oslo Accords authorized the establishment of an autonomous Palestinian government (the Palestinian Authority) in Gaza and designated areas of the West Bank.

Likud adamantly opposed the 1993 Oslo Accords, and Likud leader Binyamin Netanyahu regularly criticized them. However he had little choice but to operate within the framework they created once he was elected in 1996. For all intents and purposes, this meant an implicit recognition of Palestinian claims to the WBG. In 1997 Netanyahu signed the Hebron Protocol, which redeployed Israeli forces out of most of that city, and in 1998 he signed the Wye River Memorandum, which entailed further redeployments in the West Bank. However, Netanyahu slowed down the Memorandum's implementation, and much of its stipulations were not executed. By the late 1990s, most of the party opposed a Palestinian state and withdrawal from the area not on historical-religious grounds, but on security grounds.

In 1999 Labor won the election, and Prime Minister Ehud Barak came to office believing he could end the Israeli–Palestinian conflict. He withdrew all Israeli forces from southern Lebanon in 2000, then embarked on a hurried negotiation process with the Palestinians at Camp David in July 2000 and at Taba, Egypt, in January 2001. The bargaining dynamics of both meetings is the subject of intense disagreement, with policymakers, analysts, and pundits putting blame for the failure of the talks on different parties.[9] What is clear, though, is that Barak put unprecedented concessions on the table, including an (eventual) Israeli withdrawal from over 90 percent of the West Bank and a political division of Jerusalem. The right was incensed, fearing that Barak was giving away Israel's entire ancient homeland and its most holy religious site (the Western Wall in eastern Jerusalem), and not obtaining any concrete security guarantees in return. When the Second Intifada broke out in September 2000, Israeli public opinion turned against the concessions Barak, with the support of U.S. President Bill Clinton, had offered. Barak resigned on December 10, 2000, thereby necessitating a special election for Prime Minister. In February 2001, he was trounced by Likud's Ariel Sharon, 62 to 38 percent. The public's association of Labor with the failure of the peace process helps explain why Labor has done so poorly at the polls since then. The widespread belief that Labor continues to ignore Palestinian intransigence augments this perception.

As Prime Minister, Sharon engaged in a forceful military response to Palestinian attacks. Israeli troops reoccupied parts of the West Bank it had withdrawn from and hemmed in PLO head Yasser Arafat at his compound in Ramallah. In 2002 Sharon (reluctantly) began construction of the security barrier, and in 2003 he (reluctantly) accepted the Road Map, a document put together by the international community as a plan to reach an Israeli–Palestinian agreement. By then Sharon was increasingly convinced that the demographic balance between Arabs and Jews in the space between the Mediterranean Sea and the Jordan River was tipping against the Jews, raising concerns about Israel's future as a Jewish state. In summer 2005 he implemented his disengagement plan, pulling all Israeli soldiers and settlers out of the Gaza Strip and from four small settlements in the northern West Bank. When Sharon indicated he had plans to do the same in the rest of the West Bank, Netanyahu led a revolt against him within Likud. Sharon then left the party, taking several Knesset members with him, and established Kadima. Though he became ill before the 2006 election, his deputy, Ehud Olmert, campaigned on a platform of implementing the disengagement plan and led Kadima to victory in the election, winning 29 seats in the Knesset compared to 19 for Labor and only 12 for Likud. Olmert formed the government, but the outbreak of a war with Hezbollah in summer 2006 and a war with Hamas in 2008–2009, as well as corruption investigations into his activities, led to the fall of his government.

In the 2009 election Kadima received one more seat than Likud (28 to 27), but it could not convince a majority of Knesset members to support it in a coalition government. President Peres asked Netanyahu, by then head of Likud, to form the government. Though Labor under Ehud Barak joined the coalition, little progress in peace talks was made. At the same time, the moderates in Likud (those more open to negotiation and territorial compromise) were gradually losing influence in the party's governing institutions to both hardliners who mistrusted the Palestinians and to those committed to retaining Israeli control over the West Bank. This process was completed in the Likud primaries of November 2012 (see Chapter 9).

In January 2013 new elections were held, in which the Likud–Yisrael Beiteinu list won 31 seats and formed the government. Though domestic social and economic issues were major issues for voters in this election (see Chapter 10), security/foreign policy issues became important in the coalition negotiations that followed. Joining the coalition were Hatenua, which was formed solely to push the peace process forward, and Bayit Yehudi, which staunchly opposes an independent Palestinian state. Yesh Atid also joined the government, but its leader, Yair Lapid, seemed uninterested in foreign affairs and mostly tried to remain either noncommittal or within the general consensus on such issues.

From July 2013 to April 2014, U.S. Secretary of State John Kerry led (some argue imposed) peace talks between Israel and the Palestinian Authority. Hatenua was the only party in the Israeli government enthusiastic about the process. Netanyahu reluctantly participated, but during the course of the talks he adopted a pragmatic position on some issues (such as borders) and a hardline position on others (the division of Jerusalem). He also felt constrained by his coalition, particularly the opposition within Likud and from Bayit Yehudi. Ultimately, under pressure from nationalists and Religious Zionists in his coalition, Netanyahu agreed to release hundreds of convicted Palestinian terrorists rather than freeze settlement building in the West Bank.[10] The talks have not been renewed, and in the context of rocket attacks on Israel from Gaza and the ensuing war with Hamas in summer 2014, Netanyahu stated that "there cannot be a situation, under any agreement, in which we relinquish security control of the territory west of the River Jordan."[11] Since this scenario would leave a Palestinian state so truncated as to be meaningless, some observers have argued that Netanyahu has closed the door for good on an independent Palestinian state in the WBG.

During his 2015 election campaign, in an attempt to woo voters from Bayit Yehudi, Netanyahu proclaimed his opposition to a Palestinian state—in contradiction to a 2009 speech he delivered at Bar-Ilan University—telling an interviewer, "I think anyone who is going to establish a Palestinian state and to evacuate territory is giving radical Islam a staging ground against the State of Israel."[12] Though foreign affairs was not the deciding factor in the election, the victory of a right–center-right government led by Likud left peace talks very low on the policy agenda.[13]

Whether Likud opposes a Palestinian state in the WBG for security or for ideological reasons, over time it has come to engage in negotiations with the Palestinians—however reluctantly. In this sense, the big parties have converged on the peace process. Still, they remain far apart on the specific details of the negotiation process, what a Palestinian state should look like, and the timing of its establishment. The result of the alternation in power between the big parties, then, has been an unstable foreign policy tied closely to the political contest between them. In other words, it is easier to speak of *party* policies toward the Israeli–Palestinian conflict than to speak of *Israeli* policies, though Labor's inability to craft an alternative message to Likud policy in 2013 and 2015 makes the distinction murkier. This is best captured by the different interpretations of Israel's position in the international system expressed by Yitzhak Rabin of Labor and Yitzhak Shamir of Likud during the 1992 election campaign. Shamir saw Israel as surrounded by enemies, in a world of unrelenting hostility. In contrast, Rabin contended that "no longer are we necessarily 'a people that dwells alone,' and no longer is it true that 'the whole world is against us.'"[14]

THE DEFENSE ESTABLISHMENT

In addition to their political struggles, Israel's parties have also been subject to the influence of a third actor in the decision-making process: the defense establishment (sometimes referred to as the national security establishment). In Chapter 11 we identified the security network as an interest group in Israeli politics. While the defense establishment is composed of the security institutions of the state (the Defense Ministry, the Israel Defense Forces, and the intelligence agencies) and their officials, the security network is broader and includes retired officers who have moved into other areas of work, such as academia, the private sector, and politics.[15]

The defense establishment is intimately involved in Israeli decision-making. Because of the precarious security situation Israel was born into, it was immediately necessary to prioritize security affairs, which required that the military and intelligence agencies play a direct role in the analysis of information and presentation of options. Early on, the IDF especially was required to construct efficient decision-making procedures to cope with the wars, border skirmishes, and terror attacks that regularly broke out. It was very successful at the tactical level, though less so at the strategic level. And, like any bureaucratic institution, the IDF wanted to maintain its independence. Together, these various factors created a large space for the military and security establishment within the civilian decision-making arena.

The centralized nature of decision-making in foreign affairs also facilitated the military's place in the policymaking process. Because Israel faced serious security threats so early and so often, the government was given wide latitude to deal with threats as they arose, with little expectation of public consultation. The defense establishment's ability to shape foreign policy, then, stems from its high levels of organization and its control over expertise and resources.[16] In Cabinet meetings on major diplomatic and security issues, the IDF or a member of the defense establishment usually briefs the ministers. Often this representative presents a single option to a particular problem that must be accepted or not, with little input from other agencies or the chance to alter what is on the table.

Israel's top leadership regularly comes from the defense establishment. Of 12 Prime Ministers who served for a year or more, three (Rabin, Barak, and Sharon) were high-ranking military officers or war heroes, one (Peres) came from a long career in the Defense Ministry, two (Begin and Shamir) led paramilitary groups during the Mandate period, and one (Netanyahu) "only" served in an elite combat unit. Of Israel's 16 Defense Ministers—a position considered to be the country's most important political office apart from the Prime Minister—nine attained the equivalent rank of general in the IDF before entering politics. These ministers bring with them their connections to former colleagues, while their familiarity with military procedures and expertise prompts them to lean on the security agencies rather than "going outside" the military to civilian agencies such as the Foreign Ministry. A National Security Council, similar to the American version, was established in 1999 to address these deficiencies, but it remains relatively weak compared to other state agencies, particularly the IDF.

There are many examples of the defense establishment's role in policymaking. Once the secret talks held in Oslo in 1993 between Israeli academics and PLO negotiators became serious enough to warrant Prime Minister Yitzhak Rabin's attention, he insisted that Joel Singer—a military lawyer who had worked with Rabin in the Defense Ministry—be brought into the talks to look through what had been agreed on and identify any concerns. Rabin trusted Singer intimately because of their shared military background. The IDF was similarly closely involved in the 2000 Camp David talks. During the 2006 war with Lebanon, in addition to prosecuting the war itself, it was the military that defined the objectives of the conflict and laid out the diplomatic options.

Other examples of the defense establishment's role in policymaking are found in the country's activist military doctrine, which frames solutions to foreign policy problems in military terms. At times this approach has meant a greater suspicion of enemies' intentions than might otherwise have been the case with a broader deliberative process, and a consequent closing off of options or reliance on the use of force as a response.[17]

This tendency was evident in Israel's response to the flotilla of ships that tried to break the blockade on Gaza in May 2010. The flotilla comprised mostly humanitarian activists, but it also contained militants from a Turkish terrorist organization. Israel was determined to prevent the ships from reaching Gaza and gave them advance warning to turn back, offering to transfer the aid in their cargos to ground transportation to carry it across the land border. When the flotilla refused to change course, Israel launched a military raid to stop it. One ship, the *Mavi Marmara*, resisted, and its members attacked Israeli soldiers as they tried to board the ship. The violence that followed resulted in the deaths of eight Turkish citizens and one Turkish-American. The killings sparked a major international outcry and damaged Israel's relations with Turkey. The Turkel Commission, set up by the Israeli government to investigate what had happened, noted that the military had failed to account for the chance of violent resistance by militants and activists and what this might mean for Israel's position in the international legal structure. This poor planning resulted in part from insufficient civilian oversight of the military operation.[18]

PUBLIC OPINION

Our understanding of the role of public opinion in shaping Israeli international policy reflects what has been learned in the study of public opinion elsewhere. In his study of the effect of public opinion on American foreign policy, Richard Sobel argued that public opinion does not make specific policy but rather "has a guiding or limiting influence on policy. Support permits or facilitates, while opposition limits or deters, policymakers' discretion."[19] A similar dynamic exists in Israel.

Speaking broadly, the executive in Israel has been able to ignore public opinion when it comes to security and foreign policy.[20] The security situation has facilitated the need for quick, secret decision-making, and the public has generally understood and accepted this. Israeli Prime Ministers also exert considerable personal control over international affairs, relying for advice primarily on small groups of individuals (referred to as "kitchen cabinets"). Although Israeli Prime Ministers do check the polls or otherwise reference public opinion as a constraint on their ability to pursue certain policies,[21] the Israeli public—like populations in other countries—is malleable when it comes to major decisions of war and peace. It often follows government policy, even when there may not be broad support for that policy beforehand. Examples can be seen in the public reaction to Menachem Begin's decision to withdraw from the Sinai as part of the 1979 Egypt–Israel peace treaty, Yitzhak Shamir's policy of nonretaliation to Iraqi Scud missile attacks in 1991, Yitzhak Rabin's decision to sign the 1993 Oslo Accords, Ariel Sharon's decision to disengage completely from the Gaza Strip in 2005, and Binyamin Netanyahu's decision not to expand the military operation in Gaza in summer 2014. In each case, public opinion was either opposed to or noncommittal on these policies (in the last case, public opinion supported the expansion of military activity in Gaza), but after the government decided on an opposite course of action, public opinion was found to be supportive of it. When it comes to the peace process, these conclusions are consistently borne out by public opinion surveys. The February 2014 Peace Index found that a majority of the Jewish Israeli public would accept an agreement with the Palestinians that "goes against my political position but is approved by the government and the referendum"; among those who identify as left, 92.3 percent would support such an agreement, as would 80.9 percent of those in the center and even 58.4 percent of those on the right. A non-IDI poll in July 2014 found that 60 percent of the public would support an agreement that entailed a Palestinian state alongside Israel if the Prime Minister reached that agreement.[22]

While it is true that Israelis seem to be less supportive of an agreement with the Palestinians once discussion shifts to the details of such an accord,[23] it is also the case that levels of support for talks in general and for the specific concessions Israel puts on the table have been dependent on external events and the party in power. For example, during moments of intense violence support tends to decline, particularly when the government is headed by Likud, which has pursued peace talks only reluctantly and without any enthusiasm. In addition, the role of the Prime Minister is important. The historical evidence indicates that Israeli leaders can bring public opinion along on a policy even when it is reluctant or opposed. The public's willingness to follow the government means that if Israel does decide to push the peace process forward in an earnest manner, and if there is a serious offer from the Palestinians, the public is unlikely to serve as an obstacle.

SUMMARY

Multiple variables influence Israeli policy toward the set of issues that are part of the Israeli–Palestinian relationship, including the peace process, the settlements, and the use of force. Israeli leaders operate in a context of an uncertain security environment that is given greater salience by collective memories of the Jewish past; the struggle between opposing ideas about these issues, represented by the

Labor and Likud parties; a defense establishment that dominates the policymaking process; and public opinion that can be molded by the leadership. Of course, other factors not discussed here—particularly the actions of the Palestinians themselves—are also relevant and can push Israeli policy in specific directions. There is good reason to be pessimistic about the prospects of resolving the Israeli-Palestinian conflict at the time of this writing. Still, given the complexity of these variables, much can change over even a relatively short period of time.

KEYWORDS

Israeli–Palestinian conflict, collective memories, security threats, hawks and doves, defense establishment, public opinion, peace process

NOTES

1. Good sources on the conflict include Neil Caplan, *The Israel-Palestine Conflict: Contested Histories* (Malden, MA: Wiley-Blackwell, 2009); Alan Dowty, *Israel/Palestine*, 3rd ed. (Cambridge: Polity Press, 2012); David W. Lesch, *The Arab-Israeli Conflict: A History* (New York: Oxford University Press, 2008); Benny Morris, *Righteous Victims: A History of the Zionist-Arab Conflict, 1881–2001*, 2nd ed (New York: Vintage Books, 2001); and Mark Tessler, *A History of the Israeli-Palestinian Conflict* (Bloomington: Indiana University Press, 1994).

2. Asher Arian, *Israel and the Peace Process: Security and Political Attitudes in 1993*, JCSS Memorandum no. 39 (Tel Aviv: Jaffee Center for Strategic Studies, February 1993).

3. Personal communication with author.

4. David Horovitz, *Still Life with Bombers: Israel in the Age of Terrorism* (New York: Alfred A. Knopf, 2004).

5. Anthony H. Cordesman and Aram Nerguizian, *The Arab-Israeli Military Balance: Conventional Realities and Asymmetric Challenges* (Washington, D.C.: Center for Strategic and International Studies, June 29, 2010), 5.

6. Israel has never admitted it has nuclear weapons, but its possession of them is considered an open secret. Its official policy is opaqueness, in order to not be the first state to introduce nuclear weapons into the region. See Avner Cohen, *Israel and the Bomb* (New York: Columbia University Press, 1998).

7. Alan Dowty, *The Jewish State: A Century Later*, updated ed. (Berkeley: University of California Press, 2001).

8. Ehud Eiran and Martin B. Malin, "The Sum of All Fears: Israel's Perception of a Nuclear-Armed Iran," *Washington Quarterly* 36 (2013): 77–89.

9. Jeremy Pressman, "Visions in Collision: What Happened at Camp David and Taba?" *International Security* 28 (2003): 5–43.

10. Ben Birnbaum and Amir Tibon, "The Explosive, Inside Story of How John Kerry Built an Israel-Palestine Peace Plan—and Watched It Crumble," *New Republic*, July 20, 2014, http://www.newrepublic.com/article/118751/how-israel-palestine-peace-deal-died.

11. *Times of Israel* Staff, "Netanyahu: Gaza Conflict Proves Israel Can't Relinquish Control of West Bank," *Times of Israel*, July 11, 2014. http://www.timesofisrael.com/netanyahu-gaza-conflict-proves-israel-cant-relinquish-control-of-west-bank/

12. Jewish Telegraphic Agency, "Netanyahu: No Palestinian State on My Watch," March 16, 2015, http://www.jta.org/2015/03/16/news-opinion/israel-middle-east/netanyahu-no-palestinian-state-on-my-watch.

13. In a November 9 meeting with U.S. President Barack Obama, Netanyahu declared he remained committed to a Palestinian state, though it would have to be demilitarized and recognize Israel as a Jewish state.

14. See Brent E. Sasley, "Affective Attachments and Foreign Policy: Israel and the 1993 Oslo Accords," *European Journal of International Relations* 16 (2010): 698.

15. Gabriel Sheffer and Oren Barak, *Israel's Security Networks: A Theoretical and Comparative Perspective* (Cambridge: Cambridge University Press, 2013); Uri Ben-Eliezer, "A Nation-in-Arms: State, Nation, and Militarism in Israel's First Years," *Comparative Studies in Society and History* 37 (1995): 264–285.

16. Charles D. Freilich, *Zion's Dilemmas: How Israel Makes National Security Policy* (Ithaca, NY: Cornell University Press, 2012), 60–71; Yehuda Ben-Meir, *Civil-Military Relations in Israel* (New York: Columbia University Press, 1995).

17. Zeev Maoz, *Defending the Holy Land: A Critical Analysis of Israel's Security & Foreign Policy* (Ann Arbor: University of Michigan Press, 2006); Yoram Peri, *Generals in the Cabinet Room: How the Military Shapes Israeli Policy* (Washington, D.C.: United States Institute of Peace Press, 2006).

18. See *The Public Commission to Examine the Maritime Incident of 31 May 2010*, http://www.turkel-committee.com/index-eng.html.

19. Richard Sobel, *The Impact of Public Opinion on U.S. Foreign Policy Since Vietnam: Constraining the Colossus* (Oxford: Oxford University Press, 2001), 10.

20. Asher Arian, David Nachmias, and Ruth Amir, *Executive Governance in Israel* (Houndmills, Basingstoke, Hampshire and New York: Palgrave, 2002).

21. Yehudit Auerbach and Charles W. Greenbaum, "Assessing Leader Credibility during a Peace Process: Rabin's Private Polls," *Journal of Peace Research* 37 (2000): 33–50.

22. Nir Hassan, "Despite It All, Most Israelis Still Support the Two-State Solution," *Haaretz*, July 7, 2014.

23. Dahlia Scheindlin, "Polls: Two State Solution Was a Casualty, Even before the War," *+972 Magazine*, July 12, 2014, http://972mag.com/polls-two-states-was-a-casualty-even-before-the-war/93418/.

ֳ

CHAPTER 17

The Changing Israeli Political Arena

Israel is still a relatively new country. Although its political system began to function long before the state was declared in 1948, the country's politics and government have been regularly buffeted by internal and external challenges. For one thing, the country has yet to entrench a constitution. The Basic Laws do provide a framework, but they remain incomplete, and there is no completion date in sight. The relationship between the Prime Minister and the coalition has long been problematic, but the major attempt to deal with the issue (the direct election of the Prime Minister) failed, and the matter has not been addressed successfully since then. Other longstanding problems that bear directly on the character of the political system remain unresolved, occasionally grabbing headlines as the country attempts to confront them. Prominent examples include military service for haredim and the conversion of immigrants who qualify under the Law of Return but are not halachically Jewish. The result of all this is that it can be difficult to delineate Israeli politics at any particular point in time. Nevertheless, based on observations of developments since Israel's founding, it is possible to reach some conclusions about the way in which the political process is evolving.

Clearly, politics is not a static process; rather, it is dynamic, shaped by internal demographic changes, shifts in regional politics, and other new developments and catalytic events. Therefore we can cautiously attempt to identify and generalize about the direction of Israeli politics. Some trend lines can be discerned, so it makes sense to list and comment on some of the main ones that have characterized Israeli politics over recent decades. The major points that must be addressed include the changing socioeconomic structure, the macroeconomic transformation, major developments with regard to security and foreign relations, a relationship with the Palestinians that is constantly in flux, the decline in importance of traditional ideologies, the challenge of creating a unified political culture, the always-complex party system, the passing of charismatic leadership, renewed political consciousness in the domestic Arab sector, and a more vigorous judiciary.

A MORE COMPLEX SOCIETY

Comparing Israeli society in 2015 to that in 1948 makes the changes that the country has undergone rather graphic. Compared to the present, the Jewish sector of society at the founding was relatively homogeneous: most of the people were Ashkenazim who had immigrated from Europe between the 1880s and 1948 or were descendants of such Ashkenazim. There were some who traced their roots in Eretz Yisrael to earlier centuries, but they were a small minority. There was also an Arab minority that constituted about 20 percent of the population. In contrast, contemporary Israeli society consists of about 37.7 percent Jews of Middle Eastern, Asian, or African origin; 35.6 percent Jews with origins in Europe, the Americas, or South Africa (including 2.1 percent from North America); 1.7 percent Jews from Ethiopia; and 20 percent Arabs. The last group's percentage of the population has not much changed in 67 years, but it is much more politically active than it was in 1948 and increasingly identifies as part of the Palestinian people and with Palestinian nationalistic goals, despite its aversion to any thought of relinquishing Israeli citizenship. Mizrachim are more integrated into the Israeli political, social, and economic structures today than they were in 1948, though in many cases they are still underrepresented. Finally, now there is a much larger and more assertive haredi sector (representing about 10 percent of the total population) than ever before, with a real political impact. The net result of all these changes is that Israelis have multiple political identities, which makes the promotion of a common Israeli identity challenging. In political terms, this makes much of public policymaking highly politicized. A key question is whether the passage of time will attenuate some of these group identities and allow a more unified population to emerge or whether these strains will pull Israeli society apart.

In socioeconomic terms, the country surely shows more evidence of affluence for some sectors of the population, while poverty remains a persistent problem in other sectors. The gap between the affluent and the impoverished is wide and represents a central societal concern, even as the country searches for a solution.

AN ECONOMIC TRANSFORMATION

The economy today is much more solid and stable than it was in the early years. More importantly, there has been a shift from a state-run economy and a traditional focus on agriculture, which had ideological significance at the state's beginning, to a free market economy with diverse industrial strengths that is more consumer oriented but tends to focus on high-tech and military industries. Moreover, for the first time in its history, Israel can foresee a time when it could be energy independent. Indeed, it is on the verge of becoming an energy exporter. The country, once heavily dependent on external economic support, especially from Jews in the diaspora, is increasingly self-sufficient. One measure of increasing confidence in the economy was a 2014 proposal to allocate a substantial annual sum from government coffers to foster Jewish identity in diaspora Jewish communities. This represents a 180-degree turn from the situation in the early years, when diaspora Jewry looked at Jewish Israelis as poor relatives who constantly needed material assistance.

For years, culminating in its eventual membership in the OECD, Israel made significant economic gains and greatly improved its economic performance relative to other states in similar positions. As a result, it was able to improve its trade balance and increase its level of trade overall. This process was facilitated by the conclusion of free trade agreements, primarily with other developed states, and by the shift to a free market economy. The sounder economic base, coupled with the discovery and development of energy resources, has enabled Israel to become an economic performer of international significance. One indicator of its economic prowess is that Israel has become the second–most productive country in terms of foreign firms listed on the NASDAQ stock exchange. Over the long run these developments are likely to have positive political consequences for the country, though they will be undercut if the large wealth disparities and increasing poverty are not addressed at the same time.

TRANSFORMATION OF THE SECURITY SITUATION

From the beginning, Israel's main focus was prospering in a hostile neighborhood where the survival of the state itself could not be taken for granted. With neighbors who were enemies and could not be definitively defeated, Israel's very existence appeared conditional, not only during the 1948–1949 period, but for years afterward. The survival of the state appeared to be at stake in both the 1967 and the 1973 wars, and the conditionality of the country's existence colored most political decision-making for the first two decades. However, Israel's stunning victory in the 1967 Six-Day War, followed by its recovery from the brink of defeat to emerge victorious in the 1973 Yom Kippur War, served to transform the fundamental security situation. Since 1973 Israel has not had to fight a general war involving conventional armies. Indeed, Israel's major enemies—the ones it engages in military confrontation—are nonstate actors like Palestinian terrorist groups, Hamas, and Hezbollah, though Iran is considered the country's primary strategic threat. While terrorism on an individual level continues to pose a challenge, the country's military superiority in the region has led to a more flexible political situation in which matters other than security can at times be the major focus. These developments have also lessened the country's dependence on retired generals for political leadership, even if some former military men continue to seek political careers.

On the other hand, the improving security situation with regard to conventional warfare since the Egypt–Israel peace treaty in 1979 opened up to many Israelis the possibility of widespread debate over strategic policy, thereby reducing the traditional sense of national unity that was the understandable response to the intense existential threat dating back to 1948. The emergence of Peace Now and other groups critical of government policy, dating back to the 1970s, reflects this diminished consensus.

The other security challenge that Israel has had to face as the threat of conventional warfare has diminished is terrorism, which began in the 1950s with *fedayeen* attacks in the south. From then until the 1990s there were isolated incidents in various parts of the country, some quite consequential in terms of casualties and the threat they posed to aviation, but there were not many attacks in the country's heartland. That changed with the Palestinian terror offensives of the 1990s and 2000s, which brought death and danger into the centers of Jerusalem, Tel Aviv, and Haifa, as well as other cities in which suicide bombings and other attacks were carried out in public spaces such as buses, cafes, city squares, and restaurants. Although the terrorist threat was eventually neutralized, it could reappear if Palestinian militants decide to revert to such tactics or adopt "lone gunman"–style attacks; indeed, this occurred on a smaller scale in October and November 2015, during a series of knife attacks against Israelis. In addition, the more regular threat now comes from rocket and mortar fire from Hezbollah in Lebanon and terrorist groups in Gaza, which are aimed at Israel's population centers.

The upshot of all this is that the military and security services remain central foci of policy and government activity. Yet despite the continuing reliance on the army by the political echelon, in recent years the military has not produced political leaders of the caliber of Moshe Dayan, Yitzhak Rabin, or Ariel Sharon, two of whom became Prime Ministers and all of whom played prominent roles in politics, based in part on the charisma that they acquired through their military exploits. Nevertheless, the ongoing challenges of the security situation necessitate close cooperation between the military and the political leadership, which often results in crossovers from the former to the latter. And of course, military considerations continue to affect many areas of policymaking, including domestic matters such as whether to subject haredim to conscription and the government budget.

Changes in the security situation have affected foreign policy as well. It was only after 1967 that the relationship with the United States became the cornerstone of Israeli foreign policy. Since then the relationship has had its ups and downs but has remained resilient. Under President Barack Obama and Prime Minister Binyamin Netanyahu existing strains have intensified, raising some concerns for policymakers. For years Israel has tried to broaden its horizons to include Europe, the developing world, and, most recently, China, India, and even some Arab states, such as Saudi Arabia, with which it does not have formal diplomatic relations. As a result, foreign affairs remains a critical concern but, like domestic policy, is increasingly subject to intense domestic debate.

THE ISRAELI–PALESTINIAN RELATIONSHIP

The issue of the Israeli–Palestinian relationship involves not just the Palestinian people, but also some of the territories that came under Israeli control during the Six-Day War. Control over the territories, now mainly the West Bank, but earlier the Gaza Strip as well (though Israel maintains control over Gazan air space, sea-lanes, and most of the land border), has created dilemmas for Israeli policymakers ever since 1967. Although most Israelis do not want to rule over the Palestinians indefinitely, there are some who want to retain all or part of the West Bank, which has religious significance and is historically part of Eretz Yisrael. The Israeli public is concerned with security issues as well. The Palestine Liberation Organization was recognized by the Arab League as the "sole, legitimate" representative of the Palestinian people in 1974, but it was not until the 1980s that most of the rest of the world followed suit. This was also the decade when settlements in the West Bank began to expand more rapidly and the First Intifada broke out. Many analysts have argued that it was during this decade that the territories became the primary issue in Israeli elections and one of the major criteria for classifying the various political parties.

Most of the parties have shifted their positions significantly during the past quarter-century, but the inability of various governments and the Palestinian leadership to resolve the many issues that confront them leaves the matter high on the country's priority list. Indeed, aside from the Iranian nuclear threat, this relationship is Israel's major foreign policy concern, and a very controversial one at that. Politically, the significance of the issue is exacerbated because there is no military solution, and any political solution is bound to be both risky and divisive for society. Doing nothing is not a long-run option. But though their attitudes toward the Palestinians have converged over time, the major parties still disagree over the best policy to take regarding the Palestinians, the timing of a possible settlement, and the shape of a final agreement. In the meantime, continuing pressure from the settlers and their political backers results in more settlement construction, with all the attendant complications. The significance of settlement activity remains a source of division within Israeli society. Furthermore, Israel's development of Jerusalem makes the resolution of the city's status a particularly challenging and sensitive issue to negotiate. The legacy of the Six-Day War, then, has left Israel divided on a number of key issues, presenting a formidable challenge to the political leadership and threatening national unity.

DAMPENING OF IDEOLOGY

Even before formal statehood was achieved, ideological approaches to Zionism were a defining characteristic of the Zionist movement and the Yishuv. The party system was categorized in part by competing concepts of what Zionism meant. Over the decades since 1948, the intensity of the traditional Zionist ideological fervor has notably diminished, and the traditional struggles no longer generate the same intensity. What was once clearly an ideological political system has gradually been transformed into a more pragmatic one.

Historically, the main divisions were the choice of socialism versus a free market system and the debate over whether the state should have religious significance; sometimes foreign policy toward other states or actors mattered. If any single ideological dispute now predominates, however, it is the stance toward the territories and how to settle the conflict with the Palestinians, though the question of the relationship between religion and the state remains provocative and divisive. The socialism/capitalism question has essentially been resolved, though some aspects of socioeconomic policy, especially income inequality, remain a source of political contestation. As for Religious Zionism, it remains an option for some but does not really challenge the belief systems of the vast majority of Israelis.

Other ideological issues, though, have emerged and taken on greater prominence. In the background is the larger ideological issue of collectivism versus individualism. Historically, Israeli society put a great deal of emphasis on the well-being and success of the collectivity, even if that meant sacrificing the realization of individual goals. Although its followers never constituted more than a few percent of the ¡population, the kibbutz movement symbolized this choice. For many, the ideals of the kibbutz symbolized what Israel was all about: subordinating one's individual objectives to the achievement of societal goals. Such values had a large effect on the evolution of the military. Not coincidentally, kibbutzniks played a disproportionate role in the IDF during the early years of statehood and helped to shape the values of the military.[1]

A related matter is the decline in enthusiasm for Zionism in certain sectors of society, as well as the growth of communities that are not especially Zionist or might even be considered anti-Zionist. In the early years, the veterans of the Yishuv, who generally were strongly committed to Zionism, set the tone for the rest of society. The policies of Mapai reinforced that orientation by bringing new immigrants into the Zionist fold. But in later generations the enthusiasm for Zionism in some circles dissipated and was replaced by acceptance of, but not necessarily strong commitments to, the official state ideology. Moreover, the haredi sector had never been Zionist. Although there are some appearances of Zionist ideology among haredim now, they are limited.

As the haredi sector grew, it became one of three significant parts of the population that were not oriented toward Zionist ideology and goals, the others being Arab Israelis and immigrants from the FSU. In principle, the general Arab public does not embrace the idea of a Jewish state, while most of the leadership outright rejects it, even though they may value their citizenship. Their parties and other organizations from within the Arab community generally support measures that would reduce the Jewish character of the state, thereby undermining the relevance of Zionist ideology. Indeed, the four Arab parties that are currently represented in the Knesset as part of the Joint List each reject the basic Zionist principles that serve as the basis for Israeli statehood. Finally, most of the immigrants from the former Soviet Union who arrived during the 1990s were primarily seeking refuge rather than coming to Israel because of Zionist commitments. Their children may well be socialized into a Zionist ideological position, but that remains to be seen. In addition, an estimated 300,000 of what are usually referred to as the "Russian immigrants" are not Jewish according to Jewish religious law and may not have much Jewish consciousness, regardless of their halachic status. They are hardly likely to commit themselves strongly to the Zionist principle that Israel is the Jewish state, although their children are increasingly being socialized in that direction.

In the long run, given Israel's stated objectives, the size of its non-Zionist communities poses problems for its continued character as a Jewish state, which is reflected in struggles in the political arena. Without broader socialization into a Zionist ethos—which would be difficult in the case of the Arab and the haredi communities—the country risks a situation in which Zionists might well be in the minority. If the Ethiopian experience is suggestive, integration into the Zionist political culture is possible; Ethiopian Israelis have developed a strong commitment to the Israeli state. However, they are a very small part of the population.

POLITICAL CULTURE AND THE PARTY SYSTEM

David Ben-Gurion understood the challenge of bringing together a disparate population that, although united (except for the Arabs) by its Jewishness, was divided in a multitude of ways. The early emphasis on mamlachtiut particularly reflected Ben-Gurion's conviction of the need to instill unifying values among citizens. The Israeli political culture came to reflect widespread, though not complete, identification with the values and goals of the state and to feature broad participation in the political process, with notably high voter turnout for decades. Israelis displayed a high degree of civic engagement that fostered patriotism, loyalty, active involvement in the military, including reserve duty for decades after one's conscription period had ended, and support for state institutions. In addition, civil society eventually began to flourish as the traditional party structure weakened, leaving openings for new kinds of organizations. The expansion of civil society lessened the need for traditional party connections, which in turn fostered many new types of opportunities for political expression.

The political culture, which had always been closely related to ideology, eventually began to reflect the movement away from collectivism and toward greater individualism. Demographic changes, particularly the increased proportion of Mizrachim in society, contributed to the decline of the Labor-dominated party system and the emergence of a more competitive system. In addition, the legitimation of alternative attitudes on the Palestinian question contributed to greater policy flexibility. These developments in turn enabled voters to consider a wider range of party options than had traditionally been available.

The party system was reasonably stable from 1948 through 1977. The variables were clear, as were the orientations of the various parties. Of course there were numerous small groupings that appeared on the scene from time to time, but overall there was substantial continuity in terms of the composition of the government and representation in the Knesset. However, once Likud won an election in 1977, other possibilities began to become available. The result has been a more complex party system that has gone beyond the conventional division between left and right. Importantly, since 1977 various centrist parties have appeared from time to time and in fact have become a semi-permanent feature of the party system.

Another feature of the new party system is the success of religious parties, and particularly haredi parties, after 1984. The venerable National Religious Party made a comeback in the guise of Bayit Yehudi in 2013. The religious sector, although far from unified, has demonstrated considerable staying power, is backed by a highly motivated and loyal electorate, and has emerged with some clear policy preferences after playing a decidedly secondary role in the first decades of statehood. Indeed, aside from national unity governments, it is probably imperative to include at least one of the religious parties in every government.[2]

Taking the long view, it is more difficult to form a coalition government now than it was in the early years of the state. The possibility that a rightist, centrist, or leftist party may emerge as the likely leader of the coalition in any given election creates uncertainty, though also opportunity. Furthermore, since the 1980s smaller parties have generally increased their share of the total votes at the expense of the larger parties, thus making it more challenging for the larger parties to form stable coalition governments. Finally, the difficulty of categorizing the various parties along all the dimensions that might be meaningful to voters detracts from the clarity of the party system. The system does have the virtue of offering voters a wide range of choices—probably too many. But that virtue in turn leads to an excessive number of parties in the Knesset and occasional awkward, even unstable, coalitions.

A related issue concerns centrist parties. Traditionally, the central part of the ideological spectrum has not been well represented in Israeli politics, with leftist and rightist parties predominating. That situation began to change with the surprise showing of the Democratic Movement for Change, a party dedicated to electoral reform, in the 1977 election. Subsequently Shinui made a breakthrough in 2003, running on a strongly secularist platform but situating itself toward the middle of the party system. That success was followed by Kadima's victory in 2006, which provided Israel with the only centrist government in its history. While it might be argued that Kadima was a flash in the pan, succeeding thanks to the reflected glory of its founder Ariel Sharon, it did garner the most votes in 2009 before utterly failing in 2013. Nevertheless, it demonstrated that there was a constituency for a centrist orientation, thereby paving the way for Yesh Atid in 2013 and Kulanu in 2015. The parties mentioned here obtained double-digit seat totals in six different elections, indicating that even though none of them have demonstrated staying power, there are citizens who are prepared to vote for a centrist party. Yesh Atid dropped from 19 to 11 seats between the 2013 and 2015 elections. Kulanu made up for that decline, winning 10 seats in 2015. If the last two elections are an indication of the future direction of the Knesset, then, while the centrist parties themselves may not be permanent, a constituency of voters who gravitate toward them may be. It remains to be seen whether this floating, centrist vote can be harnessed over a long period of time, though the short lives of the centrist parties to date make this improbable.

THE PASSING OF A HEROIC GENERATION

Israeli political leaders may not have been exactly what Max Weber had in mind when he wrote about charisma some 100 years ago,[3] but there is little doubt that the founding generation of the state did have some special qualities that helped certain leaders attain almost mythic status. For some, that was due to their remarkable military achievements, but leaders like David Ben-Gurion, Shimon Peres, and Menachem Begin, none of whom had military careers, did command a dedicated following as well. Among the top military leaders, Moshe Dayan, Yitzhak Rabin, and Ariel Sharon stand out. Precisely because they were involved either in the founding of the state or in its early struggle for survival, they were often seen, at least by their partisan followers, as having special character traits. Yet all of these leaders eventually lost the luster that had once distinguished them and came to be perceived as no different from the rest of the political leadership, which of course meant that they were not immune from criticism. Ben-Gurion foundered over the Lavon Affair; Dayan lost credibility as people learned about his personal life and his political fickleness became evident; Rabin fell victim to financial irregularities during the 1970s and then became a lightning rod for the hatred of the right over the Oslo Accords; Begin suffered because of the reaction to the war with Lebanon; and Sharon was tarnished by the Sabra and Shatilla refugee camp affair and later severed ties with his rightist backers by engineering the withdrawal from Gaza in 2005.

All of these leaders enjoyed a charismatic period, but all ran into difficulties that dissipated the adoration of the citizens. (After returning to politics Rabin and Sharon were removed from the scene by assassination and illness, respectively, so it is difficult to properly assess their second chances.) And, of course, others in the political leadership and the military high command have never achieved the followings of those mentioned here. The result is that contemporary political leaders and aspiring leaders must fight for and earn the support of voters rather than having it bestowed on them, which may contribute to a sense among voters that politicians cannot be trusted. The decline in voter turnout rates from 1999 to 2013 may reflect this increasing distrust, although the 2013 and 2015 elections saw an increase in turnout. It is not clear yet which is the long-term trend.

A MORE CONSEQUENTIAL ARAB SECTOR

During the early years of statehood, everyone was aware of the Arab sector, which was under military government for 18 years, but it was not a high priority on the political agenda. Over the years since 1966, when military rule ended, issues regarding Arab Israelis gradually became more salient, a process that accelerated after the First Intifada in the late 1980s. While the First Intifada (and the Second Intifada as well) was carried out by Palestinians in the territories, such actions had an impact on Arabs in Israel, many of whom saw themselves as closely aligned with their Palestinian kin. Indeed, it is no longer unusual to observe Arabs self-identifying as Palestinian citizens of Israel. In addition, the Arab political parties that emerged during the 1980s became more assertive over time, while their supporters began to articulate their own political goals within Israel.

The result was that even though Jewish politicians have remained reluctant to contemplate any Arab party as a possible coalition partner, awareness of the political significance of the Arab minority has increased greatly.[4] Consequently, the Arab issue, in one form or another, is always on the political agenda, at least informally. Arab Israeli leadership, which still cannot gain access to the inner corridors of power, is much more articulate and demanding today than in the past. While the Arab leadership in the Knesset, reflecting four distinct parties, may not necessarily focus on its constituents' most pressing concerns, other voices in the Arab community are beginning to do so, and Jewish political leaders are certainly much more conscious of the issues concerning this community than they were in the past.

TRANSFORMATION OF THE JUDICIARY

As the political system was originally understood, the judiciary played a decidedly secondary role to other branches of the government, with few political consequences.

Within a system based on parliamentary supremacy, that much was to be expected. But several developments over the decades have helped to transform the role of the courts, with the result that the Supreme Court has become a high-profile and activist body, a force to be reckoned with politically. The most important changes have involved increased consciousness regarding the meaning of constitutionalism, creative interpretation of some of the Basic Laws, the establishment of the principle of judicial review, and activism in the High Court of Justice that has challenged government actions on a number of fronts, including policy toward Palestinian noncitizens in the West Bank and (before 2005) Gaza.

The effect of these changes is that the Court, doing double duty as the highest appellate court and, when sitting as the HCJ, a court of original jurisdiction, has established itself as a consequential political force that is fiercely independent of the government and the Knesset, one that is not afraid to challenge prevailing political views on issues as highly charged as security, relationships with the Palestinians in the territories, treatment of prisoners, and the route of the security barrier in the West Bank.[5] The assumed role of the Court definitely complicates policy-making and decision-making for those in the government. Furthermore, it probably complicates the process of completing a constitution, which in any event is proceeding very slowly, in part because of apprehension about what the Court might do with such a document once it is entrenched. Moreover, the judiciary became an issue during the campaigns for the 2015 election when Bayit Yehudi called for a reassessment of judicial review. However, soon after the new government was formed, the Justice Minister, that party's Ayelet Shaked, stated that it was unlikely that the government would tackle this issue given the current political landscape.

CHANGE VERSUS CONTINUITY

With all of the previously mentioned points in mind, we can now begin to address the question of how they fit together. Viewing the totality of these issues, is Israel a different kind of society and polity than it was in 1948? Has it changed more than other states have changed during the comparable period?

The short answer is that Israel has certainly evolved—and significantly so— but does maintain continuity with its founding principles. Perhaps the foremost of those principles is the idea that the country is both a Jewish and a democratic state. While most Israelis have taken this principle for granted since the beginning of its existence, the issue—or at least the Jewish aspect—is front and center in the negotiations between Israel and the Palestinians, as well as in internal debates between the secular and the religious, and the Jewish and the Arab sectors, and is the basis for the proposed controversial Basic Law on the Jewish State, which was placed on the back burner by the new government in 2015. Although some groups, such as many post-Zionists in Israel, do question the Jewish character of the state, their position has not gained a great deal of traction with the general public and has certainly not achieved representation in the Knesset.

While the basic ideological framework of the state remains substantially the same, the society has changed significantly, with the most noticeable shift being one from an emphasis on collective accomplishments to a focus on individual achievement. The society is also increasingly diverse, despite the unifying element of Jewish national identity for about 75 percent of the population. The country has a much more sophisticated and advanced economy than it did in 1948 and is now able to compete internationally in the areas of scholarship, research and development, and technological innovation.

Politically, the country functions in a manner that is substantially similar to what was in place during the early years, albeit with some changes in the party system and a more assertive judiciary. Israel is still plagued with an electoral system that is dysfunctional in some respects, despite numerous and continuing efforts to fix it. Externally, the country is a regional military powerhouse that no longer faces the kinds of military challenges that confronted it in the beginning. Nevertheless, the threat of the Iranian nuclear program and the difficulties in dealing with nonstate actors that engage in terrorism are reminders that Israel's quest for security remains unresolved. And of course, the lingering issues arising from the Six-Day War continue to confound legions of would-be peacemakers.

Beneath Israel's superficial identification as the state of the Jewish people lies a very complex society that has changed greatly since the beginning of statehood, and this has had clear effects on the political system. There is certainly a great deal of continuity in the country's evolution, but also much more change than would have been expected in a more established state over the same period of time. In comparison with other states, even ones of roughly the same age, the amount of change that has occurred in Israel has generally been greater.

KEYWORDS

collectivism, individualism, political culture, economic development, heroes and charisma, peace process, ethno-national consciousness, judicial activism

NOTES

1. Stuart A. Cohen, *Divine Service? Judaism and Israel's Armed Forces* (Burlington, VT: Ashgate, 2013), 8.
2. Daniel J Elazar, *Israel: Building a New Society* (Bloomington: Indiana University Press, 1986).
3. Max Weber, *From Max Weber: Essays in Sociology* (New York: Routledge, 2009).
4. The Rabin government lost its majority in 1993 but was propped up from outside the coalition by the Arab parties because they supported its promotion of the Oslo peace process.
5. Another example is the High Court of Justice's rejection of government-supported laws regarding migrants who entered the country illegally. The Court twice struck down immigration laws in 2014 on constitutional grounds and in the process attracted considerable criticism.

CHAPTER 18

✋

Confronting the Meaning
of a Jewish State

It is an exciting moment to study Israeli politics, but it is also a daunting one. While we have detailed the processes, actors, and issues in Israeli politics, we have not yet discussed what all this means for Israel itself. If one thing is clear from the preceding discussion, it is that questions of identity continue to be hotly disputed by different segments of the population, and these disputes are reflected in the political arena. Israel was founded to be a Jewish state, but there was never general agreement on what this meant in practice, even among the Jewish public, and as the country's demographics have changed, the differences between groups' preferences have become more acute. This chapter ties ideas laid out in the book together by setting out three questions about Israel that Israelis still struggle to best answer to their satisfaction. These are: the political question (can Israel exist as a Jewish and democratic state?), the social question (who is, or can be, a member of the Israeli collective?), and the academic question (how should we think about Israel?).

THE POLITICAL QUESTION:
WHAT IS JEWISH AND DEMOCRATIC?

At its creation Israel was proclaimed to be "a Jewish state." The Declaration of Independence also affirmed that Israel would "foster the development of the country for the benefit of all its inhabitants; it will be based on freedom, justice and peace as envisaged by the prophets of Israel; it will ensure complete equality of social and political rights to all its inhabitants irrespective of religion, race or sex; it will guarantee freedom of religion, conscience, language, education and culture."

The word "democracy" does not appear in the Declaration, but the priorities that document set out are widely considered to be key elements in a genuine democracy. Israeli governments have regularly reinforced this notion. The Basic Law: Human Dignity and Liberty and the Basic Law: Freedom of Occupation both refer to "the values of the State of Israel as a Jewish and democratic state." Given that the

Supreme Court has elevated the Basic Laws to constitutional status, a strong argument can be made that Jewishness and democracy are pillars of Israeli identity.

Yet elements of the Jewish component of the state are given priority. The state's symbols (e.g., the flag, the national anthem), political norms (the continued exclusion of Arab parties from governing coalition), rules on land appropriation and ownership, budgetary expenditures, and the nature of the military draft all favor Israeli Jews over Israeli Arabs. The process of the founding of Israel helps explain why this should be neither surprising nor, when we think about many other countries in the world, seen as abnormal. The practical issue is what this means for domestic harmony and for the rights of minorities.

Sammy Smooha has written of Israel as an "ethnic democracy," a model he applies to other countries in Europe as well.[1] For Smooha, Israel has elements of both an ethnocracy and a democracy. In his conception, citizenship is separated from nationality, which is based on specific ascriptive and physical characteristics. But the state is dominated by a specific nation in what he calls an "ethnic ascendancy," while members of other nations are viewed as a threat to the hegemony of the dominant community, and perhaps even to the state's existence as the political representation of that nation. All citizens of the state have full political and civil rights, and the minority group has some communal rights as well, such as language rights and some control over education. But because the dominant ethnic group has *more* rights, there cannot ever be full equality. The state is defined according to one ethnic group, rather than belonging to all its citizens.

For some this is an intolerable situation that must be changed as soon as possible. Critics of this state of affairs point to a myriad of laws and norms that discriminate against Arab citizens because they privilege Jewish citizens.[2] Others add that the occupation of the West Bank and continued settlement building there blur the Green Line, and that therefore no meaningful distinction can be made between democracy within Israel and occupation/repression within the West Bank.[3] The fiercest critics call Israel racist and colonialist.

Many in Israel share these concerns about the irreconcilability of Israel as a Jewish and a democratic state, but they approach the issue from another angle: they want to emphasize the Jewish element over the democratic element. The haredi population has long prioritized halacha over the state's temporal authority. Members of this community contend that the state already has a constitutional document, the Torah. In contrast, the secular nationalist community believes the state should represent Jewish nationalism without necessarily elevating Judaism over civil law. Religious Zionists agree with parts of both arguments. Some of those concerned with the Jewish character of the state have argued in recent years that while the Declaration of Independence does declare Israel to be both the homeland of the Jewish people and a Jewish state, there is only vague constitutional protection for either status, because there are no Basic Laws dedicated to enumerating these specific principles of identity.

In 2011, Avi Dichter, an MK from Kadima, submitted a bill to create a new Basic Law on Israel as the Nation-State of the Jewish People. This legislation would declare Israel as the homeland of the Jewish people, enshrine Jewish symbols and calendrical events as the symbols and calendar of the state, and compel the state to use Jewish religious law as a source of inspiration. The proposal was heavily criticized by those who believed that it would upset the existing balance between Jewish and democratic values, thereby depriving Palestinian citizens of legal protections.

The bill did not make it through the Knesset, but the idea gained momentum. In May 2014, Prime Minister Binyamin Netanyahu announced that he would submit a bill that "would provide a constitutional anchor for Israel's status as the national state of the Jewish people." It was widely assumed that this proposal was in response to Netanyahu's failure to convince Palestinian President Mahmoud Abbas during peace talks to formally recognize Israel as a Jewish state. Lawmakers from the right quickly picked up on Netanyahu's announcement, and by the end of the month MKs Ze'ev Elkin (Likud), Yariv Levin (Likud), and Ayelet Shaked (Bayit Yehudi) had said that they would submit new proposals on the topic. Levin and Shaked submitted a bill that explicitly calls Israel a "Jewish and democratic state" (addressing then-Justice Minister Tzipi Livni's [Hatenua] concern about emphasizing Jewish identity over democratic identity) but proclaims that "the State of Israel is the national home of the Jewish people, where they realize their aspiration for self-determination according to their cultural and historical legacy." Though all citizens are guaranteed "personal rights," only Jews have collective rights.[4] Detractors contended that the effect would still be to discriminate against the Arab minority, and, in any event, the law does not address the specific meaning of Jewish state. The bill did not reach the Knesset for a vote before the government fell and new elections were called. As of November 2015, the new Likud-led government had put the issue aside in the face of opposition from Moshe Kahlon (Kulanu) and the haredi parties, all of which oppose the effort.

Opponents of Israel as a Jewish state often point to discrimination against the Arab minority as proof of the inherent problem of such an identity. Zionists and others who believe that Israel can exist as both a Jewish state and a democracy in which all citizens share the same freedoms and rights argue that all countries contain elements of social inequality, including Western civic democracies. Nor is the privileging of one identity over others uncommon. Even in the United States, for example, the calendar is based on the Gregorian model, with Christian holidays marking time. Countries like Armenia, Germany, Greece, Ireland, and Poland give individuals who share the same ethno-national identity as the country's hegemonic community certain privileges in obtaining citizenship. While the struggle to find an effective balance between majority and minority rights continues, elevation of one communal identity over another does not disqualify Israel from being a democracy. Nor, though lamentable and in immediate need of rectification, does discrimination. Inequality is not a form of identity, nor can intent be presumed from outcomes. Governmental policies can be changed. In the case of Israel, there has been greater attention in recent years to the Arab community's needs and the imbalance in resources, with a particular focus on job training and improvements at the municipal level.

These issues are complicated by the Israeli occupation of the West Bank, which Israel never annexed but over which it has expanded its military and legal control. In order to rectify the imbalance within the state, many argue that a two-state solution—the establishment of a Palestinian state in the West Bank and Gaza that is at peace with Israel—is therefore an important component not only of resolving Israel's security situation, but also of saving Israel's Jewish character—and Zionism itself.[5] This is sometimes phrased as a question of whether Israeli identity is based on the State of Israel or the Land of the Israel. But however it is conceived, it complicates the political question by situating it in two different spheres: the domestic and the foreign.

For some Israelis, the answer to the question of how to address the close relationship between the domestic and the foreign spheres in the context of Israel as a Jewish state is to rethink Israeli sovereignty and politics. On the left, many have argued that Israel cannot remain a Jewish-Zionist state if it continues to occupy the West Bank. Writers at the left-wing blog +972 Magazine have wrestled with this issue, and although individual bloggers have come to different conclusions, they all point in the same direction. Noam Sheizaf writes that he no longer thinks in terms of the one- or two-state solution, because the ultimate controlling power in both Israel and the WBG is the Israeli government; given current reality, it does not make sense to think in such abstract terms. Dahlia Scheindlin argues that the terms "Zionism" or "Zionist" are meaningless, because groups within the movement fight viciously over how to define them—and over which territories and which groups get to be included in the definitions. Both Sheizaf and Scheindlin contend that it is better to think in terms of "rights," which focuses attention on who has and who does not.

Such ideas remain outside the mainstream in Israel, however, and for some on the right they are tantamount to betrayal. Thinkers like Sheizaf and Scheindlin are part of a still small but growing community among the Israeli left, but their ideas have been pushed into the public debate. In addition, mainstream leftist groups—those that still firmly identify as Zionists, believe in Israel as a Jewish and democratic state, and support the two-state solution—have both absorbed some of these ideas and worry that they complicate their own message of compromise. Organizations like Peace Now and Molad and political parties like Labor and Meretz all work to establish two states (a Jewish-majority Israeli state and a Palestinian-majority state in most of the West Bank and Gaza[6]) both because they believe Palestinians deserve self-determination too and to make sure Israel remains a Jewish and democratic state. The believers and the doubters continue to debate the issue among themselves, but while both are convinced their approach is the right one, the believers worry that the lack of progress toward a resolution of these issues is making it more difficult to promote such mainstream views, and that Israelis are beginning to confuse the believers with the doubters. Indeed, the moderate left has had great difficulty in finding a message along these lines that the Israeli public can identify with; the rise of the center and its preference for right-leaning parties is evidence of this challenge.

On the right and far right, individuals and organizations have come at the political question from a different angle. Naftali Bennett, leader of Bayit Yehudi, actively promotes a plan, which he calls the Israel Stability Initiative, to annex all of Area C of the West Bank, retain Israeli security control over the rest of the territory, and help establish a Palestinian state in Areas A and B.[7] Other right-leaning activists, such as former head of the Yesha Council Dani Dayan, advocate for granting Israel sovereignty over the West Bank but allowing Palestinians living there political rights in Jordan (for example, the right to vote in Jordanian elections), while many others, such as members of Likud's new young guard Danny Danon and Ze'ev Elkin, want Israel to annex most of the West Bank and leave something more like an autonomous area rather than an independent state for the Palestinians. Still others, like Likud's Tzipi Hotovely, argue that the number of Palestinians in the West Bank is small enough that even giving them all full rights under Israeli sovereignty would not endanger the Jewish identity of the state.

Given the intensity of the debate, one could be forgiven for thinking there is no mainstream or centrist position between these views. But there is, and it has been laid out in previous chapters. The majority of Israelis today believe Israel is, and should remain, a Jewish state; they want Israel to remain democratic; they do not want to remove the Arab minority's rights; and they support the establishment of a Palestinian state in the West Bank and Gaza, though they do not see how that is possible in light of the effects of the withdrawals from Lebanon and Gaza and continued hostility from various Palestinian groups. More specifically, they are not likely to see a specific connection between the foreign sphere (the Israeli–Palestinian conflict) and the domestic sphere (social and economic problems).[8] The two parties that best represent the mainstream, in addition to the various centrist parties that emerge in different elections, are Likud and Labor. Unlike these two parties, groups further to the left and to the right are more likely to emphasize the direct connection between Israel and the WBG, and propose solutions on that basis.

The mainstream is increasingly unable to control the public debate. In part this is because the issues are complex and difficult to unravel, and in part it is because the Palestinians are divided too and share the blame for the lack of progress in peace talks, which makes Israelis more suspicious of their intentions. Moreover, the status quo does not support the mainstream preference: the Israeli presence in the West Bank deepens each year, while the raft of bills put forward by two right-leaning governments in a row (2009–2013, 2013–2015) have sought to restrict the space necessary for democracy to flourish. Most important, Jewish Israelis—including those in the mainstream—have not yet defined what, precisely, being a Jewish state means, that is, what it would look like in practice. It is important to note, too, that while questions of Israel's Jewish identity have been around since the establishment of the state, they have taken on greater urgency and political relevance particularly since the 1980s, when the shift from a collectivist culture to a more individualist ethos—grounded in what we think of today as liberal democratic values—really took root.

It has been said that Israel can be a Jewish state, a democratic state, or an occupying state (in reference to the West Bank), but it cannot be all three at once. It will have to choose two. It is this choice that Israelis are struggling to make.

THE SOCIAL QUESTION: WHO BELONGS?

If the identity and political structure of the state are debatable, then the question of who belongs in the Israeli community—that is, who is an Israeli—and who gets to set those boundaries must also be addressed. As a movement of national liberation, Zionism facilitated the return of the Jews to their ancient homeland and brought them self-determination. But as a political project, it also constructed boundaries of both national belonging and acceptable politics. In the Yishuv and during the first decades of the state, the secular Ashkenazi elite dominated the state. Communists and Arabs were more or less excluded from playing an active role in politics—they could form parties and vote, but they were never serious contenders for participation in the government and they were not seen as contributors to the Zionist project; indeed, many saw them as opponents to it. In the later years of the state, other groups—including Mizrachim and Ethiopians—were also marginalized in one way or another. And although haredi parties did participate in the political system, the community as a whole was less interested in affiliating with the state.

The question of who is an Israeli is complicated by the dual nature of Israeli identity, as captured by the difference between halachic and civic definitions of who is a Jew, a debate that has implications for citizenship of non-Jews. The struggle over this question was discussed in Chapter 6. Citizenship in Israel is governed by the Nationality Law, which sets out how an individual can obtain Israeli citizenship: by birth (being born in Israel or to an Israeli mother or father), through the Law of Return, through residence (for citizens of Mandatory Palestine), and by naturalization. Prior to 2005, the identification card (te'udat zehut) that all adult Israelis are required to carry listed them not as Israeli but rather according to the specific group (le'om, which can be translated as "ethnicity" or "nation") to which they belong: Jewish, Arab, Druze, or Circassian. This categorization was removed after 2005, though the same type of group designation is still made in the state's population registry.

In October 2013, the Supreme Court rejected an appeal by a group of citizens to be listed on their identity cards as "Israeli" on the basis that they do not belong to a specific ethnic or religious group but are citizens of the Israeli state. The Court's ruling underlined questions about the relationship between Jewishness, citizenship, and belonging. The Court ruled that there was no such thing as an "Israeli people," while one judge (Hanan Melcer) wrote in his response that changing the category "was against both the Jewish nature and the democratic nature of the State." In other words, being "Israeli" requires belonging to two legally bound communities at once: the Israeli state and the ethno-religio-national community.

In addition to complicating national identity, this question has clear implications for Israeli Palestinians. Separating Israeli citizens into different categories and then tying the state's identity to one specific community (Jews) is meant to privilege the citizens of that community over citizens of other communities (Arabs). Attaching citizenship to Jewish identity has implications for non-Arabs, as well. The status of the Russian and Ethiopian communities has already been discussed; placing them into the "Jewish" category means forcing them to adapt to the Orthodox interpretations of Jewish law that govern Jewish citizens of the state—for example in personal status affairs such as marriage, conversion, burial, and divorce. So far these groups have been resistant to these efforts.

Normally, questions of national identity do not include noncitizens, even if they move legally into the country. But in Israel's case, Israelis themselves have implicated two groups of noncitizens in the debate over Israel's identity: foreign workers and African migrants/refugees.[9] In the aftermath of the First Intifada (1987–1993), Israel imposed increasingly frequent and prolonged closures of the borders of the West Bank and Gaza, preventing what had until then been a normal routine: the passing of tens of thousands of Palestinians across the Green Line into Israel to work in various industries, particularly in low-skill or unskilled areas such as construction, manufacturing, and food service. With the loss of this labor force, Israel actively sought out replacements from abroad—a sharp switch from the importance of Hebrew labor promoted by socialist Zionists in the Yishuv as necessary for the building of the state and Jewish peoplehood.

By some estimates, this led to the influx of about 350,000 to 400,000 foreign workers, both legal and illegal migrants, by 2004. According to Israel's 2013 *Statistical Abstract*, the number of legal workers has dropped somewhat since then. At the end of 2012 there were 109,000 workers in Israel with a work permit, and another 93,000 who had come to work on a tourist visa. They come mainly from Asia (the Philippines, Thailand, Sri Lanka, and Turkey) and southern and eastern Europe (the former Soviet Union, Bulgaria, and Romania).

Originally regarded as a temporary solution, little thought was given to these workers' effect on Israel's social makeup. Because they are not citizens, their access to welfare services is constrained. Yet the sheer size of the community makes it difficult to ignore their needs—particularly once they began starting families in Israel. This has led to the creation of cultural "bubbles"—small communities, concentrated in Tel Aviv, that are bound together by their identity as noncitizens. They continue to follow their own communal practices—including establishing houses of worship—and exist as separate social and political entities but are economically integrated into Israel. At first ignored by the Israeli public and government, this group has received considerable attention since 2000. Efforts to grant members social services—particularly the children born in Israel—have picked up pace. Other efforts have focused on the integration of children of foreign workers into schools with Israeli children.

There is some space in the Nationality Law for individuals to acquire citizenship by residence, but Israel's priority has been to provide citizenship to Jews. Some have argued that allowing foreign workers to remain in Israel as citizens will affect the demographic balance between the Jewish and non-Jewish population, and therefore undermine the Zionist project.

But if the presence of foreign workers has made some Israelis concerned for the future of Zionism and the Jewish state, the influx of African migrants and refugees since 2005 has sparked outright fear and racism among some. By most estimates, there were approximately 60,000 Africans—primarily from war-torn Sudan and Eritrea—in Israel by the beginning of 2012; the Hotline for Refugees and Migrants, a nongovernmental organization, put that number at 48,000 at the end of 2014. These migrants entered Israel illegally, without the state's authorization, through Egypt's Sinai Peninsula. Some of them were seeking employment opportunities, but because the countries they came from were in the throes of intense violence and there was genuine fear of persecution if they returned, they have occupied a zone of uncertainty (that is, as non-Jewish refugees) in the Israeli public space. Most of them, regardless of their reasons for coming to Israel, ended up taking on employment there, particularly in Tel Aviv, as dishwashers, laundry workers, and other menial laborers.

It is not clear what sparked the sudden interest in their presence, but in 2012 right-wing politicians began to rail against the Africans, accusing them of lying about being refugees in order to work, and of increasing the rate of crime in the country. In May 2012, MK Miri Regev (Likud) referred to African refugees as a "cancer" in the Israeli body. (She later apologized for any offense her comment gave, without retracting the comment itself.) That same month, Prime Minister Binyamin Netanyahu declared at a Cabinet meeting that the presence of the Africans "threatens the social fabric of society, our national security and our national identity." Former Shas leader Eli Yishai called for all Africans to be rounded up and deported. At a small rally in December 2012, far-right politicians Michael Ben-Ari and Arieh Eldad called for Israel to "banish the darkness" (i.e., African migrants). These arguments imply that the Africans represent a threat to the country's identity, though many rightist politicians have also blamed them for crime—such as theft, rape, and other acts of violence—and therefore cast them as a threat to the security of Israelis.[10]

In contrast, left-wing activists and human rights organizations argue that statistics do not bear out the claim that the African community has led to an increase in crime, and that the small number of Africans cannot pose a threat to the state's Jewish character. They add that helping the dispossessed and refugees is the right thing for Israel to do, not least because the Jews themselves were not long ago refugees in need of aid. Furthermore, they say, Israel is obligated to help, since it is a signatory to a number of international treaties on refugees. They criticize the government for ignoring or slowing down the applications for asylum that have been submitted.

Unlike the community of foreign workers, the government has made a concerted effort to address the presence of African migrants. In June 2012 the Knesset passed an amendment to the Anti-Infiltration Law, used in the 1950s to deal with Palestinian terrorists crossing into Israel, with the aim of using it as the main vehicle in a multipart campaign to detain and deport Africans. The law allowed the government to put the migrants in jail for a minimum of three years. In September 2013 the High Court of Justice ruled against the amendment. In December 2013 the Knesset passed another amendment stipulating that asylum-seekers who enter Israel will be jailed for one year (without trial) and then transferred to a large facility at Holot in the Negev Desert built to house migrants and refugees; refugees already in the country must also report to the detention center. Residents of the facility are allowed to leave during the day—but cannot work—and must report back at various times in the day for a roll call. There is no set period after which they must leave. The government also shut down the border with Sinai, sent notices of deportation to places Africans are known to live and work, and offered up to $3,500 in cash to those who left the country. In September 2014, the High Court again ruled against the government, ordering it to shut down the Holot center within 90 days. Interior Minister Gideon Sa'ar (Likud) proclaimed in response that "we won't have a Jewish democratic state because our borders will be overrun . . . with illegal infiltrators."[11]

In December 2014 the Knesset passed yet another government amendment, which shortened the time Africans would be imprisoned to three months and the time spent at Holot to 20 months. Any wages earned would also be taxed. In August 2015 the Supreme Court ruled again on the law. It accepted now that the law was constitutional, pursuant to specific changes in its stipulations. It ruled that 20 months in Holot was disproportionate and gave the Knesset six months to set a shorter period. It also ordered that over 1,000 Africans who had been detained there for more than a year had to be released within 15 days. Other elements of the law were also altered, for example reducing the number of roll calls Holot residents had to attend.

The African community has become more visible in the last year not only because of attention from politicians. At the end of 2013 and beginning of 2014 they adopted the Israeli tactic of protest. Leaving their (illegal) jobs, they marched by the hundreds, protesting against accusations of criminal behavior, racism, and efforts to deport them. They have drawn support from many other Israelis, but the government has continued its effort to detain and deport them. At the moment of writing, it may be that the government has slowed down its process, but it does not seem that the effort to close Israel to African migrants will stop completely.

Certainly all states must deal with questions about citizenship and belonging, particularly those that contain a hegemonic ethno-national group. For its part, Israel has not been able to satisfactorily reconcile different, and competing, understandings of national identity. Even those in the center or mainstream have different ideas about what being a Jewish or democratic state means in practice. The 2013 Israeli Democracy Index, for instance, asked Jewish Israelis whether a "Jewish" or "democratic" state was more important. 32.3 percent of respondents said that a Jewish state was more important, 29.2 percent said that a democratic state was more important, and 37 percent said both are "equally important." But it is not clear what "both" entails in practice.[12] The survey then narrowed down "Jewish" to Jewish religious principles and laws and asked which should have priority when they conflict with each other: "democratic principles" or "Jewish religious law." Among respondents, 42.7 percent said that "it is preferable in all cases to uphold democratic principles," 28.2 percent said that it is preferable in all cases to adhere to the precepts of Jewish religious law, and 21.1 percent said it depends on the circumstances. Just over 2 percent said there is no conflict between the two. As the IDI points out, these results could be read in two ways: either close to a majority strongly support democracy over other values, or a majority do not think democratic principles matter as much or are separable from Jewish halacha.[13]

That Israelis continue to openly struggle with these issues is a sign of Israel's maturity and allows for the interplay of creative ideas. For example, the growth of Israeli cinema in the last decade, as a result of an influx of government and private funds and more creative young directors and producers, has led to an explosion of well-done Israeli films. These productions touch on many of the sensitive subjects discussed in this chapter, bringing the issues into the public conversation. *Turn Left at the End of World* (2004) explores the discrimination faced by non-Ashkenazi

Jews who came to Israel in the aftermath of the establishment of Ashkenazi hegemony and their trials and tribulations in a development town in the Negev Desert. *Noodle* (2007) tells the story of a foreign worker who is deported for staying in Israel after her visa expires. Her former aloof boss helps the child who was left behind reunite with his mother in China. *Ajami* (2009) brings together Jewish Israelis, Arab Israelis, and Palestinians from the West Bank in a web of plotlines that converge in Ajami, a neighborhood in Jaffa. These films blur the lines between the various communities under Israeli control, raising hope that if art is an imitation of life, perhaps "real life" Israelis can follow suit.

THE ACADEMIC QUESTION: WHOSE HISTORIOGRAPHY?

The effort to define Israel is closely tied to the study of Israel. Not only do writers and academics pass their ideas on to their students, but their work provides information to the public, influences popular attitudes, and provides an alternative narrative to official government statements. A tug-of-war has taken place in Israel over school textbooks, for example, between right-wing and left-wing Education Ministers who want to portray Israel's history in different ways. This, in turn, has changed what Israelis learn, and therefore think, about their country and themselves.

Until the early or mid-1980s, most studies of Israel—and most Israelis— followed an "official" interpretation of the country's founding. This largely identified Israel as a small David fighting the much larger Arab Goliath. The War of Independence was one of survival, and Israel survived and flourished against all odds. Since then, the narrative continues, Israel has stretched out its hand in peace, which the Arabs have rejected with violence. Yet Israel continues to fight its wars of defense to protect itself, and nothing it can do will change the hostility arrayed against it.

By the 1980s a small number of "new historians" (the initial group was composed of Benny Morris, Avi Shlaim, Simha Flapan, and Tom Segev) had begun to dissect the official narrative about the founding of Israel through a more critical approach facilitated by the opening of previously classified historical and state archives.[14] The new historians' work was soon supplemented by similar approaches in sociology and political science. These researchers have focused on a wide range of issues: Morris, Shlaim, and Segev have explored the founding of the state and the 1948 War, Gershon Shafir and Michael Shalev have focused on Israel's political economy, while the late Baruch Kimmerling examined the construction of Israeli identity. The purpose of their work was to challenge Jewish Israelis' dominant assumptions, founding myths, and collective memories.

Many Israeli academics have absorbed the lessons of the new historians and others and have continued to raise questions about the direction the country is taking. For example, Oded Löwenheim, a scholar of international relations at the Hebrew University of Jerusalem, has written about mountain biking through trails in the Jerusalem area. *The Politics of the Trail* is a discussion of his reactions to the ruins of Palestinian houses he comes across, the separation barrier that impedes his access, and the interaction between Palestinians from the West Bank and Israeli Border Police and soldiers he witnesses. He considers the use of violence and occupation and what it means for Israeli identity, Israeli politics, and the future of the country, and he ponders his role as a student of Israel in changing or maintaining these conditions.[15]

The new historians have not gone unchallenged. Efraim Karsh has demonstrated serious methodological problems with some of their work.[16] He has, for example, highlighted a proclivity to take sections of a quote from a Zionist leader and extrapolate not just a larger meaning but a specific policy from it. Anita Shapira has raised important questions about these scholars' motivations, claims to originality, and unfortunate mixing of scholarship with ideology.[17] Nevertheless, most of the new historians' empirical findings have been accepted today, even if their conclusions and assumptions of intent have not. For example, most Israelis accept that the Zionists committed some mass killing during the 1948 War, though they might disagree over how to define these (as self-defense or atrocity).[18]

From academia this effort has been refracted, through the media and the arts, into the political arena and the public conversation as post-Zionism. Post-Zionism is a much broader exercise—it is a worldview.[19] Post-Zionists have sought to raise questions not just about Israeli policy but about Israel's moral character and appropriate future. They argue that the Zionist project has succeeded—Jews are no longer endangered—that it was never a legitimate project, or that it has become so corrupted that, *ipso facto*, it should not be allowed to continue. In all cases, post-Zionists believe the time for a Jewish state has ended, and, particularly given the privileging of Jewish identity over Palestinian identity (or, for some, the suppression of Palestinian identity and rights), a new state should be created that incorporates Israel, Gaza, and the West Bank without regard for ethnic, national, or religious distinctions. Critics respond that this is a fundamental misunderstanding of both Zionism and of nationalism in general; that there is no indication that either Jews or Palestinians want to give up their separate identities or quest for self-determination; and that all countries make mistakes but that is not a reason for the country to be erased, particularly against its population's wishes.

Although there is no sign that post-Zionism has attracted enough support to become a factor in elections, it has played a role in public debates and governmental policy. "Post-Zionist" has become a pejorative term used most often by rightists against those they think are too critical of Israel. Consequently it must be considered in any discussion of modern Israeli politics.

Both the new historians (most of whom considered themselves Zionists) and post-Zionists emerged from the process of Israeli development and social changes over time. First, a new generation of citizens and scholars came of age that was not "burdened" with the "baggage" of the past—the Arab riots in the Yishuv, the shadow of the Holocaust, the War of Independence, and the sense of insecurity that pervaded Israel until the 1980s. They were, then, more willing to question the dominant narrative of Israel's history. For this generation, Israel was the strongest military power in the region.

Second, this same generation felt stifled by the collectivist ethos that had dominated Israeli life. The notion of sacrificing the self for the collective good seemed quaint in an era when the kibbutz was no longer the symbol of the state, when per capita income was on par with that of other Western countries, when consumer goods were readily available, and when free market capitalism encouraged levels of individualism unheard of in Israel's early years. That many kibbutzim had turned away from the socialist-collective experiment by the 1980s and adopted capitalist methods of development only underscored this shift.

Third, there was a broad-based awakening of two different identities at odds with the Ashkenazi identity that had governed the country since its founding. Arab citizens and Mizrachi citizens, long marginalized in different ways, had become more acclimatized to the political system, better mobilized, and more assertive in pressing for a more equitable distribution of resources (see Chapters 5 and 7). Much of the population became more accepting of their cultural practices, as well. Mizrachi music, for example, long derided as "bus station music" because the major record stores would not sell it, instead relegating it to kiosks in bus stations, became popular in the 1990s.

Fourth, changes in the nature of Israel's wars led to an unprecedented questioning of both Israel's moral authority and mandatory service in the military. The Israel Defense Forces (IDF) prides itself on its "purity of arms," that is, its pursuit of military aims with as much humanity as possible. This ethos was captured in the widely repeated notion of "wars of no choice"—wars that were imposed on Israel and forced it to defend itself. The 1982 invasion of Lebanon and the use of the IDF to put down the demonstrations of the First Intifada called these concepts into question for many.[20] Certainly the Palestinians committed violence, sometimes terrible violence. But the general image was of stone-throwing Palestinian youth against Israeli tanks—the reversal of the traditional David and Goliath image.

A good example of how post-Zionism has gotten tangled in broader public and political debates is the story of the study of Tantura. Based on a 1998 master's thesis by a Haifa University student, Teddy Katz, in January 2000 the Israeli newspaper *Maariv* ran a story on "The Massacre in Tantura." The report used Katz's information and claimed that the IDF had killed about 200 unarmed Palestinian prisoners during the 1947–1949 War. Members of the unit accused of the war crime, the Alexandroni Brigade, immediately sued for libel. In the public trial that followed, the lawyers for the veterans of the Brigade uncovered several errors in Katz's research, including the alleged fabrication of quotes to support the claim of massacre. The suit was settled out of court, though Katz continued to receive threats for what his detractors consider the defaming of Israel's heroic generation. Haifa University then ordered Katz to rewrite the thesis, with a new committee assigned to examine it. Ultimately, the thesis was failed for not proving what it claimed it would (that a massacre in Tantura had taken place). In this episode, then, a piece of academic research became a major debate in the courts, in the media, and in the political arena once some politicians tried to put forward a bill facilitating legal action against any publication that defames the IDF.[21]

CONCLUSION

This chapter has raised three broad questions about what kind of country Israel is and should be, what it means to be an Israeli, and how students of Israel should approach these questions. All three questions are centered on the role of Jewish-Zionist identity in the Israeli state. The Jewish component of the state is also made more consequential given Palestinian Arab political activism and efforts by some on the far right to push tribal Jewish ethnocentrism. Many Israelis have recognized the difficulty of squaring this circle. In the process of trying to, a number have begun to think more deeply about these issues. Some of them have published those thoughts in English, making their deliberations accessible to those outside the country.

In *Rubber Bullets*, Yaron Ezrahi highlighted a number of questions about the end of the "Zionist dream," particularly regarding the decline of collectivism in Israeli culture and the consequences of the occupation of the West Bank and Gaza.[22] In response to the types of criticisms Ezrahi raised, Yoram Hazony wrote *The Jewish State: The Struggle for Israel's Soul* as a sort of manual for how to overcome this needless despair put forward by the post-Zionists whom, he thought, had penetrated every element of Israeli life.[23]

The later 2000s have seen a proliferation of such ruminations, particularly those written from a critical perspective. Bernard Avishai (*The Hebrew Republic*), Ari Shavit (*My Promised Land*), and Gershom Gorenberg (*The Unmaking of Israel*) have all argued that among Israel's most pressing problems are its occupation of the West Bank, its discrimination against the Arab minority, and the entanglement of Judaism in the state and the public sphere.[24] Only by directly addressing these (and other issues) can Israel secure its future. Each author offers a set of prescriptions for how to proceed.

Avishai's is the most radical. He wants Israel to become a secular Hebrew republic, which would diminish the Jewish character of the state. Such a republic would remove Jewish identity from its privileged place in the system and replace it with liberal democracy. As the "Hebrew" in the title suggests, the state would still have plenty of Jewish values, ideas, and practices in it. But it would not be, in Sammy Smooha's words, an ethnic democracy anymore.

Shavit wants a realistic appraisal of Israel's past and present in order to move on from a collective angst to an acknowledgment that Israeli life is complex and difficult and simply will be so for some time to come.[25] Gorenberg adopts a more middle-of-the-road position. He thinks Israel can be both Jewish—since the state is populated primarily by Jews, Jewish culture and practices will inevitably remain popular—and a liberal democracy that provides full individual rights for all citizens. Such a project would not be easy, given Israeli history, but there is no *a priori* reason why it cannot be done. For Gorenberg, ending Israel's presence in the West Bank is particularly urgent.

All three authors have been subject to critique. It is also not clear how much of a following they have in Israel, with the exception of Shavit, a well-known journalist. Yet the ideas they discuss have increasingly made their way into the public debate through the political struggles mentioned previously.

Many multicultural democratic states—the United States, Britain, Australia, and Canada, among others—have also been wrestling with questions of national identity in the face of changing patterns of immigration. But in Israel the tensions are heightened because the country has not defined to the satisfaction of a critical mass of its citizens what it means to be a Jewish and democratic state. Maintenance of a state of limbo regarding the West Bank—over which Israel has slowly but steadily extended military and judicial control, yet has not formally annexed—has encouraged questions about Israel's ability to remain Jewish and democratic while its borders remain unsettled. Unlike other democratic states, too, the persistence of external threats to Israel exacerbates these difficulties. That these questions continue to matter to actors in Israeli politics, and that those actors have the space to explore possible answers, says something about the maturity and liveliness of the state's democracy.

To understand a country, one must understand not just the structures and processes of its political system, its major social groups, and its political culture, but also the deeper questions that touch on the very meaning of the state for its inhabitants, and that shape and, perhaps, alter its very identity. Because these are among the largest debates in Israel today, students of Israeli politics should consider them as well.

Yet it is also important to note that despite the weaknesses in the Israeli political system, the social divisions that play such an important role in its politics, and the security concerns that continue to plague the country, Israelis are among the most content societies in the Organisation for Economic Co-operation and Development—including those states not engaged in any of these kinds of protracted struggles or identity questions. That, too, is worth studying.

Table 18.1 "Life Satisfaction" Rates in the OECD, on a 10-point scale (10 Being the Highest)

	SATISFACTION
1. Denmark, Iceland, Switzerland	7.5
2. Finland, **Israel**, Norway	**7.4**
3. Australia, Canada, Netherlands, New Zealand	7.3
4. Sweden, United States	7.2
5. Germany, Ireland	7.0
6. Austria, Belgium, Luxembourg	6.9
7. United Kingdom	6.8
8. Chile, Mexico	6.7
9. Czech Republic, France, Spain	6.5
10. Slovak Republic	6.1
11. Italy	6.0
12. Japan	5.9
13. Korea, Poland	5.8
14. Slovenia	5.7
15. Estonia , Turkey	5.6
16. Portugal	5.1
17. Hungary	4.9
18. Greece	4.8

Source: Organisation for Economic Co-operation and Development, "Life Satisfaction," *Better Life Index,* http://www.oecdbetterlifeindex.org/topics/life-satisfaction/

KEYWORDS

Jewish state, Jewish and democratic, Israeli identity, Jewish identity, foreign workers, African refugees, historiography, new historians, post-Zionism

NOTES

1. Sammy Smooha, "The Model of Ethnic Democracy: Response to Danel," *Journal of Israeli History: Politics, Society, Culture* 28 (2009): 55–62; "The Model of Ethnic Democracy: Israel as a Jewish and Democratic State," *Nations and Nationalism* 8 (2002): 475–503. For a counterargument, see Alexander Yakobson and Amnon Rubinstein, *Israel and the Family of Nations: The Jewish Nation-State and Human Rights* (London: Routledge, 2009).

2. Oren Yiftachel, *Ethnocracy: Land and Identity Politics in Israel/Palestine* (Philadelphia: University of Pennsylvania Press, 2006). Adalah maintains a list of these laws. See "Discriminatory Laws," n.d., http://adalah.org/eng/Articles/1771/Discriminatory-Laws.

3. As'ad Ghanem, Nadim N. Rouhana, and Oren Yiftachel, "Questioning 'Ethnic Democracy': A Response to Sammy Smooha," *Israel Studies* 3 (1998): 253–267.

4. This echoes the Balfour Declaration, which referred to a "national home" in Mandatory Palestine for the Jewish people, but not for the Arab population, who were to be guaranteed only "civil and religious rights."

5. Peter Beinart, *The Crisis of Zionism* (New York: Times Books, 2012); Yuval Diskin, "Israel Nears Point of No Return on Two-State Solution," *Jerusalem Post*, July 13, 2013.

6. A further issue is whether some Jewish settlers—those who want to live in what they view as the Land of Israel—can or will remain in an eventual Palestinian state.

7. The division of the West Bank comes from the Oslo II Accord. Area A is under full Palestinian civil and security control; Area B is shared between Palestinian civil control and Israeli security control; and Area C, which contains most of the settlements, is under full Israeli civil and security control.

8. See, for example, Aviad Rubin, Doron Navot, and As'ad Ghanem, "The 2013 Israeli General Election: Travails of the Former King," *Middle East Journal* 68 (2014): 248–267.

9. The term used to describe the Africans is highly politicized. Some on the right call them "infiltrators," implying a nefarious motivation and recalling Palestinian terrorists who in the past crossed into Israel from neighboring countries for murderous purposes. Most refer to them as "migrants," implying an economic motive, or as "refugees."

10. Regev's comments cited here: Ilan Lior and Tomer Zarchin, "Demonstrators Attack African Migrants in South Tel Aviv," *Haaretz*, May 24, 2012, http://www.haaretz.com/news/israel/demonstrators-attack-african-migrants-in-south-tel-aviv-1.432262. On Netanyahu's Cabinet declaration: Ministry of Foreign Affairs, "Cabinet Communique," May 20, 2012, http://mfa.gov.il/MFA/PressRoom/2012/Pages/Cabinet_communique_20-May-2012.aspx. For Yishai's calls for deportation, see: Gabe Fisher, "Eli Yishai: Round Up and Expel African Refugees," *Times of Israel*, May 16, 2012, http://www.timesofisrael.com/eli-yishai-deport-african-refugees/. On the far-right demonstration, see: Ben Hartman, "MKs Hold 'Banish the Darkness' Anti-Migrant Rally," *Jerusalem Post*, December 10, 2012, http://www.jpost.com/National-News/MKs-hold-banish-the-darkness-anti-migrant-rally.

11. Marissa Newman, "In Dramatic Ruling, High Court Rejects Israel's Policies on Illegal Migrants," *Times of Israel*, September 22, 2014, http://www.timesofisrael.com/in-dramatic-ruling-supreme-court-rejects-israels-policies-on-illegal-migrants/.

12. Israel Democracy Institute, Israeli Democracy Index 2013, 61–62, http://en.idi.org.il/media/2720081/Democracy%20Index%20English%202013.pdf

13. Ibid., 64–65.

14. Benny Morris, "The New Historiography: Israel Confronts Its Past," *Tikkun* (November–December 1988), 19–23, 99–102.

15. Oded Löwenheim, *The Politics of the Trail: Reflexive Mountain Biking Along the Frontier of Jerusalem* (Ann Arbor: University of Michigan Press, 2014).

16. Efraim Karsh, *Fabricating Israeli History: The "New Historians,"* 2nd rev. ed. (London: Routledge, 2000).

17. Anita Shapira, "The Past Is Not a Foreign Country," trans. William Templer, *New Republic* (November 29, 1999), 26–36.

18. In an interesting postscript to the emergence of the new historians, one of the most respected of them—Benny Morris, whose work laid the foundation for contemporary post-Zionism—has recently been accused of apostasy for turning his criticism from Israel toward the Palestinians. In the aftermath of the Second Intifada, Morris has condemned the Palestinians for always saying "no" in negotiations and resorting to violence. In several interviews after that period, he also argued that at least some of the forced expulsions of Arabs during the 1947–1949 War were necessary in order to create the Jewish state. See, for example, Ari Shavit, "Survival of the Fittest? An Interview with Benny Morris," *Haaretz*, January 8, 2004.

19. For a discussion of post-Zionism, see Laurence J. Silberstein, *The Postzionism Debates: Knowledge and Power in Israeli Culture* (New York: Routledge, 1999).

20. Mira M. Sucharov, *The International Self: Psychoanalysis and the Search for Israeli-Palestinian Peace* (Albany: SUNY Press, 2005).

21. For a full description of the story, see Batya Ungar-Sargon, "In 2000, a Newspaper Headline Opened a Wound in Israeli Society. It Still Hasn't Healed," *Tablet*, May 19, 2014, https://tabletmag.creatavist.com/tantura.

22. Yaron Ezrahi, *Rubber Bullets: Power and Conscience in Modern Israel* (Berkeley: University of California Press, 1997).

23. Yoram Hazony, *The Jewish State: The Struggle for Israel's Soul* (New York: Basic Books, 2001).

24. Bernard Avishai, *The Hebrew Republic: How Secular Democracy and Global Enterprise Will Bring Israel Peace at Last* (Orlando: Harcourt, 2008); Ari Shavit, *My Promised Land: The Triumph and Tragedy of Israel* (New York: Spiegel and Grau, 2013); Gershom Gorenberg, *The Unmaking of Israel* (New York: Harper, 2011).

25. Shavit, *My Promised Land*, 131.

٭

List of Parties

Achdut Ha'Avodah: Unity of Labor. A socialist party, founded in 1919, that promoted more maximalist demands regarding the Land of Israel and preferred a more activist foreign policy in the Arab–Israeli conflict. It united with another socialist movement in 1930 to form Mapai. In 1946 it split from Mapai and worked with Mapam; in 1955 it split from Mapam and ran as an independent party. In 1965 it rejoined Mapai on a joint list called the Labor Alignment. It joined together with Mapai and Rafi in 1968 to form the Israel Labor Party.

Agudat Yisrael: Union of Israel. A non-Zionist haredi party established in 1912, it now comprises Hasidic and yeshivish elements. Since the 1990s it has run on a joint list with Degel HaTorah.

Alignment (1): A list, officially called the Labor Alignment, composed of Mapai and Achdut Ha'Avodah that ran in the 1965 election.

Alignment (2): A list composed of Labor and Mapam, which lasted from 1969 to 1988.

Atzmaut: Independence. A five-member bloc of MKs who left the Labor Party in January 2011. Led by Ehud Barak as a personal vehicle for remaining within the Likud-led government, the party is considered to have contributed to the near death of Labor. It dissolved before the 2013 election.

Balad: Acronym for National Democratic Assembly. A nationalist Arab party.

Bayit Yehudi: Jewish Home. The party was formed for the 2009 election, originally out of a merger of the National Religious Party and several small right-wing parties. Primarily a Religious Zionist party oriented toward the settler community in the West Bank, it has incorporated a number of nonreligious voters and candidates.

Center Party: A small centrist party. It lasted only for one election (in 1999).

Degel HaTorah: Banner of the Torah. A non-Zionist, non-hasidic Ashkenazi haredi party that has often run on a joint list with Agudat Yisrael.

Democratic Movement for Change: A centrist party—also known by its acronym, Dash, or DMC—that drew from both Labor and Likud. It did very well in the 1977 election, contributing to the electoral victory of Likud by siphoning off votes from Labor, but broke up before the next election.

Fighters List: The short-lived party that represented the disbanded Lehi in the first Knesset. Its platform was too extreme for most Israelis, and it failed to win a seat in any more elections.

Gahal: Acronym for Herut-Liberal Bloc. The main right-wing party, it was formed in 1965 out of a merger between Herut and the Liberals. In 1973 it became the core of Likud.

General Zionists: A catchall party composed of several nonaffiliated Zionist groups with an economically right-wing (i.e., capitalist) platform. In 1961 it merged with the Progressive Party to form the Liberal Party.

Gil: Acronym for Pensioners of Israel to the Knesset. It campaigned for more social welfare services in Israel and did surprisingly well in the 2006 election, but then broke apart and failed to win seats in subsequent elections.

Hadash: Acronym for the Democratic Front for Peace and Equality, which also means "New." This Communist party, composed mostly of Arab politicians, was formed by Rakah, the Black Panthers, and other smaller leftist parties, though Rakah was the primary force within it.

HaPo'el HaMizrachi: Mizrachi Workers. The socialist wing of the Mizrachi movement. In 1956 it merged with Mizrachi to form the National Religious Party.

Hatenua: The Movement; officially, The Movement Chaired by Tzipi Livni. This is a difficult party to place. Formed strictly as a political vehicle for Livni in 2012, its sole issue has been the Israeli–Palestinian conflict. It argues for withdrawal from most of the West Bank and working with Palestinian Authority President Mahmoud Abbas. Livni is more right than left oriented, but the second and third spots on the party's list were filled by Amram Mitzna and Amir Peretz, former Laborites. In 2015 Hatenua ran with Labor on a joint ticket called Zionist Union.

Herut: Freedom. The major right-wing (Revisionist) party in Israel, formed out of the Irgun. It advocated maximalist territorial demands (the entire Land of Israel) and a more capitalist economic policy. It later folded into Gahal, and then Likud, but remained the core of both mergers.

Ichud Leumi: National Union. A far-right party, originally formed in 1999 and composed of Moledet, Tekuma, and Herut (a breakaway faction from Likud).

Herut left before the 2003 election, but Yisrael Beiteinu ran on a joint list with it. The latter ran separately in the 2006 election and was replaced with Mafdal. For the 2009 election, Mafdal and National Union both folded into Bayit Yehudi, but dissatisfied individual members then broke away and reformed National Union.

Independent Liberals: A breakaway group that left the Liberal Party when it merged with Herut to form Gahal. The Independent Liberals' electoral fortunes steadily declined, until it folded into Labor in 1984.

Joint List: A single ticket formed in 2015 by the four Arab parties—Ra'am, Ta'al, Balad, and Hadash. Its existence is largely the result of the increase in the electoral threshold in 2014, representing an effort to ensure its constituent parties won representation in the Knesset. In English it is often, though erroneously, called the Joint Arab List.

Kach: Thus. A small, extreme right-wing party. It was led by Rabbi Meir Kahane, a militant American immigrant to Israel, who promoted the transfer of Arab Israelis out of Israel. The party reflected his advocacy of violence and was banned from participating in elections for incitement to racism after the 1984 vote.

Kadima: Forward. A centrist party formed by Ariel Sharon in 2005, drawing from both Labor and Likud. It advocated a two-state solution and promoted withdrawal from the West Bank and Gaza in order to facilitate an independent Palestinian state. It was willing to dismantle Jewish settlements toward this end. Though it did well in the 2006 and 2009 elections, it all but collapsed in 2013 and did not compete in 2015.

Kulanu: All of Us. A centrist party established in 2015 by the popular Moshe Kahlon. Its platform is focused on lowering the cost of living, particularly for middle-class Israelis. It did well in its first election, taking 10 seats.

Labor: The Israel Labor Party. A center-left party created in 1968 out of a merger between Mapai, Achdut Ha'Avodah, and Rafi. It formed a brief merger with Meimad and Gesher for the 1999 election called One Israel; when Gesher left soon after, it was renamed Labor–Meimad, though Labor was the major part of the alliance. When that alliance broke up, Labor ran independently in the 2009 election and then with Hatenua in 2015 as the Zionist Union.

Liberal Party: Formed from a merger between the General Zionists and the Progressive Party. In 1965 it merged with Herut to form Gahal and then later helped form Likud.

Likud: Consolidation. A center-right party formed out of a merger including Gahal, the Free Center, the State List, and the Movement for Greater Israel. Herut and the Liberals have always remained the largest factions within the party. Unlike most other major parties, it has rarely run on an electoral list with other parties, though it did so in 2013 with Yisrael Beiteinu.

Maki: Acronym for Israeli Communist Party. It has always been non-Zionist and was originally composed of Jews and Arabs. The party became increasingly divided between the two, until the Arab members mostly left in 1965 and established Rakah. Maki was disbanded as an independent party when it folded into Moked for the 1973 election. In 1989, Rakah renamed itself Maki.

Mapai: Acronym for Worker's Party of the Land of Israel. A center-left socialist party, created in 1930 out of a merger between Achdut Ha'Avodah and HaPo'el HaTzair. In 1965 it formed the Labor Alignment with Achdut Ha'Avodah. In 1968 it was the major faction in a merger with Achdut Ha'Avodah and Rafi that established Labor.

Mapam: Acronym for United Workers Party. A socialist party to the left of Labor. It was formed out of the merger of several smaller leftist movements in 1948. Originally Marxist and pro-Stalin, in 1969 it formed the Alignment with Labor, in which it remained until 1988. It helped form Meretz for the 1992 election and formally disbanded in 1997.

Meimad: Acronym for Jewish State, Democratic State. A dovish, left-wing Religious Zionist party established in 1999, it ran on a joint list with Labor until 2009, after which it drifted among other smaller leftist parties.

Meretz: Acronym for Mapam and Ratz, which means "Vigor." It is a socialist party further left than Labor. Originally an alliance between Mapam, Ratz, and Shinui, in 1997 its constituent parties merged fully into Meretz, which in turn merged with the New Movement in 2008 to form New Movement–Meretz. By the 2013 election it was back to Meretz.

Mizrachi: A Religious Zionist party founded in 1902. In 1956 it merged with HaPo'el HaMizrachi into the National Religious Party.

Moledet: Homeland. A small, highly ideological far-right party known for advocating the transfer of Palestinians out of the West Bank to make room for Jewish sovereignty. It was founded in 1988 and helped form Ichud Leumi in 1999. It contributed to the formation of Bayit Yehudi but left before the 2009 election to join a renewed Ichud Leumi.

National Religious Party: Also known as Mafdal, the acronym for the National Religious Party, or simply the NRP. Historically the main Religious Zionist party in Israel, formed from a 1956 merger between Mizrachi and HaPo'el HaMizrachi. It was finally and completely dissolved before the 2009 election. Elements of it are represented in Bayit Yehudi.

Po'alei Agudat Yisrael: Agudat Israel Workers. A socialist haredi party, it alternated between forming a joint list with Agudat Yisrael called Religious Torah Front, and running in elections alone. It merged permanently into Agudat Yisrael in 1981.

Progressive List for Peace: Far-left party composed of both Jews and Arabs.

Progressive Party: An economically right-wing party. In 1961 it merged with the General Zionists into the Liberal Party. When the Liberal Party merged with Herut into Gahal, most former members of the Progressive Party left and established the Independent Liberals.

Ra'am (1): Acronym for United Arab List. An Arab party formed in 1977. It won only one seat in the 1977 election and disbanded after the 1981 election.

Ra'am (2): Acronym for United Arab List. Formed in 1996 from a merger between the Arab Democratic Party and elements of the Islamic Movement; it thus serves as the Movement's political representation. In 2015 it ran with the other three Arab parties as the Joint List.

Ra'am–Ta'al: A joint list composed of Ra'am and Ta'al that existed from 1996 to 2015. It broke up just before the election that year.

Rafi: Acronym for Israeli Workers List. Formed in 1965 when David Ben-Gurion led a breakaway group out of Mapai. In 1968 it merged with Achdut Ha'Avodah and Mapai into Labor.

Rakah: Acronym for New Communist List. It was created in 1965 when most of the Arab members of Maki left that party (though it still retained some Jews). It formed a joint list in 1977 with the Black Panthers and other small leftist groups called Hadash, and remains the major faction within Hadash. In 1989, Rakah changed its name back to Maki.

Ratz: The Citizens Rights Movement, sometimes called the Movement for Civil Rights and Peace. A small left-wing party formed in 1973 out of the Alignment. Over the next several years it merged into and split from a number of other groups and parties. In 1992 it formed Meretz with Mapam and Shinui.

Shas: Acronym for Sephardi Torah Guardians. A non-Zionist, haredi party formed in 1984 to represent Mizrachi haredim and traditional Sephardi voters. Most of its electoral support comes from non-haredi sectors of the population.

Shinui: Change. A secular leftist party, accused by some of being anti-religious. First formed in 1978 as a breakaway group from the Democratic Movement for Change, it has changed its name several times, though it has usually kept "Shinui" in its title. It formed Meretz in 1992 with Ratz and Mapam, but when these three parties officially dissolved themselves in 1997, a breakaway faction reestablished Shinui. The party fell apart before the 2006 election, and none of its factions passed the electoral threshold.

State List: Also known as the National List. Formed in 1969 by David Ben-Gurion out of Rafi after Rafi joined the Alignment that year. Ben-Gurion resigned in 1970, and in 1973 the party merged into Likud.

Ta'al: Arab Movement for Renewal. A small Arab nationalist party. In most elections it runs on a joint list with other Arab parties.

Tami: Acronym for Movement for the Heritage of Israel. Founded in 1981 by a former member of the NRP, it primarily represented Sephardim. After the 1984 election it merged into Likud.

Tehiya: Revival. A small right-wing nationalist party founded in 1979 primarily to promote Jewish settlement in the West Bank. It ran on a joint list with Tzomet for the 1984 election but became independent by the 1988 election. It ran but did not win any seats in 1992, and dissolved soon after.

Third Way: A short-lived centrist party formed in 1996 as a breakaway from Labor. After it could not win a seat in the 1999 election it was disbanded.

Tzomet: Crossroads. A far-right, nationalist, secular party formed in 1983. It first ran on a joint list with Tehiya but then ran as an independent party in 1988. In 1996 it joined a list called Likud–Gesher–Tzomet and then ran independently again in 1999 but failed to win any seats. Since 1999 it has consistently failed to pass the necessary threshold.

Yachad: Together. Formed as a breakaway party from Shas in 2014, it ran together with a small, far-right party widely considered a manifestation of the old Kach. It did not pass the threshold in 2015 but probably cost Shas three seats.

Yahadut HaTorah: United Torah Judaism. An alliance of Agudat Yisrael and Degel HaTorah, formed in 1992. It split briefly in 2004 but rejoined for the 2006 election.

Yesh Atid: There Is a Future. Formed for the 2013 election as a centrist party, it has sometimes been difficult to place. On the traditional left–right divide (i.e., regarding the peace process) it is more right than left, but its list is composed of a number of doves and social activists.

Yisrael B'aliyah: Israel by Aliya, more loosely understood as Israel for Immigration. Originally formed in 1996 to represent the Russian immigrant community, it folded into Likud in 2003 after its electoral fortunes declined and it became more rightist.

Yisrael Beiteinu: Israel Is Our Home. A right-wing, nationalist party that also claims to represent immigrant communities, particularly Russians. Formed in 1999, it ran independently in the election that year; in 2003 it ran on a joint list with National Union, and in 2013 it campaigned on a joint list with Likud.

Zionist Union: A list composed of Labor and Hatenua, formed to challenge Likud in the 2015 election.

National Election Results in Israel, 1949–2015

PARTY/LIST	1949	1951	1955	1959	1961	1965	1969	1973	1977	1981	1984	1988	1992	1996	1999	2003	2006	2009	2013	2015
Mapai	46	45	40	47	42															
Mapam	19	15	9	9	9	8						3[1]								
United Religious Front	16[2]																			
Herut	14	8	15	17	17															
General Zionists	7	20	13	8																
Progressive Party	5	4	5	6																
Sephardim and Edot Mizrachi	4	2																		
Maki	4	5	6	3	5	1	1													
Democratic Party of Nazareth[3]	2																			
Fighters List	1																			
WIZO	1																			
Yemenite Association	1	1																		
Hapo'el Hamizrachi		8																		
Democratic List of Israeli Arabs	3[4]		2																	
Agudat Yisrael	3				4	4	4		4	4	2	5								
Po'alei Agudat Yisrael	2				2	2	2		1											
Mizrachi	2																			
Kidmah Va'avodah[5]	1		2																	
Hakla'ut Ufituah[6]	1	1	1																	

292

PARTY/LIST	1949	1951	1955	1959	1961	1965	1969	1973	1977	1981	1984	1988	1992	1996	1999	2003	2006	2009	2013	2015
Kidmah VePituah[7]				2	2	2	2	2												
National Religious Front[8] / NRP[9]			11	12	12	11	12	10	12	6	4	5	6	9	5	6				
Achdut Ha'Avodah			10[10]	7	8															
Religious / United Torah Front[11]			6	6				5												
Shituf Ve'ahvah[12]				2	2	2	2													
Liberal Party					17[13]															
The Alignment						45[14]	56[15]	51	32	47	44	39								
Gahal[16]						26	26													
Rafi						10														
Independent Liberals						5	4		1											
Rakah						3	3													
Ha'olam Hazeh-Koah Hadash						1	2													
State List							4													
Hamerkaz Hahofshi							2													
Likud								39[17]	43	48	41	40	32	32[18]	19	38	12	27	31[19]	30
Ratz								3	1	1	3	5								
Moked								1												
Arab List for Bedouin and Villagers[20]								1												
Democratic Movement for Change									15											

(Continued)

PARTY/LIST	1949	1951	1955	1959	1961	1965	1969	1973	1977	1981	1984	1988	1992	1996	1999	2003	2006	2009	2013	2015
Hadash									5	4	4	4	3	5	3	3	3	4	4	
Flatto-Sharon									1											
Shlomzion									2											
Mahaneh Sheli									2											
Ra'am (1) & (2)									1[21]					4[22]	5					
Tami										3	1									
Tehiya										3		3								
Telem										2										
Shinui										2	3	2			6	15				
Tehiya–Tzomet											5									
Shas											4	6	6	10	17	11	12	11	11	7
Yahad											3									
Progressive List for Peace											2	1								
Morasha–Po'alei Agudat Israel[23]											2									
Kach											1									
Ometz											1									
Tzomet												2	8							
Moledet												2	3	2						
Degel HaTorah												2								
Arab Democratic Party												1	2							
Labor[24]													44[25]	34	26[26]	19	19	13[27]	15	
Meretz													12	9	10	6	5	3	6	5

PARTY/LIST	1949	1951	1955	1959	1961	1965	1969	1973	1977	1981	1984	1988	1992	1996	1999	2003	2006	2009	2013	2015
United Torah Judaism[28]													4	4	5	5	6	5	7	6
Yisrael B'aliyah														7	6	2				
The Third Way														4						
Center Party															6					
Ichud Leumi															4[29]	7[30]				
Yisrael Beiteinu															4		11	15		6
Balad															2	3	3	3		
Am Ehad															2	3				
United Arab List																2				
Kadima																	29	28	2	
Ichud Leumi–Mafdal																	9			
Gil																	7			
Ra'am–Ta'al																	4	4	4	
New Movement–Meretz																		3		
Bayit Yehudi																		3	12[31]	8
Yesh Atid																			19	11
Hatenua (Tzipi Livni)																			6	
Zionist Union[32]																				24
Joint List[33]																				13
Kulanu																				10

[1] Mapam left the Alignment and ran separately.

[2] All religious parties—Mizrachi, Hapo'el HaMizrachi, Agudat Yisrael, and Po'alei Agudat Yisrael—ran together on a single list for this election only.

3 Associated with Mapai.

4 Associated with Mapai.

5 Associated with Mapai.

6 Associated with Mapai.

7 Associated with Mapai.

8 The merged party list of Mizrachi and Hapo'el HaMizrachi.

9 During and after the 1959 election, until its dissolution in 2008, the party became the National Religious Party (Miflaga Datit Leumit—Mafdal or NRP).

10 Until this election the party had been part of Mapam.

11 A merger of Agudat Yisrael and Po'alei Agudat Yisrael.

12 Associated with Mapai.

13 Union of the General Zionists and the Progressive Party.

14 This first version of the Alignment was formed when Mapai and Achdut Ha'Avodah ran together for the 1965 elections.

15 This second version of the Alignment included the Israel Labor Party and Mapam.

16 Merger between Herut and the Liberal Party.

17 A list that included Gahal, Free Center, National List, and Greater Israel.

18 For this election Likud led a list called Likud-Gesher-Tzomet.

19 In this election Likud formed an electoral alliance with Yisrael Beiteinu.

20 Associated with the Alignment.

21 The first Ra'am (1) was a merger between Kidmah VePituah and the Arab List for Bedouin and Villagers. It was associated with the Alignment.

22 The second version of Ra'am (2) included the Arab Democratic Party and members of the Islamic Movement.

23 Composed of one former member each from Mafdal and Po'alei Agudat Yisrael.

24 Officially called Labor–Meimad for the 2003 and 2006 elections.

25 For the first time, the Israel Labor Party ran on its own; previously, it had been part of the Alignment.

26 The list was officially called One Israel and included Labor, Gesher, and Meimad.

27 In January 2011, five Labor MKs left the party to form Atzmaut (Independence), leaving Labor with eight seats.

28 The list combined Degel HaTorah and Agudat Yisrael.

29 A list composed of Moledet, Herut, and Tekuma.

30 In this election Yisrael Beiteinu ran on this list.

31 In 2013 Bayit Yehudi incorporated some members of Ichud Leumi.

32 An electoral alliance between Labor and Hatenua.

33 A single ticket comprised of Ra'am, Ta'al, Hadash, and Balad.

✒

The Balfour Declaration

November 2nd, 1917

Dear Lord Rothschild,

I have much pleasure in conveying to you, on behalf of His Majesty's Government, the following declaration of sympathy with Jewish Zionist aspirations which has been submitted to, and approved by, the Cabinet.

"His Majesty's Government view with favour the establishment in Palestine of a national home for the Jewish people, and will use their best endeavours to facilitate the achievement of this object, it being clearly understood that nothing shall be done which may prejudice the civil and religious rights of existing non-Jewish communities in Palestine, or the rights and political status enjoyed by Jews in any other country."

I should be grateful if you would bring this declaration to the knowledge of the Zionist Federation.

Yours sincerely,
Arthur James Balfour

꜀

The Declaration of the Establishment of the State of Israel

May 14, 1948

ERETZ-ISRAEL was the birthplace of the Jewish people. Here their spiritual, religious and political identity was shaped. Here they first attained to statehood, created cultural values of national and universal significance and gave to the world the eternal Book of Books. After being forcibly exiled from their land, the people kept faith with it throughout their Dispersion and never ceased to pray and hope for their return to it and for the restoration in it of their political freedom.

Impelled by this historic and traditional attachment, Jews strove in every successive generation to re-establish themselves in their ancient homeland. In recent decades they returned in their masses. Pioneers, *ma'pilim* and defenders, they made deserts bloom, revived the Hebrew language, built villages and towns, and created a thriving community controlling its own economy and culture, loving peace but knowing how to defend itself, bringing the blessings of progress to all the country's inhabitants, and aspiring towards independent nationhood. In the year 5657 (1897), at the summons of the spiritual father of the Jewish State, Theodore Herzl, the First Zionist Congress convened and proclaimed the right of the Jewish people to national rebirth in its own country.

This right was recognized in the Balfour Declaration of the 2nd November, 1917, and re-affirmed in the Mandate of the League of Nations which, in particular, gave international sanction to the historic connection between the Jewish people and Eretz-Israel and to the right of the Jewish people to rebuild its National Home.

The catastrophe which recently befell the Jewish people—the massacre of millions of Jews in Europe—was another clear demonstration of the urgency of solving the problem of its homelessness by re-establishing in Eretz-Israel the Jewish State, which would open the gates of the homeland wide to every Jew and confer upon the Jewish people the status of a fully privileged member of the comity of nations.

Survivors of the Nazi holocaust in Europe, as well as Jews from other parts of the world, continued to migrate to Eretz-Israel, undaunted by difficulties, restrictions and dangers, and never ceased to assert their right to a life of dignity, freedom and honest toil in their national homeland.

In the Second World War, the Jewish community of this country contributed its full share to the struggle of the freedom- and peace-loving nations against the forces of Nazi wickedness and, by the blood of its soldiers and its war effort, gained the right to be reckoned among the peoples who founded the United Nations.

On the 29th November, 1947, the United Nations General Assembly passed a resolution calling for the establishment of a Jewish State in Eretz-Israel; the General Assembly required the inhabitants of Eretz-Israel to take such steps as were necessary on their part for the implementation of that resolution. This recognition by the United Nations of the right of the Jewish people to establish their State is irrevocable.

This right is the natural right of the Jewish people to be masters of their own fate, like all other nations, in their own sovereign State.

ACCORDINGLY WE, MEMBERS OF THE PEOPLE'S COUNCIL, REPRE-SENTATIVES OF THE JEWISH COMMUNITY OF ERETZ-ISRAEL AND OF THE ZIONIST MOVEMENT, ARE HERE ASSEMBLED ON THE DAY OF THE TERMINATION OF THE BRITISH MANDATE OVER ERETZ-ISRAEL AND, BY VIRTUE OF OUR NATURAL AND HISTORIC RIGHT AND ON THE STRENGTH OF THE RESOLUTION OF THE UNITED NATIONS GENERAL ASSEMBLY, HEREBY DECLARE THE ESTABLISHMENT OF A JEWISH STATE IN ERETZ-ISRAEL, TO BE KNOWN AS THE STATE OF ISRAEL.

WE DECLARE that, with effect from the moment of the termination of the Mandate being tonight, the eve of Sabbath, the 6th Iyar, 5708 (15th May, 1948), until the establishment of the elected, regular authorities of the State in accordance with the Constitution which shall be adopted by the Elected Constituent Assembly not later than the 1st October 1948, the People's Council shall act as a Provisional Council of State, and its executive organ, the People's Administration, shall be the Provisional Government of the Jewish State, to be called "Israel."

THE STATE OF ISRAEL will be open for Jewish immigration and for the In-gathering of the Exiles; it will foster the development of the country for the benefit of all its inhabitants; it will be based on freedom, justice and peace as envisaged by the prophets of Israel; it will ensure complete equality of social and political rights to all its inhabitants irrespective of religion, race or sex; it will guarantee freedom of religion, conscience, language, education and culture; it will safeguard the Holy Places of all religions; and it will be faithful to the principles of the Charter of the United Nations.

THE STATE OF ISRAEL is prepared to cooperate with the agencies and rep-resentatives of the United Nations in implementing the resolution of the General Assembly of the 29th November, 1947, and will take steps to bring about the eco-nomic union of the whole of Eretz-Israel.

WE APPEAL to the United Nations to assist the Jewish people in the building-up of its State and to receive the State of Israel into the comity of nations.

WE APPEAL—in the very midst of the onslaught launched against us now for months—to the Arab inhabitants of the State of Israel to preserve peace and par-ticipate in the upbuilding of the State on the basis of full and equal citizenship and due representation in all its provisional and permanent institutions.

WE EXTEND our hand to all neighbouring states and their peoples in an offer of peace and good neighbourliness, and appeal to them to establish bonds of cooperation and mutual help with the sovereign Jewish people settled in its own land. The State of Israel is prepared to do its share in a common effort for the advancement of the entire Middle East.

WE APPEAL to the Jewish people throughout the Diaspora to rally round the Jews of Eretz-Israel in the tasks of immigration and upbuilding and to stand by them in the great struggle for the realization of the age-old dream—the redemption of Israel.

PLACING OUR TRUST IN THE "ROCK OF ISRAEL", WE AFFIX OUR SIGNATURES TO THIS PROCLAMATION AT THIS SESSION OF THE PROVISIONAL COUNCIL OF STATE, ON THE SOIL OF THE HOMELAND, IN THE CITY OF TEL-AVIV, ON THIS SABBATH EVE, THE 5TH DAY OF IYAR, 5708 (14TH MAY, 1948).

꙳

Basic Laws

Basic Law: The Knesset (1958)

Sets out the structure and mechanics of the Knesset, the responsibilities and requirements of Members of Knesset, and some elements of lawmaking.

Basic Law: Israel Lands (1960)

Claims all lands within Israel belong to the state and/or to *Keren Kayemet LeYisrael* (the Jewish National Fund). These lands cannot be sold.

Basic Law: The President of the State (1964)

Lays out the duties of the President and the manner by which one is elected to that office.

Basic Law: The State Economy (1975)

Introduces taxation, sets parameters on the making of the state budget, gives the state the power to print currency, and provides the State Comptroller the legal authority to inspect the economy.

Basic Law: The Army (1976)

Prescribes the military's subordination to civilian authority and lays the groundwork for a compulsory draft and the state's monopoly on the use of force.

Basic Law: Jerusalem, the Capital of Israel (1980)

States that "Jerusalem, complete and united, is the capital of Israel" as well as the seat of government. It also gives the city special status for development and expands its municipal boundaries.

Basic Law: The Judiciary (1984)

Sets out the structure of the court system, the process by which judges are selected, and the Supreme Court's duty to sit as the High Court of Justice.

Basic Law: The State Comptroller (1988)

Describes the duties and strictures of this position. The main purpose of the State Comptroller is to "audit the economy, the property, the finances, the obligations and the administration of the State, of Government Ministries, of all enterprises, institutions, or corporations of the State, of Local Authorities, and of bodies or other institutions."

Basic Law: Human Dignity and Liberty (1992)

Enshrines basic human rights and liberties, including protection of the physical body, property, dignity, personal liberty, freedom of movement, and privacy "in order to establish in a Basic Law the values of the State of Israel as a Jewish and democratic state." It stipulates that, in the event of a state of emergency, these rights can be restricted for a limited period.

Basic Law: Freedom of Occupation (1994)

Ensures that Israeli citizens and residents have "the right to engage in any occupation, profession or trade" in line with "the values of the State of Israel as a Jewish and democratic state." It also amends the Basic Law: Human Dignity and Liberty by adding the following section: "Fundamental human rights in Israel are founded upon recognition of the value of the human being, the sanctity of human life, and the principle that all persons are free; these rights shall be upheld in the spirit of the principles set forth in the Declaration of the Establishment of the State of Israel."

Basic Law: The Government (2001)

Sets out the nature, structure, duties, and formation of the government and of individual ministers, including provisions for votes of no-confidence. It also stipulates the conditions under which a state of emergency may be declared. This Basic Law replaces two previous Basic Laws on the government, including the 1992 Basic Law that created the direct election for Prime Minister.

Basic Law: Referendum (2014)

In the event of a government decision or international agreement to cede any piece of sovereign Israeli territory, requires a national referendum on that particular decision—unless 80 Members of Knesset have already voted in favor of the decision or agreement. The West Bank, not part of sovereign Israel, is not subject to the law.

Official Summary of the Or Commission

INTRODUCTION

1. The events of October 2000 shook the earth. The riots in the Arab sector inside the State of Israel in early October were unprecedented. The events were extremely unusual from several perspectives. Thousands participated, at many locations, at the same time. The intensity of the violence and aggression expressed in the events was extremely powerful. Against security forces, and even against civilians, use was made of a variety of means of attack, including a small number of live fire incidents, Molotov cocktails, ball bearings in slingshots, various methods of stone throwing and the rolling of burning tires. Jews were attacked on the roads for being Jewish and their property was destroyed. In a number of incidences, they were just inches from death at the hands of an unrestrained mob.

In a number of instances, attempts were made to enter Jewish towns in order to attack them. Major traffic arteries were blocked for long periods of time and traffic to various Jewish towns was seriously disrupted, sometimes even severed, for long periods of time. In a large number of instances, the aggression and violence was characterized by great determination and continued for long periods. The police acted to restore order and used a variety of means to disperse the crowd. As a result of the use of some of these means, which included firing rubber bullets and a few instances of live fire, Arab citizens were killed and many more injured. In the second wave of events, some places saw retaliatory Jewish riots against Arabs.

During the events, 12 Arab and one Jewish citizen were killed. One resident of the Gaza Strip was also killed. Such riots could have developed—heaven forbid—into a serious conflict between sectors of the population, such as the interracial conflicts with their attendant results that we have seen in distant locales. The fact is that, in a number of locations in Israel, these developments did lead to retaliatory Jewish riots.

2. The riots inside the state coincided with serious riots in Judea, Samaria and the Gaza Strip. Prominent personages from the Arab sector indicated this was not coincidental, and reflected interaction between Palestinians inside the Green Line

and Palestinians on the other side of the demarcation. Even this combination of events is unprecedented. Against the background of these aspects, the events were considered an "intifada" that exceeded the definition of local uprisings.

3. The events, their unusual character and serious results were the consequence of deep-seated factors that created an explosive situation in the Israeli Arab population. The state and generations of its government failed in a lack of comprehensive and deep handling of the serious problems created by the existence of a large Arab minority inside the Jewish state.

Government handling of the Arab sector has been primarily neglectful and discriminatory. The establishment did not show sufficient sensitivity to the needs of the Arab population, and did not take enough action in order to allocate state resources in an equal manner. The state did not do enough or try hard enough to create equality for its Arab citizens or to uproot discriminatory or unjust phenomenon. Meanwhile, not enough was done to enforce the law in the Arab sector, and the illegal and undesirable phenomena that took root there.

As a result of this and other processes, serious distress prevailed in the Arab sector in various areas. Evidence of the distress included poverty, unemployment, a shortage of land, serious problems in the education system and substantially defective infrastructure. These all contributed to ongoing ferment that increased leading up to October 2000 and constituted a fundamental contribution to the outbreak of the events.

Another cause was the ideological-political radicalization of the Arab sector. These processes were expressed in various expressions of identification with and even support of the Palestinian struggle against the state. This radicalization process was related to the increasing strength of Islamic politics in Israel in the period preceding the events. Serious conflicts existed between Muslims in Israel and governing authorities on matters like the Waqf's property; worsening conflicts between Muslims and the government on the issue of the Temple Mount; and cheers, primarily from the radical branch of the Islamic movement, for Islamist organizations that are Israel's enemies, including Hezbollah and Osama bin Laden.

4. The behavior of the Arab sector leadership contributed to the depth of the events and their force. The leadership did not succeed in directing the demands of an Arab minority into solely legitimate democratic channels. It did not succeed in understanding that the violent riots, obstruction of traffic arteries and identification with armed activity against the state and its citizens, constitute a threat against the state's Jewish citizens and substantially damaged the delicate fabric of Jewish–Arab relations in Israel. This created the mold for the threat of serious violence and the use of violence to achieve various goals, as evident in house destructions and land expropriation, and concerning negotiations regarding Jerusalem and the status of the Temple Mount. In various mosques, messages were transmitted delegitimizing the state and its security forces, and serious hostility and antagonism toward its symbols were expressed. Various circles raised demands to grant autonomy in some areas to the Arab minority, and to abolish the definition of the state as a Jewish state and make it "a state for all its citizens." This blurred more than once the line between the Palestinians in Judea and Samaria and the Arab citizens of the state.

Prior to and during 2000, there was a recognizable increase in the frequency of conflicts with the police and their force. The violent conflicts were a regular norm. In the first stage, organizations representing the Arab sector declared strikes and demonstrations, protesting processes and policies of various authorities. At the second stage, assemblies and processions were held in certain locations. At the third stage, youth left the masses to throw stones at vehicles, burn tires and damage facilities they felt symbolized the government. At this stage violent clashes with the police developed, after police arrived to restore order. Despite the fact that the slide from orderly demonstrations to unrestrained riots consistently reoccurred, the Arab leadership took no precautions to prevent the deterioration into violence, and did not warn against violating the law at demonstrations and processions it had initiated.

5. Various events that took place in the course of 2000 stridently signaled that the latent potential in these processes was getting out of control in practice. Although the police understood this and took certain steps to address this possibility, its commanders and the politicians failed in not making suitable preparations for the outbreak of widespread rioting that did take place, and in not addressing the tactical and strategic aspects involved in this possibility. The failure was evident in a lack of clear policy in handling the events during their first two, critical days. It was evident in a lack of sufficient operational or psychological training of police forces for any disturbances, and for events of the sort that occurred in particular. It was evident in a lack of appropriate police riot gear. It was evident in the police center of gravity relying on a very problematic means—rubber-coated cylinders that generally contain three separate bullets—whose various dangers were not sufficiently elucidated to those using them and those deciding to use them as a central and sometimes sole tool for handling riots. Not enough was done in order to assimilate as much as possible the need to avoid bodily injury to citizens, even rioting citizens.

6. A series of deeds and omissions close to the events and during them combined to actualize the explosive potential that grew with time. Ariel Sharon's visit to the Temple Mount led to serious responses to it from the Arab sector leadership inside Israel and from the Palestinian leadership in Judea and Samaria and the Gaza Strip. One day later, there was serious unrest at the site, and during its dispersion by the police, some were killed and many injured. Against this backdrop, serious riots began in Judea and Samaria, in which residents were killed and many were injured. The Higher Arab Monitoring Committee chose, in this sensitive situation, to send the masses into the streets and call for processions and demonstrations. With this backdrop, and in light of what was already known on the continuing processes and serious events that occurred in 2000, the police and those responsible for it, commanders and politicians, failed in not ordering appropriate preparation prior to Oct. 1, 2000. Police forces were not prepared at the locations known in advance to be possible sources of unrest.

As a result, the riots began with no response at all, and in other places, police forces were unable to handle the riots properly. By the time the police came to its senses, the events had built up momentum and begun to cause bodily injury, which added to the flames. Even at this stage, the Monitoring Committee and the government could have prevented further escalation by preventing a general strike on the one hand, and resolute action to restrain security force response in order to prevent further injury, on the other. Only after the bloody Oct. 2, 2000, did the government and other entities in the Arab sector leadership take action to moderate events and stop them. Even after this point, the serious events did not cease immediately, and five citizens were killed in riots that took place after October 2. Nonetheless, the exceptional nature of the events did moderate and order returned gradually.

7. The committee sent cautions according to Clause 15 of the Investigative Commissions Law to 14 persons and officeholders. These personages and officeholders were given the opportunity to bring evidence and make arguments in order to rebut the content of these warnings. The gist of the committee's conclusions will be described here, according to the order of the personages decided under Clause 15.

APPENDIX G

Research Institutes, Think Tanks, and Media in Israel

GOOD GOVERNANCE, RIGHTS, EQUALITY

Adalah: The Legal Center for Arab Minority Rights in Israel: http://adalah.org/eng/
Association for Civil Rights in Israel: http://www.acri.org.il/en/
Israel Democracy Institute: http://en.idi.org.il/
Sikkuy: The Association for the Advancement of Civic Equality: http://www.sikkuy.org.il/?lang=en

SOCIAL, ECONOMIC, AND PUBLIC POLICY

Adva Center: http://adva.org/en/
Jewish People Policy Institute: http://www.jppi.org.il/
Molad: The Center for the Renewal of Israeli Democracy: http://www.molad.org/en/indexarch.php
Reut Institute: http://reut-institute.org/en/Default.aspx
Taub Center for Social Policy Studies in Israel: http://taubcenter.org.il/
Van Leer Jerusalem Institute: http://www.vanleer.org.il/en

FOREIGN AND SECURITY POLICY

Begin-Sadat Center for Strategic Studies: http://besacenter.org/
Institute for National Security Studies: http://www.inss.org.il/
Israel-Palestine Creative Regional Initiatives: http://www.ipcri.org/
Jerusalem Center for Public Affairs: http://jcpa.org/
Leonard Davis Institute for International Relations: http://davis.huji.ac.il/en/
Moshe Dayan Center for Middle Eastern and African Studies: http://www.dayan.org/
Mitvim: http://www.mitvim.org.il/

ENGLISH-LANGUAGE ELECTRONIC MEDIA

Haaretz: http://www.haaretz.com/
Globes: http://www.globes.co.il/en/
i24news: http://www.i24news.tv/en/
Israel Hayom: http://www.israelhayom.com/site/today.php
Jerusalem Post: http://www.jpost.com/
Times of Israel: http://www.timesofisrael.com/
TLV1: http://tlv1.fm/
Ynetnews: http://www.ynetnews.com/home/0,7340,L-3083,00.html

Glossary

Aliya Literally, ascending; plural, **aliyot**. Immigration to the Land of Israel. There have been several waves of immigration since the early 1880s.

Ashkenazim Jews whose families originated in Europe, mainly eastern and central Europe.

Balfour Declaration The policy announced by the British government in 1917 that it supported the creation of a Jewish National Home in Palestine. This statement was the first recognition of Zionist goals by a major government.

Basic Law One of fifteen laws (of which three have been superseded) adopted by Israel since 1958 that are understood to comprise the elements of an eventual constitution.

Biltmore Program The 1942 decision by a special Zionist conference held in New York City that statehood was the movement's goal. This was official Zionism's first declaration of that objective.

British Mandate The period from 1922 to 1948 during which Britain governed Palestine, acting under the authority granted by the League of Nations. The Mandate incorporated the Balfour Declaration.

Camp David Accords An agreement between Israel and Egypt, reached with the assistance of the United States in 1978, that the two countries would sign a peace treaty and that Israel would withdraw from Egyptian territory taken in the 1967 Six-Day War. It included a plan for autonomy for Palestinians in the West Bank and Gaza.

Council of Torah Sages A body of rabbis from the Hasidic movements and the yeshiva world that provides direction to the Agudat Yisrael party.

Eretz Yisrael Land of Israel, a term derived from the Bible. There are various definitions of the precise boundaries of this land, but in contemporary practice Jews use the term to refer to the modern State of Israel plus the West Bank. Also sometimes referred to as the Holy Land.

Greater Israel Eretz Yisrael Hashelema—Israel from the Mediterranean Sea to the Jordan River. This term became a slogan of the nationalist right and settlers after the Six-Day War who wanted Israel to retain the West Bank.

Gush Emunim Bloc of the Faithful. An interest group formed during the early 1970s to settle areas that came under Israel's control in the 1967 Six-Day War. The group was originally motivated by religious concepts of messianism developed by Rabbi Zvi Yehuda Kook. Its major focus was on the West Bank.

Hagana Defense. A paramilitary group organized primarily by the Labor Zionists in the Yishuv in 1920 that became the main military force among the Jews of Palestine. In 1948 it was transformed into the Israel Defense Forces.

Halacha Jewish religious law. It is used to govern personal status matters among Jews in Israel.

Haredi(m) Literally, people who tremble in awe of God. It is the most common term used for ultra-Orthodox Jews.

Histadrut General Federation of Laborers in the Land of Israel. Founded in 1920, it was the umbrella organization for labor unions and was an economic powerhouse during the years of Mapai dominance.

Hovevei Zion Lovers of Zion. A group oriented toward immigration to the Land of Israel that was founded in Russia in the mid-1880s and had chapters in many cities. Considered one of the forerunners of the Zionist movement.

Intifada An uprising by Palestinians against Israel and its post-1967 occupation. The First Intifada lasted from 1987 to 1993, while the second ran from 2000 to about 2005.

Irgun Tzvai Leumi National Military Organization, also known as Etzel or the Irgun. Founded in 1931, it was the military arm of the Revisionists, but was absorbed into the IDF after statehood in 1948.

Israel Defense Forces The Israeli military, combining army, navy, and air force units. It was founded in 1948 and absorbed the Hagana and the smaller Jewish paramilitary groups of the Yishuv.

Jewish Agency for Israel (1) During the Mandate, the institution that represented the Yishuv to the British authorities. (2) Since 1948, a body that raises funds in the diaspora to support specified projects in Israel, especially immigration and absorption.

Kibbutz(im) A collective agricultural settlement in which all property is owned by the community. Kibbutzim were an important part of the culture during the pre-state period and for some time thereafter. They represented an idealistic approach to promoting Zionism. Most have since shifted away from the collectivist structure.

Knesset Assembly. It is the name of the 120-member parliament of Israel.

Lavon Affair Named for Mapai Defense Minister Pinchas Lavon, who was serving in 1954 when an espionage operation in Egypt was botched. The issue reverberated for years in Israeli politics and especially engaged Prime Minister David Ben-Gurion.

Law of Return Law passed by the Knesset in 1950 that gives any Jew and certain relatives of Jews the right to immigrate to Israel and automatically become citizens.

Mamlachtiut Translated as statism. The general approach to building the institutions of the state after 1948, especially during the 1950s. David Ben-Gurion was its prime architect.

Mizrachi A Religious Zionist organization founded in 1902 that became part of the Zionist movement. After 1948 it was one of the key founding elements of the National Religious Party.

Mizrachim Israeli Jews with roots in North Africa and the Middle East. This term is now more commonly used than **Sephardim**.

Al-Nakba The Catastrophe. The term used by Arab Israelis to describe the events of 1947–1949, including the collapse of Palestinian Arab society and the displacement of several hundred thousand Arabs, who became refugees.

New Zionist Organization Body established by Ze'ev Jabotinsky in 1935 as the embodiment of the Revisionist movement. It was a rival of the Mapai-dominated organizations.

Oslo Accords A 1993 agreement between Israel and the Palestine Liberation Organization that committed the parties to a negotiated resolution of their conflict within five years.

Post-Zionism An intellectual and political exercise that focuses on critiquing dominant Israeli narratives and assumptions, with the specific goal of demonstrating either the failure or the completion of the Zionist project. Most post-Zionists believe Israel should no longer be a Jewish state.

Protektzia A term of Russian origin that describes the gaining of benefits depending upon whom one knows. People with good connections are said to have protektzia.

Security network A loose grouping of serving and former military, security, and intelligence officers who share a broadly similar outlook on strategic affairs. The network's involvement in civilian decision-making is the subject of study, as is the extent and influence of this involvement.

Sephardim Jews who trace their family histories back to the Jews who lived in the Iberian peninsula before the 1492 expulsion. This term was commonly used to also refer to Jews from Arab countries. It has largely been replaced by the term **Mizrachim** for ethnic purposes in modern Israel.

Status Quo Agreement An agreement made between David Ben-Gurion and Agudat Yisrael in 1947 to clarify the religious situation in advance of statehood. The parties agreed that there would be no change in a number of religious practices in the new state. Topics covered included communal Sabbath and dietary laws observance, rabbinical control over personal status (marriage, divorce, and conversion) issues, and the establishment of a state-supported religious school system.

Vaad Leumi National Council. During the Mandate period, this was the executive power of Knesset Yisrael, the political expression of the Yishuv.

Western Wall The only remaining structure from the Second Temple in Jerusalem, considered the holiest site in Judaism. Since it came under Israeli control in 1967 it has become a focus of Jewish communal worship.

White Paper A policy statement issued by Britain in 1939 that indicated its plans for the Palestine Mandate. It was widely reviled by the Jews because it sharply limited Jewish immigration and dashed hopes for British support for Jewish independence.

World Zionist Organization Established in 1897 by Theodor Herzl, the major official representation of the Zionist movement.

Yeshiva A religious educational institution that focuses on Talmudic learning for males.

Yishuv The Jewish community in Palestine from the late nineteenth century through the end of the Mandate. The Jewish community that existed there before the onset of Zionism is sometimes referred to as the Old Yishuv.

Zionist Congress The supreme body of the Zionist movement, bringing together Jews from Israel and the diaspora. The First Congress was convened by Herzl in 1897. Since statehood the Congress has continued to meet regularly, but with less frequency than before 1948.

Bibliography

Adalah. n.d. "Discriminatory Laws." http://adalah.org/eng/Articles/1771/Discriminatory-Laws.

Al-Haj, Majid. 1995. *Education, Empowerment, and Control: The Case of the Arabs in Israel.* Albany: SUNY Press.

Arian, Asher. 1993. *Israel and the Peace Process: Security and Political Attitudes in 1993.* JCSS Memorandum no. 39. Tel Aviv: Jaffee Center for Strategic Studies.

———. 1995. *Security Threatened: Surveying Israeli Opinion on Peace and War.* Cambridge: Cambridge University Press.

———. 2005. *Politics in Israel: The Second Republic,* 2nd ed. Washington, D.C.: CQ Press.

Arian, Asher, and Michal Shamir, eds. 1995. *The Elections in Israel: 1992.* Albany: State University of New York Press.

———. 1999. *The Elections in Israel: 1996.* Albany: State University of New York Press.

———. 2002. *The Elections in Israel: 1999.* Albany: State University of New York Press.

———. 2005. *The Elections in Israel: 2003.* New York: Transaction Books.

Arian, Asher, and Michal Shamir. 2008a. "A Decade Later, the World Had Changed, the Cleavage Structure Remained: Israel 1996–2006." *Party Politics* 14: 685–705.

———, eds. 2008b. *The Elections in Israel: 2006.* New York: Transaction Books.

———. 2011. *The Elections in Israel: 2009.* New York: Transaction Books.

Arian, Asher, David Nachmias, and Ruth Amir. 2002. *Executive Governance in Israel.* Houndmills, Basingstoke, Hampshire and New York: Palgrave.

Arian, Asher, Ilan Talmud, and Tamar Hermann. 1988. *National Security and Public Opinion in Israel.* Israel: Jaffee Center for Strategic Studies/ Jerusalem Post Press.

Aronoff, Myron J. 1993a. "The Origins of Israeli Political Culture." In *Israeli Democracy Under Stress,* ed. Ehud Sprinzak and Larry Diamond, 47–63. Boulder, CO: Lynne Rienner.

———. 1993b. *Power and Ritual in the Israel Labor Party: A Study in Political Anthropology,* 2nd ed. Armonk, NY: M. E. Sharpe.

Aronson, Janet Krasner, Annette Koren, and Leonard Saxe. 2013. "Teaching Israel at American Universities: Growth, Placement, and Future Prospects." *Israel Studies* 18:158–178.

Association for Civil Rights in Israel. 2013. "Position Paper on Raising the Electoral Threshold." September 29. http://www.acri.org.il/en/wp-content/uploads/2013/10/Electoral-Threshold-Position-Paper.pdf.

Auerbach, Yehudit, and Charles W. Greenbaum. 2000. "Assessing Leader Credibility During a Peace Process: Rabin's Private Polls." *Journal of Peace Research* 37:33–50.

Avishai, Bernard. 1985. *The Tragedy of Zionism: Revolution and Democracy in the Land of Israel*. New York: Farrar, Straus and Giroux.

———. 2008. *The Hebrew Republic: How Secular Democracy and Global Enterprise Will Bring Israel Peace at Last*. Orlando, FL: Harcourt.

Avineri, Shlomo. 1981. *The Making of Modern Zionism: Intellectual Origins of the Jewish State*. New York: Basic Books.

Avner, Yehuda. 2010. *The Prime Ministers: An Intimate Narrative of Israeli Leadership*. 3rd ed. New Milford, CT: Toby Press.

Barnett, Michael, ed. 1996. *Israel in Comparative Perspective: Challenging the Conventional Wisdom*. Albany: SUNY Press.

Barnett, Michael. 1999. "Culture, Strategy and Foreign Policy Change: Israel's Road to Oslo." *European Journal of International Relations* 5:5–36.

Barzilai, Gad. 1996. *Wars, Internal Conflicts and Political Order: A Jewish Democracy in the Middle East*. Albany: State University of New York Press.

Beinart, Peter. 2012. *The Crisis of Zionism*. New York: Times Books.

Ben-David, Dan, ed. 2013. *State of the Nation Report: Society, Economy and Policy in Israel, 2013*. Jerusalem: Taub Center for Social Policy Studies in Israel. http://taub-center.org.il/tauborgilwp/wp-content/uploads/Taub-Center-State-of-the-Nation-Report-2013-ENG-8.pdf.

———. 2014. *A Picture of the Nation: Israel's Society and Economy in Figures, 2014*. Jerusalem: Taub Center for Social Policy Studies in Israel. http://www.israel-braingain.org.il/Uploads/Attachments/6675/a_picture_of_the_nation_2014_eng_taub.pdf.

Ben-Eliezer, Uri. 1993. "The Meaning of Political Participation in a Nonliberal Democracy: The Israeli Experience." *Comparative Politics* 25:397–412.

———. 1995. "A Nation-in-Arms: State, Nation, and Militarism in Israel's First Years." *Comparative Studies in Society and History* 37:264–285.

Ben Porat, Guy. 2008. *Israel Since 1980*. Cambridge: Cambridge University Press.

Ben Solomon, Ariel. 2013. "Arab Israeli Voters 56% Turnout Defies Expectations." *Jerusalem Post*, January 25.

———. 2014. "FM Liberman Calls for Boycott of Israeli Arab Businesses Who Strike for Gaza." *Jerusalem Post*, July 21.

Ben Zion, Ilan. 2012. "Religious Zionist Schools Adopt Stricter Modesty Rules." *Times of Israel*, August 20. http://www.timesofisrael.com/religious-zionist-schools-adopt-stricter-modesty-rules/.

Biale, David. 1987. *Power and Powerlessness in Jewish History*. New York: Schocken Books.

Birnbaum, Ben, and Amir Tibon. 2014. "The Explosive, Inside Story of How John Kerry Built an Israel-Palestine Peace Plan—and Watched It Crumble." *New Republic*, July 20. http://www.newrepublic.com/article/118751/how-israel-palestine-peace-deal-died.

Blass, Nachum. 2013. *Trends in the Development of the Education System: Pupils and Teachers*. Policy Paper No. 2013.11. Jerusalem: Taub Center for Social Policy Studies in Israel. http://taubcenter.org.il/wp-content/files_mf/trendsinthedevelopment2013.pdf.

Brecher, Michael. 1972. *The Foreign Policy System of Israel: Setting, Images, Process*. New Haven, CT: Yale University Press.

———. 1975. *Decisions in Israel's Foreign Policy*. New Haven, CT: Yale University Press.

Caplan, Neil Caplan. 2009. *The Israel-Palestine Conflict: Contested Histories*. Malden, MA: Wiley-Blackwell.

Cherry, Robert. 2014. "Increased Constructive Engagement Among Israeli Arabs: The Impact of Government Economic Initiatives." *Israel Studies* 19:75–97.

Cohen, Avner. 1998. *Israel and the Bomb*. New York: Columbia University Press.

Cohen, Stuart A. 2013. *Divine Service? Judaism and Israel's Armed Forces*. Burlington, VT: Ashgate.

Cordesman, Anthony H., and Aram Nerguizian. 2010. *The Arab-Israeli Military Balance: Conventional Realities and Asymmetric Challenges*. Washington, D.C.: Center for Strategic and International Studies.

Dieckhoff, Alain. 2003. *The Invention of a Nation: Zionist Thought and the Making of Modern Israel*. Trans. Jonathan Derrick. New York: Columbia University Press.

Diskin, Avraham. 2003. *The Last Days in Israel: Understanding the New Israeli Democracy*. London: Frank Cass.

Diskin, Hanna, and Abraham. 1995. "The Politics of Electoral Reform in Israel." *International Political Science Review* 16:31–45.

Diskin, Yuval. 2013. "Israel Nears Point of No Return on Two-State Solution." *Jerusalem Post*, July 13.

Divine, Donna Robinson. 2009. *Exiled in the Homeland: Zionism and the Return to Mandate Palestine*. Austin: University of Texas Press.

Don-Yehiya, Eliezer. 1999. *Religion and Political Accommodation in Israel*. Jerusalem: Floersheimer Institute for Policy Studies.

Dotan, Yoav, and Menachem Hofnung. 2001. "Interest Groups in the Israeli High Court of Justice: Measuring Success in Litigation and in Out-of-Court Settlements." *Law and Policy* 23:1–27.

Dowty, Alan. 2001. *The Jewish State: A Century Later*. Updated ed. Berkeley: University of California Press.

———. 2012. *Israel/Palestine*. 3rd ed. Cambridge: Polity Press.

Drezon-Tepler, Marcia. 1990. *Interest Groups and Political Change in Israel*. Albany: State University of New York Press.

Edelman, Martin. 1994. *Courts, Politics, and Culture in Israel*. Charlottesville: University Press of Virginia.

Eiran, Ehud, and Martin B. Malin. 2013. "The Sum of All Fears: Israel's Perception of a Nuclear-Armed Iran." *Washington Quarterly* 36:77–89.

Eisenstadt, S. N. 1985. *The Transformation of Israeli Society: An Essay in Interpretation*. London: Weidenfeld and Nicolson.

———. 2008. "Collective Identities, Public Spheres, Civil Society and Citizenship in the Contemporary Era—With Some Observations on the Israeli Scene." *Citizenship Studies* 12:203–213.

Elazar, Daniel J. 1986. *Israel: Building a New Society*. Bloomington: Indiana University Press.

Elazar, Daniel J., and Shmuel Sandler, eds. 1990. *Israel's Odd Couple: The 1984 Knesset Elections and the National Unity Government*. Detroit: Wayne State University Press.

———. 1995. *Israel at the Polls, 1992*. Lanham, MD: Rowman and Littlefield.

———. 1998. *Israel at the Polls, 1996*. London: Frank Cass.

———. 2001. *Israel at the Polls, 1999*. London: Frank Cass.

Etzioni-Halevy, Eva. 2002. *The Divided People: Can Israel's Breakup Be Stopped?* Lanham, MD: Lexington Books.

Ezrahi, Yaron. 1997. *Rubber Bullets: Power and Conscience in Modern Israel*. Berkeley: University of California Press.

Freedman, Robert O., ed. 2009. *Contemporary Israel: Domestic Politics, Foreign Policy, and Security Challenges*. Boulder, CO: Westview Press.

Freilich, Charles D. 2012. *Zion's Dilemmas: How Israel Makes National Security Policy*. Ithaca, NY: Cornell University Press.

Frisch, Hillel. 2011. *Israel's Security and Its Arab Citizens*. Cambridge: Cambridge University Press.

Galnoor, Itzhak. 1982. *Steering the Polity: Communication and Politics in Israel*. Beverly Hills, CA: Sage.

Garfinkle, Adam. 1997. *Politics and Society in Modern Israel: Myths and Realities*. Armonk, NY: M. E. Sharpe.

Gavison, Ruth. 2003. *Constitutions and Political Reconstruction? Israel's Quest for a Constitution*. Beverly Hills, CA: Sage.

Gazit, Shlomo. 1995. *The Carrot and the Stick: Israel's Policy in Judaea and Samaria, 1967–68*. Washington, D.C.: B'nai B'rith Books.

Gelpe, Marcia. 2013. *The Israeli Legal System*. Durham, NC: Carolina Academic Press.

Ghanem, As'ad. 2001. *The Palestinian-Arab Minority in Israel, 1948–2000*. Albany: SUNY Press.

Ghanem, As'ad, Nadim N. Rouhana, and Oren Yiftachel. 1998. "Questioning 'Ethnic Democracy': A Response to Sammy Smooha." *Israel Studies* 3:253–267.

Goldberg, Elisheva. 2012. "Likud: The Party of Annexation." *Daily Beast*, November 27. http://www.thedailybeast.com/articles/2012/11/27/likud-the-party-of-annexation.html.

Gorenberg, Gershom. 2006. *The Accidental Empire: Israel and the Birth of the Settlements, 1967–1977*. New York: Times Books.

———. 2011. *The Unmaking of Israel*. New York: Harper.

Haaretz and Jonathan Lis. 2014. "MK Zoabi: Israeli Combat Pilots Are No Better Than Islamic State Beheaders." *Haaretz*, October 19.

Haklai, Oded. 2007. "Religious-Nationalist Mobilization and State Penetration: Lessons from Jewish Settlers' Activism in Israel and the West Bank." *Comparative Political Studies* 40:713–739.

———. 2011. *Palestinian Ethnonationalism in Israel*. Philadelphia: University of Pennsylvania Press.

Halpern, Ben, and Jehuda Reinharz. 1998. *Zionism and the Creation of a New Society*. New York: Oxford University Press.

Harkov, Lahav. 2014. "Zoabi: Kidnappers Are Not Terrorists, They're Fighting Occupation." *Jerusalem Post*, June 17.

Hassan, Nir. 2014. "Despite It All, Most Israelis Still Support the Two-State Solution." *Haaretz*, July 7.

Hazan, Reuven, and Gideon Rahat. 2008. Special Issue: Israeli Party Politics: New Approaches, New Perspectives. *Party Politics* 14 (6).

Hazan, Reuven, and Moshe Maor, eds. 2000. *Parties, Elections and Cleavages: Israel in Comparative and Theoretical Perspectives*. London: Frank Cass.

———. 2010. *Democracy Within Parties: Candidate Selection Methods and Their Political Consequences*. Oxford: Oxford University Press.

Hazony, Yoram. 2001. *The Jewish State: The Struggle for Israel's Soul*. New York: Basic Books.

Hermann, Tamar, Ella Heller, Chanan Cohen, Gilad Be'ery, and Yival Lebel. 2014. *The Israeli Democracy Index, 2014.* Jerusalem: Israel Democracy Index. http://en.idi.org.il/media/3823043/democracy_index_2014_Eng.pdf.

Hermann, Tamar, Ella Heller, Nir Atmor, and Yival Lebel. 2013. *The Israeli Democracy Index, 2013.* Jerusalem: Israel Democracy Index. http://en.idi.org.il/media/2720081/Democracy%20Index%20English%202013.pdf.

Hertzberg, Arthur, ed. 1997. *The Zionist Idea: A Historical Analysis and Reader.* Philadelphia: Jewish Publication Society.

Herzl, Theodor. 1988. *The Jewish State.* New York: Dover Publications.

Horovitz, David. 2004. *Still Life with Bombers: Israel in the Age of Terrorism.* New York: Alfred A. Knopf.

———. 2014. "Netanyahu Finally Speaks His Mind." *Times of Israel*, July 13. http://www.timesofisrael.com/netanyahu-finally-speaks-his-mind/.

Horowitz, Dan, and Moshe Lissak. 1978. *Origins of the Israeli Polity: Palestine Under the Mandate.* Trans. Charles Hoffman. Chicago: University of Chicago Press.

———. 1989. *Trouble in Utopia: The Overburdened Polity of Israel.* Albany: State University of New York Press.

Inbar, Efraim. 1991. *War and Peace in Israeli Politics: Labor Party Positions on National Security.* Boulder, CO: Lynne Rienner.

International Crisis Group. 2004. *Identity Crisis: Israel and Its Arab Citizens.* Middle East Report No. 25. Washington, D.C.: International Crisis Group.

———. 2012. *Back to Basics: Israel's Arab Minority and the Israeli-Palestinian Conflict.* Middle East Report No. 119. Washington, D.C.: International Crisis Group.

Israel Central Bureau of Statistics. 2013. "Population of Israel on the Eve of 2014—8 Million." Jerusalem: Central Bureau of Statistics. http://www1.cbs.gov.il/reader/newhodaot/hodaa_template_eng.html?hodaa=201311357.

———. 2015. "Annual Data 2015." Jerusalem: Central Bureau of Statistics. http://www1.cbs.gov.il/reader/shnatonenew_site.htm.

Israel. *The Public Commission to Examine the Maritime Incident of 31 May 2010.* http://www.turkel-committee.com/index-eng.html.

Israel Democracy Institute. *Peace Index.* http://en.idi.org.il/tools-and-data/guttman-center-for-surveys/the-peace-index/.

Israel Hayom Staff. 2013. "Study: Haredi Schools Teach Less Than an Hour a Day of Core Studies." *Israel Hayom*, July 2.

Israel National Elections Studies. 1969–2013. http://www.ines.tau.ac.il/.

Jamal, Amal. 2008. "The Political Ethos of Palestinian Citizens of Israel: Critical Readings in the Future Vision Documents." *Israel Studies Forum* 23:3–28.

———. 2011. *Arab Minority Nationalism in Israel: The Politics of Indigeneity.* London: Routledge.

Jewish People Policy Institute. 2014. *Jewish and Democratic: Perspectives from World Jewry.* http://jppi.org.il/uploads/jewish_and_democratic-eng.pdf.

Kabalo, Paula. 2006. "Constructing Civil Society: Citizen Associations in Israel in the 1950s." *Nonprofit and Voluntary Sector Quarterly* 35:161–182.

Karsh, Efraim. 2000. *Fabricating Israeli History: The "New Historians."* 2nd rev. ed. London: Routledge.

Kashua, Sayed. 2014. "Why I Have to Leave Israel." *Observer*, July 19. http://www.theguardian.com/world/2014/jul/20/sayed-kashua-why-i-have-to-leave-israel.

Kenig, Ofer. 2005. "The 2003 Elections in Israel: Has the Return to the 'Old' System Reduced Party System Fragmentation?" *Israel Affairs* 11:552–566.

Kenig, Ofer. 2009. "Democratizing Party Leadership Selection in Israel: A Balance Sheet." *Israel Studies Forum* 24:62–81.

Kenig, Ofer, and Assaf Shapira. 2012. "Primary Season in Israel." Israel Democracy Institute. http://en.idi.org.il/analysis/articles/primary-season-in-israel/.

Kenig, Ofer, and Gideon Rahat. 2014. "Selecting Party Leaders in Israel." In *The Selection of Political Party Leaders in Contemporary Parliamentary Democracies: A Comparative Study*, ed. Jean-Benoit Pilet and William P. Cross, 206–221. London: Routledge.

Khalidi, Rashid. 1997. *Palestinian Identity: The Construction of Modern National Consciousness*. New York: Columbia University Press.

Kimmerling, Baruch. 1989. *The Israeli Society: Boundaries and Frontiers*. Albany: State University of New York Press.

———. 2001. *The Invention and Decline of Israeliness: State, Society, and the Military*. Berkeley: University of California Press.

Kimmerling, Baruch, and Joel S. Migdal. 2003. *The Palestinian People: A History*. Cambridge: Harvard University Press.

Klein Halevi, Yossi. 2013. *Like Dreamers: The Story of the Israeli Paratroopers Who Reunited Jerusalem and Divided a Nation*. New York: HarperCollins.

Konrad Adenauer Program for Jewish-Arab Cooperation and Moshe Dayan Center for Middle Eastern and African Studies. 2015. "Main Findings of Public Opinion Survey on the Arab Vote to the 20th Knesset." http://www.kas.de/wf/doc/kas_15350-1442-2-30.pdf?150315131309.

Koren, Annette, and Emily Einhorn. 2010. *Searching for the Study of Israel: A Report on the Teaching of Israel on U.S. College Campuses 2008–09*. Brandeis University: Cohen Center for Modern Jewish Studies. http://www.schusterman.org/wp-content/uploads/Searching-for-the-Study-of-Israel_January-2010.pdf.

Koren, Annette, Nicole Samuel, Matthew Boxer, and Ellie Aitan. 2013. *Teaching and Learning About Israel: Assessing the Impact of Israeli Faculty on American Students*. Waltham, MA: Cohen Center for Modern Jewish Studies.

Kornberg, Jacques. 1993. *Theodor Herzl: From Assimilation to Zionism*. Bloomington: Indiana University Press.

Laqueur, Walter. 2003. *A History of Zionism: From the French Revolution to the Establishment of the State of Israel*. New York: Schocken Books.

Lehman-Wilzig, Sam N. 1990. *Stiff-Necked People, Bottle-Necked System: The Evolution and Roots of Israeli Public Protest, 1949–1986*. Bloomington: Indiana University Press.

———. 1992. *Wildfire: Grassroots Revolts in Israel in the Post-Socialist Era*. Albany: State University of New York Press.

Lesch, David W. 2008. *The Arab-Israeli Conflict: A History*. New York: Oxford University Press.

Levinsohn, Hanna, and Elihu Katz. 1993. "The *Intifada* Is Not a War: Jewish Public Opinion on the Israel-Arab Conflict." In *Framing the Intifada: People and Media*, ed. Akiba A. Cohen and Gadi Wolfsfeld, 53–63. Norwood, NJ: Ablex.

Liebman, Charles S. 1997. *Religion, Democracy and Israeli Society*. Amsterdam: Harwood Academic Publishers.

Liebman, Charles S., and Eliezer Don-Yehiya. 1983. *Civil Religion in Israel: Traditional Judaism and Political Culture in the Jewish State*. Berkeley: University of California Press.

———. 1984. *Religion and Politics in Israel*. Bloomington: Indiana University Press.

Lis, Jonathan. 2010. "Arab MK Slams Holocaust Denial, Wins Praise from Jewish Colleagues." *Haaretz*, January 27.

Lomsky-Feder, Edna, and Eyal Ben-Ari, eds. 1999. *The Military and Militarism in Israel Society*. Albany: State University of New York Press.

Löwenheim, Oded. 2014. *The Politics of the Trail: Reflexive Mountain Biking Along the Frontier of Jerusalem*. Ann Arbor: University of Michigan Press.

Lowrance, Sherry. 2006. "Identity, Grievances, and Political Actions: Recent Evidence from the Palestinian Community in Israel." *International Political Science Review* 27:167–190.

Lustick, Ian. 1980. *Arabs in the Jewish State: Israel's Control of a National Minority*. Austin: University of Texas Press.

———. 1988. *From the Land of the Lord: Jewish Fundamentalism in Israel*. New York: Council on Foreign Relations.

Mahler, Gregory. 1990. *Israel After Begin*. Albany: State University of New York Press.

Makovsky, David. 1996. *Making Peace with the PLO: The Rabin Government's Road to the Oslo Accord*. Boulder, CO: Westview Press.

Maoz, Zeev. 2006. *Defending the Holy Land: A Critical Analysis of Israel's Security and Foreign Policy*. Ann Arbor: University of Michigan Press.

Medding, Peter Y. 1972. *Mapai in Israel: Political Organisation and Government in a New Society*. Cambridge: Cambridge University Press.

———. 1989. *Israel: State and Society, 1948–1988*. New York: Oxford University Press.

———. 1990. *The Founding of Israeli Democracy, 1948–1967*. Oxford: Oxford University Press.

Mendilow, Jonathan. 2003. *Ideology, Party Change, and Electoral Campaigns in Israel, 1965–2001*. Albany: State University of New York Press.

Meydani, Assaf. 2014. *The Anatomy of Human Rights in Israeli Constitutional Rhetoric and State Practice*. New York: Cambridge University Press.

Migdal, Joel S. 2001. *Through the Lens of Israel: Explorations in State and Society*. Albany: SUNY Press.

Morris, Benny. 1988. "The New Historiography: Israel Confronts Its Past." *Tikkun* (November–December 1988), 19–23, 99–102.

———. 2001. *Righteous Victims: A History of the Zionist-Arab Conflict, 1881–2001*. 2nd ed. New York: Vintage Books.

———. 2008. *1948: The First Arab-Israeli War*. New Haven, CT: Yale University Press.

Nasser, Riad, and Irene Nasser. 2008. "Textbooks as a Vehicle for Segregation and Domination: State Efforts to Shape Palestinian Israelis' Identities as Citizens." *Journal of Curriculum Studies* 40:627–650.

National Committee for the Heads of the Local Arab Authorities in Israel. 2006. *The Future Vision of the Palestinian Arabs in Israel*. Nazareth: National Committee for the Heads of the Arab Local Authorities in Israel.

Navot, Suzie. 2007. *The Constitutional Law of Israel*. New York: Kluwer Law International.

Netanyahu, Benjamin. 2009. "Address by PM Netanyahu at Bar-Ilan University." Speech delivered June 14. http://mfa.gov.il/MFA/PressRoom/2009/Pages/Address_PM_Netanyahu_Bar-Ilan_University_14-Jun-2009.aspx.

Newman, Marissa. 2014. "In Dramatic Ruling, High Court Rejects Israel's Policies on Illegal Migrants." *Times of Israel*, September 22. http://www.timesofisrael.com/in-dramatic-ruling-supreme-court-rejects-israels-policies-on-illegal-migrants/.

Oz, Amos. 2004. *A Tale of Love and Darkness*. Trans. Nicholas de Lange. Orlando, FL: Harcourt.

Peleg, Ilan, and Dov Waxman. 2011. *Israel's Palestinians: The Conflict Within*. Cambridge: Cambridge University Press.

Penslar, Derek J. 1991. *Zionism and Technocracy: The Engineering of Jewish Settlement in Palestine, 1870–1918*. Bloomington: Indiana University Press.

———. 2006. *Israel in History: The Jewish State in Comparative Perspective*. London: Routledge.

Peres, Shimon, in conversation with David Landau. 2011. *Ben-Gurion: A Political Life*. New York: Schocken.

Peri, Yoram. 1983. *Between Battles and Ballots: Israeli Military in Politics*. Cambridge: Cambridge University Press.

———. 2004. *Telepopulism: Media and Politics in Israel*. Stanford, CA: Stanford University Press.

———. 2006. *Generals in the Cabinet Room: How the Military Shapes Israeli Policy*. Washington, D.C.: United States Institute of Peace Press.

Pindyck, Shira, Moran Yarchi, and Amnon Cavari. 2014. "The *New York Times* Coverage of Israel: 1981–2013." Presentation delivered at the Annual Convention of the Association for Israel Studies Meeting, Sde Boker, Israel, June.

Pressman, Jeremy. 2003. "Visions in Collision: What Happened at Camp David and Taba?" *International Security* 28:5–43.

Ram, Uri. 2005. "Post-Zionist Studies of Israel: The First Decade." *Israel Studies Forum* 20:22–45.

Rahat, Gideon. 2008. *The Politics of Regime Reform in Democracies: Israel in Comparative and Theoretical Perspective*. Albany: State University of New York Press.

Ravitzky, Aviezer. 1993. *Messianism, Zionism, and Jewish Religious Radicalism*. Trans. Michael Swirsky and Jonathan Chipman. Chicago: University of Chicago Press.

Rebhun, Uzi, and Chaim I. Waxman, eds. 2004. *Jews in Israel: Contemporary Social and Cultural Patters*. Hanover, NH: Brandeis University Press, 2004.

Reich, Bernard. 2005. *A Brief History of Israel*. New York: Checkmark Books.

Reinharz, Jehuda, and Anita Shapira, eds. 1996. *Essential Papers on Zionism*. New York: New York University Press.

Rekhess, Elie. 2002. "The Arabs in Israel after Oslo: Localization of the National Struggle." *Israel Studies* 7:1–44.

———. 2007. "The Evolvement of an Arab-Palestinian National Minority in Israel." *Israel Studies* 12:1–28.

———. 2013. "Islamization of Arab Identity in Israel: The Islamic Movement, 1972–1996." In *Muslim Minorities in Non-Muslim Majority Countries: The Islamic Movement in Israel as a Test Case*, ed. Elie Rekhess and Arik Rudnitzky, 53–65. Tel Aviv: Konrad Adenauer Program for Jewish-Arab Cooperation.

———. 2014. "The Arab Minority in Israel: Reconsidering the '1948 Paradigm.'" *Israel Studies* 19:187–217.

Rettig Gur, Haviv. 2014. "Facing Extinction, Israel's Arab Parties Move Toward Unity . . . and Growth." *Times of Israel*, October 12. http://www.timesofisrael.com/facing-extinction-israels-arab-parties-move-toward-unity-and-growth/.

Rivlin, Paul. 2011. *The Israeli Economy from the Foundation of the State through the 21st Century*. New York: Cambridge University Press.

Rouhana, Nadim, and As'ad Ghanem. 1998. "The Crisis of Minorities in Ethnic States: The Case of Palestinian Citizens in Israel." *International Journal of Middle East Studies* 30:321–346.

Rubin, Aviad, Doron Navot, and As'ad Ghanem. 2014. "The 2013 Israeli General Election: Travails of the Former King." *Middle East Journal* 68:248–267.

Rubin, Barry. 2012. *Israel: An Introduction*. New Haven, CT: Yale University Press.

Rubin, Lawrence. 2014. *Islamic Political Activism in Israel*. Analysis Paper Number 32. Washington, D.C.: Brookings Institution.

Rubinstein, Amnon. 1984. *The Zionist Dream Revisited: From Herzl to Gush Emunim and Back*. New York: Schocken.

Sachar, Howard M. 2007. *A History of Israel: From the Rise of Zionism to Our Time*. 3rd ed. New York: Alfred A. Knopf.

Sandler, Shmuel, Ben Mollov, and Jonathan Rynhold, eds. 2004. *Israel at the Polls, 2003*. London: Routledge.

Sandler, Shmuel, Hillel Frisch, and Manfred Gerstenfeld, eds. 2011. *Israel at the Polls, 2009*. London: Routledge.

Sandler, Shmuel, Jonathan Rynhold, and Manfred Gerstenfeld, eds. 2008. *Israel at the Polls, 2006*. London: Routledge.

Sasley, Brent E. 2010. "Affective Attachments and Foreign Policy: Israel and the 1993 Oslo Accords." *European Journal of International Relations* 16:687–709.

———. 2013a. "The Domestic Politics of Israeli Peacemaking." Middle East Channel. *Foreign Policy*, July 22. http://mideastafrica.foreignpolicy.com/posts/2013/07/22/the_domestic_politics_of_israeli_peacemaking.

———. 2013b. "Still Going Strong." *Foreign Affairs*, December 6. http://www.foreignaffairs.com/articles/140328/brent-e-sasley/still-going-strong.

Sasley, Brent E., and Mira Sucharov. 2011. "Resettling the West Bank Settlers." *International Journal* 13:999–1017.

Sasson, Theodore. 2013. *The New American Zionism*. New York: New York University Press.

Schafferman, Karin Tamar. 1999. "Participation, Abstention and Boycott: Trends in Arab Voter Turnout in Israeli Elections." Israel Democracy Institute. http://en.idi.org.il/analysis/articles/participation-abstention-and-boycott-trends-in-arab-voter-turnout-in-israeli-elections/.

Scheindlin, Dahlia. 2014. "Polls: Two State Solution Was a Casualty, Even Before the War." *+972 Magazine*, July 12. http://972mag.com/polls-two-states-was-a-casualty-even-before-the-war/93418/.

Seeds of Peace. 2003. "The Official Summation of the Or Commission Report." Reprinted from *Haaretz*, September 2. http://www.seedsofpeace.org/?page_id=4032.

Senor, Dan, and Saul Singer. 2009. *Start-Up Nation: The Story of Israel's Economic Miracle*. New York: Grand Central Publishing.

Shafir, Gershon. 1996. *Land, Labor and the Origins of the Israeli-Palestinian Conflict, 1882–1914*. Updated ed. Berkeley: University of California Press.

Shafir, Gershon, and Yoav Peled. 2002. *Being Israeli: The Dynamics of Multiple Citizenship*. Cambridge: Cambridge University Press.

Shalev, Michael. 1992. *Labour and the Political Economy of Israel*. Oxford: Oxford University Press.

Shamir, Michal, and Asher Arian. 2011. "Introduction." In *The Elections in Israel: 2009*, ed. Asher Arian and Michal Shamir, 1–18. New York: Transaction Books.

Shapira, Anita. 1992. *Land and Power: The Zionist Resort to Force, 1881–1948*. Trans. William Templer. Oxford: Oxford University Press.

———. 1999. "The Past Is Not a Foreign Country." Trans. William Templer. *New Republic*, November 29, 26–36.

———. 2012. *Israel: A History*. Waltham, MA: Brandeis University Press.

Shapiro, Yonathan. 1976. *The Formative Years of the Israeli Labour Party: The Organization of Power, 1919–1930*. London: Sage.

Sharkansky, Ira. 1991. *Ancient and Modern Israel: An Exploration of Political Parallels*. Albany: State University of New York Press.

———. 1997. *Policy Making in Israel: Routines for Simple Problems and Coping with the Complex*. Pittsburgh, PA: University of Pittsburgh Press.

Shavit, Ari. 2013. *My Promised Land: The Triumph and Tragedy of Israel*. New York: Spiegel & Grau.

Shavit, Yaacov. 1988. *Jabotinsky and the Revisionist Movement, 1925–1948*. London: Frank Cass.

Sheffer, Gabriel, and Oren Barak. 2013. *Israel's Security Networks: A Theoretical and Comparative Perspective*. Cambridge: Cambridge University Press.

Shindler, Colin. 1995. *Israel, Likud and the Zionist Dream: Power, Politics and Ideology from Begin to Netanyahu*. London: I. D. Tauris.

———. 2008. *A History of Modern Israel*. Cambridge: Cambridge University Press.

Sikkuy. 2010. *The Equality Index of Jewish and Arab Citizens in Israel, 2009*. Jerusalem and Haifa: Sikkuy. http://www.sikkuy.org.il/wp-content/uploads/2010/12/sikkuy_eng09.pdf.

———. 2011. "Who's in Favor of Equality? Equality Between Arabs and Jews in Israel: Summary of an Opinion Survey." Jerusalem and Haifa: Sikkuy. http://www.sikkuy.org.il/wp-content/uploads/2013/12/shivion2011_english_abstract.pdf.

Silberstein, Laurence J. 1999. *The Postzionism Debates: Knowledge and Power in Israeli Culture*. New York: Routledge.

Skop, Yarden. 2013. "Forecast: Only 40% of Israeli Students Will Attend Nonreligious Schools by 2019." *Haaretz*, August 7.

Smooha, Sammy. 2002. "The Model of Ethnic Democracy: Israel as a Jewish and Democratic State." *Nations and Nationalism* 8:475–503.

———. 2005. *Index of Arab-Jewish Relations in Israel, 2004*. Haifa, Israel: University of Haifa, Jewish-Arab Center.

———. 2009. "The Model of Ethnic Democracy: Response to Danel." *Journal of Israeli History: Politics, Society, Culture* 28:55–62.

———. 2010a. *Arab-Jewish Relations in Israel: Alienation and Rapprochement*. Peaceworks No. 67. Washington, D.C.: United States Institute of Peace.

———. 2010b. *Index of Arab-Jewish Relations in Israel, 2003–2009*. Haifa, Israel: University of Haifa, Jewish-Arab Center.

———. 2013. *Still Playing by the Rules: Index of Arab-Jewish Relations in Israel, 2012*. Jerusalem: Israel Democracy Institute.

Sobel, Richard. 2001. *The Impact of Public Opinion on U.S. Foreign Policy Since Vietnam: Constraining the Colossus*. Oxford: Oxford University Press.

Sofer, Sasson. 1998. *Zionism and the Foundations of Israeli Diplomacy*. Cambridge: Cambridge University Press.

Sprinzak, Ehud. 1991. *The Ascendance of Israel's Radical Right*. Oxford: Oxford University Press.

Sprinzak, Ehud, and Larry Diamond, eds. 1993. *Israel Democracy Under Stress.* Boulder, CO: Lynne Reinner.

Sternhell, Zeev. 1998. *The Founding Myths of Israel: Nationalism, Socialism, and the Making of the Jewish State.* Trans. David Maisel. Princeton, NJ: Princeton University Press.

Sucharov, Mira M. 2005. *The International Self: Psychoanalysis and the Search for Israeli-Palestinian Peace.* Albany: State University of New York Press.

Susser, Asher. 2012. *Israel, Jordan, Palestine: The Two-State Imperative.* Waltham, MA: Brandeis University Press.

Taub Center for Social Policy Studies in Israel. 2014. *Back to Basics: Material Hardship in Israel.* http://taubcenter.org.il/index.php/publications/e-bulletin/back-to-basics-material-hardship-in-israel/lang/en/.

Tessler, Mark. 1994. *A History of the Israeli-Palestinian Conflict.* Bloomington: Indiana University Press.

Troen, S. Ilan. 2003. *Imagining Zion: Dreams, Designs, and Realities in a Century of Jewish Settlement.* New Haven, CT: Yale University Press.

Troen, S. Ilan, and Noah Lucas, eds. 1995. *Israel: The First Decade of Independence.* Albany: State University of New York Press.

Ungar-Sargon, Batya. 2014. "In 2000, a Newspaper Headline Opened a Wound in Israeli Society. It Still Hasn't Healed." *Tablet,* May 19. https://tabletmag.creatavist.com/tantura.

Vital, David. 1990. *The Future of the Jews: A People at the Crossroads?* Cambridge: Harvard University Press, 1990.

Waller, Harold M. 1988. "Israel in the International Arena." In *The Impact of the Six Day War: A Twenty-Year Assessment,* ed. Stephen J. Roth, 152–168. London: Macmillan.

———. 1989. "The 1988 Israel Election: Proportional Representation with a Vengeance." *Middle East Review* 21:9–17.

Waxman, Dov. 2008. "From Controversy to Consensus: Cultural Conflict and the Israeli Debate over Territorial Withdrawal." *Israel Studies* 13:73–96.

———. 2012. "A Dangerous Divide: The Deterioration of Jewish-Palestinian Relations in Israel." *Middle East Journal* 66:11–29.

Weber, Max. 2009. *From Max Weber: Essays in Sociology.* New York: Routledge.

Weissberg, Hila, Haim Bior, and Tali Heruti-Sover. 2013. "Labor of Love: Israelis Get Organized, Flock to Union in Record Numbers." *Haaretz,* June 5.

Wolfsfeld, Gadi. 1988. *The Politics of Provocation: Participation and Protest in Israel.* Albany: SUNY Press.

Yakobson, Alexander, and Amnon Rubinstein. 2009. *Israel and the Family of Nations: The Jewish Nation-State and Human Rights.* London: Routledge.

Yanai, Nathan. 1989. "Ben-Gurion's Concept of *Mamlahtiut* and the Forming Reality of the State of Israel." *Jewish Political Studies Review* 1:151–177.

Yiftachel, Oren. 2006. *Ethnocracy: Land and Identity Politics in Israel/Palestine.* Philadelphia: University of Pennsylvania Press.

Yishai, Yael. 1991. *Land of Paradoxes: Interest Politics in Israel.* Albany: State University of New York Press.

———. 1992. "Interest Groups and Bureaucrats in a Party-Democracy: The Case of Israel." *Public Administration* 70:269–285.

———. 1998. "Civil Society in Transition: Interest Politics in Israel." *Annals of the American Academy of Political and Social Science* 555:147–162.

———. 2001. "Bringing Society Back In: Post-Cartel Parties in Israel." *Party Politics* 7:667–687.

———. 2002. "Civil Society and Democracy." *Voluntas: International Journal of Voluntary and Nonprofit Organizations* 13:215–234.

Yuchtman-Ya'ar, Ephraim, and Yochanan Peres. 2000. *Between Consent and Dissent: Democracy and Peace in the Israeli Mind.* Lanham, MD: Rowman and Littlefield.

Zalmanovitch, Yair. 1998. "Transitions in Israel's Policymaking Network." *Annals of the American Academy of Political and Social Science* 555:193–208.

Zertal, Idith, and Akiva Eldar. 2007. *Lords of the Land: The War over Israel's Settlements in the Occupied Territories, 1967–2007.* Trans. Vivian Eden. New York: Nation Books.

Zerubavel, Yael. 1995. *Recovered Roots: Collective Memory and the Making of Israeli National Tradition.* Chicago: University of Chicago Press.

Index